Praise for *Creating a Culture of Collaboration*

"Top-down decision making is becoming a dinosaur in this era of globalization and rapid change. This outstanding book, written by international contributors, provides the pathways for successful collaborative decision making and the new wave of leadership, using practical, facilitative, and well-researched methods."

—David A. Wayne, chair, International Association of Facilitators;
chief operating officer, Tapestries International Communications, Inc.

"*Creating a Culture of Collaboration* is an excellent addition to the thinking within the profession of facilitation. It is a great follow-up to *The IAF Handbook of Group Facilitation* in the International Association of Facilitators series. The long-term process of creating the space, values, and expectations of collaboration is a serious issue in today's organizations. This book contributes much to this work."

—Jon C. Jenkins, Imaginal Training, The Netherlands;
coauthor, *The 9 Disciplines of a Facilitator*

"If you or your people are going to be crossing boundaries to work with others, then *Creating a Culture of Collaboration* has important lessons that are worth their weight in gold. Filled with insights from practitioners and frameworks that have proven their mettle, this is a handbook for success in the twenty-first century."

—Seth Kahan, executive strategy specialist

"While much has been written about collaboration over the years, this book contains important new insights and strategies. Thank you for bringing these leading practitioners together to share their knowledge with us!"

–Ingrid Bens, author, *Facilitating with Ease!*

"At last, a reference manual for civics in the post–9/11 world. Facilitating collaboration is the new *Robert's Rules of Order*—from neighborhood block clubs to Congress, and from corporate board rooms to the United Nations."

—Jim Troxel, Millennia Consulting; editor, *Participation Works*

"Insightful practices covering an amazing breadth of situations."

—Michael Wilkinson, CEO, Leadership Strategies; author, *The Secrets of Facilitation*

"Your book is a necessary and timely addition to the literature on collaboration. I especially appreciate the book's international aspect."

—David D. Chrislip, author, *The Collaborative Leadership Fieldbook*

CREATING A CULTURE OF COLLABORATION

The International Association of Facilitators Handbook

Sandy Schuman
Editor

JOSSEY-BASS
A Wiley Imprint
www.josseybass.com

Published by Jossey-Bass
A Wiley Imprint
989 Market Street, San Francisco, CA 94103-1741   www.josseybass.com

Jossey-Bass books and products are available through most bookstores. To contact Jossey-Bass directly
call our Customer Care Department within the U.S. at 800-956-7739, outside the U.S. at 317-572-3986,
or fax 317-572-4002.

Jossey-Bass also publishes its books in a variety of electronic formats. Some content that appears in print
may not be available in electronic books.

Library of Congress Cataloging-in-Publication Data
Cataloging-in-Publication data has been applied for.

Printed in the United States of America
FIRST EDITION
HB Printing   10 9 8 7 6 5 4 3 2 1

THE JOSSEY-BASS

BUSINESS & MANAGEMENT SERIES

CONTENTS

PART TWO: APPROACHES TO COLLABORATION

PART THREE: COLLABORATION IN ACTION

ANNOTATED CONTENTS

PART ONE: THE BASES OF COLLABORATION

2 Renewing Social Capital:
   The Role of Civil Dialogue   41

James M. Campbell

This chapter explores the relationship among social capital, social trust, confidence, and civil dialogue. It seeks to demonstrate the need for facilitated processes to ensure effective civil dialogue. A community rich in social networks with most of the population participating in these networks is rich in social capital and maintains a high level of confidence. Social capital is not a property of social trust; it is a function of confidence in a particular system and is based on familiarity. Because of the relationship between social trust and confidence, social trust can lead to social capital, but it has to do so indirectly by building confidence in the system. Networks of trust need to be created within society and through them new modes and systems of confidence (social capital). The key strategy to do this is communication. An operating definition of civil dialogue is cosmopolitan social trust building that engenders new shared values across the existing conflicting memberships. Thus effective civil dialogue enables individuals to develop cosmopolitan social trust, which then has the potential to move them toward a situation of renewed confidence and social capital. The failure of civil dialogue is a failure of process. It is a failure to appreciate and understand the complexity of the dialogue process and the need to provide people with a process and setting that moves toward cosmopolitan social trust. Effective civil dialogue happens when effective group facilitation is taking place.

3 The Development of Cross-Sector Collaborations
   in a Social Context of Low Trust   55

Mladen Koljatic, Mónica Silva, Eduardo Valenzuela

This chapter addresses the form that collaboration takes in contexts of low social confidence, as well as the special conditions that collaborative efforts require in societies that are characterized by low or weak levels of trust. Social confidence levels and the ease of relating to strangers vary in different societies according to their historical and cultural patterns. Examples are drawn from collaborative endeavors in Chile, a nation that is characterized by low levels of social confidence that weaken the possibility to enter into relationships with strangers and diminish the chances of association and collaboration beyond the circle of family members and acquaintances. In this context, many collaborative initiatives and alliances between businesses and civil society organizations stem from acquaintance and family relationships. For collaborative efforts to prosper, the environment of distrust and suspicion that prevails beyond the tight-knit circle of close acquaintance and family relationships must be overcome. The insights explored in this chapter may be useful for facilitators and consultants working in situations where low social confidence prevails.

4 Exploring the Dynamics of Collaboration in Interorganizational Settings   69

Ignacio J. Martinez-Moyano

The dynamics of collaboration in interorganizational settings was explored using system dynamics and group model building in an action research project to develop an information system prototype. The formal system dynamics model that was constructed provides insights into collaboration as a function of the recursive interaction of knowledge, engagement, results, perceptions of trust, and learning over time. In this sense, the way to improve collaboration is to pay attention to how knowledge is managed in collaborative efforts, results are produced and understood, and communication can enable the creation of trust. The theory and formal model of collaboration that emerged can be used to explore diverse elements related to collaborative work.

5 Equity, Diversity, and Interdependence: A New Driver for Societal Transformation   87

Michael Murray, Brendan Murtagh

If civil society is to embrace inclusiveness more fully and respect the diversity of citizens, the service support organizations with which it interacts must do the same. This applies to the delivery agencies of central government, local authorities, and partnership bodies, as well as to voluntary and community-based social service organizations. A core part of their shared mission is to promote the well-being of individuals and groups in society who are economically disadvantaged and socially marginalized. While legislation can ensure minimum standards of behavior and outcomes, meaningful organizational progress beyond the legal imperatives of equality requires authentic dialogue based on values of equity, diversity, and interdependence. These are powerful components for organizational change and ultimately of deeper societal transformation. Within the context of Northern Ireland's divided society, this chapter presents an empirical analysis of and prescriptive agenda for collaborative conversations that can build good relations. The insights provided go far beyond this territory and have a profound relevance for other societies struggling to emerge from conflict, racism, and social separation.

6 What Keeps It Together: Collaborative Tensility in Interorganizational Learning   105

Hilary Bradbury, Darren Good, Linda Robson

New ways of organizing have been increasing in response to the complex demands of the global marketplace. The inquiry in this chapter on one such organizational form: collaborative interorganizational learning efforts. The authors look specifically at how collaboration is fostered and sustained in the unstable environment of cross-boundary alliances. The chapter highlights the relational aspects of collaboration in a consortium of multinational corporations dedicated to grappling with issues of sustainable development. In developing a conceptual model, special emphasis is placed on the relational elements that facilitate and impede learning-oriented collaboration to present an emergent theory of collaborative tensility.

Mirja P. Hanson

Successful group deliberation and engagement require more than a "state of the art" process or a charismatic facilitator. Three make-or-break players inhibit or enhance the effective exchange of ideas, power, resources, opinions, and solutions for the sake of determining collective priorities—the participants, the facilitators, and the sponsors of collaboration processes. Project sponsors position a meaningful project by making sure that collaborative efforts connect to official decision making and influence mainstream actions. Facilitators design and deliver a unifying "due process" for consensus development. Participants contribute the engagement, intellect, and passion needed to transform problems into solutions that have the support of all affected parties. The findings and conclusions in the chapter are based on the testimonials and insights of thirty-five professionals from across the United States who engaged in four separate collaborative processes that were convened to address high-conflict environmental issues. According to these insiders, the process of collaboration relies heavily on intense and official acts of individual leadership not only out in front of the process but also backstage, where participants relax, strategize, brief, debrief, caucus, and prepare for action at the table. This chapter examines the on- and off-stage roles of the three key players and how each adopts a unique mix of assertiveness and cooperativeness to tackle the quest for "win-win" solutions.

PART TWO: APPROACHES TO COLLABORATION

Gervase R. Bushe

This chapter shows how the nature of experience and the human process of sense making make it difficult to create cultures of collaboration. It introduces the notion of interpersonal mush, the normal condition in organizations that makes creating cultures of collaboration difficult even among well-intentioned people who want to collaborate. The remedy for this is interpersonal clarity. Gaining interpersonal clarity, however, requires that people interact in self-differentiated ways and have organizational-learning conversations. The process of a learning conversation is described, and thirteen cultural assumptions required for collaborative relationships based on interpersonal clarity are offered.

Carol Sherriff, Simon Wilson

Metaphors are a shorthand or code for how we think about our past, present, and future. Studies of organizational metaphors and practical descriptions of how to use appropriate language are useful bases for the work facilitators can undertake with metaphors. Working with metaphors gives facilitators and organizations the opportunity to address some fundamental issues involving collaborative working. Three working assumptions are identified for using metaphors in a collaborative context: (1) every organization already has its own set of metaphors, which may fall into one or more recognized categories; (2) the role of the facilitator is to develop a rich metaphorical landscape; and (3) the facilitator's job is also to ensure that the metaphor remains the property of the group. The chapter authors set forth a five-step process for using metaphors in a collaborative context: (1) catch the group's metaphor, (2) define the group's issue, (3) gain permission, (4) explore the metaphor, and (5) apply lessons from the metaphor to the issue under discussion.

10 Utilizing Uncertainty   193

Kim Sander Wright

This chapter explores how certainty and uncertainty affect stakeholder attachment to viewpoint and engagement in conflict during collaboration. Conflict is described as the paradox of collaboration, as its destructive and constructive attributes challenge individual viewpoints and bring about change. The manifestation of cooperative and competitive states of mind are shown to arise from individual uncertainty or certainty about having the right viewpoint during such conflicts. An uncertainty framework is presented to illustrate how process facilitators can use and encourage varying degrees of uncertainty and certainty at different stages of the collaborative process in order to maximize the creativity and longevity of the outcomes. Bertrand Russell said, "About three-quarters of the evils from which the world is suffering spring from the fact that people feel certainty in matters as to which they ought to feel doubt." Through exposure to different viewpoints within a climate of uncertainty, this chapter suggests that there is a way to create a culture of collaboration.

11 Sustainable Cooperative Processes in Organizations   211

Dale Hunter

Groups and group processes are dynamic: they exist and change in time and space. This chapter explores the social and ecological context within which cooperative processes occur in groups and organizations. It also explores the development cycles of cooperative processes over time through a spiraling model, FACTS, that highlights the importance of choice, alignment, congruence, authenticity, truth telling, and synergy. By widening awareness to include groups, organizations, societies, and the natural environment and by mentally encompassing time spans beyond the short term, collaborative endeavors become more than a fragmented series of disconnected acts. They become consciously part of the tapestry of unfolding human activity on the planet. As the awareness of individuals broadens to that of the group, organization, society, region, and planet, the perspectives, insights, and decisions made will alter. Such a holistic approach offers access to rich sources of information that can assist us in becoming wiser and more effective facilitators, participants, and leaders.

In a knowledge economy, human resources are the most important assets. A collaborative culture is essential for recruiting and retaining creative and talented knowledge workers because such individuals would not work in an organization where getting things done entails navigating an obstacle course. To unleash the full potential of people power, the author notes, we need to create a collaborative culture and eliminate all the unnecessary hindrances. The chapter then identifies the structural and functional problems inherent in toxic cultures. In the context of recent developments in positive psychology and positive management, the author introduces the meaning-centered approach to facilitation as a comprehensive framework for transforming toxic cultures. Finally, the chapter describes the strategy, tools, and skills that facilitators can employ to create and maintain a collaborative culture.

This chapter describes practical dialogue, an emerging family of dialogic methods for facilitating practical creativity in working groups. In addition to effective action and concrete results, these methods foster the deep collaboration described by Herb Shepard as "secondary mentality," whereby natural synergy is experienced between individual perspectives and group well-being. Schein's framework of "culture as the residue of learning" explains how collaboration becomes part of group culture as participants work on practical issues. Two unrelated instances of practical dialogue in the facilitation field—dynamic facilitation and dialogue mapping—are described, highlighting similarities and differences. The third instance, transformative mediation, is a successful nondirective approach from the field of mediation. In all three nonlinear approaches, redefining the role of the facilitator or mediator away from "managing convergence" and toward an active yet nondirective role offers distinct benefits, including the ability to fully welcome divergent perspectives; work with complexity and "wicked problems," include emotions; elicit creativity; tap intrinsic motivation; and naturally generate stronger commitment and follow-through. This has applications to the public sphere and deliberative democracy, where the working group could be a stakeholder council or a citizen deliberative council. Whether in the private or public realm, practical dialogue addresses the need to engage creatively with polarized situations and widely divergent perspectives.

While trying to create a collaborative organizational culture, leaders may interact with others and design their organizations in ways that undermine the culture they seek to create. Creating a culture of collaboration requires that parties involved jointly design ways to work together to meet their related interests, learn with and from each other, and share responsibility, authority, and accountability for achieving results. Developing and sustaining a culture of collaboration requires changing two interactive factors: the conversations whereby people interact and the structures that shape these interactions. Both factors are determined by individuals' mental models. Consequently, creating an organizational culture of collaboration typically requires a shift in the values and assumptions that are at the core of these mental models. This chapter describes how this occurs and describes the facilitative leader approach, which can be used to create an organizational culture of collaboration.

Ante Glavas, Claudy Jules, Ellen Van Oosten

The prerequisite for collaboration is providing the proper space for a culture of collaboration to be built. In this chapter, the authors propose how an intervener such as a facilitator, consultant, coach, or manager can build a culture of collaboration through the "use of self," the role they play during the intervention and in preparation for it. They focus mostly on awareness of self and others during the process. Also explained is that any work by interveners needs to start with themselves as they are embedded in the process. The proposal draws on literature from systems theories, experiential learning, and positive psychology.

PART THREE: COLLABORATION IN ACTION

Cynthia Silva Parker, Linda N. Guinee, J. Courtney Bourns,
Jennifer Fischer-Mueller, Marianne Hughes, Andria Winther

This chapter illustrates how the creation of collaborative culture can facilitate social change. The authors describe conditions and values that support collaboration for social change and how practitioners can design processes that nurture robust, collaborative culture. A case study describing a systemwide effort to eliminate the racial achievement gap in the public schools of Brookline, Massachusetts, demonstrates these principles.

Jamie O. Harris, David Straus

In this chapter, Harris describes how he and his team successfully applied Straus's five-pronged theory of change in one of the most challenging systems: the public works department of a county agency. Even this paternalistic culture, characterized by hostility and lack of trust, could be transformed to a more cooperative and supportive environment through patient application of collaborative consulting and training skills and committed leadership from within the system. The cultural change process was linked to the mission and strategy of the department, a cross-functional, multilevel team was chartered to guide the process, short-term issues were addressed collaboratively, and skill-building and just-in-time training was delivered throughout the organization.

18 Leadership for the Common Good 367

John M. Bryson, Barbara C. Crosby

Increasingly, leaders seeking to tackle major social problems or challenges are realizing that they must foster cross-sector collaboration in order to achieve broadly beneficial outcomes. Yet such collaborations are often time-consuming and fraught with tension. To manage these difficulties, leaders would be wise to foster a collaborative culture among participants and in the broader community in which the collaboration takes place. This chapter examines a collaborative leadership initiative by elected officials, public administrators, and citizens in Hennepin County, Minnesota, the county that contains Minneapolis. Called the African American Men Project, the initiative seeks to transform the life chances of African American men and to prompt cross-sector collaboration to support this transformation. The authors use the Leadership for the Common Good framework to analyze the case and offer lessons for leaders trying to build cultures of collaboration among diverse stakeholders. The lessons highlight the benefits of intensive stakeholder analysis and extensive stakeholder involvement; the importance of thoughtfully framing public problems; the difficulties of disrupting existing systems; the importance of seed money, champions, and sponsors; and the need to share leadership widely in order to build new, beneficial policy regimes.

19 Using Deliberative Democracy to Facilitate a Local Culture of Collaboration: The Penn's Landing Project 399

William J. Ball

The Penn's Landing project, conducted in 2003, represented a rare confluence of official political interest, media involvement, and extensive public participation in planning for the development of the Philadelphia waterfront. The chapter author examines the project as a case study for creating a collaborative culture in an urban planning setting using the principles of deliberative democracy. Deliberative democracy is an effort to involve citizens in public policy agenda setting and decision making through peer discussions in small group settings. Although widely advocated in both the theoretical and applied literature on political processes, deliberative principles have infrequently been put to the test in a realistic setting, as they were in the Penn's Landing project. The project is evaluated for its impact in four areas: actual impact on policy, general thinking in the political system, training of knowledgeable personnel, and interaction with the public, using both qualitative and quantitative data. Although the project's impact on policy was derailed by the intervention of unexpected political events, the Penn's Landing project did have clear impacts in other areas that illustrate the key issues facing the creation of a collaborative culture in local planning and development.

20 Avoiding Ghettos of Like-Minded People: Random Selection and Organizational Collaboration   419

Lyn Carson

Universities provide notoriously atomized work spaces and present particular challenges for collaboration. This chapter examines two strategies for cultivating a culture of collaboration in an elite, research-intensive Australian university: (1) an initiative known as Coffee with the Dean and (2) reform of the selection procedures for the Academic Board. The author designed both strategies and assumed the role of champion for only one. Both strategies involved the random selection of participants, a selection procedure that runs counter to those typically used by hierarchical institutions. Orthodox selection methods such as nomination, invitation, or self-selection tend to encourage articulate elites to assume influential positions. The author argues that randomly based strategies, in combination with dialogic underpinnings, are a powerful combination to broaden the range of discussants while deepening organizational conversations. By embedding both, hierarchical organizations can improve their overall communication and formal decision-making processes, thus fostering a culture of collaboration.

21 Involving Multiple Stakeholders in Large-Scale Collaborative Projects   435

Tasos Sioukas, Marilyn Sweet

Involving multiple stakeholders is almost axiomatic for the success of collaborative projects. Effective collaborative agents spend time partnering with their project sponsor to identify stakeholders, talk to them, and form a core project team. Yet large-scale projects at complex organizations require much more than working effectively with stakeholders on a team. They require collaboration within and across multiple groups and individuals throughout the organization. The aim of this chapter is to help readers take the steps necessary to launch and sustain a systematic approach of inclusion and effective collaboration throughout the organization. These include reviewing the role of process facilitators, understanding the various categories of stakeholders and designing a stakeholder table of the organization, and creating a plan of collaborative action that feeds information to all stakeholder groups with the purpose of testing, refining, and communicating the solution.

Sandy Schuman is a group facilitator, collaborative process advocate, and story-teller. He helps groups create shared meaning, make critical choices, and build collaborative relationships. He is an associate at the Center for Policy Research, University at Albany, SUNY, and president of Executive Decision Services. He is editor of *The IAF Handbook of Group Facilitation* (Jossey-Bass, 2005) and of *Group Facilitation: A Research and Applications Journal* and moderates *Grp-Facl, The Electronic Discussion on Group Facilitation.*

Schuman holds a doctor of philosophy degree in organization behavior; a master of public administration degree from the Rockefeller College of Public Affairs and Policy, University at Albany, SUNY; and a bachelor of science in natural resource management from Cornell University. His work has appeared in publications such as *Conflict and Consensus, Corporate Meetings and Incentives, Interfaces, Information and Management, Journal of Policy Analysis and Management, Quality Progress, Government Technology, The Search for Collaborative Advantage,* and *Organizational Decision Support Systems.* His keynotes, presentations, and workshops have been featured by many organizations, including the American Society for Public Administration, the American Society for Training and Development, the American Society of Mechanical Engineers, the Energy Research and Development Authority, the Institute for Operations Research and Management Science, the International Association of Facilitators, the International City/County Management Association, the National Storytelling Network, and the Northeast Decision Sciences Institute.

You can contact Sandy Schuman via www.exedes.com or sschuman@albany.edu.

PREFACE

Meaning is all we want.
Choices are all we make.
Relationships are all we have.

Collaboration is hot! In fields as diverse as business, science, recreation, health care, social work, engineering, governance, and libraries, collaboration is seen as the way to address problems, add value, and achieve desired outcomes. Some articles and reports focusing on collaboration published in just the past year are highlighted in Exhibit P.1.

Why is interest in collaboration surging? Perhaps it reflects a pragmatic change in strategy to accommodate a diverse, interdependent, and complicated world. Perhaps, too, it indicates support of the values, principles, and beliefs underlying collaboration. These collaborative values, principles, and beliefs, which are reflected throughout this book, warrant our attention.

However, first I should acknowledge a number of concerns about collaboration. Collaboration "with the enemy," as in the case of Nazi collaborators during World War II, gives the word *collaboration* a distasteful connotation for many (Mintzberg, Dougherty, Jorgensen, and Westley, 1996). Although this book addresses collaboration in a positive light, caution is nonetheless warranted since collaboration is often used to give one set of individuals or organizations a competitive advantage or dominant position over another. In many cases, collaboration is unlikely to work because of "dispositions against

EXHIBIT P.1. COLLABORATION HERALDED IN DIVERSE FIELDS.

Business

Business Week highlighted the collaborative efforts of Procter & Gamble, Intuit, and other corporations to achieve their business goals ("Collaboration," 2005).

Engineering

"Casting Collaboration," an article published in *Appliance Design,* highlighted the increasing use of collaborative engineering (also referred to as cooperative engineering, concurrent engineering, or joint engineering) to "lower overall cost while improving quality and production efficiency" (Baran, 2005, p. 32).

Environment

Commenting on a recent joint agreement for the protection of the 5 million–acre Great Bear Rain Forest, British Columbia premier Gordon Campbell said, "There's a new era dawning in British Columbia. You have to establish what you value and work together. This collaboration is something we have to take into the future, and it is something the world can learn from" (Krauss, 2006).

Evolution

Researchers are exploring the evolutionary and biological bases for collaboration. Recent studies show that chimpanzees collaborate effectively when they profit directly and that humans cooperate even when they don't benefit themselves (Silk, 2006).

Federal Government

The United States' Government Accountability Office found that "the federal government faces a series of challenges in the 21st century that will be difficult, if not impossible, for any single agency to address alone" and identified "key practices that can help enhance and sustain federal agency collaboration" (Government Accountability Office, 2005, pp. 5–6).

Governance

Collaborative Governance: A Guide for Grantmakers, published by the William and Flora Hewlett Foundation, described collaborative governance as "an emerging set of concepts and practices that offer prescriptions for inclusive, deliberative, and often consensus-oriented approaches to planning, problem solving, and policymaking" and, quoting Frank and Denie Weil, "a new level of social/political engagement between and among the several sectors of society that constitutes a more effective way to address many of modern societies' needs beyond anything that the several sectors have heretofore been able to achieve on their own" (Henton, Melville, Amsler, and Kopell, 2005, p. 1).

EXHIBIT P.1. COLLABORATION HERALDED IN DIVERSE FIELDS, Cont'd.

Health and Social Work

In an article published in the journal *Health and Social Work,* the authors carefully laid out the evidence for collaboration: "Nurse and physician collaborative practice in intensive care units has been found to improve patient outcomes and nurse satisfaction. . . . Teamwork among physicians, nurses, and social workers reduced readmission to the hospital, reduced physician office visits, and helped older adults with chronic illnesses maintain their health status. . . . Collaboration among social workers and psychologists, physical therapists, and other health providers has been found to enhance the ability of these providers to meet clients' service needs, to better understand clients, to solve complex problems, and to successfully implement treatment plans" (Parker-Oliver, Bronstein, and Kurzejeski, 2005, p. 280).

Library and Information Professions

"Fostering a Spirit of Collaboration," published in *Information Today,* noted that "cooperative projects between libraries and other organizations are proliferating. . . . Information professionals actively seek partners and develop projects to reach out to new groups" (Gregory, 2006, p. 42).

Medicine

"The Power of Collaboration," in the *American Journal of Medical Quality,* reviewed various mechanisms used to improve medical quality and patient safety (Keroack, 2005).

Multiple Sectors

In *Collaborative Regional Initiatives,* published by the James Irvine Foundation, evaluators found that "collaborative efforts that engage participants from multiple sectors are more likely to produce workable solutions to challenges than business-as-usual approaches" (Innes and Rongerude, 2005, p. x).

Music

A special issue of *Psychology of Music* devoted to "the collaborative aspects of music making" found a number of factors underpinning collaboration in that field: "effective communication between the participants, whether this is verbal, nonverbal and/or musical, . . . the existence of a shared frame of reference for the task accompanied by mutual understanding, . . . [and] mutual understanding at a more personal level of each other's individual styles and preferences" (Miell, 2006, p. 147).

Parks and Recreation

"Natural Collaborations," an article in *Parks and Recreation,* provided case examples showing how collaboration "can provide answers to the budgetary epidemic that is infecting our park systems nationwide" (Trute, 2005, p. 61).

EXHIBIT P.1. COLLABORATION HERALDED IN DIVERSE FIELDS, Cont'd.

Policy

The Canadian Public Health Association published a "guide to collaborative processes involved in a wide range of situations and issues in health policy development. Its purpose is to foster awareness, dialogue and action in support of sustainable collaborative relationships" (Tomlinson and Strachan, 2005).

Science

Acknowledging the growth of scientific collaboration and its "powerful transformation of scientific work" (Hackett, 2005, p. 667), the journal *Social Studies of Science* devoted a special issue to the status and future of scientific collaboration.

Storytelling

Noting that "collaboration establishes the basis for learning from experience and sharing knowledge," Steve Denning (2005, p. 175) provided extensive guidance for using storytelling to build collaborative organizations.

---

cooperating with prior adversaries, the costs of collaboration in complex social and political systems, the difficulties of engaging in deep conflicts, and leadership incentives favoring control" (McCaffrey, Faerman, and Hart, 1995, p. 603). In some cases, where belief systems are inflexible, collaboration may not work at all: "the only thing that permits human beings to collaborate with one another in a truly open-ended way is their willingness to have their beliefs modified by new facts" (Harris, 2005, p. 48). In any case, collaboration takes time and effort and involves risks (Préfontaine, 2003).

Collaborative Values, Principles, and Beliefs

This book is focused on creating a culture of collaboration, which requires more commitment and change than, say, working collaboratively during a single meeting or project. For such relatively short-term activities, it might be sufficient for the prevailing norms to be temporarily suspended or ignored, but to create a culture of collaboration requires norms that are consistent with and supportive of collaboration. The chapters in this book address, implicitly or explicitly, the values, principles, and beliefs underlying collaboration. In addition, various organizations have issued formal statements, presented in the Appendix, "Collaborative Values, Principles, and Beliefs," at the back of the book. At their root, these statements share much in common. Each says something about our role in making decisions or choices, the information we need to make those decisions in a meaningful context, and how the individuals and organizations involved should relate to one another.

The act of making choices is fundamental to human nature and the health of individuals and society. This is reflected in the Declaration of the Rights of Man, which states, "Every citizen has a right to participate personally, or through his representative, in [the Law's] foundation" (National Assembly of France, 1789). Concern about the right to participate in decision making is not limited to the law or public sector issues; a number of recent articles have focused on the workplace (Cheney and Cloud, 2006; Johnson, 2006). For example, the journal *Economic and Industrial Democracy* "focuses on the study of initiatives designed to enhance the quality of working life through extending the democratic control of workers over the workplace and the economy" (Magnusson and Ottosson, 2006). A recent article noted:

> One of the consequences [of recent corporate scandals] has been the emergence of an employee rights movement that advocates greater employee participation in corporate decision-making. . . . Workplace democracy exists when employees have some real control over organizational goal setting and strategic planning, and can thus ensure that their own goals and objectives, rather than only those of the organization, can be met. . . . We feel it is difficult to contest employees' right to have a say not only in the conduct of their jobs, but also in the wider organization of work and the company's strategic direction, when employees will potentially be most negatively affected by the decisions made [Foley and Polanyi, 2006, p. 174].

Herbert Simon ([1945] 1997), a Nobel laureate in economics, deemed decision making the central function of organizations, and some scholars view choice as central to human experience: "All students like to believe that their particular subject is the center of the universe. Doubtless, students of judgment and decision making are no different, but they may have a good argument for their view. After all, they can claim that the great moments of history all turned on someone's judgment as to what should be done and someone's decision to do it" (Hammond and Arkes, 1986, p. 1).

These views and my own experience lead me to support the claim that all individuals and interest groups, in all sectors of society, have the right to meaningful participation in decisions that affect them.

To participate in decision making inherently requires that participants have pertinent information. A choice without information is hardly a choice at all. In the words of Thomas Jefferson, "I know no safe depositary of the ultimate powers of the society but the people themselves; and if we think them not enlightened enough to exercise their control with a wholesome discretion, the remedy is not to take it from them, but to inform their discretion by education" (Lipscomb and Bergh, 1904, p. 278).

Technical, objective facts are necessary but not sufficient. The social and personal context of facts is what gives them meaning. Following World War II, Victor Frankl wrote, "Striving to find a meaning in one's life is the primary motivational force of man" ([1946] 1962, p. 99). In recent years, researchers in positive psychology have identified meaning—"attachment to something larger, and the larger the entity to which you can attach yourself, the more meaning in your life" (Seligman, 2002, p. 14)—as essential to human fulfillment and happiness. Even when there is no argument about objective facts, their meaning—their implications and the preferences and subjective judgments related to them—can vary for different individuals and groups. How those differences come to be known and how they are communicated and understood rely on the relationships among the individuals and groups involved.

Margaret Wheatley (1999) observed, "None of us exists independent of our relationships with others. . . . What is critical is the *relationship* created between two or more elements" (pp. 35–36). Relationships provide the social context in which we exchange information and make choices. The dynamic health of our relationships affects, and is in turn affected by, the quality of our information and choices. Through our relationships, the knowledge, wisdom, and understanding of each individual have the potential to contribute to greater shared meaning and choices that provide greater mutual benefit. Meanings, choices, and relationships are inextricably and dynamically interdependent and are at the core of collaboration.

What's in This Book?

"What do you think it takes to create a culture of collaboration?" So begins Sam Kaner's conversation with five CEOs in Chapter One, "Five Transformational Leaders Discuss What They've Learned." These leaders synthesize their experiences in building collaborative organizations and touch on many of the issues that are the focus of subsequent chapters. Following this far-ranging conversation, the book is organized in three parts: "The Bases of Collaboration," "Approaches to Collaboration," and "Collaboration in Action." Many of the chapters could fit comfortably in any of these sections. Nonetheless, I hope the following organization and overview will set the stage for the book and help you find the information you need.

Part One: The Bases of Collaboration

The chapters in Part One explore the foundations on which collaboration can be built. Without these elements, it would be difficult for collaboration to succeed.

Chapter Two, "Renewing Social Capital: The Role of Civil Dialogue," by James Campbell, highlights the relationships among social networks, social capital, social trust, and social confidence—all necessary foundations for a culture of collaboration—and the role civil dialogue plays in their development.

However, even when some of these social conditions are lacking, collaboration can be built, as described by Mladen Koljatic, Mónica Silva, and Eduardo Valenzuela in Chapter Three, "The Development of Cross-Sector Collaborations in a Social Context of Low Trust," which draws on studies of cross-sectoral collaborations in Chile.

The dynamic nature of collaboration and the conditions that come into play are made more explicit in Chapter Four, "Exploring the Dynamics of Collaboration in Interorganizational Settings," by Ignacio Martinez-Moyano, which presents a formal model of interorganizational collaboration dynamics.

In Chapter Five, "Equity, Diversity, and Interdependence: A New Driver for Societal Transformation," Michael Murray and Brendan Murtagh review their experiences using equity, diversity, and interdependence to help heal social divisions in Northern Ireland and provide recommendations for applying this approach in organizations.

The conditions that enable a collaborative to maintain itself—to bend and remain flexible under pressure—are the subject of Chapter Six, What Keeps It Together: Collaborative Tensility in Interorganizational Learning," by Hilary Bradbury, Darren Good, and Linda Robson, which is based on their five-year study of the Sustainability Consortium, an interorganizational learning collaboration.

Concluding this part, in Chapter Seven, "Make-or-Break Roles in Collaboration Leadership," Mirja Hanson emphasizes the importance of three roles—participants, facilitators, and sponsors—for successful collaborative problem solving.

Part Two: Approaches to Collaboration

The actual work of creating and maintaining a culture of collaboration requires more than an understanding of its bases or foundations; we need some practical approach that will help individuals and groups work together more collaboratively. This part presents several such approaches.

Gervase Bushe illustrates the use of "learning conversations" to create "interpersonal clarity" in Chapter Eight, "Sense Making and the Problems of Learning from Experience: Barriers and Requirements for Creating Cultures of Collaboration." The author identifies thirteen cultural assumptions essential for interpersonal clarity and collaborative relationships.

In Chapter Nine, "Metaphors at Work: Building Multiagency Collaboration Through a Five-Stage Process," Carol Sherriff and Simon Wilson demonstrate how organizational metaphors can be made explicit and used to build shared meaning in multiple-organization settings.

The "uncertainty framework" presented by Kim Sander Wright in Chapter Ten, "Utilizing Uncertainty," provides a way to acknowledge stakeholders' states of mind with regard to their differing viewpoints and develop collaborative processes accordingly.

Chapter Eleven, "Sustainable Cooperative Processes in Organizations," by Dale Hunter, approaches collaboration as a developmental group process with the group's widening awareness of its social and ecological context.

Paul Wong bases his strategy of cultural transformation on the positive psychology of management, presented in Chapter Twelve, "Is Your Organization an Obstacle Course or a Relay Team? A Meaning-Centered Approach to Creating a Collaborative Culture."

In Chapter Thirteen, "Practical Dialogue: Emergent Approaches for Effective Collaboration," Rosa Zubizarreta compares dynamic facilitation, dialogue mapping, and transformative mediation, three nonlinear, nondirective approaches to collaboration.

Roger Schwarz contrasts the models of unilateral control and mutual learning in Chapter Fourteen, "Using the Facilitative Leader Approach to Create an Organizational Culture of Collaboration." He suggests that a change in mind-set is key to creating a culture of collaboration.

Chapter Fifteen, "Use of Self in Creating a Culture of Collaboration," by Ante Glavas, Claudy Jules, and Ellen Van Oosten, focuses on practitioners—facilitators, consultants, coaches, and managers—and their role as instruments of change by virtue of the way they present themselves to the individuals and groups with whom they work.

Part Three: Collaboration in Action

The case studies in this part are vehicles for integrating theory and practice and providing insights into what works.

To reduce its racial achievement gap and achieve educational equity, the public school system of Brookline, Massachusetts, had to work collaboratively. The conditions, practices, and processes used are described in Chapter Sixteen, "Collaboration for Social Change: A Theory and a Case Study," by Cynthia Parker, Linda Guinee, Courtney Bourns, Jennifer Fischer-Mueller, Marianne Hughes, and Andria Winther.

The maintenance division of a county public works department, "plagued with hostility, lack of trust, a vigorous rumor mill, racial tension, and an all-white 'old boy' network" is the setting for a five-pronged effort to build a more collaborative organization in Chapter Seventeen, "Theory in Action: Building Collaboration in a County Public Agency," by Jaime Harris and David Straus.

Stakeholder analysis and involvement, the framing of public problems, the difficulties of disrupting existing systems, the need to share leadership widely, and the importance of seed money, champions, and sponsors are important lessons from Chapter Eighteen, "Leadership for the Common Good," by John Bryson and Barbara Crosby.

In Chapter Nineteen, "Using Deliberative Democracy to Facilitate a Local Culture of Collaboration: The Penn's Landing Project," William Ball evaluates this effort to involve citizens in terms of its impact on public policy, general thinking in the political system, training of knowledgeable personnel, and interaction with the public.

Lyn Carson advocates for the random selection of participants in Chapter Twenty, "Avoiding Ghettos of Like-Minded People: Random Selection and Organizational Collaboration." She illustrates its effectiveness in one case and explores why it never got off the ground in another.

Using a synthesized case in a higher education setting, Chapter Twenty-One, "Involving Multiple Stakeholders in Large-Scale Collaborative Projects," by Tasos Sioukas and Marilyn Sweet, focuses on stakeholders and how they figure into planning and implementation at various stages of a project.

At the back of the book, the Key Concepts defines ideas and terms, cross-referenced to the chapters in which they are discussed.

Acknowledgments

The IAF Handbook of Group Facilitation was months away from coming off the press when this book project was launched. My personal thanks go to the International Association of Facilitators and Jossey-Bass for their willingness to forge ahead with a second edited volume before the success of the first one was known.

Working with the thirty-eight authors who contributed to this book has been intellectually rewarding and personally gratifying. My thanks go to all of you for your insights and efforts putting them in writing. Many of the authors attended a two-day "authors conference" that gave us the opportunity to hear and talk about draft chapters. Additional thanks go to you who participated in that outstanding exchange. Jon Jenkins, head of the Publications and Communications Strategic Initiative for the International Association of Facilitators, and Kathe Sweeney, senior editor at Jossey-Bass, deserve special thanks for supporting and advising this project from its inception.

June 2006
Albany, New York

Sandy Schuman
University at Albany
Center for Policy Research
sschuman@albany.edu

References

Baran, L. J. "Casting Collaboration." *Appliance Design*, 2005, 53(11), 32–36.

Cheney, G., and Cloud, D. "Doing Democracy, Engaging the Material: Employee Participation and Labor Activity in an Age of Market Globalization." *Management Communication Quarterly*, 2006, *19*(4), 501–540.

"Collaboration." *Business Week*, Nov. 21, 2005, p. 92.

Denning, S. *The Leader's Guide to Storytelling: Mastering the Art and Discipline of Business Narrative.* San Francisco: Jossey-Bass, 2005.

Foley, J. R., and Polanyi, M. "Workplace Democracy: Why Bother?" *Economic and Industrial Democracy,* 2006, *27*(1), 173–191.

Frankl, V. E. *Man's Search for Meaning: An Introduction to Logotherapy.* Boston: Beacon Press, 1962. (Originally published 1946.)

Government Accountability Office. *Results-Oriented Government: Practices That Can Help Enhance and Sustain Collaboration Among Federal Agencies.* Document no. GAO-06-15. Washington, D.C.: Government Accountability Office, Oct. 2005 [http://www.gao.gov/new.items/d0615.pdf].

Gregory, G. M. "Fostering a Spirit of Collaboration." *Information Today,* 2006, *23*(1), 42.

Hackett, E. J. (ed.). "Scientific Collaboration." *Social Studies of Science,* 2005, *35* (entire issue 5).

Hammond, K. R., and Arkes, H. R. *Judgment and Decision Making: An Interdisciplinary Reader.* Cambridge: Cambridge University Press, 1986.

Harris, S. *The End of Faith: Religion, Terror, and the Future of Reason.* New York: Norton, 2005.

Henton, D., Melville, J., Amsler, T., and Kopell, M. *Collaborative Governance: A Guide for Grantmakers.* Menlo Park, Calif.: William and Flora Hewlett Foundation, 2005.

Innes, J., and Rongerude, J. *Insight—Collaborative Regional Initiatives: Civic Entrepreneurs Work to Fill the Governance Gap.* San Francisco: James Irvine Foundation, 2005.

Johnson, P. "Whence Democracy? A Review and Critique of the Conceptual Dimensions and Implications of the Business Case for Organizational Democracy." *Organization,* 2006, *13*(2), 245–274.

Keroack, M. A. "The Power of Collaboration." *American Journal of Medical Quality,* 2005, *20*(3), 119–120.

Krauss, C. "Canada to Shield 5 Million Forest Acres." *New York Times International,* Feb. 7, 2006 [http://www.nytimes.com/2006/02/07/international/americas/07canada.html].

Lipscomb, A. A., and Bergh, A. E. (eds.). *The Writings of Thomas Jefferson, Memorial Edition,* vol. 15. Washington, D.C.: Thomas Jefferson Memorial Association, 1904.

Magnusson, L., and Ottosson, J. (eds.). *Economic and Industrial Democracy: An International Journal* [http://www.sagepub.com/journalScope.aspx?pid=30]. 2006.

McCaffrey, D. P., Faerman, S. R., and Hart, D. W. "The Appeal and Difficulties of Participative Systems." *Organization Science,* 1995, *6*(6), 603–627.

Miell, D. (ed.). "Musical Collaboration." *Psychology of Music,* 2006, *34* (entire issue 2).

Mintzberg, H., Dougherty, D., Jorgensen, J., and Westley, F. "Some Surprising Things About Collaboration: Knowing How People Connect Makes It Work Better." *Organization Dynamics,* 1996, *25*(1), 60–71.

National Assembly of France. "Declaration of the Rights of Man," Aug. 26, 1789 [http://www.yale.edu/lawweb/avalon/rightsof.htm].

Parker-Oliver, D., Bronstein, L. R., and Kurzejeski, L. "Examining Variables Related to Successful Collaboration on the Hospice Team." *Health and Social Work,* 2005, *30*(4), 279–286.

Préfontaine, L. *New Models of Collaboration: A Guide for Managers—Risk Management in New Models of Collaboration.* Montreal: Centre Francophone d'Informatisation des Organisations, 2003.

Seligman, M.E.P. *Authentic Happiness: Using the New Positive Psychology to Realize Your Potential for Lasting Fulfillment.* New York: Free Press, 2002.

Silk, J. "Who Are More Helpful, Humans or Chimpanzees?" *Science,* 2006, *311,* 1248–1249.

Simon, H. A. *Administrative Behavior: A Study of Decision-Making Processes in Administrative Organization.* (4th ed.) New York: Free Press, 1997. (Originally published 1945.)

Tomlinson, P., and Strachan, D. *A Guide to Collaborative Processes in Health Policy Development and Their Implications for Action.* Ottawa: Canadian Public Health Association, 2005.

Trute, B. R. "Natural Collaborations." *Parks and Recreation,* 2005, *40*(11), 60–63.

Wheatley, M. J. *Leadership and the New Science Revised: Discovering Order in a Chaotic World.* San Francisco: Berrett-Koehler, 1999.

CREATING A CULTURE OF COLLABORATION

Sam Kaner, Ph.D., is regarded as one of the nation's leading experts on consensus decision making. He is the senior author of *Facilitator's Guide to Participatory Decision-Making* (New Society, 1996) and has for more than two decades been a featured speaker at the annual conferences of several professional associations, including the International Association of Facilitators and the National Organization Development Network. His corporate clients have included Hewlett-Packard, VISA International, Charles Schwab, PricewaterhouseCoopers, Symantec, and many other Fortune 500 companies. His public sector clients have included the California Supreme Court, Omidyar Network, March of Dimes, Special Olympics, Goodwill Industries, and many community-based organizations, universities, foundations, and government agencies. Since 1986, Kaner has been executive director of Community At Work, a San Francisco–based consulting firm that specializes in designing and facilitating cross-functional and cross-sector collaboration.

CHAPTER ONE

FIVE TRANSFORMATIONAL LEADERS DISCUSS WHAT THEY'VE LEARNED

Sam Kaner

You're about to read an edited transcript of two conversations over dinner among five chief executives and a moderator. The topic was "What have we learned about creating collaborative cultures in our organizations?"

The executives are three CEOs and two executive directors. All five have led their organizations through deep, systemic transformations. They have each "earned their spurs" as leaders of change, and they each richly deserve to be seen as leaders in the broad-based progressive movement to foster healthy human systems at work and in larger constituent communities. This is not to say that they have positioned themselves as public speakers or professional experts on collaboration; far from it. In fact, all five have focused their professional efforts on advancing the missions of their organizations. These are CEOs, not management gurus. Nonetheless, in their efforts to overcome the challenges presented by hierarchical authority, tradition, dependence on expertise, and the other sources of inertia that make genuine collaboration difficult, they have gained much wisdom.

The author would like to thank Susan Lubeck, Jacqueline Warner, and Sam Chapman for their assistance in the preparation of this chapter.

Since every human organization is unique, perhaps it is self-evidently true that the specific day-by-day activity of creating a culture of collaboration will also have many unique components. This raises a basic question: are there any commonalities, any challenges or insights that might resonate or apply across different sectors and different types of organization? The organizations discussed in this chapter represent a broad range of enterprise cultures: business, government, human services, academia, and politics. Yet even though their organizations' missions and strategies were uniquely different from one another, the five chiefs had no trouble establishing a commonality of experience. They immediately found their way to the central question: what does it take for people—employees, customers, boards, other stakeholders—to contribute meaningfully to the success of the enterprise as a whole? On this topic, with its many various subthemes, the five spoke as colleagues, as though they could take it for granted that they shared many assumptions and goals.

In addition to writing this paper, I was also the conversation's moderator on both evenings. I am an organization development (OD) consultant, and all five executives and their organizations were current OD clients of mine at the time of the event. I was assisted in moderating this project by Susan Lubeck, J.D., a professional colleague and senior OD consultant at our firm, Community At Work.

In what follows, I have decided to let the wisdom of the conversation speak for itself, without providing any footnotes or other editorializing comments. However, I would like to use this initial moment, before the main event begins, to share one observation that stood out for me.

More than any specific insight I heard discussed at the dinners—and there were many, as you'll see—I was struck, overall, by a quality of transformational leadership that all five of these leaders shared:

They had more questions than answers.

They were thoughtful, curious, and eager to show each other their thinking. They wanted to get a better grasp on what they did not yet have nailed down. Throughout the conversation, and also back home at their organizations, they were able to "live in the question." This is not to say that they were overly cautious or ruminative in their approaches to running their organizations. From watching them at first hand in each of their work settings, I know them all to be risk takers—a quality that I think goes with the territory of leading an organization through basically uncharted water. But what I saw at the dinners is that they did not feel they had to have all the answers.

They all understood the desirability—perhaps I could even say they all recognized the necessity—of embedding participatory, collaborative values into their organizations' mind-sets and daily practices. Yet they had acknowledged for themselves that the project of building collaborative culture is not scientific. They did not even presume that they could rely on a body of accepted practices that would work the same way in every case, with predictable results. Leading an organization to change itself into a more empowered, more inspired, healthier human system is a hope, not a formula; it's something you do, and keep doing, on faith. And you do it knowing you will face plenty of trials and errors along the way. It's an ongoing existential challenge, complete with the leader's burdens—being accountable (even if not solely responsible) for the painful, unpredicted impacts on real people and for the inevitable less-than-perfect outcomes for the system as a whole. The conversation got me thinking that where "change strategy" is concerned, living in the question is probably the only honest choice.

The five chiefs seemed to take this for granted, and it made them reflective and humble. It appeared to be clear to them, even without discussing it directly, that the unknowns of system change were deeper and more impactful than the models and techniques they employed. I suspect that this modesty is a characteristic that comes with time; it's a seasoning that I think develops after one discovers the hard way that "hip, hype, and hurry up" might get a new product out the door, but sustainable transformation is something else entirely.

I hope that message comes through in what follows. It was not the purpose of this chapter to celebrate leadership or even to propose that the leader is the key to a transformation. As Caroline Estes (1996) puts it, "Everyone has a piece of the truth."

A leader has a role to play, yes, and in that role, he or she can provide the organization with many important elements: vision, insight, expertise, focus, resources, and so on. And I think it's self-evidently important to discuss and explore the role of leadership in a collaborative context, as this project has attempted to do.

But being the formal leader in creating a culture of collaboration is not the same as being the all-seeing, all-knowing provider of the "right way" to make it work. It takes the village to raise the child. And isn't that the whole point of creating a collaborative culture to begin with?

The Participants

Deborah Alvarez-Rodriguez: President and CEO of Goodwill Industries, San Francisco, San Mateo, and Marin counties. Deborah has enabled a systemwide rethinking of the Goodwill mission in the Bay Area. The result is a profound shift from the long-standing mission—managing thrift stores that also provide job training and transitional support for people with barriers to employment—to the revitalized new mission: *Goodwill Industries creates solutions to poverty through the businesses we operate.* At this writing, Goodwill is fully profitable, with gross revenues greatly increased from its historical norms.

Kriss Deiglmeier: Executive director of Stanford University Graduate School of Business Center for Social Innovation (CSI). Kriss is responsible, along with her two academic co-directors, for creating and following through on a systemwide shift in the CSI mission and strategy and in the implementation of many new programs and services. Stanford Graduate School of Business was recently honored by the Aspen Institute with the prestigious Beyond Grey Pinstripes award. Stanford ranked as the number one full-time M.B.A. program, leading the way in integrating social and environmental stewardship into business school curricula and research.

John Harris: Founder and CEO of California Birth Defects Monitoring Program (CBDMP). CBDMP is generally regarded as the world's largest research organization that focuses exclusively on finding causes of birth defects. To further enhance the reach and power of his organization, John also founded Pediatric BioBank, an international collaborative research organization that provides the best maternal health researchers in the world with state-of-the-art technology, to collaborate across traditional disciplines in studying why some babies are born healthy and others are not.

Kathy Kneer: President and CEO of Planned Parenthood of California. This organization is primarily an advocacy organization, affiliated with the nine Planned Parenthood–affiliated operating medical clinics in California. Under Kathy's leadership since 1993, Planned Parenthood Affiliates of California has become one of the leading voices in the national movement for women's reproductive rights. Prior to 1993, Kathy was COO at CBDMP and worked side by side with John Harris for several years.

Jim Schorr: Executive director of Juma Ventures, Inc. This organization provides employment and job skills training and support to at-risk youth. Juma Ventures is frequently held up as a national model for a successful social enterprise and youth development programs. Under Jim's tenure, Juma was refocused and redesigned in a multimonth process that involved full participation from every staff person. In February 2005, Juma Ventures was cited in the *Harvard Business Review* as one of the most successful social enterprises in the United States.

The Conversation: Opening Thoughts

Sam Kaner: Well, how about if I start with the question in its most basic form: What do you think it takes to create a culture of collaboration?

Jim Schorr: I think it takes a really deep belief among the key people in the organization that a collaborative culture is the path to the best results you want to achieve. If they don't believe it, they won't help create it.

Sam: From your own personal experience, what suggests that as a key factor?

Jim: Some people, perhaps myself included, aren't collaborative by nature. They have been successful in their careers by being outstanding at what they do as individuals—by cranking out work and producing results. That attitude doesn't translate well into the leadership role. I have managers who I put into leadership roles because they're good at what they do, in their own area of competence. But once in the role, they need to develop a whole new perspective. They have to think on behalf of something larger than themselves, on behalf of the success of the organization as a whole, which is where the benefit of a collaborative culture comes in. This is a challenging bridge to help them cross—it has certainly been challenging for me!

Kathy Kneer: I agree completely. As a leader, I have to keep in mind that I'm doing this for the long-term benefit. There's surely no reason to do it for a short-term benefit.

Jim: I'm not even sure there *are* any short-term benefits. To my mind, the short term impacts are risks.

Sam: Such as . . . ?

Jim: Lost opportunities. Impatience from people with short attention spans and lots of work to do back in their own program areas. The lowering of morale that can come with that. And there's a discomfort many people feel at being expected to speak their minds when they aren't really used to talking to their peers that way. It can be polarizing in the short run.

Kathy: Yes, often the pressures to deliver a result in the near term are so strong, I have to hold back my own impulses and just keep reminding myself of the payoffs—even though those payoffs are two, three, five years away. This is a hard thing to get across to my managers. I have had to keep communicating about the value itself. And communicating about a value is always a work in progress.

Some things need to happen faster than the pace of collaboration and full participation can permit. So you have to strike a balance between short- and long-term impacts. It's a trade-off. And explaining that rationale becomes part of what needs to be communicated.

John Harris: For me, there is one key value that I want my managers to understand and endorse. There has to be shared belief among all of us that the team works better than the individual. If they can accept that value and treat it as a basic premise of our meetings and our projects, then they will have an easier time tolerating the frustration and impatience that accompany our efforts to build a shared framework of understanding.

Sam: How important is it for your groups to build a shared framework of understanding among the members?

John: It is absolutely necessary, but in practice, it is a really hard thing to do. You have to create an atmosphere where people are willing to listen and where they are willing to teach one another and learn from one another—and that's very difficult. You get into the issues of hierarchy and status, and people at both ends of the spectrum become reluctant to engage. So when I address that dynamic, I do as Kathy suggested: I communicate about the value. However, rather than try to explain to them the concept of shared understanding, I put it out as the principle that a team works better than an individual.

Kriss Deiglmeier: A favorite saying of mine is "No one is as smart as everyone." I've used that as a shorthand way to remind people to stay patient. And I've found the result to be generally worth the effort. Even if a decision takes longer to reach, the implementation has a much better chance of succeeding. Of course, like everyone else, I am dealing with many people who don't intuitively appreciate this value, so I agree. I put a lot of effort into communicating and staying committed to the value.

Kathy: Different leaders may have different reasons they think collaboration is important to their work. But once they come to that conclusion, I think there is often a period where that one person has to put himself or herself out there and stand up for the value—even in the face of a lot of people who don't support it. I remember when John and I introduced this value at CBDMP, we both had to put ourselves on the line, and for a while there, we were target practice! Regularly. And as things unfolded, we had to go through sustained periods of rebellion. We had to just keep living the value, modeling it, and not taking all the criticism personally.

Ultimately, you want a group that believes in the values of full participation, mutual understanding, and shared responsibility, but you don't start with any of that. No matter what words one communicates about the value or the benefits, it is just not real in the beginning—or for quite a while. So what you do have early on is a lot of personal risk taking by the leadership, a lot of being willing to lead by example under scrutiny. It took awhile for people to trust us enough to start taking risks themselves.

Deborah Alvarez-Rodriguez: To me, it's an article of faith. It's not a matter, exactly, of being able to achieve a linear result by a particular point in time. It comes down to faith—a fundamental belief or understanding that there is a better way. Yes, teamwork is harder, costly, slower in the short run, and yes, sometimes being autocratic is even really the better choice. But in the big picture, I just have a profound belief, a conviction, that collaboration will not only eventually get you to the best solutions but will in fact bring out the best in everyone. It will bring out the best in the organization and its people. This is what I try to get across to my people. I can put up with the level of risk and hassle because I believe in the underlying view of the world that collaboration represents. There aren't too many things in my life I'd be willing to sacrifice as much as I've sacrificed to try to build a collaborative culture in an organization. I don't want to come across sounding overly religious here, but this notion of faith and sacrifice, this is what it takes for me to get up every day and get back in there. All the operational issues, the policy meetings, the budget challenges, the personnel challenges, the lawsuits . . . all of it!

Kathy: And don't forget our boards of directors.

Deborah: Don't get me started! Sometimes it all just boggles my mind. It's like "What, you want to share another idea with me? Can you please take a number? Can't you just go away and deal with these things yourself?" And actually, it's at those very moments, when it would be so much more expedient to just forget about participatory values—those are the times that my faith kicks in. "Stop, Debbie, slow down and listen; you just might find the answer if you can just shut up and listen. You just might see someone else step up and rise to the occasion." And sometimes it happens and sometimes it does not. But if I didn't believe that it could happen, that it will happen, and that it matters—deeply—not only for my employees personally but for my basic view of the world—if I didn't believe it, I don't know if I would keep coming back to work.

Creating and Managing Participants' Expectations

Kathy: This is bringing something up for me: the issue of words versus action. I have observed leaders—and I'm sure I have been guilty of this myself—who have advertised to their staff the desire to keep everyone involved and obtain buy-in from everyone. And yet when they were under pressure, they fell back on their own instincts and made the decision. People can see through that, of course, and it becomes a setback.

Listening to Deborah, I realize that we are going to end up being true to who we are. If as a leader you are a person who operates best in a hierarchical structure, then fine—just say what's true and let yourself be as effective as you can be. I think it's a serious mistake to say one thing and act differently. And we need to be clear that what we *tell* people we want to create is what we actually *do* want to create. Especially in the early stage, when so much of our ability to make a change is based on our own behavior—on the modeling we do, not our words. We have to be careful not to communicate values that we can't model.

Deborah: I agree. This notion of "walking your talk" and being consistent with who you are is really important. People do pick up on the bull, really quickly. Even so, in my own case, my actions are not entirely consistent with my values, even though I truly do believe in them. I can jump too far out in front, and when I do, I sometimes pay the price we've been discussing.

At those times, one of the most helpful tools has been acknowledging that I made a mistake. "I made this decision based on such-and-such information and reasoning. I now see that it was not a good decision for these reasons." When I've done that, it has been very powerful; it encourages a level of risk taking in others. Just sharing and being honest about the mistakes I've made has carried enormous weight. That's been a revelation for me. If I don't walk my talk sometimes, I can acknowledge it and hopefully learn from it, and we can move on.

Sam: Well, this raises a fundamental question: how do any of you manage to walk the talk of teamwork and participation, modeling collaborative values, when at the same time you are the visionary of the group? Sometimes you are the person who has done the most thinking about the future. On the strategic plane, you may well have the best judgment in the room. And then during a discussion, all the ideas people bring up are ones you've thought about and already dismissed months ago. . . .

So tell me, how do you balance this tension?

Kathy: Let's suppose you do have a clear, compelling vision; you have already done the groundwork, the research, the background conversations, and so on. In those situations, you don't want or need your staff to be reinventing the wheel. In that case, the nature of the collaboration is to bring all the players into alignment. You want them then to find ways to turn the vision from ideas to reality.

John: In our case, to make our vision come true, I knew I needed very strong implementation skills. I'm talking about the many skills that I didn't myself have. So I was able to convey that I needed to learn from the people in the room what it would take to make our mission succeed.

The mission itself was not up for grabs—our mission is to find causes of birth defects, and even though that might sound like an easy and obvious mission to get behind, there are in fact reasons why a scientist might not like it or feel 100 per cent comfortable with it. But I learned to be really clear about what's not negotiable. At a certain point, I learned how to bracket the academic conversations and move them out of our planning sessions. At that point, I was able to focus the group's thinking, and everyone was able to relax. My message was, "I don't have the slightest idea how to make this happen; designing this certain system or process is beyond me. I need people who can help me build this research apparatus, and therefore I need you." And I genuinely believe that—I mean, I know my limits as an implementer.

Kriss: Do you believe that engaging your staff in designing the implementation will cause them to believe that they, too, helped develop the vision?

Jim: In my experience, yes, they did have that perception—because the vision actually changed slightly in the process of being implemented.

Kriss: I agree with that. Even if you have a vision that is 100 percent clear, it really ends up being about 30 percent different from what you initially brought to the group. It ends up better, in other words, because of everyone's unanticipated contributions.

John: Absolutely.

Leadership Competencies

Jim: As I listen to this conversation, a couple of themes are coming up for me: patience and accountability. These have been important learnings for me.

Sam: How so?

Jim: I'm someone who needs and wants to solve a problem as soon as it comes up. I'm not patient about discussing the issues; I want to get right to the heart of "the answer." And when I do make an effort to hold back and give people the chance to contribute, not everyone is willing to speak up and say what they really think. A few people, yes. But others seem, at times, prepared to just wait things out. Either they make statements that are innocuous, noncontroversial, or they don't say much at all. And then, because of my natural tendency, I'm often willing to jump in and fill the dead space. Then I look back later and realize I did more talking than I'd wanted to.

John: Me too, sometimes. For sure.

Kathy, Deborah: Me too!

Jim: So I have had to make a very conscious, thoughtful effort about how I carry myself at work. Every day. When I'm unprepared for a meeting—when I let myself "wing it"—I make the same mistakes: moving at my pace, not the pace of a group; giving the answers to every question that arises; not letting others wrestle with the issues. Not being a natural collaborative leader, I have had to learn to spend literally a couple of hours each night thinking about the next day's meetings. The one-to-one meetings, the supervision sessions, the group meetings. If I do think about them and focus myself on being aware of the interaction, not just the answers, I find that I'm a lot more effective in the role.

Sam: You mentioned two themes: patience and accountability. Could you say more about the latter?

Jim: I don't think a participatory process will work if people feel that it is acceptable for them to sit quietly in a meeting, keeping their opinions to themselves so they don't have to risk dealing with others who might disagree with them. I can understand that some people might feel self-conscious for various reasons. And I don't mean that I want to pressure people to perform for the sake of performing. But on the other hand, I don't think it's good for me to accommodate their passivity either. If they are silent and I just jump in to fill in the blanks, I am in effect endorsing their passivity. At those junctures, my behavior is saying, "It's OK for you to be quiet and let me talk. I'll just go ahead and do that."

This is an insight that has proved very useful to me. I want people in my groups to understand and experience that I do expect them to give us their best thinking—not just as a nice idea, but as a responsibility.

John: Again, this rings true for me.

Deborah, Kriss, Kathy: Yes, me too.

Kriss: Speaking of preparation, I did not anticipate how much time it takes to plan a collaborative process. Setting the goals, defining what's not up for grabs versus what decisions are the group's to make. And this is true also for the participation of the individuals—the issues Jim just brought up. To me, whether it is silence or a different dynamic, the sort of endless discussion that happens in academic settings, or whatever, you don't just get people to behave differently by politely asking them to. It takes structure. There is a vast depth of structure to collaboration. And designing the structure and organizing the process take a whole lot of time and concentration.

Jim: Exactly.

The Value of an External OD Consultant

Kathy: This conversation about structure and planning is reminding me of Sam's role and how it affects me. Do any of us think we could do this kind of work if we did not have external consulting? I wonder. We've all had the chance to work with Sam, a disinterested third party—not someone to tell us what to do but someone who helps us think things through. Is it realistic to expect that we could accomplish some of what we've been discussing without some degree of external coaching?

Deborah: You can use your own organization as your sounding board only to a certain extent. You can't ever lose sight of the impacts of your role and how your behavior is going to be perceived. My role, my authority, and my power affect how people engage with me, even how they look at me. I have to be careful how I phrase things. We can say, "Yes, we are all in this together," but the fact that I'm CEO carries a different weight, even when I don't want it to!

Jim: It's inherently challenging to be a CEO and to be a collaborator among others.

Deborah: That's where having a skilled person like Sam comes in. It's not just that he helps me achieve my goals; it's a lot more. I can learn—partly from our conversations and partly from watching him handle the people and the processes, in the various groups he facilitates at our company.

Basically, my relationship with Sam represents the maximum level of vulnerability I allow myself to have at work. That then becomes the context for my maximum level of "teachability." My chance to be reflective and let my guard down is wrapped together with my chance to learn and grow in this role.

Kriss: The isolation we feel is one problem; another is the challenge of wearing two hats. In my own case, I have to participate *and* facilitate. I have multiple advisory and faculty boards. They need to hear my thinking—and often I need to be thinking right alongside them. When I've got the external facilitation support, I can participate fully; when I don't have the support and therefore I have to facilitate as well, it's much harder to make my best contributions. I really notice the difference.

Deborah: Well, let's agree that the external process-consultant role is critical to success—yet there are so few people who do it well. Plus, it's difficult to fund, and it's difficult to carve out the time for it.

Kathy: I think we have all realized this is something you can't short-shrift. We can have the vision, but to really make it happen, we need to use external resources. It would be much harder if we didn't. I think this is about being honest with ourselves: are you really committed to collaboration? If so . . .

Deborah: Granted. Still, this has implications. For one, it's challenging to figure out where and when to deploy external facilitators and coaches and consultants and at what level within the organization. I want to support my middle managers and even my line staff to emerge as leaders. But it's very tricky to supply everyone with all the external support they might need. I also need to run a profitable business that aligns with market realities. So how does one multiply the "Sam Kaner effect"?

John: Part of our evolution to a collaborative culture was in the skills and tools we developed to manage our meetings. Collaborative culture is experienced in meetings, so I made it a priority for us to learn and improve those skills. I started out poor, and now I'm good at meetings. I can facilitate. So can others. Our staff uses flipchart pads. Without consulting support, this could not have happened. I had the insight to want to be better at meeting management but didn't have the skills.

Sam: You're pointing out that skill building is part of the answer to the problem of leveraging external resources. I'd like to pursue this a bit more. What are your opinions of putting a lot of employees through a two- to three-day workshop on a key topic? In your experience, how effective are those programs as a vehicle for building collaborative culture?

John: Workshops are an introduction, but the real training ground happens when you are inside a problem and you have to solve it. One time I ran an all-staff meeting that was a disaster. I walked into Sam's office the following week and said, "That's it—I'm quitting!" But actually, once I got over my initial discomfort, I found that the sense of failure gave me an enormous impetus to improve. That experience of trial and error, of falling down and learning how to get up—that was the real training. Similarly, with my managers, we have to wrestle with very difficult problems, and the experience of being frustrated, being disheartened, but still hanging in there and recovering and then learning how and why our recovery was possible—that was the training. After fifteen years of those experiences, I'm very versatile. And many people in the organization have developed their own competencies in similar ways—through real-world training, not just workshops.

Kathy: Let's acknowledge that it is important to build capacity in your organization. I think there are various ways you can do this. I routinely have consultants other than Sam who work with my staff—for planning, for big meetings, for coaching, and so on. But I want to be tenacious about the importance of investing in ourselves as leaders. At some point, we need a truly safe place for ourselves. That is the hardest part for me to think about—because it is not comfortable to make the decision to invest in myself, as an asset of the organization. I want to reiterate: if we are going to make our commitment to collaboration and participation into something real, we have to be willing to invest in the resource of a talented, trustworthy outside consultant.

Kriss: Would I be at the same stage of success now if I had undertaken to change my organization without Sam or someone like him? Who knows? But there is a significant possibility that I would not be. The complexity of what I was undertaking was vast. I couldn't see clearly. Working with the consultant, assessing, helping make the options clear—all of that enabled me to make key decisions and then move forward in a conscious and intentional way. I had a gut commitment to be inclusive and build a critical mass of support, but there were so many variables in play. Politics, personalities, structure, funders. I can't envision that I'd have been able to juggle so many variables on my own. I'd have continued with my values, yes, true. On a "successfulness scale" of one to ten, maybe I'd have gotten to a five.

Jim: Would you say that a central factor was the opportunity to slow down and think strategically?

Kriss: It's more than that. I know how to set the time aside to focus on thinking strategically. But in the complexity of my whole situation—I'm overseeing operations, I'm engaged in all the fundraising, I'm interfacing politically throughout the system—it is extremely valuable to have someone skilled who can facilitate my thinking, someone I can bounce off, someone who sees things in a different way—that's their job.

Deborah: When I first became CEO of Goodwill, I was hired with a mandate to bring a lot of change to this company. I interviewed many people before I took the job. And then after I started, I spent several weeks continuing to assess and gain a sense of the scale of the needed organizational transformation. After a couple of months, it became clear just how huge the change was going to be. And it became equally clear that I couldn't lead this transformation without someone helping me with in the ways we discussed: helping me with my clarity, my discipline, my pacing. I would have gotten caught up in details and focused on the most expedient solution, even though I really wanted to be collaborative and strategic.

Interestingly, the expenditures for consulting services introduce a level of discipline: when you're spending the time and money on this high-level consultation, it really makes you think twice about short-circuiting the collaborative process and undermining your investment. So the discipline in and of itself has been very useful to me.

Jim: I've found that my instincts are good in some areas and not so good in others. With people issues, I've been surprised at how often my instincts aren't as good as I need them to be. Working with Sam has helped me with that, helped me make better decisions, especially in the realm of various personnel issues. Dealing with the transition challenges of being successor to the founder of our organization, dealing with the human variables of building a whole new leadership team—all those types of decisions. On the people side, I don't always see the land mines. . . . That's a lot of what I get out of the relationship with Sam. In some areas, I can see pretty clearly. With human dimensions, I don't.

What Keeps You Up at Night?

Sam: As you've each been speaking about your relationships with me and what it means for you, you have also been speaking about yourselves—just as Jim just did. And you've been sharing your hopes and your fears and your sense of where you're strong and where you need help. I'd like to ask you to stay with this a bit longer—not about me, not about your relationship to a consultant, but just about yourselves as individuals in this role. You are each having to carrying the ball of being the visionary leader, but also you can't avoid being the role model for collaboration—the chief implementer of the culture change—*and* you must also be the chief implementer of the strategy itself. With all the weight and all the pressure of having to measure up on competing and sometimes contradictory roles, what is hard for you about that? What keeps you up at night? What weighs on your shoulders heavily about playing this role?

John: People. There are many people I love to learn from, and I can and do learn from them. But now and then I have to deal with people I'd basically just like to klonk!—on a good day! And they can be in positions of very high responsibility—for example, they might be high-ranking government officials, some of whom I have to deal with month in, month out. Or perhaps they are research scientists, based at a university but running studies through our organization so their influence is widely felt. And there have been senior people within my own staff, too. All these people are in their roles because they are capable at something, whether science or management. Yet for whatever reason, their personalities don't mesh well with mine.

What worries me is the way I might react to such people. I don't want to lose my objectivity, even when I'm having emotional reactions. Partly I'm concerned that I won't listen to them; I'll write them off. Or even more likely in my case, I worry that I'll overcompensate and give them too much influence on my decisions—not because they intimidate me or anything like that but because I don't want to let my anger get the best of me, so I lean in the other direction.

Sam: So it's how to manage your own feelings as you manage the relationships with the ones you're having trouble with?

John: Yes.

Sam: What's your M.O. for working with that concern, so you don't get constantly caught up in it?

John: I bought my own sound bite, believing the team works better than an individual. I have a deep belief in that. I like sports, and it works in sports. In research, it's obvious: you can't work in any way other than as a team. I really deeply believe in that. And I also deeply believe that many people can do many things better than I can.

Sam: So reaching to that belief in the power of teams and collaborating helps you get past your own personal feelings.

John: Yes—though I don't always get past them, as you know [*laughs*]. . . . Also, I think my fear of failure is another of these. It presses on me. And then I draw on my belief in the power of teams to help me override that fear.

Kathy: I too have a fear of failure—but even more than that, I have that nagging question, "Did I do enough? Maybe I should've done one more thing." That's the fear that eats at me. The stakes are high. Not just for our employees or my board but, more importantly, for all women and their health and, even beyond that, the role of women in our society. There are so many things that need to be done; so many forces and challenges coming up all the time. Did I do enough? And the issue of collaboration gets in here because it begs the question, "Am I putting enough time into developing my staff? Am I doing enough there?"

Deborah: Two questions keep me up at night: Am I doing the right thing? And am I getting too far out there, too grandiose? Both questions are undergirded by that fact that so many of our employees are vulnerable, still learning how to get on their feet. If I make bad decisions and we have to downsize, I'm hurting the person with four kids including one who's autistic—I'm contributing to messing up their lives. Should I really put so much effort and money and time into this whole transformation process? Maybe I should slow down, focus on incremental gains.

And the vision that I have been holding out—am I crazy? I want to grow a major business, a real business; I want to prove you can do business in a way that treats poor people as the essence of value creation, not as a by-product of value creation. At the end of the day, I would hate to think I was instrumental in destroying an eighty-seven-year-old organization.

Jim: That fear of screwing up an organization—I've had to work hard on getting over that one. Juma Ventures, from an external perspective, was very healthy, innovative, successful, when I took over. Of course, it had its fair share of challenges and issues—but all the same, I was succeeding the founder of a successful, reputable organization, and I did not want to screw it up.

Even so, I definitely wanted to refocus the whole enterprise. We have closed businesses to streamline the operation, we have strengthened many programs, we have positioned ourselves for a significant expansion on quite a different footing than our previous approach, and one of the features of the change has been the depth of collaboration that has been undertaken by my new team. But the subterranean worry about messing things up—that has been tough to get my hands around.

Nonetheless, there is an even bigger weight I carry. That's the solitude of the role, the feeling of being alone in the job, in so many ways. It is ironic that despite my serious effort and investment to deepen our teamwork and collaboration, I myself feel so isolated.

Being collaborative, it turns out, does not mean being deep friends. The boss is the boss, and having a staff as youthful as mine just amplifies this condition. It isn't a fear, but it's a deep, nagging loneliness that keeps me awake all the same.

Difficult Dynamics, Part One: Individuals Who Are Reluctant to Embrace a Collaborative Philosophy

Sam: At the beginning of our conversation tonight, Jim suggested that one of the critical success factors for building a culture of collaboration was a deep belief in collaborative philosophy among the key players. The way you put it, Jim, was, "If they don't believe it, they won't help create it." John, you echoed this theme a few minutes ago when you said that what keeps you up at night is the people who are not collaborative. So tell me, what happens with the people who simply don't see it the way each of you does?

Kathy: Obviously, it's not as simple as "fire them." If you did that, a wealth of knowledge and seasoning would walk out the door.

Jim: Or maybe the person is someone you recruited and cultivated for a long time, perhaps because they provide cultural balance to a workforce that needs to maintain staff diversity.

Sam: Yes. What do you do about these types of employees? You don't want to lose them, and they don't want to change. And yet your other employees are watching you. If you don't handle those people effectively, it will often be perceived as evidence that you don't walk the talk. I'd appreciate hearing you talk about this struggle.

John: I'm very conscious of this issue. I'm also very sure I don't have an answer—I'm very conscious of that too. I'm working with scientists whose main labs are based all over the world and who all share a few key assumptions of the academic-scientific culture, which are anathema to the collaborative philosophy. Being a principal investigator, a PI, is basically like being the lord of the land. In my day-to-day negotiations with PIs, I'm constantly trying to stand for a collaborative model, a model based on sharing protocols and data early on—not after studies are published but much sooner—so that we can get on with the business of actually finding causes of birth defects. And this is a very, very hard stance to take. These are people who have enormous research grants: they are tenured, they are deans, they are senior scientists in some of the largest research centers in the world, and they often don't give a damn about sharing protocols—at least, not before they publish their own findings. To them, collaboration means reading papers at conferences or corresponding about interesting questions. At most, it means working with a small group, their own individual research teams. But it does not, for example, mean sharing with their counterparts at other universities the set of raw data collected during interviews with pregnant mothers.

So I have to make trade-offs when I negotiate with these scientists. Sometimes I feel like I'm not walking the walk, I'm not consistent. I can say that I am conscious all the time of what is a collaborative arrangement and what isn't. But I don't have the . . . the what? Is it the power? The clout? I do have excellent resources and systems to share, which is why I'm even at the table. . . . I just don't have a model, I don't feel I've solved this challenge yet.

I do know and believe in my heart that science will find causes of birth defects sooner, and better, if the best thinkers in the world would do a better job of pooling resources and brainpower, and I want to make that happen as much as possible in my lifetime. But I don't know how to do it, against all the assumptions and culture and reward systems currently in effect.

Kriss: From my perspective, the answer is that there is no answer. You make your best guess, from a cost-benefit standpoint, about how to approach each test, and you evaluate whether the benefit will outweigh the cost. Because there's definitely going to be cost. There's no model for these really sophisticated challenges; these are judgment calls. And you're going to pay the consequences of whichever decision you make.

Kathy: Yes, this is life; it's reality. You can't eliminate "resisters." Sometimes they have their own important contributions to make. In those circumstances, you have to learn how to work around them, in essence, and still move the organization forward. Sometimes they may reach a point where the organization's momentum is too strong to resist; sometimes they may discover that they are in peril of being marginalized, left behind by the flow of events. Some change; some never do. Some leave.

Deborah: We have all faced this problem, I'm sure. At times the main problem is about lost opportunity, but at other times the problem is that damage is being done to the organization. In the latter case, you have to be thoughtful about how to contain the damage. Let's assume that the person is not easily "sent away"—perhaps because he or she is an expert in their area or because the person has built an important network for implementing things effectively. I have had to work with such people, to talk through the new parameters within the organization, and help them define their job and their niche differently. For some people, this might mean limiting their scope of influence; for others, it might mean coaching them to become more involved or to become more of a mentor. I calculate the potential damage they can do to the effort, and then I make the appropriate move.

Sam: The other day I was at your organization, and I saw you struggle with a version of this issue. You had a meeting of key stakeholders who were making decisions about whether to treat a certain priority as having medium importance or super importance. You personally felt it was hugely important, and you wanted to use the meeting to build alignment. Most of the people you had invited to that meeting had misgivings, but you felt optimistic. If you made your best case and if you talked things through with them respectfully and if you operated from a commitment to problem-solve in order to deal with their concerns, then you hoped that the meeting would build to a consensus outcome. However, you already knew that you were going to have trouble with one particular stakeholder. This person—whose presence was not absolutely essential—was going to come to that meeting with the openly declared intention of defeating or at least constraining your initiative.

So you had a choice to make: should you bring this stakeholder to the meeting as a full participant and pay the various costs—the extra time it would take, the inevitable periods of frustration and misunderstanding in a meeting that was originally supposed to be upbeat, and most of all, the uncertainty and risk of a potentially troubling outcome—or should you move ahead with your core group and then, once you had built a critical mass, deal with this "resister" one-on-one—offline, as some people call it. And this question you had to deal with is my question to all of you: when you are facing that situation, when you are sizing up the trade-offs of including versus not including the people whom you know will make trouble, what goes through your mind? How do you size up the trade-off?

Kriss: I think in previous positions at different organizations, in more cases than not I have moved in the direction of isolating these people. And I think I have learned a lot from doing that. In hindsight, I'd have thrown them more into the mix and designed the process to accommodate more tension and disagreement. And most important, I would want to design a process that aims at a high standard of actually thinking through and achieving a goal. I want the participants to see that I am not going to create a process that is superficial and noncontroversial just to accommodate the feelings of people who are stubborn or afraid. If someone does not want to collaborate in a well-designed process, I want all of us to see the challenge for what it is, so that we can keep thinking, keep working, accepting the reality but not becoming defeated by pretending to be "collegial" but actually being avoidant.

Jim: I had a situation last year that was of that ilk. Didn't handle it very well. I had a leadership team member who was really out of sync with me and my style and vision for the organization, just everything. This was a seasoned member of our staff—influential with the younger staff and very well-respected, for good reason. Still, we had a lot of differences, especially about vision and strategy. And rather than deal with the gap between us in a real-time, confrontational way—not in a negative, blameful put-down session but with productive confrontation—rather than do that, I chose to just observe it all and create a mental list of reasons why I couldn't work with this person. I waited till I had my whole case organized, and then I confronted her in a this-is-the-last-straw kind of way. In doing so, I created a wall between us. By design. I thought I could isolate her from the rest of the organization, and for some reason I thought that might work. Boy, did it ever not work. I essentially resisted the opportunity to confront her in small ways, in real time. Instead I let it build up to a breaking point: "Here's the way it is: you can keep your job, but you're off this leadership team. . . ." And of course the fallout was extremely negative. The isolating strategy was anything but effective. The fallout rippled all through the organization.

Sam: As you reflect on this experience, it sounds really hard to live through—for you and for everyone concerned.

Jim: You bet. If I could do it again, or if I ever come up to a situation similar to it again, I'd like to think I would handle it very differently.

Sam: One aspect of what you're sharing connects to a point you were making earlier this evening when you spoke about the theme of accountability. At that time, you were saying that it was critical, in building a culture of collaboration, to hold people accountable for saying out loud more of what they're actually thinking about key issues at work. Listening to you now, I'm hearing a closely related thread: that one of the things that goes with the territory of handling people challenges is to hold yourself accountable to engaging with them.

Jim: Exactly right. You can't call it collaboration and then withdraw when the stakes go up.

Kathy: Sometimes we might represent collaboration as a process design, a map with milestones and stakeholders and such. But I think what Jim is talking about here is a lot more than designing and implementing a process to do a project. Jim's talking about an organic way of being. As we share our thoughts about these experiences, what we have in common is that we're trying to make a certain way of being become organic, natural to the organization. In creating a culture of collaboration, there's no such thing as "OK, we're done." It's organic; it's continuous; it keeps developing and transforming. And that's really hard and taxing. And so much of it is brand new because it keeps unfolding.

John: In my situation, I'm so personally ambivalent. The mission is to find causes of birth defects. For this you need scientists—the best scientists. The core value of collaboration seems like a no-brainer to me: why would we let scientific progress crawl along at the pace of one decade at a time when we can move things exponentially faster if people would work together? But those scientists aren't collaborative. I need them, and they are who they are. So I probably do accommodate in different ways because of my two competing values: "find causes" versus "be collaborative."

Kriss: I know what you mean. In my organization, not only are we part of a university, with all of the academic culture you're describing, but we're housed in a business school. So you can imagine how many people think collaborative culture is worth striving for. I remember one incident when I really caught on to this. I was working with one of the key thinkers at my organization, and we were talking about engaging with students, faculty, and a variety of other stakeholders to get input on a major upcoming initiative. I thought we were talking about "how to," not "whether to." But I realized I was wrong when this person said, "But if we get them involved in this, they'll think it's their idea!" The reward system in the university is based on ideas, holding on to ideas and positioning oneself over who takes credit.

John: Exactly. In my own organization, I built a collaborative culture and used it during a three-year reengineering, when we cut down from studying more than one hundred types of rare birth defects and got focused on the five most common, costly, and deadly. And we reduced our "cycle time" enormously—that's the time it takes to complete a study from start to finish. And yet when it comes to the actual ongoing scientific work, even with the research being done entirely with our own scientists at my own organization, I'm still not fully clear about where to come down. The mission value is toward the scientist, but the core value is toward collaboration. I'm sure the collaborative culture gets watered down; I'm sure I am making this mistake ongoingly.

Kathy: I don't see it as a mistake; you're dealing with the way things are. And like you said, you're still conscious of it. You're not just giving in to the mainstream cultural norms. This is, I think, what we're all trying to do: change things. And real change is not going to be simple or easy. You're doing it, John.

John: Well, it's true that I'm constantly, painfully aware of the choices I keep making. I just don't have a model for making the real, lasting change more likely to come true.

Kathy: You're inventing the model. We're all inventing it. By the way, Deborah, what happened? What did you do?

Deborah: Well, in this particular case, I chose to include the person and take the gamble. I thought my chance of bringing him on board was much greater if I could use the presence and strength of the group. We would all wrestle through everything together. We had several hours set aside, and this was a big opportunity. And it turned out wonderfully! We saw his objections melt when he had the chance to be taken seriously and have his concerns dealt with thoughtfully. So yes, I made the decision to put this right in the middle of the challenge, to let all the stakeholders duke it out as needed and work things through. [This key stakeholder went on to become a strong, vocal advocate for this decision, influencing and ultimately leading a key group to endorse and implement crucial elements of the decision.]

Sam: And what was your rationale, since you have sometimes made the opposite choice?

Deborah: I thought, "Now is the time to put them in the middle. There's enough bench strength, enough dynamic support, enough good faith."

Sam: Enough "bench strength." Does that seem like a reliable criterion?

Deborah: Yes. And I have made the same decision at other times, over this past year, for a different reason. Sometimes you include people to get them to either step up or step out. Like Kriss was saying before, sometimes it's important for people to discover the situation in a living, dynamic, social context. If they're doing poorly in it, they can see their situation and it can help them choose which change to make.

Sam: And does this interface with your thought about "bench strength"?

Deborah: Yes, exactly. Several months ago, I had a group that was composed primarily of either consultants or people who were on their way out. This was not a group to do a lot of pushing and testing and pressuring with. The payoff would not have been there. I would have been investing for nothing. I had one staff person in it who was maybe or maybe not going to stay with the organization. But instead of being clear in my mind about whether to use the group as an implicit context to help him self-evaluate, I was ambivalent. I put him in for a while; I pulled him out; I left him hanging about whether he should come back in—it became a mess. He left, but it was not an easy termination. And I'm still paying consequences in terms of cleanup.

In retrospect, I should have orchestrated his departure sooner. I was hoping that putting him in this group would help resolve the situation one way or the other, but I misestimated the strength of the group. It was simply not resilient enough to engage with problematic passive-aggressive behavior by a member, not strong enough to respectfully confront that behavior and push the person to shape up.

Sam: I see a lot of heads nodding.

Kathy: This is a key insight. A participatory process can be draining on a group—especially if it's the first time they're coming around. It can be draining. You're right—there are certain things you can only do with the right mix of people. You have to be thinking about this when you make judgments like which groups to use to launch a process, and which groups to include later. Yes, this is really, really important.

Difficult Dynamics, Part Two: Working with Newcomers

Sam: What about the newcomer? There are people in key positions who are not resistant in the sense that they actively disagree with collaborative philosophy, but they are naïve about it. Maybe they are completely unaware of collaboration as a legitimate approach to management. Or maybe they know the hype about it but have never lived through the kinds of tests and character building that you've all been describing today. How do you work with the newcomer who just wants to "go off and do his or her job"?

Deborah: We're having this exact conversation now. We hired a key player, a senior manager who is excellent at the type of work we hired him to do. And he has a new team. I quickly saw that his team was going to need some attention because we're still in the process of building our culture and there was no reason to assume that this new team, led by a newcomer, was going to develop along collaborative lines. So I discussed it with him and we came to the conclusion that for a while, I would join his operations team. The idea is to make sure the team has the support and attention of the CEO to make it as successful as possible. We had to clarify that I'm not watching over him and his team; I'm offering coaching and support and vision while they invent themselves.

Jim: You're engaging with them.

Deborah: Yes, precisely. I can't afford to leave these early developments to chance.

Jim: Me too. I am so much more deeply engaged than I was a year ago.

John: About eight years ago, we did an analysis of the turnover pattern in our organization. We learned that we had a huge turnover rate among people who were in their first three years at our organization. But we also found that those who made it to the three-year mark were likely to stay forever. My strategic management team discussed this quite seriously, and we came to the conclusion, since borne out, that it takes a huge effort to build a shared framework of understanding with newcomers. For high-level people, the CEO has a major role in this. I can recall twice over the years bringing on high-level staff, whom I recruited for many months each, and then once they were hired, I moved on to other things—and in both cases they didn't last a year. At other times, I have brought in people who I have stayed closely connected to, and—surprise!—they're still here to this day. It takes an enormous commitment of senior staff to bring them in. I have seen senior staff be welcoming, and I have seen them be resistant, to the introduction of new managers, whether senior or middle managers. And you can predict the outcome, if you're paying attention.

Kathy: That goes to what Deborah was saying: she interjected herself into the situation where the newcomers were being indoctrinated with the vision and values and culture of the organization.

Kriss: At a previous job where I was COO, we went through a period during the early years when the organization was new, small, and very collaborative. Then we had a big growth spurt, and we made the mistake of thinking that collaboration was fully incorporated into the culture. We didn't systematize it. We didn't do anything intentional to integrate the way the leadership team worked with the way the rest of the organization worked. We had so many new projects and programs starting up that we just let people do things their own way. And sure enough, we paid significant consequences for that. That experience raised a question for me that I'm hoping we can spend some time on: how to institutionalize the culture.

Institutionalizing the Culture of Collaboration

Jim: Recruiting is one key, I think. It's more a question of how we recruit in a way that sets up for success. This past year, as I've been rebuilding, I am much more insistent on the alignment of values and people. I've got an idea in mind, a vision, I guess you could say, of the culture we want to create. Not the culture that currently exists, which is basically the culture that has existed for years, but rather a culture that is more in line with the type of values we have been discussing.

Kriss: It's one thing to hire good people, who at the hiring interview say they value collaboration and empowerment as a management style. I'd think, "OK, great, they're aligned with the values." But there's a large gap between statements made in a hiring interview and the ways people behave from day to day.

Jim: I may be a little delusional about how well I can assess that on the front end, but I'm making people decisions with a broader set of thinking and information than I did a year ago.

Kriss: You're right, we can do a lot of good or ill by the type of people we select to place in leadership roles. And I agree with you that conscious recruiting practices can play a strong role in institutionalizing a collaborative culture. Even so, it's a totally different thing to hold people accountable for their daily and monthly behavior. It's not at all obvious how to define objectives that pertain directly to participatory values or how to measure, monitor, and evaluate successful job performance. In other words, how do you build accountability into this value?

a project-managed, team-based culture. In fact, that's exactly the phrase I used—"a project-managed, team-based culture"—whenever I communicated about what we were aspiring to become. Well, I don't think we have done as well as I'd wanted, on the team-based side, although many people would disagree with me. But we have definitely accomplished the shift to project management. And that happened through the influence of our early adopters, who were, as I can see now, actually more aligned with project management via a "project team" model of implementation than they were aligned with a model that aimed at a deep, participatory-value-based culture.

Jim: Your experience suggests that a new culture can become ingrained even when you didn't fully understand what was taking place or how. This is both interesting and reassuring.

Deborah: It's another case of emergence rather than planfulness. The early adopters emerged as leaders and took the culture in a certain direction. Not 180 degrees different from where John had wanted to go, but not 100 percent the same either. This is the self-organizing behavior that I do believe occurs in a complex adaptive system.

Changing Systems to Institutionalize the Culture Change

Jim: Before branching in that direction, though, I would like to go back to something else. A few minutes ago, Kriss posed the question, "How can we institutionalize the culture we aspire to create?" This is a key question at Juma.

As a social enterprise organization, we've got a "double bottom line": because we are a business, we want to earn enough revenues to turn a profit or at least break even, yet our main reason for existing is to help our youth employees pull themselves out of poverty. Those two purposes are not easy to reconcile. It is much more profitable to sell ice cream when you don't have to provide additional programs and services to your ice cream vendors; yet if you just throw many of our youth into jobs without individual support, they can easily fail. We needed to take a huge leap forward—we needed to vastly improve our performance on both of our bottom lines, even though in some ways success on one side seemed like it would undercut success on the other side. In fact, this was the whole impetus for redesigning the organization in the first place.

Well, we have definitely made great strides on this: we have developed a deep, serious commitment to the principle of integration, integrating every aspect of our youth service with every aspect of how we run our business. That's the goal. And in practice, it means collaborating across functions, on every aspect of our work. My youth development staff and my business management staff have to collaborate on many, many issues. For now, we're successful at it. But this brings me back to Kriss's question, which is precisely the question I'm focused on now at Juma: "What can be done to ensure that spirit of collaboration in the long term?

So Deborah, a few minutes ago you said something I wanted to follow up on. You said we could possibly build systems and platforms that could support people to step up and take initiative, try out new ideas, collaborate across sectors, and so on.

Deborah: Yes, exactly. That's what self-organizing systems do. They build platforms that support people to behave with some degree of spontaneity and autonomy. That's exactly what we're trying to do—determine which platforms, which systems, will support the broadest distribution of leadership, initiative taking, and teamwork.

Jim: Well, good; this is what I want to explore further. Here's my question to you about that: what systems and practices, from your experience, might be the ones that have the most leverage?

Deborah: I can think of a few. I'll start with one we're deeply engaged in right now. We are looking at our HR policies and programs—the whole HR function, actually—as the backbone of any organizational culture. This is because HR helps recruit, orient, and reinforce, through many different policies and procedures, what you want in the culture. Therefore, we decided, among other things, to completely redo every part of our performance appraisal system. And that's what we're doing. As a first step, we are working on changing the entire performance appraisal system so that individual goals are aligned with their departmental-organizational goals and aligned as well with agencywide goals so you can see the connection. Just like John described.

John: That's a huge project in itself.

Deborah: You bet! And by the way, the negotiating among the various players about how to do that in a collaborative, cross-functional way has been quite a challenge too. We're getting there, but building these systems is not simple. Here's another one, Jim. Early on when I was getting the transformation under way, I made the mistake of relying on the old existing communication system. That was an absolute disaster. The messages I sent were not being repeated, the underlying philosophy was not being reinforced, and it continued to deteriorate until I faced up to what was happening—or, rather, what was not happening.

Except when I did it personally, there were no internal systemwide communications, period. So I proceeded to hire a whole new communications team, and they built completely new infrastructure to support internal communications. And they built it in a way that expressed and reinforced what I see as a core value of collaboration: open communication; dialogue; feedback. Now communication flows back and forth. The process of obtaining feedback has been built in to the communication system. I no longer worry that my messages are going to be filtered unless I do eighty million focus groups all the time.

Kathy: John and I had the same experience in the late 1980s, and we turned it around, with the same result.

John: Yes, it's true. When our internal communication systems are functioning well, the level of shared understanding is much better. And the morale is higher. People trust more. And they ask me better questions, too, and more of them.

Deborah: Another way to institutionalize our new culture is through training. We've always been big investors in training on basic technical skills for certain groups of our employees; but in this past year, we have been working hard to rethink the entire function and make it more available to more people—everyone, actually—in more modalities, such as mentoring and real-time problem solving, not just classroom training, and on different competencies, including culture-oriented skills of leadership and collaboration.

Kathy: I've been thinking along a similar line. At my organization, I've been focusing on professional development. It's related to training but more personal and more directed toward strengthening the courage and character of our emerging leaders in the movement. One of the deepest reasons I care about the culture at Planned Parenthood is because I care about the strength and effectiveness of the entire national women's movement. We need to be working to develop the next generation of leaders focused on women's rights. And collaborative processes are an incredibly powerful context for building organizational strength and a movement. So I have been pretty intentional about bringing in external coaches and facilitators such as Phyllis Watts, Wildswan Resources, and Sunny Sabbini, from Community At Work. And I don't just bring these people in for a meeting here or there; we have long-term relationships with them so that my staff can gain personal opportunities to grow, both through one-on-one sessions and through participating in challenging thinking sessions. Earlier in this session, we spoke about the importance of having external support, the importance of investing in our own professional development. As I see it, long-term contractual relationships with external consultants are definitely part of institutionalizing the value of collaboration.

Jim: This is all really, really helpful. I'm thinking, as you're speaking, of opportunities to use these as I continue to rebuild my own organization.

Deborah: One more: incentives. We're doing that now—thinking through the possible ways of creating an "incentive infrastructure." This is different from performance appraisal. The question here is, "How do we incentivize the culture of teamwork and innovation?" I don't have the answer, but we have a team now working on it.

Kriss: As the person who raised the question originally, I'm appreciating all of what I'm hearing and find myself very stimulated by it—and yet I'm struggling a bit with some of it. I'm questioning how to apply some of this thinking to a larger system like mine. For example, take compensation. The pay scales at Stanford are set far beyond my influence. The incentives and bonuses for the professors are established. Or take human resource systems and policies: same thing. My little CSI is independent in some ways, but not in those ways.

John: Us too. Much of our compensation structure and our HR policies are governed by the state of California, the Department of Health Services, the Civil Service union, the March of Dimes, the National Institute of Health, . . .

Kathy: Planned Parenthood too. In some ways, we're autonomous; yet in many regards, we voluntarily abide by norms and standards of the state and national federations.

Kriss: I guess what I'm realizing, then, is that the very concept of institutionalizing your culture is a balancing act between systems you can influence straightforwardly and those you can't. And as I think about this, I suspect that for each of us, maybe there are one or two key systems, key components, that can drive the institutionalization of culture. I'm thinking, for example, of Nordstrom. I grew up in Seattle, and I saw it grow from one store downtown through all its stages of national expansion—in fact, I was with Nordstrom when they opened up the East Coast. And through it all, at every step of the way, it is "customer service" that has kept that company alive. They have a core philosophy, as many other businesses do, a key driver that guides the development of a few critical systems. It gives the organization its spine.

Sam: So let me check to see if I'm understanding you. Are you suggesting that each of your organizations may need to find its own one or two "key drivers," as Nordstrom has?

Kriss: Yes.

Sam: So that those one or two key drivers would enable you to institutionalize the culture of collaboration in unique ways in your own systems?

Kriss: Yes. And you know, I have one other thought about this. We are all being pushed by many factors, and there is a never-ending supply of things to think about and things to do. This year we're focused on growth, next year it might be downsizing. My point is that we may never have the time to institute every one of our infrastructures perfectly. I think we each have to think for ourselves, determine and decide on the right priorities. If you want to promote a culture of collaboration, ask what are the one or two key drivers that will give you the most bang for your buck, to systematize and institutionalize collaboration.

Closing Thoughts

Sam: We're going to have to wrap up soon. First, let's see if I can summarize your thoughts on this topic—you've said a lot! Deborah mentioned four systems: performance appraisal, communications, training, and incentives. For each of those, Deborah, if I've understood correctly, you are in the midst of developing not just policies but an entire infrastructure, expressly with the intention of institutionalizing a culture of teamwork and innovation.

Deborah: Yes. We're right in the middle of all this now, so I don't know whether it will turn out to be right or wrong; I don't yet have a good sense of the

payoffs or the trade-offs. These are the four core systems we have identified to date, and I expect we'll identify others as we go along.

Sam: Earlier, Jim brought up recruiting. Jim, you reported that you were much
more aware this year than previously that you could screen for a person's
potential affinity for collaboration even before you hired the person. That
struck me as another area that might clearly strengthen the culture.

Jim: I think so. I hope so.

Sam: John, you spoke about the importance of an environment that encouraged learning and continuous improvement through such methods as
alignment of goals, tracking meetings and progress, and other project
management systems and tools. Kathy, you brought up professional development, and you reminded us to think of long-term relationships with
external change consultants as part of institutionalizing your culture.
And Kriss has offered an insight that it might be most practical and perhaps most effective to focus on one or two key drivers, based on a core
philosophy, and use those drivers to push the development of systems
and practices.

Kathy: Good job, Sam. If we had more time, I think I'd want to look carefully
at another one of these: participatory governance. Our boards play a
significant role in how we do or don't walk our talk of collaboration.

Deborah: Our executive teams, too. Yes, that would be an important topic. As
I've said, I'm working to create a distributed network model for leadership, and yet I still understand the importance of preserving a clear locus
of authority. Balancing these two, living with the dynamic tension between them, and even consciously institutionalizing it—well, we would
have a lot to talk about on this subject.

Jim: I'd want us to trade our experiences on the actual work of implementing
the various systems we've been discussing; I'm thinking about phases and
stages. At Juma, I think we had to go through some major phases before
we could become ready to undertake the transformation. I certainly had
to get ready myself; certain other alignments had to be dismantled, and
there was also a transitional period of trial and error before I even knew
what I was looking for.

Kriss: And of course at Juma you have the additional challenge of a workforce
who are mostly going to leave the organization within a couple years of
their arrival.

Deborah: Goodwill too. Almost all of our employees leave, by design.

Kathy: And what about the students at Stanford? Or for that matter, my volunteers . . . ?

Kriss: And our funders. And the faculty. Yes, there are loads of challenges about engaging the various constituencies, the stakeholders who are not our managers. This is actually the issue that most centrally affects me and my organization. Stakeholder engagement is the type of collaboration my particular effort has focused on, much more so than participatory management. And that does bring me back full circle to one other topic I touched on earlier: using early adopters to connect with these constituencies. I'd like to explore this more: what critical success factors are involved in improving and increasing your base of support with those stakeholder groups? I understand the value of early adopters; how do we substantially increase their numbers?

Kathy: I know we have to close, but I do have one response to Kriss that I really believe in. As you know, we work in coalitions all the time. It's one of my core areas of expertise. And one thing I've learned is that you don't try to convert everyone to your way of thinking; you develop a few key relationships and strengthen them. For the broader constituency, you send messages that speak to them, and you create an overall climate of common interest. But don't expect to get very many players from these other groups to take your projects seriously. They have their own projects to work on; that's where their passions are. So when you need support and effort from your other stakeholder groups, you use your key relationships to carry the water. Don't expect everyone to take responsibility for everything.

Deborah: Yes, but . . .

Sam: Excuse me, excuse me; sorry to interrupt, but we need to finish up. I see that there are many other meaningful questions we could explore. With your permission, though, I would like to override this discussion and move into a closing summary.

Everyone: Yes. Fine. Go for it!

Sam: Throughout this conversation, I noticed that each of you would take turns agreeing with something and then taking the thought in a somewhat different direction. You resonated with one another in many ways, yet you frequently had many perspectives on a single issue, and I often had the sense that you were each emphasizing different things. Kriss drew this to our attention most explicitly when she encouraged us to recognize the different needs and conditions that distinguish one organization from the next. And this simple fact—the diversity of your organizations and their structures and missions—begs the question, "Is there 'one right philosophy,' one correct model or definition, of a 'culture of collaboration'?"

We've been talking about five different organizations that share a core value of wanting to put participatory values into practice. Does this mean they each share the same meaning and vision of a culture of collaboration? I think I'm walking away tonight convinced that the answer is no. To my mind, we've been hearing that whether a particular organization leans more toward a project management culture or more toward a distributed leadership culture or more toward a stakeholder engagement culture or more toward capacity-building professional development or more toward a double-bottom-line integrative culture, all of them are manifestations, one way or another, of participatory values.

Jim: That speaks for me. I'm still not sure what the core of our long-term culture will be, although it's true that "integration" will hopefully be our driver. And your point, Sam, brings me to a closing comment of my own. I think of myself as a practical person, a person who is driven by goals and results. As a consequence of that, I became a proponent of participatory leadership not because I felt it was great in and of itself but because I have seen quite clearly that as a practical matter, it's a model that can help us achieve our highest potential. So yes, I have become a convert to participatory leadership. Thank you all for supporting my learning on this.

Deborah: For me, I'd like to end on a different note. Still hopeful, yes, and definitely inspired by all the thinking we have done here. But for me, the jury on the primacy of a culture of collaboration is still out. As I've said, I want to create a balance between planfulness and chaos, between teamwork and initiative taking, between doing really good thinking in groups and taking bold risks and sometimes even failing as individuals. I really want to work with that tension, experiment with it, use it. I agree with Sam's point about participatory values: what I want most is not any specific formulaic culture; I just want to keep finding ways to bring out the best in everyone.

Kriss: And please keep me posted on how that evolves.

John: In fact, it would be great for us all to stay in touch.

Jim: To be continued, then.

Kathy: Let's hope. And not just for ourselves and our own organizations. *Every* organization can be strengthened from within. And we're all better for it.

Sam: Thank you, everyone.

Reference

Caroline Estes, "Consensus Ingredients," Fellowship for Intentional Communities [http://www.ic.org/pnp/cdir/1995/25estes.php]. 1996.

PART ONE

THE BASES OF COLLABORATION

James M. Campbell, B.S., was born in western Pennsylvania in 1940. Upon graduating from Edinboro State University in 1962, he moved to Chile, where he lived and taught school for three years. Returning to the United States, he joined the staff of the Ecumenical Institute in Chicago (precursor of the Institute of Cultural Affairs) and worked for a number of years in the Fifth City Community Development Project on the city's west side. In 1972, he moved to Kenya, where he started up the institute's first office in Africa. Five years later, he moved to Brazil to establish an office there. Since 1982, he has been a staff member of the Institute of Cultural Affairs in Brussels, Belgium. He works as a trainer and consultant in the field of facilitation throughout Europe, mostly with the NGO community.

CHAPTER TWO

RENEWING SOCIAL CAPITAL

The Role of Civil Dialogue

James M. Campbell

The creative use of language to facilitate the practice of transparent interactions, between and among people in all walks of life, will help to assure that sensible, fair decisions can be made, based on the same shared information. Essentially, this is the foundation of liberty, individual responsibility and the free exchange of ideas and information, for all. The best hope for resolving conflicting interests so that an outcome yields the greatest benefit to both interests is through dialogue.

GINGER MCCARTHY (1997)

Because the vast majority of the audience was opposed to President Bush's suggested changes in Social Security, the speaker was all but shouted down. That was unfortunate, because it dealt another blow to our already fragile civic culture. Are all so-called town meetings to become "by invitation only," both for the participants and the questions?

CHARLES LAWTON (2005)

The two quotations illustrate the growing gap we find across the world today between what we know is required to build a more effective human community and what is really happening in local communities. While acrimonious debate has always been part of the experience of human community, we have, by and large, been able to sustain the debate and to eventually reach some resolution. When this does not happen in a community, the response ranges from distrust and antagonism to overt conflict. In many communities today, we are seeing less and less real debate, even acrimonious debate, and more and more dismissal of people we oppose as people with whom we have nothing in common and with whom no compromise is possible.

Human community depends on communication. Without communication, there is no community of any kind—even geese, elephants, or lions exist as flock, herd, or pride only because they communicate. The more complex and evolved the communication, the more complex the community's interactions can be. Given the seemingly infinite variety of human verbal interactions, we are part of the most complex community on the planet. This complexity ensures a richness and diversity that makes our community an endlessly enlivening and fascinating place. At the same time, it makes it a community that is very difficult to sustain.

The opportunities for miscommunication of all kinds are legion. We have just completed the deadliest century in our history, a century in which we chose repeatedly to communicate using bombs and bullets. And in this new century, we seem to be continuing on the same path. We have, around the world, numerous communities where dialogue of any kind, let alone civil dialogue, seldom if ever occurs.

In this chapter, I want to do two things: first, examine the nature of social capital, including its relationship to confidence and social trust, and second, reflect on the role of civil dialogue, enabled by process facilitation, in renewing social capital.

Social Capital

In economics, capital is defined as "material wealth used or available for use in the production of more wealth." When a community reaches the point where it is generating more wealth than it needs to sustain itself, it is generating capital. A healthy community is understood to be one that regularly generates capital, which is then used to renew, expand, or develop new activities to meet the community's needs. Early in the twentieth century, this concept was borrowed by social scientists and applied to the accumulated value to be found in social networks (Putnam, 2000, p. 19).

In *Bowling Alone*, Robert Putnam (2000, pp. 19–21) outlines the core concepts that delineate social capital. The following is a summary of his core concepts.

- By analogy with notions of physical capital and human capital—tools and training that enhance individual productivity—the core idea of social capital theory is that social networks have value.
- Social capital refers to connections among individuals—social networks and the norms of reciprocity and trustworthiness that arise from them.
- Just as a screwdriver (physical capital) or a college education (human capital) can increase productivity (both individual and collective), so too social contacts affect the productivity of individuals and groups.
- Social capital can thus be simultaneously a "private good" and a "public good." Some of the benefit from an investment in social capital goes to bystanders while some of the benefit rebounds to the immediate interest of the person making the investment.
- Networks of community engagement foster sturdy norms of reciprocity: I'll do this for you now, in the expectation that you (or perhaps someone else) will return the favor. "Social capital is akin to what Tom Wolfe called 'the favor bank' in his novel *The Bonfire of the Vanities*," economist Robert Frank noted (Putnam, 2000, p. 20). It was, however, neither a novelist nor an economist but Yogi Berra who offered the most succinct definition of reciprocity: "If you don't go to somebody's funeral, they won't come to yours" (p. 20). Sometimes, as in these cases, reciprocity is *specific:* I'll do this for you if you do that for me. Even more valuable, however, is a norm of *generalized reciprocity*: I'll do this for you without expecting anything specific back from you, in the confident expectation that someone else will do something for me down the road.

Thus social capital is the stored value that individuals have accumulated in their networks. If this social capital is to be maintained, people must continue to participate in their networks with the confidence that their participation will generate new social capital. When, for whatever reason, people stop participating in these networks, the community starts to deplete its stored social capital. People in a community that is depleting its social capital experience a decline in confidence and a corresponding decline in communication between groups and individuals within the community. With the depleting of social capital, the value in people's networks diminishes, and they either restrict their participation or withdraw altogether. It is in these situations that social trust and confidence become significant both in explaining what is happening and in determining how social capital can be renewed.

Social Trust and Confidence

Timothy Earle, in a paper titled "Social Trust and Confidence," makes a helpful distinction between social trust and confidence. In addition, he distinguishes between *pluralistic* social trust and *cosmopolitan* social trust.

Pluralistic Social Trust

All social trust is based on similarity. This form of social trust is based on a similarity of "current salient values" (Earle, 2002, p. 2). It is the kind of social trust that is based on similarities that are shared by a group. "You have trust within the group, but then you may have problems between groups. Pluralistic social trust in that sense can lead to ethnic conflicts and so on" (p. 2).

Cosmopolitan Social Trust

In cosmopolitan social trust, the similarity is "based on two individuals and their individual agency, free agency. The similarity is not based on any connections between any specific values or roles. It rests on a mutual acknowledgment of agency. . . . It is reflexive, multiple, forward-looking, and based on negotiation. And it is very useful for problem solving" (Earle, 2002, p. 2).

Social Trust and Confidence

"Social trust is a relation between two persons whereas confidence is between a person and an organization. Social trust is based on similarity, either existing or negotiated, whereas confidence is based on familiarity, evidence, or experience within an organization. There is no evidence or experience that you can get that would convince *me* to trust *you*. I trust you because I believe that you are the same as me. But I have confidence in an organization based on past experience" (Earle, 2002, p. 2).

"You may have confidence in [a system], but as system differentiation increases, you may reach the limit of the system, and the situation of liability and negotiability is such that the need for trust emerges" (Earle, 2002,

FIGURE 2.1. CONTINUUM OF SOCIALITY.

Cosmopolitan	Pluralistic	Confidence
Social Trust	Social Trust	
• **Based on similarity**	• **Based on similarity**	• Based on familiarity,
• **Between individuals**	• **Between individuals**	evidence, or experience
• **Based on risk-choice**	• **Based on risk-choice**	within the organization
between alternatives	**between alternatives**	• Between a person and
• Individual agency	• Shared cultural values	an organization
• Private persons	• Public persons	• Based on the past
• Mutual acknowledgment	• Below conscious level	• Can lead to overconfidence
of free agency	• Static	(not reflexivity, movement,
• Dynamic emerging relations	• Existing relations	or change)
• Across groups	• Backward-looking	
• Reflexive	• Adversarial	
• Multiple	• Problem-creating	
• Forward-looking		
• Based on negotiation		
• Useful for problem solving		

Note: Items in bold are common to both cosmopolitan and pluralistic social trust.

Source: Adapted from Earle, 2002, p. 3.

p. 2). When a system becomes widely divergent and diversified and the system starts to break down, a new system must be created. The transition between the old and new is made by trust. "Confidence must be maintained through trust. Then we can speak of a *continuum* of sociality" with cosmopolitan social trust at one end, pluralistic social trust in the middle, and confidence at the other end (see Figure 2.1). "In real life, we are moving along this dimension. Most of life for most people is spent in the condition of confidence" (p. 3).

Social Trust and Risk

Why is there a risk in trust? "You are trusting another person, and you don't know what he or she is going to do. Therefore, you are making yourself vulnerable to that person, and trust involves risk. . . . Trust properly understood is fundamentally based on risk. Without risk there can be no trust" (Earle, 2002, p. 3).

Social Trust, Confidence, and Social Capital

This distinction between social trust and confidence helps us understand the reality of social capital in a community. Social capital is created and accumulated when people participate in social networks. A community with many social networks and most of the population participating in them is rich in social capital. And in such communities, confidence is generally high. "Social capital is not a property of social trust; it a function of confidence in a particular system and is based on familiarity. Because of the relationships between social trust and confidence, social trust can lead to social capital, but it has to do so indirectly by building confidence within a system. Social capital is simply confidence within a system. . . . Networks of trust need to be created within society and through them new modes and systems of confidence" (Earle, 2002, pp. 6–7). Earle ends his paper by pointing to communication as one of the key strategies for creating these needed networks of trust and new modes and systems of confidence—that is, creating new social capital.

Civil Dialogue

As Nicholas Berger (2004, p. 1) points out:

> Much has been said in recent years about a political fatigue in Europe: an increasing percentage of the population across Europe feels entirely disconnected from local politics, let alone their national [politics]. . . . It is evident that the political processes of today—as much as we cherish and safeguard the establishment of parliamentary democracy—cannot deal with the socio-economic and environmental crisis Europe is facing. A dramatic loss of trust in politicians and democratic institutions is blatantly evident; a sense of disconnection between people and "their" representation is the feeling of the age. . . . Many have tried to find answers to this problem. One answer that has been propagated over the years is the establishment of more participatory elements that complement the political process of representative democracy. This participation is called civil dialogue—or as I prefer participatory democracy.

Ginger McCarthy (1997, p. 1) adds, "The best hope for resolving conflicts with an outcome which yields the greatest benefit to both parties is through dialogue. Each of us has a better outcome in resolving conflict this way, no matter what is at issue."

The Current Crisis

Whether we look at the local, national, or global level, we find deep divisions as one of the defining characteristics of contemporary society. "We are also challenged to have the clarity to make history—both as individuals and as members of communities and nations—through the uniquely suited tool of language [and] to engage in competition and in conflict through dialogue rather than any other more wasteful alternatives" (McCarthy, 1997, p. 2).

How can this happen when you have a community where the social capital is depleted, people are no longer participating in social networks, and confidence has evaporated? In such fragmented communities, the low stock of social capital means that people are participating in very limited social networks that primarily provide only private good and specific reciprocity; in other words, the impact on the general good and the creation of generalized reciprocity is minimal or nonexistent. An article in the London *Financial Times*, titled "When the Party's Over," noted, "From London to Ottawa, Washington to Canberra, political party membership around the world is at an all-time low. Are we heading for government by celebrity politicians and single-issue pressure groups instead?" (Bentley and Miller, 2004, p. W1). In the past, a political party was a social network that was inclusive of people from different social classes with varying interests and needs. They were, however, bound by a common vision and an understanding that participating in this social network would generate both private and public goods as well as specific and generalized reciprocity. Today, that understanding seems to have gone by the wayside, and people tend to focus on some particular issue where they have a defined position and where they can find a network of like-minded people. It is very much the situation of pluralistic social trust. They tend to have little or no confidence in people outside this network and usually feel that if you are not in the network, you are untrustworthy and in opposition to them.

These examples serve to remind us that effective civil dialogue is not happening in our communities. We are seemingly unable to engage in the sort of civil dialogue that builds cosmopolitan social trust.

The Challenge

The challenge of civil dialogue is to enable people to engage in cosmopolitan social trust, where people discover "new shared value across the existing conflicting memberships" (TRUSTNET, 2002, p. 1). This provides an operating definition of civil dialogue: the building of cosmopolitan social trust in a way that engenders new shared values across the existing conflicting memberships. Effective civil dialogue enables individuals to develop cosmopolitan social trust, which then has the potential to move them toward a situation of renewed confidence and social capital.

Charles Lawton's comment on the shouting down of a speaker, quoted at the start of this chapter, highlights this issue. "Because the vast majority of the audience was opposed to President Bush's suggested changes in Social Security, the speaker was all but shouted down. That was unfortunate, because it dealt another blow to our already fragile civic culture. Are all so-called town meetings to become 'by invitation only,' both for the participants and the questions?" The problem here is that if you bring a group of people together to talk about a contentious issue and let them make speeches at each other, the result will be little or no real communication. The assumption that all you have to do is get people together and they will share their true concerns and positions and work with others to reach an understanding that is acceptable to all may be true in a community that is rich in social capital, but it is not true where social capital has been depleted.

Also, it is important to realize that ineffective dialogues consume social capital and confidence and reinforce pluralistic social trust. People leave such a meeting feeling that there is no further value in that particular system and that they had better stick to trusting people like themselves (pluralistic social trust). It also develops an unwillingness to participate in that network again, thereby further diminishing the social capital of the community.

Process Facilitation

The fundamental issue in establishing effective civil dialogue—building the kind of social trust that engenders new shared values across existing conflicting memberships—is not the content of such dialogues; there is rarely any shortage of content issues requiring resolution. The issue is not about the *what* but about the *how.* This is the challenge of effective process facilitation. The failure of civil dialogue is a failure of process. It is a failure to appreciate and understand the complexity of the dialogue process and the need to provide people with a process and a setting that move toward cosmopolitan social trust.

Roger Schwarz's definition of group facilitation reminds us of what we mean when we speak of effective process facilitation: "Group facilitation is a process in which a person who is acceptable to all members of the group, is substantively neutral, and has no decision-making authority intervenes to help a group improve the way it identifies and solves problems and makes decisions, in order to increase the group's effectiveness" (1994, p. 4).

If we reflect on the main parts of this definition, we can identify some clues as to why process facilitation is crucial to effective civil dialogue. The first part of the definition has to do with the person in the role of facilitator. It says that he or she must be acceptable to all members of the group, substantively neutral, and have no decision-making authority. These three points (acceptable, neutral, without authority) have to do with the ability of the group to accept the facilitator as a person with no vested interest in the outcome of the process. There is a recurring situation in the American TV program *The Gilmore Girls:* the local community holds town meetings chaired by a man who is a local businessman and property owner. He is everything a facilitator should *not* be: he is not acceptable to all members of the community, he is not neutral (he always has a hidden agenda, which is inevitably exposed by the end of the episode), and he is not without decision-making authority. Fortunately, this is television, where it is all played for laughs; in real life, this community would quickly experience a collapse of social capital and deep fragmentation.

The next part of the definition is that the person must intervene to help the group improve the way it identifies and solves problems and makes decisions. The key words in this phrase are *the way.* Facilitation is about the process that enables a group to identify and solve its problems and make its decisions.

The objective of all this is "to increase the group's effectiveness." The facilitator's main task is to help a group increase its effectiveness by improving its process. "Process" refers to how a group works together; it includes such things as how members talk to each other, identify and solve problems, make decisions, make plans, and handle conflict.

A Culture of Collaboration

Finally, if civil dialogue is going to be effective in enabling social trust leading to renewed confidence and a replenished stock of social capital, process facilitation must occur in a culture of collaboration. "The best hope for resolving conflicts with an outcome which yields the greatest benefit to both parties is through dialogue." McCarthy then goes on to talk about the need for a reliance on transparency and full disclosure of all relevant information if dialogue is to be effective (McCarthy, 1997, p. 2). These two categories, along with process, give us three dynamics that interact and are fundamental to a culture of collaboration.

These categories also help us understand why a culture of collaboration is significant in the operation of cosmopolitan social trust, which is based on negotiation and is open, forward-looking, and oriented toward problem solving (see Figure 2.2). Cosmopolitan social trust, a negotiated trust between two free agents, will be enabled by transparency, full disclosure, and a process that is effective.

Transparency has to do with people's willingness to make sure that all have the information they need to participate effectively in the community. It means that people are willing to test the assumptions that inform their opinions and

FIGURE 2.2. CULTURE OF COLLABORATION.

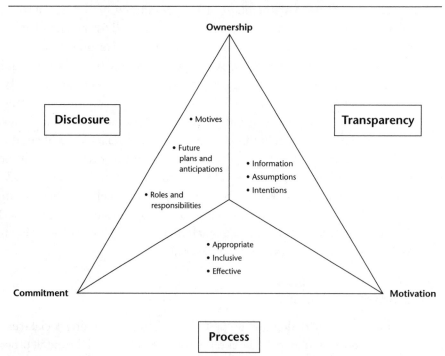

actions and to have those assumptions questioned by other members of the community. They strive to be aware of their intentions and their implications and are ready to share them with the community and to have them challenged.

Disclosure has to do with what the people feel they can reveal to each other. A community with strong social capital and confidence is a community where people are open about their motives—people explain why they are saying or doing what they are saying or doing without fear of ridicule, abuse, or retribution. They are open about their hopes and dreams. And they willingly reveal any external roles or responsibilities that might shape or inform their participation in and understanding of the community.

Process consists of the methods, ground rules, and techniques that govern how people in a community interact. A culture of collaboration depends on a process that is *appropriate* to the time frame and capacities of the community. Furthermore, it must be culturally appropriate and suitable for use in multicultural situations if necessary (for example, see Hogan, 2005). The process must also be *inclusive* in its capacity to deal with the all the relevant information and to involve all concerned parties, and it must be *effective* in accomplishing the objectives that the community has set for itself.

Conclusion

Facilitated civil dialogue has the potential to enable people to participate in situations of cosmopolitan social trust in a way that engenders new shared values across existing conflicting memberships. These new shared values are the building blocks of a growing sense of confidence in a community. As people regain their confidence, they will be more willing to engage in broader social networks, thus generating social capital. This new social capital will enable the experiencing of both private and public good and specific and generalized reciprocity. Practically, this will be experienced by community residents as a new sense of ownership of their community, empowered by a commitment and motivation to be engaged.

References

Bentley, T., and Miller, P. "When the Party's Over." *Financial Times,* Sept. 25–26, 2004, pp. W1–W2.

Berger, N. "Participatory Democracy: Organised Civil Society and the 'New' Dialogue." [http://www.fedtrust.co.uk/eu_constitution]. July 2004.

Earle, T. C. "Social Trust and Confidence." [http://www.trustnetgoverance.com.] April 2002. (See also Earle, T. C., and Siegrist, M. "Morality Information, Performance Information, and the Distinction Between Trust and Confidence." *Journal of Applied Social Psychology*, forthcoming.)

Hogan, C. "Successfully Facilitating Multicultural Groups." In S. Schuman (ed.), *The IAF Handbook of Group Facilitation*. San Francisco: Jossey-Bass, 2005.

Lawton, C. "Without Dialogue There Can Be No Insight." MaineToday.com [http://business.mainetoday.com/bottomline/050306chuck.shtml]. Mar. 6, 2005.

McCarthy, G. "Creative Response to Conflict: A Century of Dialogue." [http://members.aol.com/Altdisres/Dialogue.html]. Nov. 23, 1997.

Putnam, R. D. *Bowling Alone: The Collapse and Revival of American Community*. New York: Simon & Schuster, 2000.

Schwarz, R. M. *The Skilled Facilitator: Practical Wisdom for Developing Effective Groups*. San Francisco: Jossey-Bass, 1994.

TRUSTNET. "Social Trust: A Growing Concern." [http://www.trustnetgovernance.com/RiskG/RG3.htm]. Apr. 2002.

Mladen Koljatic, M.B.A., Ed.D., is a professor in the Escuela de Administración at the Pontificia Universidad Católica de Chile and the local leader of the Social Enterprise Knowledge Network (SEKN) project, a partnership among institutions of management education to strengthen research, teaching, and management practice in social enterprise in Latin America. His scholarly work focuses on nonprofit management with an emphasis on higher-education institutions and corporate social responsibility. Articles of his have recently appeared in *Higher Education, Psychological Reports, Scientometrics,* and several Latin American management journals.

Mónica Silva, Ph.D., is an educational psychologist. She has been associate researcher for the Escuela de Administración at the Pontificia Universidad Católica de Chile since 1999 and a member of the Social Enterprise Knowledge Network (SEKN) since 2001. Her research focuses on educational assessment and research methods, and her articles have appeared in *Evaluation and Program Planning, Health Education Research, Psychological Reports,* and *Scientometrics,* as well as local Latin American journals.

Eduardo Valenzuela, Ph.D., has been a faculty member and director of the Sociology Institute at the Pontificia Universidad Católica de Chile since 1996. He is the head of the Dirección de Estudios Sociológicos (DESUC), a center that provides consultation services and conducts surveys for local businesses and organizations. His scholarly research focuses on culture and social trust. His articles have appeared in several academic journals.

CHAPTER THREE

THE DEVELOPMENT OF CROSS-SECTOR COLLABORATIONS IN A SOCIAL CONTEXT OF LOW TRUST

Mladen Koljatic, Mónica Silva, Eduardo Valenzuela

Latin America is a continent plagued by social ills. Poverty, social discrimination, unequal access to educational opportunities, and low social mobility are some of the problems that have endured throughout its history. The state has been unable to solve these social problems, and the third sector is striving to fill the unmet social needs. How can businesses and nonprofit organizations work together and collaborate in solving social problems? Many people believe that these sectors have very distinct roles to play and that they are opposites in various aspects. Particularly, the business sector has been regarded with wariness and concern about self-interest and exploitation rather than as an agent of beneficence and caring for the well-being of the community at large. Still, despite the differences and suspicions among them, collaboration between these sectors appears to be developing (Austin and others, 2004). Cross-sector alliances between business firms and nonprofit organizations are becoming more common and more visible. Interest on the part of businesses in collaborating in social initiatives to remedy social problems

The authors are grateful to Professor James Austin for sharing his thoughts and experience on how to promote collaboration. Work on this chapter was supported in part by a grant from the Avina Foundation for the Social Enterprise Knowledge Network (SEKN) project and the Pontificia Universidad Católica de Chile.

appears to be growing. Cooperative arrangements are being forged in a number of ways, including philanthropic donations, alliances with nonprofits, and the creation of endowments or foundations. These efforts attest to the increasing connections between these two worlds, where both stand to gain through their association.

If social initiatives and businesses can gain through collaboration, the issue becomes how to promote productive cooperation between them. Preliminary research findings show that cultural characteristics may explain the differences in the origination of cross-sector collaborations in the United States and in Latin America. The differences between the two hemispheres can best be exemplified by the following scenario: during a short flight, the top executive officer of a large business corporation engages in conversation with the person next to her, who happens to be the head of an NGO. They exchange cards and arrange to meet shortly to continue exploring ways in which the business corporation can collaborate with the NGO. This is a perfectly plausible situation in the United States but would be rather unlikely in Latin America and even more improbable in Chile. The key to understanding why this kind of fruitful interaction would be so unlikely in a country like Chile is complex and is associated with the somewhat elusive concept of social trust.

Social Trust

Trust, in general, depends on certain contexts and circumstances. Just as one finds variations in trusting behavior between individuals, it is possible to find variations in social trust between cultures. Citizens in some nations appear to be more open and trusting than in others. The attitude of "innocent until proven guilty" that operates in the United States works in reverse in societies with low levels of social trust, where individuals treat each other as "guilty until proven innocent." Proverbs sometimes reflect this generalized tendency to distrust in certain societies. Such is the case with the Chilean saying "It's better to deal with a known devil than an unknown saint" and the Japanese adage "It's best to regard everyone as a thief." In such cultures, common beliefs hold distrusters as smarter, less gullible, and more successful than generalized trusters (Yamagishi, 2001).

Although there is no objective standard for measuring trust in societies, sociologists attempt to measure it through surveys applied to representative samples of people around the world. These allow for comparisons between societies. In terms of social trust, societies show high variability in their levels of interpersonal social trust. Nations like Sweden, Norway, and the United States are characterized by high or strong levels of social trust, while others, like Chile, are characterized by low or weak levels of trust. In one such ranking, only 23 percent of Chileans agreed with the statement that "most people can be trusted," compared to 66 percent of Swedes (Inglehart, Basañez, and Moreno, 1998, tab. V.94).

In terms of social trust, Chileans behave similarly to impoverished peasant subsistence communities in southern Italy, Mexico, and Peru, where family members stick together and distrust strangers (Hardin, 2002). Chile's geographical isolation may account for this phenomenon, which favors restricted personal interactions between individuals belonging to a small group of close-knit relations where "everybody knows everybody" as opposed to establishing collaborative relationships with others outside the family boundaries (Godoy, 1981).

Chileans do not trust strangers, and a majority of them believe that it is extremely unlikely that citizens will disinterestedly contribute to a good cause or perform a good deed without expecting something in return (Butazzoni, 1998). This attitude is in marked contrast to the traditions of fraternity and strong participation in the civic community that characterizes the culture in the United States. This may derive from the fact that American society has been built through successive waves of migration. In this process, migrants have lost their original family ties, and their closest associates become the other individuals who live in the same local community. Of course, immigrants often concentrate in neighborhoods that try to preserve their cultural ties. In the absence of close family ties, the neighborhood and the community become the most likely sources of mutual support and strong associative activity (Valenzuela and Cousiño, 2000). This may account for the stronger levels of association between members of a community in the United States compared to Chile and the higher levels of social trust that characterize the American population.

In Chile, the lower levels of general social trust are compensated by the strength of family ties. Chileans, compared to Americans, report a lower number of friends and greater contact with family members. A long history of suspicion and distrust of new acquaintances and even friends is reflected in the saying "Protect me, Lord, from my friends; from my enemies I can protect myself." A corollary of this attitude is the inclination to offer job positions to people with family connections rather than to strangers, a practice of nepotism that would be frowned on in other cultures. In Chile, this "job for one of the guys" practice enjoys widespread tacit approval and is condemned only when the individual in question proves to be inefficient or performs illegal or immoral acts (González, 2002). Family is the main repository of trust, with close friends running in second place. The natural wariness regarding friends and its impact in the sociability of Chileans is evident in the significantly lower average number of friends reported by them compared to the average reported by Americans. While Americans acknowledge an average of 6.2 friends, Chileans report only 3.3 (Valenzuela and Cousiño, 2000, p. 325).

Social trust is associated with confidence in institutions. Low-trust societies tend to have low levels of confidence in their institutions. Although it is not possible to establish a causal relationship between the two factors, it appears that transparency in institutions and the honorability of those who hold positions of power and authority fosters the emergence of collaborative relationships based on trust (Sztompka, 1999). In societies where corruption is rampant, social trust is eroded. However, as noted, the relationship between corruption and low social trust is not necessarily causal. Chile is a country where perceptions of corruption run low, but the culture is characterized by high levels of distrust nevertheless.

The question remains whether enhancing trustworthiness in general will increase levels of social trust. Some experts believe it will, simply because people tend to respond to the level of trustworthiness of others (Hardin, 2002). As noted in Chapter Two, social trust is not conceived as a permanent state of society. It is affected daily by destructive events, be they small or large. Social capital is created and accumulated when people participate in social networks, but the willingness to participate entails a disposition to trust. Hence interest in the study of social trust also has a pragmatic side: the possibilities of social exchange and collaboration that follow from generally trusting others (Hardin, 2001). There appears to be widespread agreement that the advantage of pursuing trust is that it eases the way to cooperative social relations (Fukuyama, 1995; Luhmann, 1980; Putnam, 1993). Without trust, only very rudimentary forms of human cooperation seem possible. A culture of trust strengthens the bonds of the individuals with the larger community, fosters collaborative relations, and increases solidarity and altruistic behavior in the solution of social problems (Sztompka, 1999).

One of the characteristics of low-trust societies is the weakness of group sanctions in the face of opportunistic behavior by its members. Ethically questionable acts are often presented as accomplishments and shared openly, indicating that such dubious behaviors are acceptable and actually credit the person who performs them. A couple of recent examples taken from local media publications illustrate this phenomenon. In one of them, a member of the House of Representatives boasted that by lying to a police officer and posing as a journalist, he was able to watch an international soccer game at a privileged location reserved for members of the press (González, 2005). Another example is provided by a letter to the editor of a local newspaper in which the author described an act of deceit whereby she and her spouse, while visiting in Rome, managed to be admitted to a public audience with the pope (Irarrázaval, 2005). Not only were these two firsthand accounts of deception published, but no one responded to any of them by pointing out the inappropriateness of the behaviors in question. In such societies, there appears to be a relaxed and tolerant attitude toward transgressions, accompanied by a generalized perception that "everybody does it." The performer of an opportunistic act, if successful in attaining its objective, is hailed as clever, resourceful, and worth imitating, while the deceived is viewed as incompetent and gullible. Thus a disposition to distrust may actually be a smart course of action in societies where opportunistic behavior is openly tolerated.

Still, even in societies with low levels of social trust, cross-sector alliances have prospered under certain conditions. The key question is how strangers can develop trust in each other and build a cooperative relationship in a culture that is characterized by low levels of social trust. Some findings in the context of a study of cross-sector collaborations and alliance formation in Chile (Austin and others, 2004) can provide clues to practitioners and consultants as to how to favor collaboration in such cultures.

The Role of Trust in Cross-Sector Alliances in Chile

The insights into the particular role of trust in alliance formation in Chile came, in part, from the study of cross-sector collaborations in the region. An academic initiative to study social enterprise in Latin America—the Social Enterprise Knowledge Network (SEKN)—was launched as part of a major research effort by a group of leading business schools in six Latin American countries and the Harvard Business School with the support of the Avina Foundation. Field-based case studies using a common interview and observation protocol served to provide a deeper understanding of the processes underlying alliance formation and maintenance in the different countries. Each business school had to select four ongoing and publicly visible alliances or partnerships between businesses and nonprofits that had endured for at least five years for an in-depth study of their characteristics.

An unanticipated finding while researching Chilean alliances was the frequent existence of prior liaisons between participants in many of the collaborative efforts, represented by family or friendship ties. When asked about the circumstances that led to the formation of the alliance, key actors involved in the Chilean cross-sector alliances mentioned a friend or family member who had served as a liaison. This was not the case in the alliances studied in other countries. One possible explanation of this distinctive feature in Chilean alliances lies in the concept of social trust. The cases that follow are examples of this phenomenon.

Friendship and Family Ties as Trust Builders

Dr. Jorge Rojas, the leader of the Corporación de Ayuda al Niño Quemado (COANIQUEM), an organization created to provide free medical treatment to children suffering burns, offered one particularly revealing account of the compensatory role of familiarity ties in breaching the low levels of trust in Chilean culture.

Rojas and his colleagues had founded COANIQUEM in 1980, but it started operating two years later after he managed to obtain financial support from ESSO-Chile. Rojas recalled the fortuitous starting point of this alliance:

> It all began [with] social connections, as is often the case in Chile. My wife and I went to my mother-in-law's birthday party, and we happened to sit next to one of my wife's cousins and her husband, who was the head of the Public Affairs Department at Esso at the time. . . . [During the party] I got carried away talking about the extremely inadequate conditions for the rehabilitation of burned children in the country and how we had created COANIQUEM to address the needs of these children but that it was still basically a dream because we had no funding. . . . [The Head of Public Affairs] said ESSO-Chile could provide funds if we presented a formal project [Koljatic and Silva, 2003b, p. 6].

According to Rojas, had it not been for this accidental encounter at the party, the partnership between COANIQUEM and ESSO-Chile might never have materialized. For one thing, Rojas had no idea that the company supported social initiatives, but even if he had known, he doubts that he would have ever knocked on its doors without any acquaintance with executives. "Why would they have trusted me, a perfect stranger?" he reflected (Koljatic and Silva, 2003b, p. 7). The reasoning and behavior of Rojas fits the pattern expected in a culture that is characterized by low levels of social trust. (It is interesting to note that the head of the Public Affairs Department took the case to his superiors and opted to abstain from any involvement in the grant assignment process. This may be explained by the fact that ESSO-Chile was a subsidiary of an American company and, unlike most Chilean companies at the time, had norms to prevent nepotism.)

Once an organization has achieved a solid public image, the likelihood of collaborative alliances is enhanced, even in societies characterized by low levels of trust. The support of ESSO-Chile paved the way for the establishment of other alliances in the community: ESSO-Chile, Rojas explains, "helped build our image at a time when we were perfect strangers in the eyes of the public. . . . When a mayor or government official sees that a major corporation such as ESSO-Chile is willing to finance a dawning initiative, it is a validation support. We had gained public credibility" (Koljatic and Silva, 2003b, p. 8).

From then on, COANIQUEM developed a number of alliances with other business companies, and the initiative grew with the support of its corporate partners. Through this network, COANIQUEM expanded across the borders of the nation to serve the needs of burned children and their families in other Latin American countries and formed a foundation in the United States: the COANIQUEM Burned Children Foundation (BCF). BCF was created to raise funds to promote the treatment of burned children in any part of the world, advance research in the field, and advocate the prevention of burn accidents.

Another interesting case that illustrates the facilitating role of preexisting ties in the emergence of collaboration is offered by the alliance between Banco de Crédito e Inversiones (BCI) and the Corporación de Crédito al Menor (CCM). Renato Ferreti, marketing manager at BCI, after watching a program on TV about abandoned and homeless children, became fixated on the idea that he had to do something about it. After some failed trials to involve the principal and parents at his children's school, he decided to give it a last try by attempting to mobilize support within his workplace. He did not have a clear idea of how to address the problem, but he knew that in order to start any kind of initiative geared toward the protection of children, he would need money. Ferreti aimed his efforts at a strategic actor: his occasional tennis partner, Hector Pozo, the bank comptroller. Pozo was an emblematic figure within BCI. He had worked at the bank for forty years, was deeply trusted by the president and the board, and was highly esteemed and trusted by managers and employees. Ferreti anticipated that gaining the support of Pozo for the initiative would greatly facilitate the selling of the idea to the other managers and to the board. Not only did Pozo endorse the initiative, but he even agreed to open a joint account with Ferreti for fundraising purposes. Pozo explained his support in the following terms: "I felt very close to Renato. . . . We were good friends. At first he used to talk to me about his project and I would listen noncommittally, but in the end I gave in to his enthusiasm [even though] it was a crazy idea" (Koljatic and Silva, 2003a, p. 4).

With the endorsement of Pozo, Ferreti went door to door asking his fellow managers to commit 1 percent of their monthly salary from then on to support this vague and uncertain initiative. Irrational as it may seem, none of the managers refused, including the "hardest nut to crack," the bank's CEO. According to Ferreti and other executives, had he been unsuccessful in gaining the adherence of Pozo, "the initiative would have been a flop." The generalized trust of bank managers in the judgment of Pozo made the difference. Eventually, CCM managed to clearly define its mission and beneficiaries, and ten years later, it operated two facilities dedicated to providing assistance to underage at-risk girls because of abuse or abandonment. About half the bank employees and executives donated 1 percent of their monthly salaries to support CCM. BCI also made generous contributions to help cover operating costs.

Exceptions to the Rule?

Exceptions to the pattern of friendship and family ties in collaborative endeavors appear to exist. What sets apart the cases that will be described is that the initiator of the cross-sector alliance was not the leader of a nascent social initiative that needed funding. Interestingly, family and friendship ties were absent in the cases where the initiator of the collaboration was a business firm that actively sought to establish a partnership with a nonprofit. In these cases, trust was built through familiarity with the nonprofit organization. In both cases, the alliance partner chosen was an established nonprofit, one that already had a presence in the community. Still, the two cases that follow may not be typical of cross-sector alliances involving local organizations since they involve foreign companies. Further research is needed to understand the differences observed between the cases that follow and those described earlier.

One Chilean case that did not fit the pattern of family or friendship ties involved the alliance between Compañía Interamericana de Seguros (CIS), an AIG affiliate that started operating in the country in the 1980s in the individual insurance policy and pension fund business, and the Fundación Las Rosas (FLR), a organization that catered to the needs of elderly poor. The initiator of the alliance was Alex Fernández, a Cuban-born and American-raised executive and CEO at CIS. Uneasy about the Chilean custom of sending "gifts" to clients at year-end, a practice he viewed as a waste of money, he decided to do away with that tradition and replace it with a monetary contribution to a charitable organization. Fernández assigned the task of finding suitable local nonprofits to the marketing manager. He analyzed several candidates, among them FLR, an organization that already enjoyed a well-deserved reputation as an efficient provider of services for the destitute elderly. This review of potential alliance candidates is a common and recommended practice in the United States (Tennyson, 2003). Once Fernández chose FLR as the donation recipient, he approached its director as he would have done in the United States and organized a meeting to deliver a check the day before Christmas. Fernández recalled, "The idea was to take a few pictures for marketing and advertising. . . . [However,] the appalling conditions of the home and the site of the elderly deeply moved me. I said, this check is not enough. You need more. I'll see what else we can do" (Koljatic and Silva, 2003c, p.4).

Twenty years after its first donation, with Fernández long gone from CIS, the company was still collaborating with FLR. Fernández also played a key role in forging another alliance between FLR and Farmacias Ahumada S.A., the largest drugstore chain in Latin America, where he was an influential board member.

Another case of a local alliance that did not involve family or friendship ties is that of General Electric (GE) in Chile and Hogar de Cristo (HC), a prestigious church-based local organization. HC was founded in the 1950s by Father Alberto Hurtado, a revered Chilean Jesuit priest, to cater to the needs of the homeless. After fifty years of operation, HC commanded enormous trust and respect in the nation. GE executives approached HC to request their collaboration in order to build trust into one of their social initiatives. GE, as part of its program of social responsibility, had designed a costly dental mobile clinic (DMC) to serve inner-city poor. The clinic was staffed by dentists and dental technicians who volunteered their time to serve low-income patients at no cost in the poorest sections of the Chilean capital, Santiago. In the earlier stages of the project, GE executives realized that to succeed, their initiative needed to be validated within the community, and the alliance with HC served that purpose. The public had to be convinced that there were no ulterior motives attached to the project, and HC played an important role in accomplishing this. The HC logo next to GE's served to instill trust and create goodwill toward the initiative in the community. The alliance not only facilitated the access of patients to the DMC but also served to ensure that the community would protect the motor vehicle and its valuable components from theft and vandalism when it was stationed in high-crime neighborhoods. In this case, GE executives employed a go-between or mediator strategy—finding a familiar person or institution to form an alliance—as a way to build trust into a nascent social initiative.

Lessons for the Development of Collaborative Efforts

Lack of trust in a culture poses significant problems and obstacles for the development of collaborative efforts. In low-trust societies, the conditions that facilitate the initiation and maintenance of collaborative efforts are far from ideal. The weak associative tendencies that characterize low-trust societies work against the establishment of the rich interpersonal networks that form the basis of a strong civil society.

Development of cross-sector collaborations is a challenge, even in societies that are characterized by high levels of social trust. The "alliance marketplace" in the United States—the meeting ground where parties interested in cross-sector partnering find good information about potential partners—is still far from ideal, being currently underdeveloped and inefficient (Austin, 2000). Often "prospective partners lack good information about each other and easy ways to seek one another out" (pp. 41–42). The challenges are multiplied in low-trust societies, where there is a pressing need to build trust between parties in order to promote cross-sector collaboration. The need to build trust appears to be particularly relevant in cases where the leaders who seek the alliance represent dawning or relatively unknown social initiatives. The ongoing study of collaborative efforts in low-trust societies can help shed light on the processes that favor the emergence of collaboration.

Chile provides an instance of a culture characterized by low levels of social trust where collaborative efforts are displayed between people who are already familiar with one another. The cases described in this chapter portray a tightly knitted society where social networks and family relations support the emergence of collaboration. The existence of prior links between parties appears to have a substantial impact on the way initial contacts unfold. These personal relationships bypass the general social distrust and associated uncertainty, provide some initial level of confidence, and pave the way for collaboration. When no personal relationship is available, it is possible to speculate that being associated with a reputable institution could provide a "guarantee" of reliability. Although merely a conjecture at this point, it is possible that in societies characterized by low levels of social trust, dawning initiatives might benefit by seeking to associate with a reputable secular or religious institution that can mediate or serve as a bridge between potential partners. The Catholic church in Chile might be a case in point since it represents a widely respected institution that has traditionally inspired confidence in the population. The role the church played in the defense of human rights during the military regime probably reinforced the confidence and respect that it instills in a majority of the population. Its endorsement of a nascent social organization could help overcome the prevalent and ingrained attitude of distrust toward the unknown.

One interesting observation that stems from the study of alliances and that merits further research is that the influence of family and friendship ties in fostering collaboration does not appear to operate in cases where multinational corporations are actively searching for potential partners or allies among local nonprofits. The selection criteria in the latter case appear to be of a more rational nature. They are based on the reputation and the image of the nonprofit in the community and its potential to create value for its business ally.

An important lesson for nonprofit consultants working outside their own culture is that levels of social trust and associative tendencies vary, and this needs to be taken into consideration when implementing strategies to foster cross-sector collaborative behaviors. The dynamics of the emergence of collaboration do not appear to follow an identical pattern across cultures. Facilitating collaborative endeavors in low-trust societies entails the heightened challenge of actively building the conditions for trust to emerge between the potential partners.

Finally, even if an alliance is engineered through preexisting social networks, it is necessary to study the mechanisms by which it is sustained over time. Important as such ties appear to be in the emergence of collaborative endeavors, it is unlikely that friendship or family connections will suffice to maintain the collaboration in the absence of positive outcomes. The challenge in societies characterized by low levels of social trust is to create conditions where cooperation and solidarity can have a path for expression in order to produce favorable consequences for social and civic life.

References

Austin, J. *The Collaboration Challenge*. San Francisco: Jossey-Bass, 2000.

Austin, J., and others. *Social Partnering in Latin America*. Cambridge, Mass.: David Rockefeller Center for Latin American Studies, Harvard University, 2004.

Butazzoni, L. *Sociabilidad y confianza en Chile* (Puntos de Referencia No 198). Santiago, Chile: Centro de Estudios Públicos, 1998.

Fukuyama, F. *Trust: The Social Virtues and the Creation of Prosperity*. New York: Free Press, 1995.

Godoy, H. *El carácter chileno: Estudio preliminar y selección de ensayos*. Santiago, Chile: Editorial Universitaria, 1981.

González, E. "La importancia de ser pariente." *Santiago Revista Ercilla*, Aug. 5, 2002, p. 23.

González, J. "Pizza con Pellegrini." *Revista El Sábado, El Mercurio (de Santiago)*, Sept. 10, 2005, p. 48.

Hardin, R. "Conceptions and Explanations of Trust." In K. Cook (Ed.), *Trust in Society*. New York: Russell Sage Foundation, 2001.

Hardin, R. *Trust and Trustworthiness*. New York: Russell Sage Foundation, 2002.

Inglehart, R., Basañez, M., and Moreno A. *Human Values and Beliefs: A Cross-Cultural Sourcebook*. Ann Arbor: University of Michigan Press, 1998.

Irarrázaval, A. "Audiencia Papal." *El Mercurio (de Santiago)*, Apr. 3, 2002, p. A2.

Koljatic, M., and Silva, M. *The Banco BCI and the Corporación Crédito al Menor* (SEKN Case Collection, Document SKE-013). Boston: Harvard Business School Publishing, 2003a.

Koljatic, M., and Silva, M. *Corporación de Ayuda al Niño Quemado and ESSO-Chile* (SEKN Case Collection, Document SKE-009). Boston: Harvard Business School Publishing, 2003b.

Koljatic, M., and Silva, M. *Farmacias Ahumada S.A. and the Fundación Las Rosas* (SEKN Case Collection, Document SKE-019). Boston: Harvard Business School Publishing, 2003c.

Luhmann, N. *Trust and Power.* Hoboken, N.J.: Wiley, 1980.

Putnam, R. *Making Democracy Work.* Princeton, N.J.: Princeton University Press, 1993.

Sztompka, P. *Trust.* Cambridge: Cambridge University Press, 1999.

Tennyson, R. *Manual de Trabajo en Alianza.* London: International Business Leaders Forum and Global Alliance for Improved Nutrition, 2003.

Valenzuela, E., and Cousiño, C. "Sociabilidad y asociatividad: Un ensayo de sociología comparada." *Estudios Públicos,* 2000, *77*, 321–339.

Yamagishi, T. "Trust as a Form of Social Intelligence." In K. Cook (Ed.), *Trust in Society.* New York: Russell Sage Foundation, 2001.

Ignacio J. Martinez-Moyano is a scientist at Argonne National Laboratory's Decision and Information Sciences Division, in its Decision and Risk Analysis Group. He is also a research associate with the Center for Policy Research of the State University of New York at Albany. His current research interests include behavioral theories of judgment and decision making under uncertainty in complex systems, the evolution of collaboration in complex systems, and the evolution of digital government. His research work has been published in academic journals including *Transactions on Modeling and Computer Simulation* (published by the Association for Computer Machinery/ACM TOMACS) and *Government Information Quarterly*. He holds a Ph.D. in public administration and policy from Rockefeller College of Public Affairs and Policy at the State University of New York at Albany; a master of science degree in systems engineering and information science, a master of business administration degree, and a bachelor's degree in industrial and systems engineering from ITESM in Mexico.

CHAPTER FOUR

EXPLORING THE DYNAMICS OF COLLABORATION IN INTERORGANIZATIONAL SETTINGS

Ignacio J. Martinez-Moyano

The Center for Technology in Government (CTG) at the State University of New York at Albany recognized that an integrative theory about interorganizational collaboration would enable the center to better fulfill one of its key goals, to help government agencies work together to integrate their information resources so as better to accomplish their overlapping public service missions. Developing this theory would increase the likelihood of success in their collaborative projects. To accomplish this task, CTG decided to use dynamic modeling as a framework for its theory-building efforts and worked in conjunction with system dynamics modelers from the Rockefeller College of Public Affairs and Policy at SUNY-Albany. The theory of collaboration presented in this chapter was developed in the course of analyzing the creation of an information system prototype for the New York State Bureau of Housing Services, the Homeless Information Management System. (Additional information about the project can be found in Cresswell and others, 2002a, 2002b, and in Black and others, 2003.)

The research presented here would not have been possible without the collaboration of Center for Technology in Government researchers and Rockefeller College modelers. David F. Andersen, George P. Richardson, and Anthony Creswell were instrumental in the development of the theory described here.

The methods used in this investigation include the system dynamics model-building process (Forrester, 1961, 1968; Richardson and Pugh, 1981; Sterman, 2000) and its group model-building variant (Andersen and Richardson, 1997; Andersen, Richardson, and Vennix, 1997). In addition, semistructured interviews were conducted during the refinement and validation stages of the theory-building effort. Brief explanations of system dynamics and group model building are provided in Exhibits 4.1 and 4.2.

EXHIBIT 4.1. SYSTEM DYNAMICS MODELING.

System dynamics is "a computer-aided approach to policy analysis and design" (Richardson, 1996, p. 657) that applies to complex problems arising in dynamic systems. System dynamics provides a way to explore feedback-rich systems (where relationships among some of the elements are circular) and is used to study how the various components of systems interact and influence each other and how they define the behavior of systems over time.

The main purpose of system dynamics is to discover the structure that conditions the behavior of systems over time. System dynamicists try to pose dynamic hypotheses that *endogenously* contribute to the observed behavior of systems by linking this behavior to a hypothesized causal structure. The aim of a system dynamics modeling effort is to generate endogenous—structurally based—explanations of the behavioral evolution of the system over time. The main focus of system dynamics is to produce insights about the linkages between the structures and behaviors of systems facilitating the discovery of leverage points of intervention.

System dynamics is essentially interdisciplinary and "grounded in the theory of nonlinear dynamics and feedback control developed in mathematics, physics, and engineering" (Sterman, 2000, p. 5). Mathematically, "the basic structure of a formal system dynamics computer simulation model is a system of coupled, nonlinear, first-order differential (or integral) equations" (Richardson, 1996, p. 657) that can be written in the form

$$\frac{dx}{dt} = \dot{x}(t) = f[x(t), u(t)]; \ x(t_0) \text{ given}$$

where $x(t) = n^{th}$-order vector of system states (or levels)

$x(t_0) = $ initial value for state vector at

$u(t) = $ vector of exogenous inputs (or parameters), and

$f(_) = $ nonlinear vector-valued function

$\frac{dx}{dt} = \dot{x}(t) = $ time derivative of the state vector

Although system dynamics uses formal mathematical models to describe the system, its main focus is on understanding the system, not on the mathematics used to represent it.

EXHIBIT 4.2. GROUP MODEL BUILDING.

Group model building deals with "the processes and techniques designed to handle the tangle of problems that arise in trying to involve a large number of people in model construction" (Richardson, 1999, p. 375). A base of literature has been developed in the area of group model building and continues to grow, presenting specific guidelines and scripts to carry out these processes (Andersen and Richardson, 1997; Andersen, Richardson, and Vennix, 1997; Vennix, 1999). According to Zagonel (2002, 2004), two main types of models may arise in group model building. *Micro-world* types of models arise when the main concern of the group is to describe their agreed-on state of the world and to capture reality for all to see. *Boundary-object* types of models arise when groups are concerned with understanding their diverse views about the world, and a model emerges as a composite of the reality that groups observe creating a negotiated social order. While logical empiricism drives micro-world modeling, collective subjectivism is the driver that determines usefulness and truth in boundary-object models.

The Homeless Information Management System

The action research context for the development of the dynamic theory of collaboration was the development of a prototype information system, an integrated information system that would consolidate information resources used in providing shelter services for the homeless population of New York State. In New York, approximately thirty thousand homeless people receive services worth an estimated $350 million per year (Center for Technology in Government, 2000). Thousands of information resources geared to providing services to the homeless were distributed across dozens of state agencies and hundreds of service providers. Furthermore, the data collected by these various actors were defined differently (for example, service providers used different terms to describe clients' ethnicity), and some desired data were collected by some actors but not by others. Standardizing and sharing the data was seen as crucial to managing resources more effectively and improving program outcomes.

Starting in 1998 and for a period of almost three years, CTG worked closely with the New York State Office of Temporary and Disability Assistance, Bureau of Housing Services, to develop an integrated information system. This system was designed to help government agencies and nonprofit organizations manage services provided to the homeless and evaluate the effectiveness of these services. One important outcome of this project was the construction of a prototype integrated information system, the Homeless Information Management System (HIMS).

HIMS was built based on preexisting data from multiple case and financial management systems of government agencies and providers of homeless services. The aim of the system was to integrate data from multiple sources and provide a single point of reference for the agencies involved in the process. For example, each shelter provided demographic data about the individuals served, the state's Welfare Management System provided payment information, and the Bureau of Housing Services provided general information about the shelters. The HIMS data repository was designed to allow decision makers at the state, local, and provider levels to manage and evaluate temporary housing and service programs for homeless families and single adults (Center for Technology in Government, 2000). A brief history of the development of the theory is presented in Exhibit 4.3. In the next section, the dynamic theory of collaboration is presented, including its components and assumptions and possible extensions.

EXHIBIT 4.3. DEVELOPMENT OF THE DYNAMIC COLLABORATION THEORY.

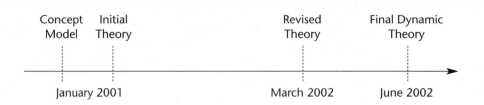

In this theory-building effort, developed over a period of eighteen months, case study research was used to generate new theory (Eisenhardt, 2002). In January 2001, researchers from CTG and modelers from Rockefeller College met for the first time to talk about interorganizational collaboration dynamics observed in the development of the HIMS prototype. A concept model was developed and later used in the process. In addition, during that same month, a new theory was developed. This theory focused on project management–related dynamics. After the January 2001 meeting, the modeler team worked on formalizing the initial theory and on understanding its dynamic implications. Model formulation and testing became critical to inform modelers and other members of the team about the structure of the model and accumulations that needed to be considered in order to replicate observed dynamic behavior. A revised theory was created during the second meeting with the team in March 2002. Three months later, the group met again, and the final dynamic theory, focused on the role and effects of knowledge accumulation on collaborative processes, was delineated.

A Dynamic Theory of Collaboration

The dynamic theory of collaboration presented here is the product of the HIMS project group's reflection about collaboration efforts carried out while developing the information system prototype. In its final form, the theory focuses on the dynamics generated by action and knowledge accumulation and how these influence the development of collaboration over time. A theoretical framework based on the identification of cross-boundary activity (Carlile, 1997, 2002; Black, 2002) was used in this process. The cross-boundary activity framework stresses the relevance of actions being carried out by collaborative partners "at the boundary" of their collaborative effort. According to Carlile (1997), in collaborative projects, knowledge is embedded in what he calls *boundary objects* that allow partners to share information and empowers them to work together. Black (2002) operationalized this thinking using system dynamics modeling (see also Black, Carlile, and Repenning, 2004).

Key insights were gained at various stages in the development of the model. Four models are highlighted here—the *concept model,* the *initial theory,* the *revised theory,* and the *final theory.* This presentation illustrates both the process of developing the models as well as the insights gained into collaboration dynamics with each model.

Concept Model

The first model created is what Andersen and Richardson (1997) describe as a *concept model.* The concept model is used to capture the attention of the group with which the modeling effort is carried out. In this case, it was built using data collected from preliminary interviews of state agency and service provider representatives. As shown in Figure 4.1, the concept model captures four feedback mechanisms that foster the creation of collaborative engagements. Consistent with system dynamics practice (Oliva, 1996), the constructs used in the model implicitly refer to a collaborative process from a high-level perspective.

Project dynamics in this model are captured with a stock of *tasks to do* that as a function of *progress rate* become *tasks done.* The more progress in the project is made, the more *trust* is built in the collaborative engagement, bringing *people productivity* up and further increasing the *progress rate.* Once *trust* is accumulated, it can be depleted via the *trust erosion rate.* When the *time for trust to erode* is long, the *trust erosion rate* is small. When the *time for trust to erode* is extremely small, the

FIGURE 4.1. CONCEPT MODEL.

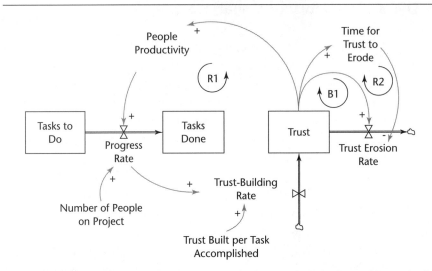

accumulated *trust* will deplete immediately, having an important effect on *people productivity*. However, the accumulation of *trust* acts as a deterrent mechanism that prevents its own erosion. Higher levels of *trust* in collaborative engagements induce a longer *time for trust to erode* and therefore low *trust erosion rates*. This reinforcing mechanism creates the possibility of experiencing virtuous cycles of *trust, people productivity,* and *progress* and *trust-building rates* (R2 in Figure 4.1), fostering collaboration.

Initial Theory

The first group meeting resulted in the creation of the initial theory (see Figure 4.2), which dealt with the mechanics of project development and their effects on collaboration and productivity (for examples of system dynamics treatments of project dynamics, see Abdel-Hamid, 1984; Abdel-Hamid and Madnick, 1991; Lyneis, 1980; Lyneis, Cooper, and Els, 2001; and Sterman, 2000). The main effects of collaboration identified in this theory are increased productivity and decreased number of unsolved problems.

The initial theory reflects the notion that effective participation in project activities fosters collaboration, which increases productivity and avoids problems. Results with fewer problems are interpreted as increased progress and added po-

FIGURE 4.2. INITIAL THEORY.

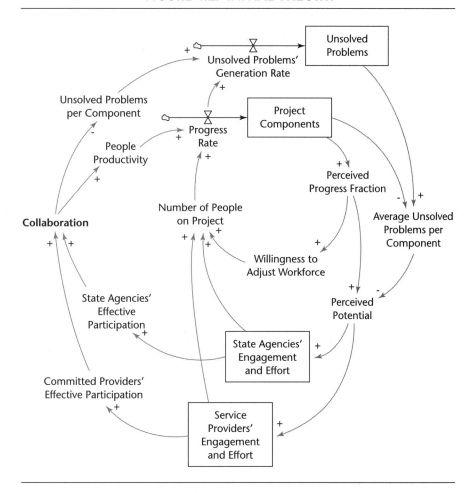

tential. Furthermore, added potential brings additional momentum to the collaborative effort, increasing engagement, which drives effective participation up further, closing a virtuous cycle. In this theory, actors' commitment spreads like a virus, causing participants to be involved in the project. This spreading theory is consistent with the experience that researchers at CTG had in the development of the HIMS prototype (Center for Technology in Government, 2000).

Revised Theory

A considerably more complex theory was developed next, moving beyond the mechanics of the work in the collaborative project. This theory, centered on the interaction dynamics of actors involved in developing the HIMS prototype, includes important behavioral elements that influence the development of collaboration in interorganizational settings. As shown in Figure 4.3, the focus of collaborative interaction is on the way collaboration, perceived risk, and the ability to work with others coevolve over time as actors work together on project development.

FIGURE 4.3. REVISED THEORY.

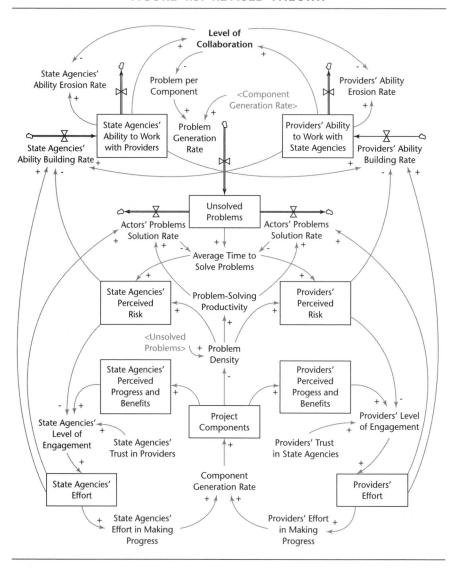

Collaboration, in this revised theory, generates both operational and behavioral influences. From an operational point of view, *level of collaboration* (at the top center of the diagram) is modeled as the combination of the accumulation of ability of the actors to work together over time, specifically, the *state agencies' ability to work with providers* combined with the *providers' ability to work with state agencies*. In turn, an increase in *level of collaboration* decreases the number of *problems per component* (a component is a working element of the prototype) due to such factors as increased communication, higher accuracy in the definition of requirements, and enhanced design interaction. Increases in *level of collaboration* indirectly influences actors' *ability to work with others* by increasing the time it takes to erode this ability, decreasing its erosion rate.

The revised theory had more explanatory power than the initial one, but the group felt it still needed refinement. The group thought that the theory needed to incorporate the actions and effects of a facilitator in the collaborative process to truly reflect the experience of building the HIMS prototype.

Final Theory

The final version of the theory highlights the interrelated roles of the accumulation of mutual knowledge, productivity, sense of progress, engagement, and trust. Each of these relationships is described.

Mutual Knowledge. Mutual knowledge is essential for collaboration to develop. Mutual knowledge "consists not only of the information itself but also the awareness that the other knows it" (Cramton, 2001, p. 347) and is able to understand and use it. In Figure 4.4, mutual knowledge is represented in the system diagram by *state agencies' knowledge about the project and about providers* and *providers' knowledge about the project and about state agencies*. *Project components* represents the accumulation of completed tasks that contributed to the overall project. In addition, the project components served as boundary objects, providing collaborative partners with a basis for communicating and exchanging information and knowledge.

In the development of the HIMS prototype, as shown in Figure 4.4, the more knowledge the actors had about the project and each other, the greater the *productivity rate*, which in turn pushed up the *work completion rate*, allowing actors to *learn by doing* and accumulate completed *project components*. This reinforcing mechanism (represented by loops R1a and R1b in Figure 4.4) generates growth in both the production of *project components* and *knowledge*. Learning by doing has long been recognized as a key mechanism to increase

FIGURE 4.4. REINFORCING CYCLE OF MUTUAL KNOWLEDGE, PRODUCTIVITY, WORK COMPLETION, AND LEARNING BY DOING.

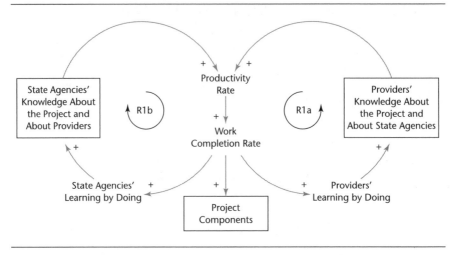

knowledge (Argyris, 1976, 1994; Argyris and Schön, 1996; March, 1981, 1988, 1999; March and Olsen, 1988; March and Simon, 1958).

Error Rates. Further, accumulation of knowledge resulted in reduced error rates, which in turn further strengthened the cycle. Figure 4.5 incorporates *error rate*, recognizing another set of reinforcing loops (R2a and R2b). These mechanisms were especially apparent during the requirements definition stage of the HIMS prototype. As the prototype was built, state agencies gained knowledge about the type of information system they needed as well as concerns that prevented the service providers from engaging in the construction of the prototype. For example, many service providers feared that disclosing information to state agencies would produce negative financial consequences for them. However, after learning more about the project, the role of the state agencies, and how the information system would be used, the providers found that their fears were unfounded, and their willingness to share key information increased substantially.

Sense of Progress and Engagement. As the service providers and state agencies collaborated effectively, their sense of progress increased, which in turn increased their level of engagement, making further accumulation of knowledge possible. These reinforcing cycles are shown in Figure 4.6, loops R3a and R3b.

FIGURE 4.5. KNOWLEDGE-REDUCES-ERRORS REINFORCING LOOPS.

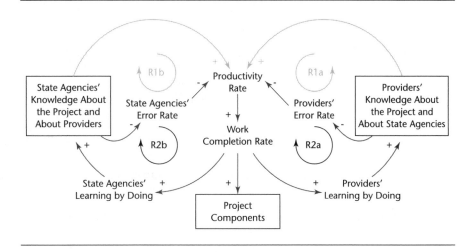

FIGURE 4.6. SENSE-OF-PROGRESS AND ENGAGEMENT REINFORCING LOOPS.

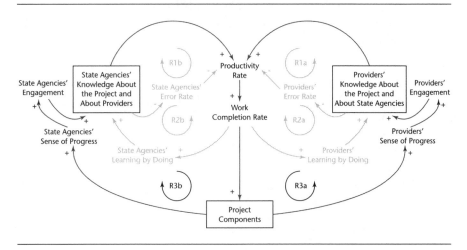

Trust. Actors' knowledge accumulation also had an effect on the level of trust between the actors. Trust, or lack of it, has been recognized as an important predictor of collaborative efforts. Powell, Koput, and Smith-Doerr (1996) argue that "a lack of trust between the parties, difficulties in relinquishing control, the complexity of a joint project, and differential ability to learn new skills" (p. 117) are all barriers to be surmounted in collaborative efforts. In the case of HIMS, as state agencies' knowledge about the project and about the role of providers in the project grew, the level of trust that state agencies had in service providers experienced a dramatic increase, creating an environment leading to higher levels of engagement (see Figure 4.7, loop R4b).

Reinforcing processes like those generating engagement and trust can become engines of growth or engines of decline in collaborative settings. If providers of services had not been able to accumulate enough knowledge about the project and about the role of state agencies in the project, generating enough trust in the process to engage and move forward, this reinforcing cycle would have prevented trust from emerging and engagement from happening.

In certain cases, especially in small, informal projects, levels of knowledge and trust required to trigger engagement of actors might be low because these projects pose little risk to the actors involved (Ring and Van de Ven, 1994). In these cases, a small amount of effort might be enough to start collaboration processes leading to interorganizational exchanges that eventually reach higher

FIGURE 4.7. KNOWLEDGE-TRUST-ENGAGEMENT REINFORCING LOOPS.

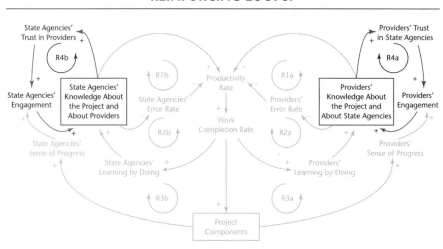

levels of shared knowledge and collaboration. In large-scale projects, however, this might be difficult to achieve.

Collaboration. In the initial theory (see Figure 4.2), collaboration was modeled as the confluence of effective participation of all actors. Effective participation was defined as a combination of engagement and effort in the collaborative process. In the revised theory (see Figure 4.3), collaboration was defined as the combination of the accumulation of the actors' ability to work with each other. Ability to work with each other accumulates over time as a function of effort, perceived risk, and interaction with other actors in the project. In the final theory, as shown in Figure 4.8, collaboration was redefined as the confluence of *engagement* of the parties involved: the higher the engagement, the higher the *collaboration* achieved. This conceptualization was identified by the group as a parsimonious and robust representation of the specific connotation of collaboration in the context of the creation of the HIMS prototype.

The group agreed that actors' engagement, as a driver of collaboration, needed to be understood in more than its operational sense. To understand

FIGURE 4.8. COLLABORATION LOOPS.

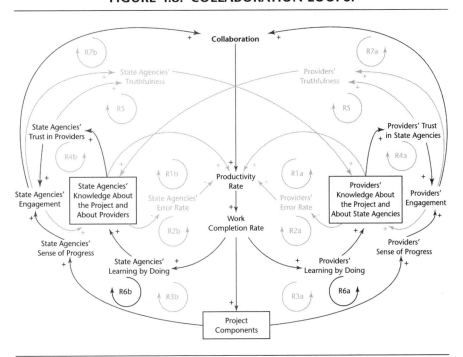

the group's thinking, it will be useful to review how engagement evolved through the early versions of the theory.

In the initial theory, engagement was driven by perceived progress, which was in turn determined by purely operational variables—feasible components and unsolved problems. In the revised theory, the definition of engagement was enriched beyond operational factors by including the effects of perceived risk in its formulation. Including behavioral elements in the formation of collaboration allowed for a richer understanding of its dynamic drivers. However, by decoupling the effect of engagement on collaboration, the theory lost definitional robustness and directness.

In the final theory, engagement has a direct influence on collaboration. The conceptualization of collaboration as a function of engagement of the actors is a way to recuperate the simplicity of the formulation without losing its richness, due to the way in which actors' engagement is conceptualized. As shown in Figure 4.8, actors' *engagement* is a function of *sense of progress* (mostly operational components) and *trust* (mainly behaviorally driven elements) gained by the accumulation of relevant *knowledge* about the collaborative project and its partners (largely cognitively driven elements). The richness of this formulation allowed the group to move forward with a simplified definition: collaboration is the confluence of engagement of actors in the collaborative project.

Simplicity in the formulation of collaboration does not come at the cost of losing feedback richness. In the computer-based simulation models that formalized each version of the theory, the number of feedback loops in which collaboration appears provides a proxy for the level of dynamic complexity captured in the model. In the initial and revised models, collaboration was part of 32 and 72 feedback loops, respectively. In the final model, collaboration is part of 21,553 feedback loops, representing a major increase in feedback complexity. (Mathematical equations for the formal model are available from the author upon request.)

The final theory captures component production, problem generation, problem solving, and learning processes in a very specific way, allowing their dynamics to have an influence on the temporal evolution of collaboration. It presents a feedback-intensive view of the collaborative process that captures the interconnections that make the collaborative endeavor a highly interactive phenomenon difficult to explore and explain in simple terms. For example, in the simulation model, *work completion rate* is part of 3,990 feedback processes, while *productivity rate* is part of 23,202 feedback paths. *Sense of progress,* the construct that captures the way in which collaborative partners estimate how the project is moving forward, is part of 27,903 feedback loops.

Final Considerations and Future Research

The theory of collaboration presented in this chapter is the result of careful examination of the case of the creation of the HIMS prototype and thoughtful reflection of the mechanisms that drove collaboration in that context. Researchers at CTG and modelers from Rockefeller College put numerous months into thinking hard about the problem and about what drivers and underlying structure created the conditions for collaboration to emerge in this case. This theory is grounded in case data, literature, and the expert judgment of CTG researchers. The case data used in this theory have been thoroughly documented by CTG researchers and have been used to continue their search for guidelines to help individuals in public and private sector organizations cope with the demands of collaborative enterprises. CTG researchers have as a priority to act as facilitators of efficient collaborative efforts in projects that involve the use of technology in government and are committed to sharing these insights. The theory presented here would have not been generated had it not been for their effort.

Collaboration is a function of the recursive interaction of knowledge, engagement, results, perceptions of trust, and accumulation of activity over time. In this sense, the way to improve collaboration is to pay attention to how knowledge is managed in collaborative efforts, how results are produced and understood, and how communication can enable the creation of trust.

This research produced a robust endogenous dynamic collaboration theory based on the HIMS prototype development case. Additional research is needed to investigate how this core dynamic engine of collaboration applies to other cases and settings. Also, investigating the intricacies of the relationship between initial levels of knowledge and accumulation of knowledge over the course of the collaborative effort seems to be important. Other areas of further inquiry include learning mechanisms, relative speeds of learning and their effects on trust formation, and the role of perception and memory in the formation of beliefs about progress in projects.

References

Abdel-Hamid, T. K. "The Dynamics of Software Development Project Management: An Integrative System Dynamics Perspective." Unpublished doctoral dissertation, Sloan School of Management, Massachusetts Institute of Technology, 1984.

Abdel-Hamid, T. K., and Madnick, S. E. *Software Project Management Dynamics: An Integrated Approach.* Upper Saddle River, N.J.: Prentice Hall, 1991.

Andersen, D. F., and Richardson, G. P. "Scripts for Group Model Building." *System Dynamics Review,* 1997, *13,* 107–129.

Andersen, D. F., Richardson, G. P., and Vennix, J.A.M. "Group Model Building: Adding More Science to the Craft." *System Dynamics Review,* 1997, *13,* 187–201.

Argyris, C. "Single-Loop and Double-Loop Models in Research on Decision Making." *Administrative Science Quarterly,* 1976, *21,* 363–377.

Argyris, C. "Good Communication That Blocks Learning." *Harvard Business Review,* July-Aug. 1994, pp. 77–85.

Argyris, C., and Schön, D. A. *Organizational Learning II: Theory, Method, and Practice.* Upper Saddle River, N.J.: Prentice Hall, 1996.

Black, L. J. "Collaborating Across Boundaries: Theoretical, Empirical, and Simulated Explorations." Unpublished doctoral dissertation, Sloan School of Management, Massachusetts Institute of Technology, 2002.

Black, L. J., Carlile, P. R., and Repenning, N. P. "A Dynamic Theory of Expertise and Occupational Boundaries in New Technology Implementation: Building on Barley's Study of CT Scanning." *Administrative Science Quarterly,* 2004, *49,* 572–607.

Black, L. J., and others. "A Dynamic Theory of Collaboration: A Structural Approach to Facilitating Intergovernmental Use of Information Technology." Paper presented at the 36th Hawaii International Conference on System Sciences, Big Island, Hawaii, Jan. 2003.

Carlile, P. R. "Understanding Knowledge Transformation in Product Development: Making Knowledge Manifest Through Boundary Objects." Unpublished doctoral dissertation, University of Michigan, 1997.

Carlile, P. R. "A Pragmatic View of Knowledge and Boundaries: Boundary Objects in New Product Development." *Organization Science,* 2002, *13,* 442–455.

Center for Technology in Government. "Building Trust Before Building a System: The Making of the Homeless Information Management System." [http://www.ctg.albany.edu/static/usinginfo/Cases/bss_case.htm]. 2000.

Cramton, C. D. "The Mutual Knowledge Problem and Its Consequences for Dispersed Collaboration." *Organization Science,* 2001, *12,* 346–371.

Cresswell, A. M., and others. "Evolution of a Dynamic Theory of Collaboration: Modeling Intergovernmental Use of Information Technology." Paper presented at the 20th International Conference of the System Dynamics Society, Palermo, Italy, July 2002a.

Cresswell, A. M., and others. "Modeling Intergovernmental Collaboration: A System Dynamics Approach." Paper presented at the 35th Hawaii International Conference on System Sciences, Big Island, Hawaii, Jan. 2002b.

Eisenhardt, K. M. "Building Theories from Case Study Research." In A. M. Huberman and M. B. Miles (eds.), *The Qualitative Research Companion*. Thousand Oaks, Calif.: Sage, 2002.

Forrester, J. W. *Industrial Dynamics*. New York: Productivity Press, 1961.

Forrester, J. W. *Principles of Systems*. New York: Productivity Press, 1968.

Lyneis, J. M. *Corporate Planning and Policy Design*. New York: Productivity Press, 1980.

Lyneis, J. M., Cooper, K. G., and Els, S. A. "Strategic Management of Complex Projects: A Case Study Using System Dynamics." *System Dynamics Review*, 2001, *17*, 237–260.

March, J. G. "Footnotes to Organizational Change." *Administrative Science Quarterly*, 1981, *26*, 563–577.

March, J. G. (ed.). *Decisions and Organizations*. Malden, Mass.: Blackwell, 1988.

March, J. G. *The Pursuit of Organizational Intelligence*. Malden, Mass.: Blackwell, 1999.

March, J. G., and Olsen, J. P. "The Uncertainty of the Past: Organizational Learning Under Ambiguity." In J. G. March (ed.), *Decisions and Organizations*. Malden, Mass.: Blackwell, 1988.

March, J. G., and Simon, H. A. *Organizations*. Hoboken, N.J.: Wiley, 1958.

Oliva, R. "A Dynamic Theory of Service Delivery: Implications for Managing Service Quality." Unpublished doctoral dissertation, Sloan School of Management, Massachusetts Institute of Technology, 1996.

Powell, W. W., Koput, K. W., and Smith-Doerr, L. "Interorganizational Collaboration and the Locus of Innovation: Networks of Learning in Biotechnology." *Administrative Science Quarterly*, 1996, *41*, 116–145.

Richardson, G. P. *Feedback Thought in Social Science and Systems Theory*. Waltham, Mass.: Pegasus, 1991.

Richardson, G. P. "System Dynamics". In S. I. Gass and C. M. Harris (eds.), *Encyclopedia of Operations Research and Management Science*. Norwell, Mass.: Kluwer, 1996.

Richardson, G. P. "Citation for Winner of the 1999 Jay W Forrester Award: Jac Vennix." *System Dynamics Review*, 1999, *15*, 375–377.

Richardson, G. P., and Pugh, A. L., III. *Introduction to System Dynamics Modeling with DYNAMO*. New York: Productivity Press, 1981.

Ring, P. S., and Van de Ven, A. H. "Developmental Processes of Cooperative Interorganizational Relationships." *Academy of Management Review*, 1994, *19*, 90–118.

Sterman, J. D. *Business Dynamics: Systems Thinking and Modeling for a Complex World*. Burr Ridge, Ill.: Irwin/McGraw-Hill, 2000.

Vennix, J.A.M. "Group Model-Building: Tackling Messy Problems." *System Dynamics Review*, 1999, *15*, 379–401.

Zagonel, A. S. "Model Conceptualization in Group Model Building: A Review of the Literature Exploring the Tension Between Representing Reality and Negotiating a Social Order." Paper presented at the 20th International Conference of the System Dynamics Society, Palermo. Italy, July 2002.

Zagonel, A. S. "Reflecting on Group Model Building Used to Support Welfare Reform in New York State." Unpublished doctoral dissertation, Rockefeller College of Public Affairs and Policy, State University of New York, Albany, 2004.

Michael Murray is a Reader in Spatial Planning at Queen's University, Belfast, in Northern Ireland, the institution at which he earned his Ph.D. His research interests include partnership governance, strategic planning, and community-led rural development. He has been a visiting scholar at Colorado State University and has collaborated with scholars and practitioners attached to University of Wisconsin-Madison and the United States Department of Agriculture. He is the author of numerous articles and has cowritten or coedited eight books including, with Brendan Murtagh, *Equity, Diversity, and Interdependence: Reconnecting Governance and People Through Authentic Dialogue* (Ashgate, 2004).

Brendan Murtagh is a Reader in Spatial Planning at Queen's University, Belfast, in Northern Ireland, the institution at which he earned his Ph.D. His research interests include planning and ethnic division, urban regeneration, and community development. He is a member of the Best Practice Panel of the British Urban Regeneration Association and has undertaken policy development and evaluation assignments on urban renewal in Northern Ireland. He has published widely on community-led neighborhood regeneration and cowritten, with Michael Murray, *Equity, Diversity, and Interdependence: Reconnecting Governance and People Through Authentic Dialogue* (Ashgate, 2004).

CHAPTER FIVE

EQUITY, DIVERSITY, AND INTERDEPENDENCE

A New Driver for Societal Transformation

Michael Murray, Brendan Murtagh

At the heart of public policy in the United Kingdom and Ireland is the drive to reduce social exclusion and promote a greater appreciation for diversity. The government's commitment to addressing social exclusion is being taken forward in Northern Ireland, where, in the context of a society long divided by politics, religions, and inequalities, it has been the view that local community groups are often dominated by one tradition, resulting in little contact with similar groups from the other tradition who may be engaged in comparable activities. This lack of contact, linked to a failure to explore difficult questions and different realities, limits addressing social exclusion in its many forms, not least social prejudice in general and sectarianism in particular.

This chapter extends a baseline assessment of attitudes, behaviors, and perceptions in relation to equity, diversity, and interdependence—or EDI for short (Murray and Murtagh, 2004). While the divided society of Northern Ireland provides the empirical laboratory for this analysis, our aim is to provoke organizational self-reflection in other settings and to highlight possible pathways for relational transformation. It is our view that the application of

The authors express their thanks to Rural Community Network and the International Fund for Ireland for their research grant in support of this project.

EDI can provide a new driver for organizational change and ultimately societal change. EDI directly confronts social exclusion and provides a basis for creating a culture of collaboration.

In this chapter, we first consider the meaning of EDI and illustrate its relevance to public policy in Northern Ireland; we then provide an organization case study of how EDI is being used as a transformational practice in the voluntary sector; and we conclude by suggesting a number of ways in which EDI can be applied in other organizational settings.

EDI, Social Exclusion, and the Northern Ireland Context

Social exclusion results from barriers to the rights of citizenship, to a basic standard of living, and to participation in the occupational and social opportunities of society. Although there is a strong relationship between social exclusion and poverty, isolation, prejudice, and discrimination, it is also recognized that system failures play an important part. Atkinson (1999) identifies four dimensions to system support: the democratic and legal system, which promotes civic integration; the labor market, which promotes economic integration; the welfare system, which promotes social integration; and the community and family system, which promotes interpersonal integration. Social exclusion occurs when one or more of these systems break down.

Equality or civil rights legislation can ensure minimum standards of practice and behavior in these matters. Thus, for example, the Northern Ireland Act 1998 establishes that due regard must be given by public bodies to the need to promote equality of opportunity (1) between persons of different religious belief, political opinion, racial group, age, marital status, or sexual orientation; (2) between men and women generally; (3) between persons with a disability and persons without; and (4) between persons with dependents and persons without. But minimum standards also tend to preclude best results from being achieved. Progression beyond these legal imperatives requires a long-term commitment to processes of authentic dialogue constructed around equity, diversity, and interdependence in order to promote good relations.

Government action as a response to social exclusion spans cities, towns, and rural areas; within each domain, it is supporting an active citizenry as evidenced by the sheer number of community and voluntary groups participating in a wide range of government-sponsored social and economic development programs. At the local level, this work is underpinned by an extensive infrastructure of service organizations. Collectively, these organizations recognize that social exclusion encompasses all the aspects of living that prevent people from being fully involved in society.

Moreover, it is accepted that the diversity of personal relationships that exist in service organizations can have implications for the way that an organization is perceived internally and externally. A key proposition in this chapter is that if local communities are being encouraged to more fully embrace ideas of inclusiveness and diversity, then the same can be said for the service organizations with which they interact. In this way, service organizations begin to create the necessary space for embedding mutual respect in all their relationships, both internal and external.

The following four illustrative documents are but a few of the many that have been issued in Northern Ireland in recent years that deal with social exclusion and diversity, the complex interdependence between governance and people, and the challenges faced by societal leaders in responding to imperatives of equality.

In January 2003, the General Synod of the Church of Ireland published *The Hard Gospel: Dealing Positively with Difference in the Church of Ireland.* This report, prepared by the church's Sectarianism Education Project Committee, presents a unique survey of attitudes toward sectarianism and other forms of difference, not least those arising out of differences in political allegiance between members of the church in the separate jurisdictions on the island of Ireland. The analysis, however, moves beyond sectarianism to also consider peace-building initiatives, ethnic differences, sexuality and relationships, and age-related issues.

In September 2004, the secretary of state for Northern Ireland issued a consultation paper, *Gender Matters,* that set out government proposals to tackle gender inequalities within the region. It pointed to amassed evidence of gender inequality, such as lower earnings for women; women constituting the majority of economically inactive persons; workforce segregation, with women dominating in sectors such as health care, social services, education, and retailing; the underrepresentation of women in government and senior public administration positions; and disproportionately higher numbers of women as victims of domestic violence. The report argued that some differences between men and women may be due to inequality of opportunity resulting from processes and structures that may appear fair but in effect lead to gender discrimination. The report proposed a process of gender mainstreaming for all areas of public service based on respect, recognition, and positive valuing.

In March 2005, the Office of the First Minister and Deputy First Minister for Northern Ireland issued draft legislative proposals that would create new and improved rights for some 330,000 disabled people in the region. Existing legislation based on the United Kingdom's Disability Discrimination Act 1995 would be amended, for example, to extend the definition of disability to include people with cancer, multiple sclerosis, and HIV and removing the requirement that people with a mental illness must show that it is a clinically recognized illness before it counts as a mental impairment.

Finally, the Community Relations Unit of the Office of the First Minister and Deputy First Minister for Northern Ireland published *A Shared Future: Policy and Strategic Framework for Good Relations in Northern Ireland* in March 2005. This explicates the government's vision for the future of Northern Ireland based on a peaceful, inclusive, prosperous, stable, and fair society. Emphasis is placed on resolving differences through dialogue and building relationships around mutual recognition and trust. The document sets out practical proposals for action at the central and local government, regional agency, and community levels. These include tackling the visible manifestations of sectarianism and racism (for example, the removal of paramilitary flags and displays), promoting shared education (for example, the development of intercultural education), building shared communities (for example, the protection of mixed housing areas and the fostering of integrated housing), giving support to cultural diversity (for example, by putting good relations at the core of services offered by libraries, museums, and galleries), and closely aligning community development and community relations work (for example, challenging approaches that reinforce segregation).

As reflected by these examples, contemporary society in Northern Ireland is stratified by multiple interlocking identities and exclusions that deepen the inequality and isolation experienced by many people and interests. Moreover, these identities and exclusions can be simultaneous and will change over time, giving rise to different impacts on people's situations and experiences. EDI, we argue, can provide a valuable vocabulary for praxis within the complex relational settings between service organizations and citizens.

EDI in Northern Ireland emerged from research and policy applications in the field of community relations. It was the Community Relations Council's 1998–2001 strategic plan that initially defined this trinity of principles.

Equity is a commitment at all levels within society to ensuring equality of access to resources, structures, and decision-making processes and to the adoption of actions to secure and maintain these objectives. Equity is about achieving equal opportunities and fairness in redressing inequalities.

Diversity can be seen in the ever-changing variety of community and individual experiences. Respect for diversity affirms the existence, recognition, understanding, and tolerance of difference, whether expressed through religious, ethnic, political, or gender background. Diversity is about being free to shape and articulate identities as well as acknowledging and valuing difference.

Interdependence requires recognition by different interest or identity groups of their obligations and commitments to others and of the interconnectedness of individual and community experiences and ambitions, leading to the development of a society that is at once cohesive and diverse. Interdependence is concerned with building better relationships and trust.

The Community Relations Council (1998) took the view that "civil society depends on a shared discourse which recognises and affirms differences, but allows these to exist in constructive relationships with each other. For this to happen, initiatives at all levels must be able to integrate these principles into their work in appropriate ways" (p. 6). In short, EDI comprises the components of a change-oriented road map for building a different and better future.

The contribution of Eyben, Morrow, and Wilson (1997) has been especially influential in articulating the value of these principles for social relations in Northern Ireland. However, they point out that activities have long focused on interpersonal and intergroup encounters at the community level rather than also embracing governmental and institutional stakeholders. The Northern Ireland Act 1998 was put in place to deal with some aspects of EDI, and as noted earlier, the legislation now places a statutory duty on public bodies to have due regard to the need to promote equality of opportunity between persons in different key category groups. The four examples given earlier in this chapter are in line with these requirements. However, the extent to which this statutory duty can be operationalized beyond "box-ticking" at the middle, delivery-oriented level, to encompass a multiplicity of Northern Ireland service organizations remains somewhat unclear. Morrow, Eyben, and Wilson (2003) describe this challenge and the necessary response in the following fashion:

"Rather than coercive legislation, which requires conformity with preordained legislative outcomes, the requirement is for measures which support the development of a culture of learning and development which encourages innovation and commitment in pursuit of an agreed vision and values. The key measure of success in such policy is in the growth of new capacity to deal with difficult but real problems rather than the absence of surface difficulties which leaves underlying issues untouched" (p. 180).

In light of this challenge, EDI brings a broad relevance to the discussion of social exclusion and reaches across the mosaic of public, private, community, and voluntary bodies that comprise contemporary governance. Assuming that the three elements of EDI become core values in that governance, it has the capacity to foster good relations within organizations and between organizations and their constituencies. In the next section of this chapter, we report on the efforts of one organization that is part of the "policy community" for rural development in Northern Ireland and whose ongoing engagement with EDI fits well with this broader need to insert relational transformation into the ethos, policies, and procedures of service organizations.

Transforming Relationships: A Case Study

Rural Community Network (RCN) is a Northern Ireland voluntary organization established by community groups from rural areas in 1991 to articulate the voice of rural communities on issues relating to poverty, disadvantage, and inequality. It receives core funding from the Department of Agriculture and Rural Development, with the remainder of its income coming from charitable trusts, membership fees, and project income. RCN has over five hundred members, consisting of community groups, Northern Ireland–wide voluntary organizations, local authorities, external bodies, consultants, and individuals. RCN sees itself as a learning organization characterized by continuous review of its work, training, and staff development and a participative management style. It abides by the following precepts:

- Rural development must be implemented at a variety of geographical scales—local, subregional, and regional.
- Voluntary participation through a community development process can contribute to better planning and delivery.
- Inequality and sectarian divisions in rural areas can be reduced by community development and the creation of social networks across communities.

- Increasing the capacity to forge new skills related to leadership, mediation, and conflict resolution is essential in building community confidence.
- Openness, accountability, and transparency are essential building blocks for the equitable development of rural areas.

RCN decided in 2000 to advance its own commitment to EDI through an ongoing process of dialogue and understanding. The initial steps RCN took to introduce an EDI framework were designed to facilitate all of the following:

- An integrated approach that would champion fairness in relation not only to religion but also to other categories of persons identified by the 1998 equality legislation
- A desire to go beyond the provisions of the equality regulations, which would demonstrate the EDI process as a real commitment to change rather than a commitment to the legislation
- A willingness to uncover the organizational culture and the subtle messages that resound around teamwork, the roles of men and women, what is talked about, who has power and influence, and the tinges of personal political preference
- An organizational learning approach in which the emphasis is on learning from experience rather than on blame and punishment
- Support for organizational change throughout the EDI process, consisting of actionable items such as policies, structures, and targets
- Recognition that an internal and voluntary process was needed before the approach could reach out to the wider community group membership of RCN

At the outset, RCN encountered a certain amount of internal resistance to "up-front" training around the issue of sectarianism. Some individuals admitted that they had had bad experiences in the past and preferred not to revisit those memories. Any effort to fully embrace EDI requires considerable courage. This is because conversations around EDI take people out of their personal comfort zone in the status quo and provide them with opportunities to talk about personal issues not usually known to others.

The RCN Analysis

As noted, RCN has had a long-standing commitment to equality and collaboration, expressed through its aims to reduce social exclusion, social prejudice, and sectarianism. Its activities over the past fifteen years or so are perceived by staff to have made a positive contribution to relational change in rural areas because of the group's emphasis on networking and involvement in the delivery of program funding. However, rural people are aware that most participants in the rural development arena have been Catholic community groups. Staff believe that this has fueled the erroneous impression that RCN is a Catholic organization whose interests are located "west of the River Bann"—a geographical metaphor for the peripheral part of Northern Ireland that is perceived as rural and nationalist.

To probe that assessment, data on perceptions of RCN corporate identity were obtained in 2001 from a survey of RCN members and nonmembers. The important point here is that this research was carried out as part of an internal dialogue on matters related to EDI. What was remarkable about the baseline survey was the degree to which the organization was prepared to expose itself to possible criticism regarding diversity and inclusion. The survey questionnaire explored perceptions of RCN as an organization in relation to religious affiliation, political opinion, gender makeup, social class, geographical spread, quality of voice for groups in rural society, and quality of support for groups in rural society. The questionnaire results confirmed some of the analysis made by RCN staff; they provided the basis for informed dialogue and a fresh understanding of EDI issues within RCN and presented new possibilities for more effectively incorporating the three elements of EDI into the organization. For example, steps have since been taken to improve the gender and religious balance of staff and board members.

Bringing EDI into RCN

The internal process of bringing EDI more deeply into RCN commenced with the participation of the senior management team in a number of facilitated daylong workshops to discover "where individuals were coming from" in terms of personal background. Issues were explored in relation to how EDI should be defined from a senior management perspective and how EDI could affect RCN and other rural interest organizations.

A similar format was used to engage development workers. After their initial three days of training, the consensus was that much had been achieved in terms of strengthening teamwork by sharing experiences and airing perceptions and grievances not raised before. The involvement of administrative staff required a different approach. A boat trip on a local waterway with a different facilitator was selected. However, this cohort of staff expressed less interest in EDI, which became apparent later when only one person on the administrative support team signed up for EDI training. The view of most administrative staff was that the EDI process was "not for them" and that time taken for dialogue was a distraction from doing their jobs.

From this early experience, senior staff recognized that applying a similar method and pace of engagement for each group of staff was inappropriate, though they still hope that all staff will eventually convene together. Furthermore, while reflections on the EDI process as a whole have been recorded, the details of the discussions remain confidential. This is because EDI requires intensive person-to-person dialogue. This communication must be based on mutual trust that what is revealed will be respected. In short, EDI conversations created the space for people to explore their own context, assumptions, and relationships and to determine behavioral choices on the basis of that assessment. Many organizational issues that might otherwise have continued to lie dormant were brought to the surface through a process linked with team building and greater openness.

This effort was formally embedded within the organization by the establishment in September 2004 of a steering group and the appointment of an external mentor to guide the EDI process. A two-year strategy and implementation plan, with monitoring and evaluation commitments, was put in place, and a statement by RCN on EDI principles in the format of a good relations policy was created in May 2005 (see Exhibit 5.1).

A program of eleven staff workshops to be held between November 2004 and March 2006 was drawn up. These included study visits, residential team building, and themed discussions around topics such as racism, politics in Northern Ireland, disability, cultural differences, and gender biases. A Good Relations officer was appointed and charged initially with drafting an organizational policy on EDI and later with reaching out to external stakeholders.

EXHIBIT 5.1. RURAL COMMUNITY NETWORK'S GOOD RELATIONS POLICY.

Rural Community Network (RCN) as a community development organisation is committed to supporting and encouraging rural communities to build good relations enabling people to live and learn, work and play together.

- RCN will promote Good Relations and Peace Building as a key objective of the organisation in helping meet the needs of an increasingly multi-cultural and diverse rural community.
- RCN will commit to undertake Good Relations and Peace Building through community development values.

RCN's core community development values and principles are as follows:

Relationships: Building respect and positive relationships through dialogue

Empowerment: All policies and programmes should be developed and delivered in ways that facilitate empowerment

Social justice: Enabling people to claim their human rights, meet their needs and have greater control over the decision-making processes that affect their lives

Participation: Facilitating democratic involvement by people in the issues that affect their lives

Equality: Challenging the attitudes of individuals and the practices of institutions and society that discriminate against and marginalise people

Learning: Recognising the skills, knowledge and expertise that people contribute and develop by taking action to tackle social, economic, political and environmental problems

Cooperation: Working together to identify and implement action, based on mutual respect of diverse cultures and contributions

RCN will ensure that its Good Relations policy is one that is promoted and delivered in order to respect and embrace diversity in all its forms. RCN's Good Relations and Peace Building approach will be built on a foundation of Equity, Diversity and Interdependence (EDI). Over the years the organisation has incorporated the values of EDI in all of its work and these principles are a critical part of the policies, procedures and ethos of RCN.

Equity, Diversity and Interdependence

- **Equity:** Equal opportunities and fairness in redressing inequalities
- **Diversity:** Acknowledging and valuing identities and difference
- **Interdependence:** Building better relationships and trust

EXHIBIT 5.1. RURAL COMMUNITY NETWORK'S
GOOD RELATIONS POLICY, Cont'd.

EDI builds on the Northern Ireland Act 1998, Section 75. In addition to high-lighting equality for the groups identified under Section 75, it has a strong focus in the "promoting Good Relations" part of the legislation.

- RCN will continue to support a dedicated staff team who are responsible for shaping the Good Relations framework within and across the organisation.

- RCN is committed to providing staff support using the EDI process through providing safe spaces for staff to have the difficult conversations and the freedom to discuss sensitive issues in a non-threatening manner.

- RCN will continue to work towards building Good Relations and ensuring an inclusive cross-community organisation through its membership at sub-regional level and at regional level through its board and staff.

- RCN will encourage and support the Rural Support Networks to respond to the challenges of building Good Relations based on the values of community development and the principles of EDI.

- RCN will encourage wider rural stakeholders and member groups to recognise the importance of building good relations within rural communities.

- RCN will ensure that effective monitoring and evaluation procedures are put in place in order to develop and strengthen Good Relations programmes and approaches.

More information about RCN can be found at http://www.ruralcommunitynetwork.org.

Some Lessons Learned

From our discussions with RCN staff, we have identified the following insights:

- Different approaches to engagement and dialogue are needed for different staff groups, and there is no single road map.
- Time and space away from the office are required for this dialogue.
- Everyone should be introduced to EDI at the beginning of the process.
- An internal steering group of senior management and other key staff should be established at the outset.
- Skilled external facilitation is perceived as very important in the early stages to demonstrate and build confidence in dialogue; however, after a period

of time, it is more appropriate to engage an EDI-skilled mentor linked with an appropriate internal facilitator to progress the implementation of an EDI action plan.

RCN hopes to share this broad approach to organizational change more widely and to include Northern Ireland Rural Support Networks and their community group members. A workbook (Rural Community Network, 2003) was designed to stimulate EDI-related conversations at the local level. Finally, RCN staff agree that this must be an ongoing and open-ended effort if it is to be successful. Thus, for example, in 2006 RCN commissioned a fresh assessment of its EDI activities, including stakeholder attitudinal research from the authors of this chapter. The RCN experience thus underlines the "learning organization" character of a dynamic, self-critical, dialogue-based EDI process.

Signposts for Practice

Six important insights drawn from our research can guide organizations seeking to reshape their operational practices around EDI.

1. Recognize Multiple Situations and Experiences

Service organizations perceive themselves as making a difference by improving the quality of life of their constituencies. At the same time, society is extremely differentiated in terms of inclusion and exclusion. In other words, there are multiple and overlapping identities and conditions that affect citizens, groups, and the relationships among them. For example, the experience of women in rural life can be classified on the basis of farming or nonfarming background, age, race, sexual orientation, family and marital status, disability, religion, political opinion, and other parameters. Our research reveals that there is often a hierarchy of difference operating in local communities and that some differences are more acceptable than others. Whereas differences in religious and political identities are more readily acknowledged, differences in relation to race, sexuality, or physical ability may be less so and give rise to verbal abuse and physical assault. These varying forms of prejudice may be related, for example, to isolation, nonrecognition, poverty, and powerlessness. An EDI process gives recognition to these multiple situations and experiences.

2. Value the Local Social Capital Environment

The local social capital environment is a powerful dynamic for change that can successfully challenge institutional and organizational inertia or caution. However, we accept that social capital within organizations, groups, and local communities has the potential to be exclusive, elitist, and conservative. Our research identifies, for example, that a support infrastructure in rural Northern Ireland for victims, survivors, and ex-prisoners is weakly developed. These are some of the most marginalized and vulnerable groups in the region, and there is resistance among mainstream community organizations to address this deeply fractured and contradictory constituency. Yet there is a danger that working with these groups as distinct interests may simply reinforce their identity as victims, survivors, or ex-prisoners and not bring about a positive change in attitude or behavior. Social capital, as a long-term, respect-oriented construct, can open up these groups to local activities and people with whom they have something in common. EDI conversations that seek to enrich the local social capital environment can help address the many hidden consequences of violence.

3. Complement Legal Conformity with Relationship Building

Organizations are now challenged to consider not just diversity in society but also the particular underlying conditions of inequality that can affect the individuals that make up their service constituencies. Because of its perceived transformational capacity within organizations and between organizations and their constituencies, the EDI approach is capable of reaching much deeper than the provisions of statutory equality schemes. More than the implementation of the provisions of equality legislation, EDI is about trying to encourage people to act in a positive way toward others who are different, not merely to meet a legal obligation but rather out of a sincere desire to change relationships for the better.

4. Incorporate Sensitivity to the EDI Process

The EDI process is slow and needs to be implemented at a pace that the key stakeholders are comfortable with, especially within their own constituencies; it should be treated not as a mandatory requirement of funding programs but as the adoption of core values that are important for their own sake. An EDI process has the potential to disturb or frighten target interests and cause initial rejection of it; this is a key issue when engaging with community groups and interest coalitions. EDI discussions must be handled with considerable tact and diplomacy. EDI is not a ready-made product that provides one answer that others must be convinced to adopt. Rather, it involves creating space for people to explore their own context, assumptions, and relationships and to determine behavioral choices on the basis of that assessment. Different situations, contexts, and groups will have different learning experiences. Critical self-assessment, which draws on perception data from organizational constituencies, can enrich this internal analysis. But confidentiality is vital, and in this context, EDI does not lend itself to early, comfortable, frank group discussion. Any perceived slight has the potential to derail a process built around trust, especially in delicately balanced political and ethnoreligious contexts. EDI involves taking risks to create confidence around having a dialogue. The approach works best when it is implemented internally before being introduced to external target groups and being aimed at external issues. At minimum, the bedding down of an EDI initiative should be completed before there is any wider engagement with an organization's constituency.

5. Obtain Visible High-Level Support

Champions for the EDI process should be identified; they should be affiliated with the organizational hierarchy for initiating, managing, and achieving change. Champions have an important role in persuasion, particularly with individuals and groups who share dynamics of fear and resistance. Commencement of the process requires committed leadership, and hence the approach must be enshrined in organizational objectives, the corporate strategy, and the review procedures. A written EDI statement, like the one featured in Exhibit 5.1, has both symbolic and practical value. EDI must also be able to command political support, especially from local authorities and area-based partnerships. EDI has a profound effect on the way in which political business is conducted, and the greatest success can be achieved through intensive work with the members of individual political parties and stakeholder groups before reaching across to engage an organization on a more collective basis.

6. Use Facilitation and Mentoring Expertise

External expertise can be vital in securing organizational commitment to a process that is both rigorous and valid. Partners who have developed the necessary expertise in a dialogue process around EDI are perceived as valuable.

But it is also important that some of the language and concepts be translated by process facilitators and mentors in a way that can be readily accessible to people with different levels of knowledge and experience. Very focused work on identification of possible outcomes, risk assessment, contingency planning, and exit strategies needs to be thought through before EDI work is implemented. Even so, precise outcomes are impossible to predict, and the process must allow a group to move in whatever direction is evolving. In other words, there must be flexibility within the EDI framework. Constant monitoring, problem anticipation, and program delivery adjustment can ensure that the implementation of EDI is dynamic, responsive, and adaptable, especially in reaction to unpredictable political events. The evaluation of EDI activities must embrace qualitative measures. However, evaluation has to be part of the journey of change and must not be constrained by artificial indicators established at the start of the process. Furthermore, EDI must be underpinned by specialist training in generic skills for building cross-community respect, including dispute mediation and resolution; this is regarded as a vital precondition before any engagement with communities is initiated. By reason of their connectedness to localities, local development networks can be significant players in this arena of change.

Conclusion

As a transformational process, EDI is an important response to the challenges of working in a divided society. It seeks to grow people's capacity to deal with complex social, economic, cultural, and political tensions regarding how society organizes itself. An EDI process can inform better organizational internal work practices and collaborative relationships. EDI can also help build external collaborative relationships, better connecting service organizations with their constituencies.

This chapter has demonstrated that EDI is much more than a conventional interpretation of community relations that is built around making people and communities apolitical. In that regard, EDI has a broader relevance across the vast sweep of social diversity. An EDI process can help expose contexts, identify where alliances are possible, and support and ultimately strengthen fragile connections through dialogue and trust. Ultimately, EDI is a prescriptive project and has relevance well beyond Northern Ireland, especially in societies struggling to come out of conflict or come to terms with racial and social separation.

References

Atkinson, R. "Countering Urban Social Exclusion: The Role of Community Participation in Urban Regeneration." In G. Haughton (ed.), *Community Economic Development.* London: Stationery Office, 1999.

Community Relations Council. *Into the Mainstream: Strategic Plan, 1998–2001.* Belfast: Community Relations Council, 1998.

Department of Agriculture and Rural Development. *The Rural Development Programme, 2001–2006.* Belfast: Department of Agriculture for Northern Ireland.

Eyben, K., Morrow, D., and Wilson, D. *A Worthwhile Venture? Practically Investing in Equity Diversity and Interdependence in Northern Ireland.* Coleraine, Northern Ireland: University of Ulster, 1997.

General Synod of the Church of Ireland. *The Hard Gospel: Dealing Positively with Difference in the Church of Ireland: A Scoping Study Report to the Sectarianism Education Project.* Belfast: Church of Ireland Press, 2003.

Morrow, D., Eyben, K., and Wilson, D. "From the Margin to the Middle: Taking Equity, Diversity and Interdependence Seriously." In O. Hargie and D. Dickson (eds.), *Researching the Troubles: Social Science Perspectives on the Northern Ireland Conflict.* Edinburgh, Scotland: Mainstream, 2003.

Murray, M., and Murtagh, B. *Equity, Diversity and Interdependence: Reconnecting Governance and People Through Authentic Dialogue.* Aldershot, England: Ashgate, 2004.

Office of the First Minister and Deputy First Minister for Northern Ireland. *Gender Matters: A Consultation Document—Towards a Cross-Departmental Strategic Framework to Promote Gender Equality for Women and Men, 2005–2015.* Belfast: Office of the First Minister and Deputy First Minister for Northern Ireland, 2004.

Office of the First Minister and Deputy First Minister for Northern Ireland. *A Shared Future: Policy and Strategic Framework for Good Relations in Northern Ireland.* Belfast: Office of the First Minister and Deputy First Minister for Northern Ireland, 2005.

Rural Community Network. *Workbook on Equity, Diversity and Interdependence (EDI) in Rural Society: Addressing Our History of Hear No Evil, See No Evil, Speak No Evil.* Cookstown, Northern Ireland: Rural Community Network, 2003.

Hilary Bradbury, Ph.D., is a research member of the Society for Organizational Learning. Her research, scholarly activism, and teaching focus on the human and organizational dimensions of sustainable development. Until December 2005, she was associate professor of organizational behavior at Case Weatherhead School of Management in Cleveland, Ohio, and director of the Weatherhead Institute for Sustainable Enterprise (WISE; www.weatherhead.cwru.edu/wise). Since moving to Southern California in 2004, Hilary has been elected to the governing board of Pasadena City College and is affiliated with the University of Southern California's Center for Sustainable Cities, where she is teaching and continuing to foster an action research or community design approach to sustainability. She coedited the best-selling *Handbook of Action Research* (Sage, 2001) with Peter Reason and is currently working on a second edition; she is also one of the founding editors of the international peer-reviewed Sage journal *Action Research.* Her articles have appeared in *Organization Science, Academy of Management Executive, Journal of Management Inquiry,* and *Organization Development Practitioner,* among other journals.

Darren Good, M.A., is a doctoral candidate in organizational behavior at the Weatherhead School of Management, Case Western Reserve University. He obtained his master's degree in clinical psychology from Pepperdine University in 2002. His research interests include mindfulness, employee engagement, executive coaching, and values.

Linda Robson, M.A., is currently a doctoral student in organizational behavior at the Weatherhead School of Management, Case Western Reserve University. Her master's degree in anthropology was earned at New Mexico State University. Her areas of research interest are sustainability and interorganizational collaboration.

CHAPTER SIX

WHAT KEEPS IT TOGETHER

Collaborative Tensility in Interorganizational Learning

Hilary Bradbury, Darren Good, Linda Robson

In the relatively short period of the past decade, technological advances, coupled with global economic and social transformations, have spawned novel ways of working. Two emergent organizational trends, receiving attention in both academic and applied circles, are interorganizational collaborations and learning organizations.

Within both of these new organizational forms, we see flatter structures that are characterized by horizontal information flows, adept use of virtual communication, networking, and diversity of all types. Our research focuses on the intersection of these two emergent trends: interorganizational efforts that espouse a learning orientation (Lawrence, Hardy, and Philips, 2002; Powell, Koput, and Smith-Doerr, 1996). We believe that the capacity to collaborate and learn across traditional boundaries provides a strategic advantage that better enables partnering organizations to address the shared challenges of a changing environment, particularly challenges that cannot solely be addressed by any single organization (Trist, 1983; Kuwada, 1998; Vangen and Huxham, 2003).

This study was funded and supported by National Science Foundation grant no. SES NSF 0080643. Coinvestigators were Peter Senge and John Carroll.

Intrigued by the challenges and opportunities presented by these new organizational forms, we have sought to explore the conditions necessary to create and maintain them. More specifically, we wondered what conditions enhance collaborative "tensility," the ability of interorganizational learning collaborations to bend and remain flexible under pressure (Dutton and Heaphy, 2003).

This chapter offers findings from our five-year study, which began with the instigation of a consortium of multinational companies. The consortium continues beyond our formal study. Our data consist of field notes and interviews conducted with members of the consortium. We share the details of the consortium and why it offers a unique case for our research question. We then reflect on a more general level, drawing on literature from the domains of positive organization studies, collaboration, and learning. We end with suggestions for scholars and practitioners, which include implications relating to future research and measures for improving the chances that new interorganizational collaborative efforts will be successful.

Development and Operation of the Consortium

The development and operation of the consortium was dependent on three critical aspects: the invitation to participate, skillful meeting design and facilitation, and active engagement of participants in developing their own collaborative activities. We discuss each of these aspects in detail.

Invitation to Interorganizational Collaborative Work

In 1998, an invitation to participate in the Sustainability Consortium was extended to company representatives who were members of an organizational learning network called the Society for Organization Learning (SOL), an alliance of organizational leaders (http://www.solonline.org). The invitation was made by a small group inside SOL in hopes of attracting like-minded members and facilitating knowledge sharing and learning across companies. The Sustainability Consortium aims to help member organizations deal more effectively with issues related to sustainable development. It encompasses all three facets of sustainability: a concern for profits, balanced against environmental and social issues. Its goal is "to nurture the desire and capacity . . . to build knowledge for achieving . . . sustainability [through] engaging people committed to leadership and learning to collectively [redirect] commerce, education, and technology" (Schley and Laur, 2000, p. 22). The organizers' original vision was for an inclusive consortium that would represent the "whole ecology of organizational life" (p. 22).

The first meeting was held at SOL headquarters in Cambridge, Massachusetts, in 1999. The organizers facilitated the meeting and invited business participants to be active from the start. About twenty-five people attended, most representing organizations from the corporate world that had expressed an interest in embracing a broader business mandate. Most of the member companies were large corporations such as Ford, General Motors, Nike, Shell, BP, and Unilever, but there were exceptions such as Plug Power, a small fuel-cell company, and the World Bank. The first meeting was cast as an inquiry into the need for developing a consortium that would allow for companies to send representatives, who, over time, would work on interorganizational projects, both conceptual and action-oriented, that would facilitate companies pursuing their agenda of sustainable development.

Over time, the consortium members established structures and routines, including a steering committee, a set of goals, membership fees, and an evolving set of practices around meetings and projects. The major consortium activities have evolved since 1999 to include semiannual meetings and projects. Member organizations rotate responsibility to host the semiannual meetings, typically choosing a site near the host company's corporate headquarters. Approximately fifty representatives meet for two or three days, about one-third of whom are new to the consortium. Roughly two hundred individuals from the member companies have participated in meetings since 1999, including executives, line managers, internal consultants, engineers, and other individual contributors. Meetings provide opportunities to create new projects, which have grown over time in numbers and size. Not all organizations participate in all projects, but the organizers encourage such participation. One of the distinctive characteristics of the consortium is that projects are carried out by volunteers from the member organizations. Overall, the consortium is characterized less by transactional modes of relating based on appraisals of costs and benefits and more by shared commitment to the goals of sustainability.

From the start, it was evident that some participants were more fully committed than others to the core purpose of the consortium. A few were deeply knowledgeable about and committed to seeing their companies embrace the broader business mandate associated with sustainability. For many, the application of ideas about sustainable development to their companies was somewhat "fuzzy." A couple of participants who were mainly concerned with the financial aspects of sustainability decided not to participate in further meetings. The emerging core group was strongly committed to sustainability and interested in developing projects inside their companies. Toward the close of that initial meeting, all participants were invited into a spirit of active participation, a sense of "if we do this, we do it together." This influenced attitudes regarding working together in the future and the meaning of a commitment to consortium development, in contrast to adopting the stance of "wait and see what others can deliver." The success of the meeting was to be judged by whether a company representative would step up and host the next meeting. Some weeks after the meeting, a host did emerge. Thus the consortium came into being, with the next meeting scheduled six months later.

Using the virtual communication system that SOL had previously developed, invitations were sent out, along with a description of the purpose of the consortium. It was hoped that those who were already actively engaged in the purpose or saw its potential importance in their company would attend. From the beginning, the consortium highlighted its inquiry and dialogue approach in meetings so that those invited could expect a "safe place" to explore the issues they cared about.

Skillful Meeting Design and Facilitation

Facilitation of consortium meetings has always been "light-handed," meaning that it was rare for a facilitator to intervene directly beyond the need for time management. The original power of facilitation was in the meeting design. Ground rules were articulated to promote a learning format from the first meeting and have since become permanent. These included an invitation to all participants to be in "inquiry mode," meaning that advocacy of opinion or facts needed to be balanced by openness to inquiry into those opinions or facts so that dialogue might promote collective thinking and creativity. An appreciative orientation was achieved by emphasizing people's strengths rather than the challenges they faced in their companies. Such ground rules, along with a relaxed dress code, humor as a common mode, and facilitators' concern for participant comfort, encouraged people to feel they could speak honestly.

As the consortium grew, new participants requested more training for "inquiry" and "dialogue skills." Facilitators therefore began to set aside time at the start of meetings in which they employed an adult experiential approach to teaching (Kolb, 1984) and offered a number of exercises for participants to reflect on their own skills. In addition to these "primers," and drawing original participants from SOL, facilitators could refer with some ease to principles of organizational learning and dialogue. Specifically, the work of Peter Senge (1990; Senge and others, 1994) guided dialogues on the development of new business practices, which incorporate concern for broader social and environmental issues.

Importantly, facilitators "deputized" those who attended such workshops to encourage the use of dialogue and to intervene in any difficult conversations among other participants. Thus a repertoire of behavioral norms has come to be voluntarily enacted by those who participate as they find it a useful way to create common ground among participants.

Active Participation

Now entering its seventh year, the Sustainability Consortium has developed sufficient critical mass. Not only do members attend meetings, but increasingly, member companies are investing resources in collaborative enterprises with other consortium participants. In the early stages of the consortium, participants engaged in mostly dyadic experiential-learning exercises in which members from different companies shared insights and experiences about responding to specific business challenges. Over time, many of the dyads developed into partnerships beyond the consortium meetings, taking the form of projects with corporationwide reach. In one example, a fuel company and a home furnishing company teamed up to find a way to reduce the home furnishing company's carbon emissions. In another, members from several companies joined up first to share information about chemical feedstocks in their products and subsequently to begin the process of redesigning these feedstocks without using the toxic materials typically employed. Generally, we can say that the work moved from a dyadic to collective and from abstract to increasingly broad-reaching and concrete projects.

Methods and Data Collection

Data were collected through semistructured interviews from a sample of consortium participants. The transcribed interviews were analyzed through a content analysis, and four codes emerged: learning space, relational quality, aligning vision and values, and benefit.

Interviews

Our data are in the form of participant interviews and field notes taken during meetings of the Sustainability Consortium. The interviews were semi-structured interviews with two groups of consortium participants, ten longtime members and ten newcomers. All interviews were recorded and transcribed, except in one case where audio equipment malfunctioned and we used the detailed interviewer notes as a substitute for the actual interviewee's words. We began the interview by soliciting narratives of collaborative activities using the critical incident technique (Flanagan, 1954). We did this to gain information about what the interviewees experienced as successful and unsuccessful collaborative endeavors and the conditions they felt were responsible for those outcomes. We sought a very high level of detail regarding the collaborative events selected by the respondents, probing for specific details of how projects and events unfolded (Motowidlo and others, 1992). The final part of those interviews included reflections about collaboration in the consortium and responses to scale items on the importance of various factors for collaboration.

Analysis

In research of this type, theory is derived "emergently" (Yin, 1994) from content analysis. We reviewed and integrated data to describe and visualize the relational underpinnings of the interorganizational collaboration. We asked ourselves questions Strauss and Corbin (1998) recommend for uncovering processes, including "What conditions have contributed to the context in which the participants collaborate?" "What conditions or activities connect the categories?" and "How do the consequences of one set of behaviors and interactions play into subsequent implementation of collaborative projects?" As our qualitative research process unfolded, we found ourselves referring to a variety of disciplines, research paradigms, and theoretical perspectives from which research in interorganizational collaboration is tackled.

Huxham (2003) reminds organizational scholars and practitioners of some of the challenges to theory development and research in interorganizational collaboration. Specifically, Huxham asserts that the language of collaboration is so subject to varied interpretations that there seems to be little agreement over usage of terms such as *alliance, network, partnership, collaboration,* or *interorga-*

nizational relations. Taking this advice, we endeavored to create flexible, yet clear, thematic categories.

Our process involved reading through interviews several times and scanning the text for relevant keywords and phrases using content analysis software (NVivo). In so doing, we initially assembled a large collection of themes, clustering apparently similar data items and interpretations into broad thematic categories, giving titles to the clusters, and successively trying out ways to frame and write about the emerging theory of collaborative tensility (Huxham, 2003). We met on a weekly basis over the course of five months, engaged in a process of refining our original themes. This included revisiting the interviews three times beyond the first analysis and coding. At each stage, we reread hard copies of the interview texts, without coding anew, to test whether our evolving thematic categories continue to fit the intent of the respondent.

As in a darkroom, an image of collaborative tensility began to emerge from the data. Given the broad and inclusive practice of our early analysis, a complex matrix of thematic categories took shape. Gradually, as a result of continued conversations, memos, and weekly meetings, we eliminated much of the overlap. Through this iterative course of analysis, four thematic categories emerged: learning space, relational quality, aligning vision and values, and benefit. Interrater reliability was measured at 89 percent.

Table 6.1 shows how often these themes were present in the twenty interviews comprising our data set. As noted earlier, due to a recorder malfunction during one interview, this interview was coded using detailed notes taken during the interview process.

TABLE 6.1. COLLABORATIVE TENSILITY: THEME FREQUENCY.

Theme	Interview Transcripts Coded ($n = 20$)	Paragraphs Coded	Passages Coded
Learning space	18	78	59
Aligning vision and values	16	51	40
Relational quality	13	36	36
Benefit	8	13	12

Categories Comprising Collaborative Tensility

Respondent comments and observations relating to learning space were the most frequent across our data, occurring in 90 percent ($n = 18$) of our twenty interviews. Broadly, the comments coded as learning space describe the environment of the collaborative space in addition to the experience of participating in the consortium as a learning organization. Stories falling into this category include behaviors, interactions, observations, and experiences in the meetings and beyond.

The next most frequently occurring theme was aligning vision and values, which was present in 80 percent ($n = 16$) of our twenty interviews. Aligning vision and values groups together stories and observations about shared or congruent belief systems or principles. It includes experiences of shared intent, passion, ideals, and motivations among the members of the consortium, which were almost always about sustainability.

Relational quality came in next, encompassing reflections about how relationships either impede or facilitate collaboration and how relationships among members affect the overall tensility of the organization. Often respondents expressed a sense of personal connectedness among participants and social interactions within and outside the formal meetings. Comments about relational quality occurred in 65 percent ($n = 13$) of our twenty interviews.

Our last thematic category, benefit, was evident in 40 percent ($n = 8$) of the twenty interviews. Responses in this group conveyed a sense of benefit resulting from interactions, collaborations, projects, and consortium membership, including actual projects. However, given the focus of the consortium, it was often about relationship development, network building, learning, or the fulfillment of members' expectations and sense of value derived from participation in the consortium.

The remainder of this section provides a more thorough explanation of each theme, including quotes from the interviews that illustrate how each theme builds toward tensility for collaboration.

Learning Space

The intent of this thematic category is to describe the environment of the collaborative space, specifically, the experience of participating in the consortium as a learning organization. Both positive and negative perceptions are encompassed, but with a preponderance of the positive. When describing the learning space of the consortium, many members spoke of "a sense of safety in the room" or "a sense of openness in the room." The organizers' facilitation techniques and how meetings were formatted and conducted were also mentioned.

Indicators of a positive learning space include remarks about communication styles and balancing inquiry with advocacy. Argyris (1990, 1993), describes such styles as "Model II" characteristics in that they support examination of difficult communication or failure so that better, learning-oriented styles can be developed. This contrasts with covering up personal difficulties or moving ahead without thorough investigation. The latter way of communicating is referred to as Model I and is thought to be more common in the general population.

> We make sure everyone is heard. It's more inquiry-oriented than advocacy.

> I think the organizational learning piece is quite important, in order to have effective collaboration. . . . [We] talked about some of the organizational learning techniques, and I think understanding those enables you to interact and communicate more effectively, which in turn hopefully leads to more effective and successful collaborations.

Furthermore, remarks clustered within learning space referred to the role that personal connection or developing relationships have on the respondent's learning.

> [It's] important to create an environment that inspires collaboration. And how that's done exactly I'm not sure, but I know it requires open space and dialogue and pointing out to people the thread, about why they've come together, so that you can at least give people someplace to start, because they're coming in thinking that "I'm nothing like you; we have nothing in common." But you can say, "Well, you do have this one thing. So let's at least use that as a basis." And then [build on] that.

Learning space includes description of methods and experiences of participating in the consortium. As such, this category may refer to specific behaviors, such as the willingness to try something new and inquiry-centered communication practices. Examples consist of participants' sharing their own experience of willingness as well as stories and observations of other participants.

"Cool Fuel" . . . [is an example of] an interesting kind of collaboration between those two companies that presumably wouldn't have happened [without the consortium], getting these people to meet together in a non-threatening and kind of learning, organizational-learning environment.

Learning space also encompasses negative experiences that detracted from learning. Sometimes a sense of guardedness or defensiveness was experienced by Consortium members in response to consultants attending meetings. A sense of safe learning space was impeded by perceptions of an interlocutor having a solution to "sell" rather than listening and figuring out together what is needed.

Aligning Vision and Values

Aligning vision and values includes experiences of mutual intent, passion, ideals, and motivation among the members of the consortium. Among our data, the topic of passion, ideals, and values is almost always about sustainability. Illustrating this, one participant recalled:

When I walked in there, I knew at minimum we all were thinking about the same thing, . . . we were all there sort of with this thread of environmental sustainability. And at the start, I didn't feel like I maybe had much more in common with anybody else in the room, but as [time] went on, I found that there really was a lot more commonality in our hopes and our fears and our dreams and our passions and our goals.

Positive incidents of aligning vision and values describe a shared sense of calling or purpose and comments about consistency between one's personal values and professional work.

I think we're trying to represent the best interests of the planet.

What I had in common with [other members of the consortium] is we're all very interested and committed to sustainability and they've chosen their jobs as roots to try to lead to change toward sustainability.

As with the other three categories in our coding scheme, both positive and negative indicators of alignment are included. Negative occurrences of this label include experiences wherein participants realized or perceived a difference in beliefs, motivations, or principles.

> It was not clear that everyone had the same aims and I think it's [natural] not to try to have conflict but try to see what we're all doing together, but in fact, I think people . . . did have different visions of what we were about.

Furthermore, negative indicators of aligning vision and values included respondents' descriptions of being disillusioned.

> I also think that there was a group [that] was rather reactive. . . .[I] didn't quite know how to feel with it all. . . . We probably didn't have as much relatedness because we didn't feel the same set of personal beliefs around [sustainability] and our companies were going in quite different ways.

Relational Quality

Once people convene and experience the consortium as more positive than negative, relationships can develop that in time will sustain the consortium. The category of relational quality is concerned with how relationships either impede or facilitate collaboration and the overall resilience of the collaborative. It encompasses statements that speak to the importance of relationship development among members.

> Well, you have to go slow to go fast. You have to establish a common bond or common areas of interest, and you need to reinforce those. [It's the] whole aspect of communication, cooperation, and collaboration as being a progression. Respect, understanding—it's very complicated. . . . results is the key part, but it's also about process, it's also about relationships.

> The other thing is to really form some strong relationships with people that I really trust and like working with and use them as touchstones. I can't tell you how many times I've called up [a colleague in the consortium] and said, "So this is what we're thinking. I just want to run this by you because

I want to see if there are any big holes or if I'm really missing anything or I'm too far in left field."

This category includes references to personal ties built through conversation and social interactions at the consortium's formal meetings as well as elsewhere.

> We . . . had the trusted space because we were all in the same room and over the course of the three days we got to know one another and have a beer together and all that kind of social interaction.

> [At] the end of the day, . . . I think the reason this was more collaborative was that we were put in an environment where collaboration could occur and there weren't a lot of agendas going on and because we all really wanted to, we were all willing to contribute.

Relational quality encompasses positive and negative indicators. Positive incidences of relational quality include descriptions of relationship development among members, rapport and trust built as a result of seeing the same people at meetings, and peer-to-peer interactions. One respondent described her experience as follows:

> You have to have a sense of cooperation, to get the collaboration. And my sense is that I think the communication has gone well. I think that's established a spirit of cooperation and that we're all in this together; and there's less of a client-vendor relationship and it's more we're on an equal level. We're peers.

A negative indicator of relational quality includes remarks about the inconsistency of members' participation, illustrated in this quote:

> If I don't know people, I don't know how they're going to treat information I might provide. And for me, that's a big determinant of how successful collaboration is.

This and other such sentiments illustrate the difficult balance the consortium must maintain in convening a learning space that is open to newcomers and new ideas yet simultaneously fosters ongoing relationships and commitment.

Benefit

Benefit refers to the degree to which respondents' expectations are fulfilled and perceptions of value derived from participating in the consortium. Positive indicators of benefit include comments about gaining new perspectives or insight from consortium members and facilitators. Perhaps most important, it reflects tangible engagement with concrete projects across companies that could not come into existence without the consortium.

> I think being part of the consortium helped us . . . think more broadly about what success might look like.

> [Members] know how to make the connections, that they can borrow and share ideas from each other, from other industries, that you could then take and apply, take from say the oil industry into the IT industry. You wouldn't think that there was anything that you could share from those two, but I think in fact that there [are things you can share].

Participants frequently refer to the inspiration they get from other members and from attending consortium meetings, which they perceive as a major advantage of their membership.

> [The] benefits are that people can really inspire one another to do stuff. Like [a particular company], which was just getting into this whole Sustainability Consortium when they came to the Aspen meeting—I mean, they're on fire. And when those guys are on fire, man, there's nothing that can stop them. And they've been really inspired by the efforts of the other companies.

Complementary to the other categories, respondents point to the benefits of an increased and diversified professional and social network, as well as an experience of increased legitimacy in the sustainability arena.

> [First] of all, it was really great to find other people that do something similar to what I do within companies because it's a little bit unusual and it tends to be kind of hard to find those people. But the conversations were really helpful too because [people] were talking about subjects that I myself have grappled with. Everything from what position you take on Kyoto and

your philosophy overall about the government affairs approach or piece of the environmental job. So I really enjoyed the opportunity to just be able to talk with other people that were thinking about the same issues that I was thinking of and that also were coming with really different perspectives based on their experiences in their unique businesses.

I expanded my network, which means for me that now I have more people, that have deeper understanding of the area that I spend my workdays focusing on, that I can tap in to, that can help me do a better job within my day-to-day work.

Negative indicators of benefit include descriptions of a lack of perceived value from participation.

[The] rest of the meeting to me seemed, I don't know what the best term is, maybe "fuzzy." It was just people talking about idealist types of things that really didn't have much grounding in terms of actually taking action and making things happen.

The consortium is a very high-level group of people, [and] there's a lot of concepts that are discussed, but not a lot of action, not a lot of doing.

Relational Bases of Collaborative Tensility

As framed to this point, the SOL Sustainability Consortium presents a unique organizational form. The consortium involves collaborative learning across industry and organizational boundaries. This emphasis on interorganizational collaboration by its nature lacks the traditional qualities of imposed structure, titles, and formal hierarchies. Adding further distinction, as opposed to emphasizing transactional motivations for participating in the organization, members of the consortium tend to be driven by a desire to be part of a community of learners around a shared value system.

Across our data, respondents' perceptions and stories began taking a more dynamic form of interrelated experiences of learning space, aligning vision and values, relational quality, and tangible benefit. Referring to Strauss and Corbin (1998), we examined the thematic categories, looking for sequences and effects of interactions, seeking to understand how the four categories varied in response to changing conditions.

Learning space, aligning vision and values, relational quality, and benefit comprise a necessary set of relational bases for developing the collaborative tensility required to support new organizational forms, such as the consortium. We further believe that they are interdependent and self-reinforcing. To better understand the interactive and collaborative nature of these relational bases, we developed a conceptual model, which we shall explain in detail.

Our model, as shown in Figure 6.1, is based on the experience of participants who responded to an invitation by a core group and entered what was initially a space with little but potential to meet their needs. With some simple ground rules aimed at promoting a sense of safety and inquiry, facilitation aimed at helping the group develop behavioral norms (for example, promoting inquiry) that enabled participants to create something together with a positive goal. This allowed participants to engage each other more deeply and share their own purpose and developing vision of what the consortium might portend for them.

FIGURE 6.1. RELATIONAL BASES OF COLLABORATIVE TENSILITY.

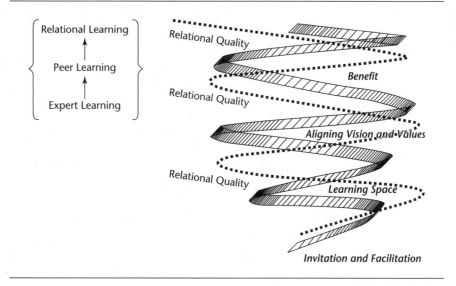

The model illustrates the development of collaborative tensility as a spiral to suggest an iterative and interactive process of establishing and supporting learning space, aligning vision and values, relational quality, and benefit. Underpinned by the creation of the organization as a forum for learning and the initial invitation, the cycle of learning begins. Aided by skillful facilitation, learning space is created that fosters a sense of safety and openness, enhanced by the learning process itself and by the early development of relationships with others in the consortium. As the relational quality increases and the learning space is maintained, these two relational bases build on each other, furthering the creation of the organization's collaborative tensility; therefore, the model depicts relational quality as a theme that exists throughout all parts of the model.

Relationship development, trust, and a sense of safety in learning encourage participants to take an active role in shaping their learning experience. Still aided by light-handed facilitation, participants begin taking greater degrees of responsibility in the consortium, which includes a shift from a focus on "expert learning," where knowledge is passed on from expert to learner, to "peer learning" (Vygotsky, 1978), where knowledge is shared among participants. As shown in the model, throughout the cycle of interaction and experience, if positive relational experiences accrue, the momentum of the process is maintained. Further, a sense of benefit from membership is identified by each participant, be it about an increased network of professional contacts or belonging to a community of learners who share congruent belief. Peer-to-peer learning expands into what we refer to as relational learning, wherein knowledge is created among peers, in an environment characterized as egalitarian.

As the cycle of supportive learning space, senses of aligning vision and values, increasing relational quality, and perceptions of benefit gains momentum, it promotes and strengthens the development of collaborative initiatives and the overall organizational form. That is to say, as positive experiences of the four components increase, so does the consortium's ability to remain flexible during periods of stress or conflict, thus enhancing collaborative tensility.

The challenge of presenting a cyclical process in an illustrated format, as Figure 6.1 attempts to do, is that the simultaneity of the process—the development, reinforcing, and interdependent nature of the relational bases—is difficult to capture. For this reason, in addition to the conceptual model's narrative, we have included direct quotations from field notes to give a clearer sense of the larger context in which the work originated and developed, specifically in connection with the first meeting of the consortium, its early facilitation, and evolving active participation.

The model in Figure 6.1 suggests an interplay among the thematic categories of learning space, relational quality, aligning vision and values, and tangible benefit. Thus the existence of one of these characteristics enhances the capacity for the other experiences to emerge. For example, the quality of the learning space, which has been consciously created and supported by the consortium organizers and members, creates a platform on which relational quality, tangible benefit, and aligned vision and values can rest. The model is not meant to illustrate a true linearity but does suggest that collaborative tensility emerges temporally between the invitation and the experience of the four themes in any number of orders and intensities.

Learning space alone does not increase relationship quality—feelings of trust and willingness to disclose personal or proprietary information. Positive learning space and high relational quality are influenced by perceptions of aligned vision and values. Consortium members develop a rich sense of safety as they realize that alignment of vision is present. Such alignment and understanding of a superordinate goal likely leads to assumptions of other similarities (Sherif, 1966; Byrne, 1971), which in turn deepen feelings of trust and safety, which result in more acts of disclosure. It is arguable that the mutually supportive and cyclical relationship among these factors will lead to improved relational quality and better learning space as deeper interconnectedness lessens participants' need to protect themselves and practice advocacy.

It is the concept of benefit that consortium members must reflect on most intently in order to recommit to and restart the cycle of collaborative learning. If members accrue benefits, they are more willing to reenter the learning space and in so doing nurture their relationships and align their values with others'. Participants generate a sense of benefit from the networks and relationships they have created, experience of being with like-minded individuals, aligning of visions and values, or the generation of new ideas or new projects. Usually some combination is in play.

The positive emotions that come from the open learning space and developing relationships in turn reinforce more positive affect, signaling to others the potential for further relational involvement. Overlapping the learning space created and supported in the consortium, the high relational quality, and positive emotional responses, benefit is produced and in turn provides an important catalyst for continued participation.

Discussion

This study has several implications for practice and research. For practitioners working with similar consortia and learning organizations, it is advised to pay special attention to alignment of participant's vision and values and potential shifts in perceived alignment as membership in the consortia continues to grow. Our findings suggest the importance of establishing an open and safe environment that is inquiry-focused as opposed to encouraging positions of self-advocacy.

This study suggests that future research is needed to elucidate contributing factors and necessary conditions that enable successful and tensile collaboration across organizational boundaries. Here we discuss some of the implications this study holds for future endeavors of practitioners and researchers.

Implications for Similar Consortium-Building Endeavors

To create a positive climate for learning and relationship development, much attention must be devoted to the design and facilitation of a learning space in which quality relationships can flourish. While the existence of trusting relationships between partners is arguably the ideal situation, it appears that caution, rather than psychological safety, between partners is the typical starting point (Doz and Hamel, 1998). Therefore, supporting inquiry and appreciation in an emergent learning space, along with identifying similarity, in the form of recognizing areas of alignment in vision, values, or beliefs, makes tensile collaboration easier to achieve and sustain.

Our data suggest that the realization or emergence of different beliefs, values, and attitudes in established relationships is a double-edged sword: beneficial when it signals similarity and problematic when it signals that certain beliefs and expectations are no longer mutual (and perhaps never were). Agreement on what constitutes a beneficial joint outcome may be difficult to achieve where the latter circumstance predominates.

Linking the importance of shared vision, beliefs, and values to the strength of relationships will help facilitate the cycle of relational organizational learning. The detection of similarity often results in positive emotional responses (Byrne, 1971), which are known to encourage "broaden and build" behaviors underlying the formation of social relationships (Fredrickson, 1998) and therein the open learning space.

Whether or not benefit or value has been derived, once realization of divergent values, principles, vision, or beliefs occurs, this will have a negative impact on the quality of the relationships and in turn the learning space, reinforcing the cyclical interplay of factors argued in our model. This makes clear the real challenge to conveners, facilitators, and participants in collaboratives of diverse participants, highlighting the ongoing need for intentional, explicit communication about expectations and assumptions, for example, balanced inquiry and advocacy.

Implications for Research

In the past two decades, collaboration among organizations of all types has become more abundant. Huxam and Vangen (2000) quote Trist's assertion that significant social issues necessarily sit within the interorganizational domain and cannot be tackled by any one organization acting alone." Yet even with so many years of practice and reflection, interorganizational arrangements remain difficult to manage and often fail to meet expectations (Himmelman, 1994; Meschi, 1997).

Most salient in our analysis was the consistent interplay between learning space and relational quality. Easterby-Smith and Araujo (1999) assert that "good learning" takes place in climates of openness, in which "political" agendas and behavior are minimized. Concurrently, a positive learning space and relationships of high quality facilitate a climate within which consortium members feel safe and enact a shared set of behavioral and communication norms. Baumeister and Leary (1995) support this notion, finding the need to form and maintain strong, stable, interpersonal relationships a fundamental human motive. Buck (1985) explained this positive "virtuous cycle" when he suggested that during initial collaborative encounters, positive affect induced by reciprocal gains and the ease of coordination results in "spontaneous expressive tendencies" (p. 405). Similarly, Fredrickson (1998) wrote that positive emotions "broaden and build" behaviors underlying the formation of personal relationships and encourage creativity, exploration, and the investment of time, energy, and effort.

According to the evolutionary psychology perspective (see, for example, Tooby and Cosmides, 1996), individuals are predisposed to value similarity in close relational partners because shared preferences and behaviors convey an important adaptive advantage. Individuals who share a belief system or principles are more likely to share common goals, referents, and assumptions. The importance of such perceived common knowledge in facilitating collaboration has been investigated across a variety of disciplines (see Mehta, Starmer, and Sugden, 1994; Planalp and Garvin-Doxas, 1994; and Schelling, 1960), finding that alignment of vision and values, often in the midst of apparent diversity, catalyzes continued participation in collaborative initiatives simply because people go with what they know (Krauss, Fussell, and Chen, 1995). Accordingly, one participant's behavior is more likely to converge or coincide with others who happen to share similar expectations, referents, and assumptions. Kelley and Thibaut (1978) explored the importance of similarity, with respect to creating correspondent outcomes among interdependent parties, agreeing that perceptions of likeness promote cooperative behaviors. Moreover, Berscheid (1985) noted that similarity allows for greater prediction, control, and coordination. Thus it's crucial in the learning space to encourage positive behaviors beyond what people already know through engendering a culture of inquiry and openness to new ways of looking at issues together.

Perceived similarities are powerful in facilitating collaboration, but organizations exist in an increasingly diverse realm, surrounded by differences, such as ethnicity, amount of resources, or industry. While it is true that collaborations across the ages have leveraged alliances, what is unique about the Sustainability Consortium and potentially many other cross-boundary collaborations is the climate, which consciously supports collaborative tensility through the development of learning space and relational quality. We posit that this type of environment is necessary for successful *tensile* collaboration, knowledge sharing, and knowledge creation in collaborative relationships, such as interorganizational alliances.

Interorganizational collaborations like the consortium are examples of emerging approaches to organizing. Because they lack traditional structure or institutional girders, such as organizational hierarchy, shared physical space, or salaried administrators, they must rely more heavily on establishing and maintaining a high-quality community space and relational climate. Future research is needed to reveal contributing factors and necessary conditions that enable more successful tensile collaboration across organizational boundaries. Potential studies might draw on literature from such diverse fields as relationship management, group dynamics, and organizational systems theory.

We have asserted in this chapter that when relationships are strong and a climate of learning together has been created, collaborative initiatives and nontraditional organizational models are more likely to weather the lack of immediate received benefits. We have used the SOL Sustainability Consortium to illustrate the importance of relational quality and learning space, aligning vision and values, and benefit in fostering and sustaining collaborations that cross organizational lines and hence lack traditional organizational support structures. High-quality relationships, a supportive culture of learning, perceptions of shared vision and values, and tangible benefits work in concert to facilitate the tensility and flexibility of the interorganizational collaboration.

References

Argyris, C. *Overcoming Organizational Defenses: Facilitating Organizational Learning.* Boston: Allyn & Bacon, 1990.

Argyris, C. *Knowledge for Action: A Guide to Overcoming Barriers to Organizational Change.* San Francisco: Jossey-Bass, 1993.

Baumeister, R., and Leary, M. "The Need to Belong: Desire for Interpersonal Attachments as a Fundamental Human Motivation." *Psychological Bulletin,* 1995, *117,* 497–529.

Berscheid, E. "Interpersonal Attraction." In G. Lindzey and E. Aronson (eds.), *The Handbook of Social Psychology,* Vol. 2. (3rd ed.) New York: Random House, 1985.

Buck, R. "Prime Theory: An Integrated View of Motivation and Emotion." *Psychological Review,* 1985, *92,* 389–413.

Byrne, D. *The Attraction Paradigm.* San Diego, Calif.: Academic Press, 1971.

Doz, Y., and Hamel, G. *Alliance Advantage: The Act of Creating Value Through Partnering.* Boston: Harvard Business School Press, 1998.

Dutton, J., and Heaphy, E. "The Power of High-Power Connections." In K. Cameron, J. Dutton, and R. Quinn (Eds.), *Positive Organizational Scholarship: Foundations of a New Discipline.* San Francisco: Berrett-Koehler, 2003.

Easterby-Smith, M., and Araujo, L. "Organizational Learning: Current Debates and Opportunities." In M. Easterby-Smith, M. J. Burgoyne, and L. Araujo (eds.), *Organizational Learning and the Learning Organization: Developments in Theory and Practice.* London: Sage, 1999.

Flanagan, J. "The Critical Incident Technique." *Psychological Bulletin,* 1954, *51,* 327–354.

Fredrickson, B. "What Good Are Positive Emotions?" *Review of General Psychology,* 1998, *2,* 300–319.

Himmelman, A. "Communities Working Collaboratively for a Change." In P. Herrman (ed.), *Resolving Conflict: Strategies for Local Government:* Washington, D.C.: International City/County Management Association, 1994.

Huxham, C. "Theorizing Collaboration Practice." *Public Management Review,* 2003, *5,* 401–423.

Huxham, C., and Vangen, S. "Ambiguity, Complexity, and Dynamics in the Membership of Collaboration." *Human Relations,* 2000, *53,* 771–806.

Kelley, H. H., and Thibaut, J. W. *Interpersonal Relations: A Theory of Interdependence.* Hoboken, N.J.: Wiley, 1978.

Kolb, D. *Experiential Learning.* Upper Saddle River, N.J.: Prentice Hall, 1984.

Krauss, R. M., Fussell, S. R., and Chen, Y. "Coordination of Perspective in Dialogue: Intrapersonal and Interpersonal Processes." In I. Markova, C. F. Graumann, and K. Foppa (eds.), *Mutalities in Dialogue.* New York: Cambridge University Press, 1995.

Kuwada, K. "Strategic Learning: The Continuous Side of Discontinuous Strategic Change." *Organization Science,* 1998, *9,* 719–736.

Lawrence, T., Hardy, C., and Philips, N. "Institutional Effects of Interorganizational Collaboration: The Emergence of Proto-Institutions." *Academy of Management Journal,* 2002, *45,* 281–290.

Mehta, J., Starmer, C., and Sugden, R. "Focal Points in Pure Coordination Games: An Experimental Investigation." *Theory and Decision,* 1994, *36,* 163–185.

Meschi, P. "Longevity and Cultural Differences in International Joint Ventures: Toward Time-Based Cultural Management." *Human Relations,* 1997, *50,* 211–227.

Motowidlo, S. J., and others. "Studies of the Structured Behavioral Interview." *Journal of Applied Psychology,* 1992, *77,* 571–587.

Planalp, S., and Garvin-Doxas, K. "Using Mutual Knowledge in Conversation: Friends as Experts on Each Other." In S. Duck (ed.), *Dynamics of Relationships: Understanding Relationship Processes,* Vol. 4. Thousand Oaks, Calif.: Sage, 1994.

Powell, W., Koput, K., and Smith-Doerr, L. "Interorganizational Collaboration and the Locus of Innovation: Networks of Learning in Biotechnology." *Administrative Science Quarterly,* 1996, *41,* 116–146.

Schelling, T. C. *The Strategy of Conflict.* Cambridge, MA: Harvard University Press, 1960.

Schley, S., and Laur, J. "The SOL Sustainability Consortium." *Reflections,* Summer 2000, pp. 22–23.

Senge, P. M. *The Fifth Discipline: The Art and Practice of the Learning Organization.* New York: Currency/Doubleday, 1990.

Senge, P. M., and others. *The Fifth Discipline Fieldbook: Strategies and Tools for Building a Learning Organization.* New York: Currency/Doubleday, 1994.

Sherif, M. *In Common Predicament: Social Psychology of Inter-Group Conflict and Cooperation.* Boston: Houghton-Mifflin, 1966.

Strauss, A., and Corbin, J. *Basics of Qualitative Research: Techniques and Procedures for Developing Grounded Theory.* (2nd ed.) Thousand Oaks, Calif.: Sage, 1998.

Tooby, J., and Cosmides, L. "Friendship and the Banker's Paradox: Other Pathways to the Evolution of Adaptations for Altruism." *Proceedings of the British Academy,* 1996, *88,* 119–143.

Trist, E. "Referent Organizations and the Development of Interorganizational Domains." *Human Relations,* 1983, *36,* 269–284.

Vangen, S., and Huxham, C. "Nurturing Collaborative Relations: Building Trust in Interorganizational Collaboration." *Journal of Applied Behavioral Science,* 2003, *39,* 5–31.

Vygotsky, L. *Mind in Society: The Development of Higher Psychological Processes.* Cambridge, Mass.: Harvard University Press, 1978.

Yin, R. *Case Study Research: Design and Methods.* (2nd ed.) Thousand Oaks, Calif.: Sage, 1994.

Mirja P. Hanson is a facilitator, consultant, instructor, and author with over thirty years of experience in community development, multiple-stakeholder decision making, policy consensus building, interorganizational partnerships, and strategic planning. She has worked with public and private organizations, including more than fifty federal, state, and local agencies; numerous education institutions; the U.S. House of Representatives; town meetings in over one hundred U.S. municipalities; corporations such as USX and 3M; the United Nations Sustainable Development Program; and Habitat for Humanity. She recently wrote *Clues to Achieving Consensus: A Leader's Guide to Navigating Collaborative Problem Solving* (Rowman & Littlefield, 2005). Hanson holds a doctorate in education from the University of Saint Thomas, a master of business administration from the University of Minnesota, and a bachelor of art degree from the Metro State University. She is an adjunct faculty member at the University of Saint Thomas and a founding member of the International Association of Facilitators.

CHAPTER SEVEN

MAKE-OR-BREAK ROLES IN COLLABORATION LEADERSHIP

Mirja P. Hanson

We must devise a system in which peace is more rewarding than war.

ATTRIBUTED TO MARGARET MEAD

As many leaders, administrators, and managers may be discovering, successful and sustainable group deliberation and engagement require more than a "state of the art" process or a charismatic facilitator. Social capital and political will must be built among the stakeholders. My experience tells me that this can only happen with the leadership of three vital players: the participants, facilitators, and sponsors of collaboration processes.

Management scientists Quinn and Guile (1988) studied the dynamics of how and why innovations survive, thrive, or die. They concluded that like babies, innovations require proactive, flexible, and attentive care of three agents—parents, guardians, and pediatricians. They found that venture teams composed solely of dispassionate experts are not effective. Because innovations are just as unpredictable and vulnerable as babies, Quinn and Guile concluded that they succeed only when the same key players provide customized attention, judgment, and maintenance:

- A *parent* who loves the project irrationally
- A *guardian* who protects the project with resources and authorization
- A *pediatrician* who contributes advice and technical assistance about project development

I believe that collaborative problem solving can be viewed as innovations that similarly require multiple caretaker roles: process sponsors (as guardians), facilitators (as pediatricians), and participants (as parents) (see Figure 7.1).

The project *sponsors* are the *guardians* who position a meaningful project. Sometimes known as *conveners*, they authorize the collaborative effort and support the work group with resources and authorization.

The *facilitators* are the *pediatricians*: they do not have a stake in the project outcome but know about building collaboration and consensus in general. They are dedicated to providing state-of-the-art advice and leadership in designing and delivering a unifying process and guiding consensus development.

The *participants* serve as the *parents*. Without their engagement and passion, problems cannot be transformed into solutions that make sense in the real world and are supported by everyone.

How do these participants, facilitators, and sponsors either inhibit or enhance the effective exchange of ideas, power, resources, opinions, and solutions for the sake of determining collective priorities? What do collaborative

FIGURE 7.1. KEY ROLES IN COLLABORATIVE PROBLEM SOLVING.

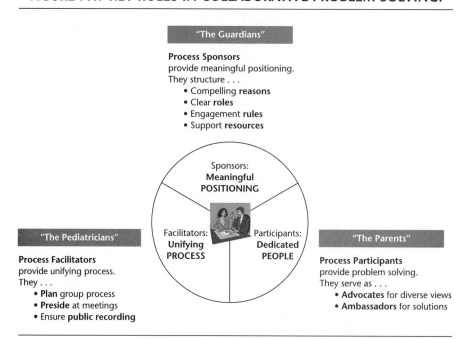

"The Guardians"

Process Sponsors
provide meaningful positioning.
They structure . . .
• Compelling **reasons**
• Clear **roles**
• Engagement **rules**
• Support **resources**

Sponsors:
**Meaningful
POSITIONING**

"The Pediatricians"

Facilitators:
**Unifying
PROCESS**

Participants:
**Dedicated
PEOPLE**

"The Parents"

Process Facilitators
provide unifying process.
They . . .
• **Plan** group process
• **Preside** at meetings
• Ensure **public recording**

Process Participants
provide problem solving.
They serve as . . .
• **Advocates** for diverse views
• **Ambassadors** for solutions

efforts really look and feel like from the perspective of the people who have been involved in each of these roles?

I had some idea of the view of a facilitator, but my curiosity about the participants' and sponsors' insider experiences led me to study the consensus process from their point of view. In 2000, I interviewed thirty-seven people from across the United States who had participated in four separate collaborative processes addressing high-conflict environmental issues, two of which I facilitated (See the appendix to this chapter for a description of the research methodology.) Their testimonials, stories, and insights contributed greatly to ideas in this chapter.

The Participant Role: Serving on the Front Line in Forging Collaboration

The consensus participants I interviewed had wide discretion in the way they fulfilled the job of representing stakeholder interests in consensus building. Everyone seemed to agree with one key point: the visible actions at the table are just the tip of the political iceberg. Just as the majority of an iceberg rests hidden under water, strong influence is exerted behind the scenes. The process of collaboration relies heavily on earnest and official acts of individual leadership not only on the *front stage* of the process but also on the *back stage*, where participants "let their hair down," strategize privately, brief, debrief, caucus, and prepare for the front-stage action at the table. The successful or unsuccessful outcome of the collaborative process is very heavily influenced by the degree to which participants individually engage their private passion and energy while enacting their public role.

Front-Stage Activity

The front stage is where representatives participate in business meetings or other official activities at the table. According to the interviews, the representatives found front-stage work extremely intense and challenging. After one exhausting day, one member remarked, "In these participation processes, the power really belongs to the guys that can stay alert and aggressive all day and then have enough energy to explain everything to the folks back home." In assessing the participants' experiences, front-stage duty involved three main functions: absorbing background information, participating in deliberations, and holding formal feedback meetings with their constituencies.

Backstage Activity

Backstage activities are crucial to the success of any collaborative effort. Official front-stage meetings are in effect the mechanisms by which informal backstage conversations, proposals, and resolutions are formally acknowledged, exchanged, and processed. As one person put it, "If you wait until the front-stage meetings, you've missed the most important places to affect what is going to end up happening. You have to work the issue between the meetings. I do not think it is wrong to meet between sessions. I think you have to recognize that it is going to happen. It is a matter of getting in there and mixing it up with everybody else who is going to be doing it. And you can't assume naively that you can just wait until the meeting and then count votes because it just doesn't work that way." According to participants, "Working the issue between meetings" meant preparing for consensus deliberations, developing participant relationships, advocating position proposals, and promoting collaborative solutions.

Participants I interviewed concurred on the importance and influence of front-stage and backstage activity, but there were significant differences in how participants engaged on the two stages. In the next section, I will take you deeper into the various ways that participants contributed to the quest for collaborative solutions.

More Than One Way to Serve as Advocates and Ambassadors

All representatives around the table were chosen by their interest groups because they were effective advocates, good communicators, and committed to seeking mutually beneficial and agreeable solutions in a collaborative way. But there were significant differences in how the players approached "collaborative" participation. Participants believed they put in a "good faith effort" to collaborate at the consensus table, but each adopted a unique mix of *assertiveness* and *cooperativeness* to find common ground in the midst of differing perspectives.

Participants chose a particular style of interaction based on their familiarity with the subject matter, experience with group process, relationships with other members, time and other resources available, and individual characteristics such as personality traits, temperament, and interaction preferences. Ideologies did not dictate how participants chose to execute their advocacy role in the quest for collaboration. In other words, participants with differing views on a given issue could adopt a similar style of engagement in the deliberations. I concluded that one style of collaborating is not better or more righteous than another. Furthermore, the collaboration styles were not static; some participants changed their engagement strategies several times in response to the way the discourse evolved and intensified.

The variance in collaborative styles revealed an interesting pattern. Even though all the participants perceived themselves to be interacting within the collaborative mode described in the Thomas-Kilmann Conflict Mode Instrument (Thomas and Kilmann, 1974), they demonstrated at least four distinct approaches to collaborative problem solving: a *competing* way (the boundary guards), an *avoiding* way (the team players), an *accommodating* way (the boundary spanners), and a *collaborating* way (the solution brokers). Interestingly, the diverse interaction approaches within the collaborative mode mirrored the four major quadrants of the Thomas-Kilmann Conflict Mode Instrument, as shown Figure 7.2. A similar pattern may exist in the other three modes, but that is for other studies to pursue and prove. In the following section, I will describe the differing ways in which collaborative problem solvers tackled the quest for "win-win" solutions.

Boundary Guards. Boundary guards adopted a style of collaborative representation that was highly assertive and minimally cooperative. They viewed the collaborative process as a contract negotiation. They felt that collaboration was best achieved if all parties bargained aggressively for their positions. Their goal was to guard or expand their scope of influence on the given issue. They did not want to lose ground in fronting their interest. They were willing to consider solutions that stayed within the sacred boundaries of acceptable outcomes. As one boundary guard professed, "I was careful not to give anything up." Other participants described boundary guards as "soldiers of fortune," "confrontational and impatient," "Darth Vaders," "extremists," or "people that were interested more in protecting their turf than finding solutions."

They aimed to win big, but at the least, they hoped to come through with specific and tangible gains that would expand their domains. According to one observer, "Many of us wanted results a slice at a time, but [the most extreme boundary guards] wanted the whole loaf, to blow up the ovens and burn the

FIGURE 7.2. FOUR STYLES EMPLOYED BY CONSENSUS BUILDERS.

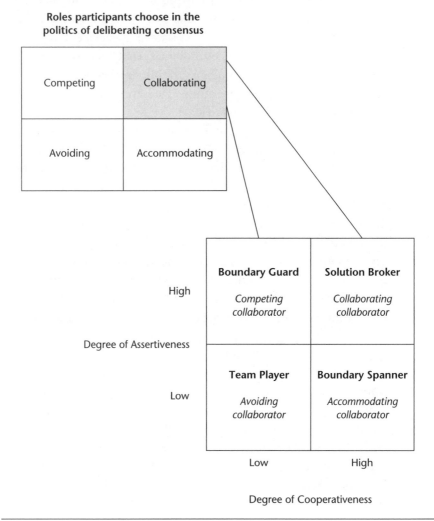

Roles participants choose in the politics of deliberating consensus

Competing	Collaborating
Avoiding	Accommodating

Degree of Assertiveness

High

Boundary Guard

Competing collaborator

Solution Broker

Collaborating collaborator

Team Player

Avoiding collaborator

Boundary Spanner

Accommodating collaborator

Low

Low   High

Degree of Cooperativeness

Source: Adapted from Thomas and Kilmann, 1974.

wheat fields. We just can't deal with that. We can deal with evolution but not revolution." For the boundary guards, collaboration meant letting others have it their way.

To the very end, the boundary guards behaved like missionaries, hoping to convince or convert others to their truths. The imperative was to win more political territory and expand their constituent boundaries. For them, the ends justified the means. They were skillful communicators who used all of the allotted time and available tactics to make their case, keep the debate moving, and ensure a substantive decision-making process. One member explains the aggressive style of participation of many boundary guards as follows: "When I walk into a collaborative process, part of my intent was to intentionally throw in a hand grenade, and part of the reason for doing that was to flush these issues on the table. I know it makes the job tough for facilitators, but we can have a love fest and accomplish nothing, or we can put the issues on the table and try to deal with them" (Hanson, 2001, p. 288).

The boundary guards were always conscious of the power bases connected to the diverse array of stakeholder groups and their major positions or ideologies related to an issue. They were constantly guarding the power balance and watching how the various sides were influencing the decisions. In experiencing and hearing about this approach, I was tempted to disqualify boundary guards as members of the collaboration quadrant of the Thomas-Killman model. However, the participants who fit the boundary guard designation perceived themselves as collaborators. As mentioned before, their goal was to negotiate "in good faith" to find mutually agreeable solutions. They pointed out that they were forgoing many adversarial tactics to participate around the table.

Team Players. The team players adopted a "wait and see" collaborative style that was minimally assertive and minimally cooperative. For them, the collaborative process was like a high-level committee, jury duty, or a board meeting—a place where recommendations, verdicts, or policies are decided after a thorough airing of ideas, evidence, or motions. They played on two teams and switched allegiances based on the substantive merits of the discussion. Sometimes they resonated with the arguments of the stakeholder interests or ideology they represented (their "home" team). At other times they aligned closely with the consensus areas or new paradigms that were emerging around the table (the "collaboration" team). Team players waited until all the evidence was in or the time was up to make up their minds.

Team players felt that the way to conduct a fair, collaborative process and to fulfill their duty was to participate wholeheartedly in front-stage activities. They faithfully attended all meetings of the consensus-building group and their constituency group. They diligently shared reports between those groups but were perceived by others as "nonplayers" when it came to the ultimate brokering of resolutions and agreements. In the interviews, some participants referred to team players as "hand raisers" or "freelancers." However, in talking to the team players, it is clear that their silence and/or deliberativeness did not reflect a lack of participation. As confirmed by this account, they did not consider themselves mere followers: "The amount of time spent speaking is not necessarily indicative of effective participation. I was able to offer some practical solutions as I saw them from a policy perspective and practitioner's perspective" (Hanson, 2001, p. 291).

The team players' power base was their mystery. They were selected by their constituencies to represent a particular perspective, but they were not zealots. They preferred to give all sides the benefit of the doubt during the deliberation. They were the "undecided voters" who could decide the outcome of the election. Other participants came to realize that the only way to gain team players' support was to make a compelling case for the views they were presenting. Team players followed the advice of the anonymous sage who said, "A good hunter changes his way as often as he needs to."

Boundary Spanners. The boundary spanners were extremely cooperative and minimally assertive on behalf of a particular interest. Their special interest was the good of the whole. They were dedicated spokespersons for building bridges across ideological, geographical, jurisdictional, or other boundaries. If they did represent a narrower interest, they felt that the interest of their stakeholder group would be best served by reaching as much common ground as possible. As illustrated in the following account, many boundary spanners felt that success in collaboration requires people who specialize in "keeping the group together": "You have to have people whose bottom line is in representing their interest, but you also have to have people whose heart, soul, and bottom line is keeping the group together. Anybody who thinks that the latter is not important, that the process should just include a bunch of interests, should take a look at some of the other unsuccessful examples of collaboration. I believe they fell apart because they did not have a mix of participants" (Hanson, 2001, p. 295).

Other participants nicknamed the boundary spanners "big-picture leaders," "free agents," or "moderating influences."

The boundary spanners were faithful ambassadors for the collective product. Like the team players, their primary stage of action was the meetings. They approached the consensus-building activity like a policy think tank or a planning retreat. The group could count on them to help identify and synthesize points and then make compelling cases for bridge-building solutions.

Given this type of commitment to minimizing boundaries, the boundary spanners were always ready to find and support the emerging areas of common ground. Their role was appreciated by other consensus builders. One member felt "we gained from the presence of some skillful synthesizers, . . . members with a big-picture attitude."

Boundary spanners tended to focus their activism on the front stage but did lobby offstage if it helped the common cause. In this excerpt, one boundary spanner "pleads guilty" to going above and beyond the front-stage duties to fight for solidarity:

> I tried to play a constructive, supportive role. I thought this was a good thing. I do remember that when we got down to the wire, I will plead guilty to making a phone call or two myself. I called one person once because I knew he was wrestling with whether to support the consensus product or not. As a matter of conscience, I thought it was a good thing for as many people as possible to support it. We had done a lot of hard work. So I called him and said, "I know you're struggling with this, and I'm not trying to twist your arm, but if there's anything that I could possibly do to help you be more comfortable about this, I'd like to let you know I'm available." Hopefully, I helped make him a bit more comfortable [Hanson, 2001, p. 296].

Solution Brokers. The solution brokers advocated aggressively in both directions; they lobbied for their own interests but listened intently in order to find clues to substantive agreements or innovative ways to ensure that some forward movement was achieved in the collaborative process. They were proactive architects, contractors, and deal makers in the pursuit of collaborative solutions. For them, the collaborative process was like a legislative session, a forum where one could use any means possible to influence individual judgments. They were boundary spanners and guards. This role was extremely difficult and labor-intensive. At the table or away from the table, they worked overtime to serve as evangelists for their interest group as well as the collaborative cause.

Like the boundary guards, they had a lot at stake and used every means possible to make sure that the process would produce results that made a temporary or lasting difference in "achieving a mutually beneficial future." They were described by others in the process as "skillful synthesizers," "extremely constructive about trying to find a middle ground," "trying to figure out ways of solving the problems," "really putting their hearts into it thinking it will make a difference," and "most interested in seeking agreement." One participant described their role as "negotiators."

> There were some friendly and unfriendly elements, but we were pretty civilized most of the time. . . . Also, in any group like that, there were a few people that rise to the top and use their voices to help unify things. And my role was that of a negotiator. . . . When things got tough and it looked like we were going to fracture in the consensus group, a few of us would work out the negotiation. It's not quite that overt in some processes, but there are always the voices with more experience that are willing to engage for the good of the whole [Hanson, 2001, p. 298].

They were pragmatists as they went about their brokering work and knew the importance of not burning any bridges that would hamper future effectiveness: "We were not going to do something that would really set off any key organization. We wanted to play nice with them because we were going to have to work with them once we got to implement the consensus recommendations" (Hanson, 2001, p. 297).

Solution brokers took the long view. Early in the consensus-building process, Solution brokers identified the degree of surmountable and insurmountable differences. They analyzed the battles at hand and chose which were best fought now and which were better left for later. Then they began to navigate a search for the best possible agreements that bridged the boundaries between ideological territories.

No matter which style a consensus representative adopted, I learned that for more than half the participants, serving as an agent of collaboration was not like any professional or volunteer duty that they had experienced before. Often the costs were high and rewards long-range, but no one defected. Despite the obstacles, representatives persevered because they cared about the issue at hand. Not all collaborative problem-solving experiences last a year or more like those in my study, but to some degree, success in any collaborative process depends on what participants do at and away from the table.

There is no question that the participant role is a make-or-break variable in achieving consensus. The participants are the human magic behind success. The success of the collective product is directly related to the individual participants' choices about their style and level of engagement—the degree to which they commit their effort, knowledge, and imagination to the quest for honest common ground. The challenge for sponsors is to find stakeholder group spokespersons who are willing and able to undertake the dual roles of advocate and ambassador in a collaborative effort. Because participants do not really show their propensities until the collaboration is under way, the best strategy for sponsors is to educate potential participants about their role prior to selecting groups for collaboration projects.

The Facilitator Role: Ensuring an Equitable and Effective Field of Play

The facilitator exerts political influence to the extent that he or she levels the political playing field and enables all participants to engage equitably and respectfully in the deliberation. The three primary duties of a facilitator are careful *planning* of the overall process, *presiding* over the formal meetings, and creating a *public record* of the discourse. The most visible aspect of a facilitator's job is in front of the room, directing the discussion of a group of people. But much of the work of facilitation takes place offstage.

The Politics of Planning

In complex environmental conflicts such as those that formed the basis for my study, the sponsor typically determines the basic reasons, roles, rules, and resources of a consensus engagement, and facilitators translate these "specifications" into a fair, meaningful, and timely political forum. They customize a fair field of play for working through issues and developing action solutions. Specific tasks include determining the best methods and techniques, making sure the process is easy to understand, clarifying and enforcing the steps for achieving agreement, and managing science and data proactively. It also means empowering the participants by making the process truly participant-friendly and building in the time for the consensus builders' political work.

The Politics of Presiding

Once the basic process plan is constructed, a facilitator's key political role is presiding over the forum and knowing when changes to the process plan must be made along the way. Even with the best-laid plans, managing the exchange of views, ideas, powers, resources, and so on is a "full-contact sport." When the collaborators gather, wills converge, and conflict ignites, a facilitator must be prepared to referee the political forum while simultaneously tracking all levels of discourse, including issue content, opinions, emotions, time, meeting space, participant comfort, and informal input.

A facilitator is a nonvoting member but influences the outcome by maintaining a fair and relevant political process. Since consensus building has no codified rules and regulations, content and process are both variable elements. The fairness and relevance of a process is constantly under evaluation by participants, sponsors, the facilitator, and any other stakeholders that choose to weigh in. The two major challenges in the politics of presiding fairly involve ensuring that all voices are heard and knowing when to play by the rules or change them.

The Politics of Public Documentation

A facilitator has a great deal of influence in his or her most invisible and silent role: representing the substance and spirit of the deliberation in recording the discourse proceedings. Translating flipcharts, legal pads, notes, minutes, tape recordings, memory, sticky notes, individual worksheets, and other raw records into findings, conclusions, and recommendations is an important part of process politics. Consensus is always fragile. It will evaporate like steam if participating stakeholders do not have a common public record of what happened.

The political challenges of preparing reports include representing the state of the group will in a fair, accurate and reader-friendly manner; writing an account that is not too lengthy or too brief; and making sure the record of collaborative discourse is publicly acceptable. The document is the main link between those who represented interest groups at the table and all the other members of the stakeholder groups. Its function is to enable present and future participants to become insiders in the whats, whys, and hows of the collaboration process.

The Sponsor Role: Linking Collaborative Efforts to Mainstream Decisions

Community and organization administrators, officials, managers, and other leaders who sponsor collaborative processes may play the most critical part in fostering collaboration because they determine the role of participants and facilitators. They can either inhibit or enhance the power of consensus ventures by the manner in which they set up a participative exchange. Motivation to participate in cooperative efforts is greatly diminished if the interaction is not connected to real-world operations in a meaningful way.

A sponsor or convener of an effective consensus process takes on the role of an organizational architect. The goal is to design group decision making that equalizes power and voice among the various stakeholders to promote authentic dialogue and inclusiveness among groups with inherently different roles. This question was at the heart Scott Bauer's research in "Creating a Level Playing Field" (1997). Twenty design teams from New York school districts were charged to develop "rules of the game" that would make the best shared decision-making policies for the needs and nuances of their district: "Instead of looking at the routinized adoption of a *standard model*—site-based management means devolving decision-making authority over budget, staffing, and curriculum to a site council made up of principal, teachers, and perhaps parents—research needs to focus on how to fit site-based processes into existing school system cultures and the ways to use this restructuring as a lever for improvement. This depends, in part, on devising ways to create forums that invite frank, open discourse on issues of importance to the school" (p. 5).

Sponsorship Formats

Consensus building can be sponsored in several ways. Some common sponsorship formats include leader-directed, commissioned, convened, and grassroots approaches.

Leader-Directed Process. The leader of a team, department, function, school, district, company, community, or other group calls together a consensus process for planning, problem solving, input, or other group decision-making effort. Some common examples include organizationwide planning efforts or interfunctional project or problem-solving teams.

Commissioned Projects. One or more public or private organizations convene and sponsor a process for making collaborative decisions or policies and initiate interorganizational partnerships. One example is a state senate that commissioned stakeholders of forty organizations to develop recommendations for the state's forest policy. They specified the outcomes and began scripting the process. They appointed the meetings managers and assigned the executive branch agencies to implement the process. Another example is a sixty-member advisory committee for encouraging home ownership by minorities and new immigrants commissioned by the state housing agency, the Federal Reserve, and Fannie Mae.

Convened Projects. When there are no official decrees to start a collaborative effort, multiple entities can convene a potential cross-boundary partnership. Many cross-organization partnerships are convened by a lead organization or team of organizations. The convening organization hosts the launching steps, and other participating organizations will eventually share resources to launch and operate the partnership by using pooled resources.

For example, a school board and superintendent of the district convened meetings to begin a multiyear initiative to involve the entire "village" in education improvement. The parent-teacher association, community groups, public organizations, employers, and foundations who agreed to participate offered support and resources to plan and implement shared strategies for building a "world-class school system."

In another example, a regional planning agency served as an "initiator" for a controversial effort to establish procedures for water quality decision making among forty-eight stakeholders, including agricultural, industrial, and recreational water users; local and municipal governments; federal and state agencies, water providers; and the water and sanitation districts. Due to past conflicts, all organizations were hesitant to step up as the sponsor. Even the initiating agency wished not to take on the role because it had often been a litigant in water court. A planning group representing a microcosm of the stakeholder system was created to steer the collaborative problem solving.

Grassroots Sponsorships. In many voluntary collaboration situations, a group of community people sponsors self-facilitated processes. On an as-needed basis, the group brings in other people and entities to present information, conduct research, lead meetings, and help with other meeting-leadership and support duties. In the environmental community, the Quincy Library Group is a legendary example of a grassroots group that has met for years to debate and resolve local environmental disputes. It took its name from its meeting place. The group chose the library setting to make sure that everyone abides by the ground rules that require listening and never shouting or attacking other participants. Another example is a group of five rural communities in northeastern Minnesota that decided to form a partnership known as the East Range Service Alliance to share municipal and township public services.

Sponsorship Duties

Regardless of who sponsors the collaborative problem solving, the duties include determining the *reasons, roles, rules,* and *resources* of the consensus process. If the effort makes sense to people, they are willing to play the game.

Determining Reasons. The importance of a meaningful mission applies to any project or endeavor. If you cannot easily answer why the process is needed, who needs it, and what it should achieve, it is better not to start. To attract stakeholders, there must be something at stake and a readiness to engage. Without a concrete link between the "input, throughput, and output" (Harrington, 1978), stakeholders cannot gauge their own incentives for participation. Sponsors must envision the project from beginning to end and identify how to gain buy-in and get to a worthy destination. Even when a dispute, problem, or partnership seems evident or urgent, a process should not be commissioned until a meaningful purpose has been identified. If the projected or promised benefits don't exceed the cost of involvement, consensus building will not have the incentives to succeed. Also, consensus needs to be integrated into mainstream operations instead of an "attachment" to official decision making and management. For example, at a large mining operation, assets were saved from a slow death when all two hundred managers became insiders in the improvement effort. The new general manager set up biweekly planning and coordination sessions that developed recommendations for executive decision making. This was a departure from the traditional top-down style in the industry. A rigorous participatory planning process helped identify improvement options, select priorities, and make a compelling case for receiving funds from the parent company. As a result of formally linking broad-based managerial input to executive-level decisions, the mine and plant were transformed.

The importance of integrating consensus processes into the fabric of the organization is echoed in L. Dean Sorenson's study of site-based management, *Avoiding Disaster While Sharing Decision Making* (1995). Sorenson warns against superficial empowerment:

> The term *empowerment* saturates the educational literature and evokes a variety of operational definitions. Sergiovanni (1992) stressed that before

empowerment can be meaningful, there must be agreement within the organization or a shared covenant. A covenant that is the product of consensus among a representative group of school stakeholders helps define the organization's collective values, vision, mission, educational objectives, organizational priorities, and operating principles. Developing consensus on a shared covenant and reshaping school culture requires open and honest communication among stakeholders and an honest assessment of organizational strengths and weaknesses as they relate to the preparation of students [p. 11].

Once a process is mobilized, sponsors need to serve as an active political link between the collaboration process and its future results by staying visible and vigilant as the consensus builders carry out their charge. The linking role will be augmented by some of the consensus participants. For example, the representatives of a large state agency that sponsored an environmental issues process built receptiveness to eventual recommendations by regularly debriefing more than two dozen agency managers and legislative stakeholders during a yearlong process.

Clarifying Roles. Designating the individual and collective roles for participants is another major political responsibility of sponsors. One of the mistaken assumptions about consensual approaches is that everyone must make decisions about everything. All types of decision-making roles are fair game as long as they are clear up front. Nothing destroys group trust and productivity faster than conflicting role expectations between sponsors, participants, and facilitators.

Setting Rules. Once it is clear why a problem needs solving, who should do it, and the end result should look like, the remaining question is "how?" Litigation or parliamentary procedures come with meticulously prescribed steps for conducting the process. Consensus engagements have some familiar building blocks, but each situation needs a unique, rigorous, and custom-crafted process.

Sponsors set the political parameters and protocols for how a consensus-based decision is defined and developed, including what science, data, or background information needs to inform the discussion and what ground rules are used to determine collective choices. Constructing effective consensus process means that sponsors should work closely with the process facilitator to ensure a fair field of play.

Securing Resources. Securing adequate resources for supporting a collaborative process is often the most difficult background duty for a sponsor. Acquisition of resources tests the importance of a given project within a sponsoring organization. The cost-benefit scrutiny is often quite intense because most entities have few surplus resources. The leadership of sponsoring organizations needs to be convinced that group dialogue will deliver the returns that merit an investment of precious organizational resources. Bauer (1997) points to resource allocation as a common pitfall of effective shared decision making in schools: "Issues of 'insufficient capacity' are often cited as explaining the failure of site-based management. 'Capacity' equates to district support for site teams in terms of providing authority, training, time, information, and other resources necessary for team operation. Districts rush to implement site-based management without considering what it takes to make the transition from traditional decision-making structures" (p. 3).

Negotiating, lobbying, and adjusting the budget or other "creative financing" activities can be extremely challenging. However, this political step helps transform a good idea into an institutional or mainstream priority.

Conclusion

The proactive efforts of sponsors, facilitators, and participants can significantly increase the chance for successful collaboration between diverse parties. Each player, engaging fully in his or her role, can help rekindle trust in citizen participation by ensuring that each public forum is utterly meaningful and productive. Participants will contribute if they can see that their investment of time and energy actually influences the decisions that affect them. No one can guarantee the outcomes of political activity, but if we fail to properly construct the *input, throughput,* and *output* mechanisms of consensus decision making, the result will be failure. We do not want to see further examples where input does not make a difference. Each meeting, planning session, or roundtable is an opportunity to build public trust in participation or damage it further.

Appendix: Research Methodology

The research cited in the chapter is from the study presented in my dissertation, "Constructing Sustainability Policy Through Collaboration" (Hanson, 2001). The following is a description of the research process.

Scope and Subject

The data, findings, and analysis in this study are based on the experiences of about seventy collaborative process pioneers. They are among thousands of people across the nation and the world who have participated as citizen representatives in panels, partnerships, committees, roundtables, councils, forums, task forces, and other public decision-making ventures. Their charge was to develop cooperative solutions to address long-standing environmental disputes. They are people from all walks of life who decided to take on a new kind of "jury duty," to assist formal leaders at all levels of government to deliberate on matters that are too nebulous, complex, or contentious to be solved by existing jurisdictions or democratic mechanisms. The interview participants of this research participated in four environmental projects:

> The Minnesota Process: The Timber Harvesting Roundtable
>
> The Tennessee Process: The Forest Management Advisory Panel
>
> The Southwest Oregon Process: The Applegate Partnership
>
> The Northwest Minnesota Process: The Red River Basin Work Group

The featured projects shared an overall scope and process. With respect to scope, each project group tackled a complete system of environmental and social issues rather than addressing a specific problem. Regarding process, the case studies were similar—in terms of duration, membership, and outcomes. None were positioned as quick fixes. All were hefty undertakings that called for an enormous investment of human resources. The formal portions of the four deliberations lasted between a year and a decade. Follow-up activity continues to this day. The membership of each effort involved a team of about fifteen to thirty-five people, representing multiple interest groups with a strong stake in the sustainability dialogue. As far as project outcomes are concerned, each project successfully accomplished its short-term mission and gave rise to some form of long-term commitment to ongoing sustainability dialogue.

Data Collection and Sources

The research data originated from four sources: (1) *participant observation* of the processes facilitated by the author (Forestry projects in Minnesota and Tennessee), (2) extensive *document review* of formal and informal records related to each project, (3) a *literature review* of other cases in multiple-stakeholder environmental disputes, and most useful of all, (4) a series of in-depth *interviews* with thirty-seven people who participated in four different environmental projects in various parts of the United States.

In conducting the interviews, every effort was made to ensure that they elicited a full range of recollection, reactions, interpretations, and resolutions from participants. The researcher identified several potential barriers to effective interviews, such as the tendency to jump to conclusions, level of recall, and the time and patience to discuss old events. To address these barriers, a question sequence was constructed to enable people to remember and speak freely. The open-ended questions guided the participants through various levels of their experience without leading them in any particular direction:

What really transpired in the consensus-building process?

As "official representatives," what stake or interest did consensus-process members see themselves representing?

How did members fulfill their role?

How did the experience of the "representative duty" compare with member expectations?

What did members do to forge consensus between very diverse views?

What did members do between meetings?

How did process resolutions translate into implementation?

What do members consider successes and failures, and why?

How did the ends and means of the process hurt or benefit their interests and constituencies, and why?

What difference did the agreements make in resolving issues?

How does the experience of consensus participants shed light on understanding and conducting consensus making about environmental issues?

What helped or hindered the achievement of the consensus-building task?

References

Bauer, S. "Creating a Level Playing Field: Structuring Shared Decision Making to Promote Authentic Dialogue." Paper presented at the annual meeting of the American Educational Research Association, Chicago, March 1997.

Hanson, M. "Constructing Sustainability Policy Through Collaboration: A Multi-Site Case Study of Decision-Making Processes That Seek Sustainable Solutions for Statewide Forests or Local Watershed Development." Doctoral dissertation, School of Education, University of Saint Thomas, 2001.

Harrington, S. Presentation on the steps of effective group decision making, Institute of Cultural Affairs Training Session, Minneapolis, Minn., Mar. 1978.

Quinn, J., and Guile, B. *Managing Innovation: Cases from the Service Industries.* Washington, D.C.: National Academy Press, 1988.

Sergiovanni, T. J. "Moral Authority and the Regeneration of Supervision." In C. D. Glickman (ed.), *Supervision in Transition.* Alexandria, Va.: Association for Supervision and Curriculum Development, 1992.

Sorenson, L. D. "Site-Based Management: Avoiding Disaster While Sharing Decision Making." Paper presented at the annual meeting of the American Association of School Administrators, New Orleans, Feb. 10–13, 1995.

Thomas, K. W., and Kilmann, R. H. *The Thomas-Kilmann Conflict Mode Instrument.* Tuxedo, N.Y.: XICOM, 1974.

PART TWO

APPROACHES TO COLLABORATION

Gervase R. Bushe is an associate professor of management and organization studies in the Segal Graduate School of Business at Simon Fraser University in Vancouver, Canada. A leading organization development scholar, his research is widely cited. His early work was in developing collaborative labor-management relations and the re-design of large bureaucratic organizations toward team-based forms of organization. More recently, he has focused on changing cultures and developing leadership re-quired for new, collaborative forms of organization. He has won four best-paper awards from journals and the Academy of Management. He is on the editorial boards of the *Journal of Applied Behavioral Science* and *Organization Development Practitioner*. A skilled OD practitioner, he has more than twenty-five years' consulting experience in the areas of large systems change, organizational redesign, team building, and lead-ership development. He has consulted in Canada, the United States, Europe, Australia, and Africa, mainly to businesses. For more information, visit www.gervasebushe.ca.

CHAPTER EIGHT

SENSE MAKING AND THE PROBLEMS OF LEARNING FROM EXPERIENCE

Barriers and Requirements for Creating Cultures of Collaboration

Gervase R. Bushe

This ideas in this chapter come from thirty years of working with and studying business organizations, attempting to foster greater collaboration and the difficulties they encountered. In many chapters in this book, we see that collaboration is a complicated relationship that requires ongoing maintenance to sustain itself. When we talk about building *cultures* of collaboration, we are interested in creating environments that will sustain those kinds of relationships over the long term. It's not enough that collaboration occurs episodically in facilitated gatherings; it needs to be part of the day-to-day experiences of people for it to be part of the culture.

Cultures of Collaboration Are Hard to Create

This chapter rests on the premise that a culture of collaboration is one where certain basic assumptions are shared (Schein, 1992), including those that are required for the maintenance of collaborative relationships. I'll begin with a story about a work group that wants to be collaborative and whose manager describes it as collaborative but that over time has not been able to implement the maintenance processes required for real collaboration to take hold.

Lynette's Story

This story takes place in a business unit whose manager prides himself on teamwork and collaboration. In the unit's weekly meeting, Lynette, a new manager of the customer service group, describes her group's poor performance results and what she intends to do to improve them. As she talks, other managers listen politely, and a few ask questions "for clarification." At the end of her presentation, the boss thanks her, encourages the rest to pitch in with solving the problems, and says he looks forward to reviewing the results of her plans next quarter, and the meeting moves on. But many things have not been said. More than one manager at the meeting does not really agree with Lynette's analysis of the problems but says nothing about it. Some say nothing to avoid embarrassing Lynette, others to avoid being seen as quarrelsome. Doug wonders if Lynette is competent and if she really understands the situation. Marlene believes Lynette knows perfectly well what is going on but has chosen not to talk about the whole story to protect people in her department. Bruce thinks Lynette is trying to protect herself by covering up the real problems in her group. Sondra thinks Lynette is well intentioned but taken advantage of by her employees. Others have other thoughts and opinions, all of which they keep to themselves.

After the meeting, some of them get together in smaller gatherings, over coffee or lunch, and conversation turns to what they think is really going on in Lynette's department, what Lynette is really going to do about it, and why she is saying some things about it but not others. Differing opinions are examined and discussed, and in future interactions with Lynette, people look for tips and clues to support or refute different opinions about her real thoughts and feelings. In time, these managers come to develop firm opinions about Lynette's real motivations and competence. None of this is ever discussed or checked out with Lynette. Over the next few months, an image of who Lynette is, her strengths and weaknesses, her motivations and agenda, develop among each of the smaller groups, and these guide future interactions with Lynette.

Lynette is fully aware of what is going on in her department and has some excellent ideas about what to do about it. Due to perceptions she had developed of her current boss before becoming his subordinate, however, she believes it is not a good idea to be completely truthful, especially since some of his behaviors are part of the problem. She is a little surprised by the lack of cooperation she is receiving from her peers. They're nice and verbally supportive, but she notices a lack of follow-through on things she thought they had agreed to. She attributes this to overwork, lack of resources, and forgetfulness, unaware that the others are actually concerned about the accuracy of her analysis of the problems and the motivations behind her plans. Why waste energy and resources on a doomed effort is the thinking behind much of the noncooperation.

After months of frustration with the slow pace at which others are moving, Lynette, at another meeting, brings up her need for more support from others to improve performance. A certain nervous tension fills the room, and her boss, a "team player," moves quickly to smooth things over. Lynette's complaint is not examined in much detail, and everyone professes a willingness to be more supportive. Although Lynette's coworker are well intentioned, their behaviors, and the beliefs behind them, don't really change. A cycle of lunchtime conversations, unexamined assumptions, and avoidance of issues results in continued mediocre results and increasing stress from all the gossip and politics at work.

Interpersonal Mush Versus Interpersonal Clarity

If this sounds at all familiar to you, then you understand the territory of this chapter. I believe that in this story lies the basis of group and organizational dysfunction and the inability of smart and well-intentioned people to create the collaborative work cultures they say they want. I describe this group as living in *interpersonal mush*. Interpersonal mush occurs when people's understanding of one another is based on fantasies and stories they have made up, thinking that they are facts. I will argue that over time, interpersonal mush diminishes the capacity for collaboration. I will describe how *interpersonal clarity*, the antidote to interpersonal mush, is the basis for sustaining long-term collaboration. By *collaboration*, I mean a relationship in which two or more people are committed to the success of whatever project or process they are jointly engaged in and use assumptions and behaviors consistent with interdependence while pursuing those outcomes.

The model I will describe echoes a stream of thinking about organizational learning (Argyris and Schön, 1974, 1996; Schutz, 1994; Senge, 1990; Short, 1991; Torbert, 1973, 1981) that emphasizes the need for trust and authenticity in maintaining effective working relationships. It blends social constructionism, cognitive psychology, and family systems therapy to offer a perspective on why so little authenticity is found in normal working relationships and a novel, practical solution for increasing clarity and promoting group and organizational learning. I will begin by describing two aspects of normal cognitive functioning that I think create interpersonal mush and diminish the capacity for collaboration: the nature of experience and the nature of sense making. I will then describe why sustainable collaboration requires interpersonal clarity, what makes it difficult to achieve, and a process for increasing it. I'll conclude by offering thirteen "shared assumptions" whose presence in a culture support interpersonal clarity. I will mainly talk about this in the context of work organizations, although I think it applies to all systems of collective action.

We Create Our Own Experience

We have at least two very different ways of using the word *experience* in the English language. One refers to things that happened to us in the past, things we put on our résumés. The other refers to the moment-to-moment stream of perceptions, emotions, desires, and observations going through us. In this article, I will be using the word *experience* exclusively in the latter sense. From this perspective, experience only happens in the here and now. Things that happened in the past are *memories* of experience. I further define *experience* as consisting of four elements: observations, thoughts, feelings, and wants (Bushe, 2001a). At any moment, one can be aware (or only partly aware) of the totality of the experience one is having: the things one sees and hears, one's perceptions and cognitions, the sensations and emotions taking place in one's body, and the desires and motivations animating these.

As each of you reads this chapter, you will be having a unique experience—a multithreaded stream of observations, thoughts, feelings and wants—that is different from everyone else's. Some of that moment-to-moment experience will be related to this chapter and some to your environment, history, interest in this topic, recent coffee consumption, and many other factors. This is true of every interaction. As the interaction takes place, each of us has a personally unique experience.

In a group of people, during the same event, the experience of each person is different, sometimes dramatically so. Most of the managers I have worked with will quickly agree that this happens, but relatively few have thought through the implications for collaborative relationships. Perhaps the most important implication is that experience is not what happens to people but what they do with what happens to them (Short, 1998). Events occurring outside the person combine with internal cognitive maps, biases, emotional states, and motivations to result in their moment-to-moment experience. So each person, in effect, creates his or her own experience. This generates a dilemma for people trying to collectively learn from their experience together. As many chapters in this book demonstrate, collaboration endures only when partners learn about and adapt their relationship in an ongoing manner.

Learning from experience is often framed as an attempt to analyze the past in order to develop conceptualizations that will better guide future actions (see, for example, Kolb, 1984). If each person is continuously having a personally unique, self-created experience, how do we decide which experience to analyze? Who is having the "right" experience? What are the important thoughts, feelings, and wants for the people in the group to have? Learning from collective experience is a lot more complicated than reflecting on individual experience. (Later I offer a different image of learning from experience, with a different process and purpose for it.)

I believe that one reason why formal, hierarchical structures are so prevalent is that they solve the problem of who is having the right experience—the boss is having the right experience. Cultures of collaboration are inherently based on a different logic, where each person's experience has equal status and people are supposed to come to agreement through interaction and mutual adjustment. Without an understanding of the nature of experience and how interpersonal mush is created and overcome, the array of experiences occurring at any one moment creates conditions for misunderstandings, poor alignment, and increasing distrust. I believe that this is one reason why so many "successful" experiments in creating collaborative work systems don't, over time, fulfill their promise (Heller, Pusic, Strauss, and Wilpert, 1998; Weiss and Hughes, 2005). To create cultures of collaboration, we need to figure out how to organize collective action while recognizing that everyone will be having a different experience and treating each person's experience as legitimate as anyone else's.

We Need Self-Differentiation

Another serious impediment to clarity and collaboration occurs when people hold others responsible for their experience. When I blame you for my feelings, I'm holding you responsible for my experience. Instead of operating on the assumption that I am creating my experience of you, I'll either try to avoid you (so I won't have those feelings) or try to get you to change so I can have a better experience. Well-intentioned attempts to discuss and work out inter-personal problems don't often make relationships better if people are holding one another responsible for their own experience. The resulting frustration can lead people to think that such conversations are not useful (they're right) and reduce future attempts to clear things up.

If the parties attempting to build cultures of collaboration hold themselves responsible for others' experiences, which seems to me to be fairly prevalent, they will try to "fix" it when others are having "bad" ones. Taking responsibility for other people's experience is a dilemma for persons who are building cultures of collaboration, because it has both positive and negative effects. On the negative side, many people don't like it when others try to "fix their experience"—for example, by giving them a pep talk when they are afraid, trying to make them happy when they are sad, trying to get them to see things differently when they feel remorse, explaining why they shouldn't want something they are frustrated about, and so on. When one person tries to fix another's experience, it creates a transactional imbalance in which the one doing the fixing is the "parent," has their act together, and the one being fixed is the "child," needing help. The person being fixed can feel violated, defensive, or diminished and may resolve to be less forthcoming about his or her experience in the future. Then there are people who like it when others look after their experience. They are quite willing to snuggle into a relationship where, over time, real interdependence is replaced by more or less virulent forms of codependence. In either direction, the motivation to get clear about our different experiences wanes, and interpersonal mush increases and reduces the ability to maintain collaboration over time.

The dilemma is that personal effectiveness requires learning about the impact one has on others and revising one's behavior to have the effect one wants. To be effective, people need to learn about the experience they create in others, work to get their meaning across with minimal distortion, and check to find out if the message received was the message intended. Since personal effectiveness increases one's capacity for collaboration, collaborators face the paradoxical dilemma that sustainable collaboration requires both taking responsibility for other people's experience and not taking responsibility for other people's experience.

In practice, the way out of this dilemma seems to require attaining a state of self-differentiation in relationships (Bowen, 1978). A self-differentiated interaction is one in which you are at once both connected to and separate from the other. You are connected enough to be interested in and listen to the other's experience but separate enough to not be emotionally hooked and to know your own thoughts, feelings, and wants independent of the other person. Self-differentiation rests on the ability to be aware of your own experience and to be curious about others in a detached way. Valuing and practicing self-differentiation, especially by leaders, appears to be indispensable in organizations in which clarity flourishes (Short, 1991). If people are too connected to each other, holding others responsible for their experience or themselves responsible for other people's experience, they will be afraid of hearing or speaking the truth about anyone's experience because it is too threatening to the relationship. If they are too separate and don't pay attention to the experience of others, they will neglect the maintenance that collaborative relations need. Self-differentiation is the basis for leadership that can create interpersonal clarity and support sustained collaborative relationships. (Bushe, 2001b, 2002).

We Make Up Stories About Each Other's Experience

A related problem we face in creating cultures of collaboration is that we are all sense-making beings (Weick, 1995). All of us work at making sense of whatever is important to us until we are satisfied. In practice, we make up stories about other people's experience to fill in the gaps of what we know or think we know.

In Lynette's story at the start of this chapter, Lynette's colleagues are trying to make sense of her behavior. Notice a few common elements of sense-making processes. One is that her actions are being placed in a larger context: the perceptions people have about the problems in her area. In order to "make sense" of something, it has to fit with what people already believe to be true, the bigger picture. Another is that what she doesn't say or do is given as much scrutiny as what she does say and do. Nonverbal actions are given meaning. Notice that people are making up fantasies about her experience, about what she is thinking, feeling, and wanting. Lynette is, of course, also engaged in sense making about the others. For example, she has a story about why people aren't following up on agreements. Her view of her boss is based on past perceptions of him. To be satisfied with our sense making, current stories have to fit with past sense making. Finally, people are talking to others to try to make sense of Lynette. This is one of the key barriers to creating cultures of collaboration: where there is interpersonal mush, people rarely go to the person they are trying to make sense of to check out their stories. Instead they seek out third parties. When the event they are trying to understand is new or different, they seek out someone else to help make sense of it. They may seek out others in the organization or others outside the organization, such as a spouse or close friend.

The sense-making process is over when one has a story that one now treats as "the truth." One no longer treats the story as a possible scenario but as what actually happened and bases future perceptions and actions on these "facts" unless new information surfaces that forces a revision of the story. If the new information is vague and ambiguous, however, it can be easy to ignore or distorted to fit.

So We End Up in Interpersonal Mush

Interpersonal mush is an attribute of an interaction. It exists when two or more people interact on the basis of stories they have made up about each other but not checked out. Given the nature of experience and our compulsion to make sense of those around us, interpersonal mush is the normal, everyday, taken-for-granted climate in which most people live, at home and at work (Bushe, 2001a). Interpersonal mush makes it difficult, perhaps impossible, to create a culture of collaboration even among well-intentioned, highly motivated people.

Interpersonal mush happens when people don't describe the "truth of their experience" and don't inquire into other people's experience but instead make up a story about it. For the most part, this happens because people are afraid of negative repercussions if they do tell the truth about their experience. These include things like hurting other people's feelings, being misunderstood, causing others to act defensively, being forced to justify their experience, and being judged negatively. Since people don't normally describe all or most of their experience, others are compelled to make it up.

Sense making in an environment of interpersonal mush might be neutral if we were as likely to err on the positive as on the negative. Theoretically, it is possible that the story one person makes up gives the other person credit for being more courageous, more concerned, more honest, or more trustworthy than is actually the case. When this happens, people end up on a pedestal that they really don't merit. But that isn't often what happens. Unfortunately, the stories people make up tend to be more negative than the reality. In a vacuum of information, people tend to assume the worst, and this is particularly true in work organizations. As a result of interpersonal mush, what people believe about the organizations they work in and the people they work with is usually worse than the reality. In my thirty years of consulting and studying organizations, I find that executives are often perceived as more heartless and more cruel than they really are, organizations as more political and unbending than they are, coworkers as more insensitive and uncaring than they are, and subordinates as lazier and more careless than they are. This is one reason why, in toxic environments, getting people to share their experience is almost always a powerfully positive intervention (see, for example, Rosenberg, 2004).

Interpersonal mush has numerous negative impacts (Bushe, 2001a). One particularly related to collaboration is the impact on making and keeping agreements. When people who work together don't tell the truth about their experience, organizational meetings fall into a predictable spiral. In formal sessions, things get said, lists get made, and decisions are agreed on. Then people meet in small groups outside the meeting with trusted others to talk about what they really think and feel and want about the topics discussed at the meeting. They say things they don't believe would be acceptable if said during the meetings—usually expressing doubts, concerns, and questions about the topic of discussion. Under conditions of interpersonal mush, what appear to be agreements and consensually made decisions don't get implemented very well, if at all, because people haven't really committed to them. The lack of follow-through decreases people's trust in each other, which feeds the interpersonal mush, and on it goes.

Interpersonal Clarity Is the Antidote

Interpersonal clarity is a state in which each person is aware of his or her own experience, the other's experience, and the differences between them. In practice, that means that each person knows what he or she observes, thinks, feels, and wants and has listened to the other person describe what he or she observes, thinks, feels, and wants without either of them trying to change the other's experience.

The need for interpersonal clarity in ongoing collaboration makes three demands on participants:

- It requires them to explore their own *thinking and observing* and those of others and understand similarities and differences in vision, strategies, goals objectives, and mental maps (Argyris and Schön, 1996). The more such things are on the table for inspection, the greater the ability to find real alignment and support mutual success.

- It requires them to be honest with themselves and others about what they *want* without thinking that simply stating it makes others, especially leaders, responsible for fulfilling it. All forms of win-win conflict resolution and problem solving require clarity about needs and interests in finding successful solutions (Fisher, Ury, and Patton, 1991).

- It requires them to be honest with themselves and others about what they *feel* because people react to each other and make decisions about what to say and do based on what they feel and what they think the other feels (Barrett and Salovey, 2002).

Interpersonal clarity is not the same thing as being "open and honest." In fact, I believe that advising people to be "open and honest" doesn't really work. People think being open and honest is risky; they equate it with being honest about their judgments or expressing their feelings—both of which can damage work relationships. Hurling judgments at others is rarely useful for building any kind of relationship and more often leads to hard feelings and deteriorating relations. That's why people learn not to be open and honest in the first place. Expressing feelings (hugging others when happy, crying when sad, storming about when angry) in nonintimate relationships can push people away because of the power strong feelings can have on irrational behavior. Interpersonal clarity is not about being intimate—it does not require telling others about your life and your hopes and dreams or expressing the fullness of your being in their presence.

Interpersonal clarity is about being "transparent," about letting others know what your in-the-moment experience (observations, thoughts, feelings, wants) is so that they will make up more accurate stories about you. It's about calmly and dispassionately describing (not expressing) what you are feeling. It's about putting on the table the observations and mental maps that are leading you to your judgments without assuming that your judgments and maps are "the truth" or that the other person has the same observations or maps as you.

If the purpose of collaboration is supporting mutual success, collaborators need to be clear about all the elements of experience, what each observes, thinks, feels, and wants. Creating a relationship where people are willing to tell each other the truth about their experience requires assuming that each of us is having a different experience, we all have a right to our own experience, we are not responsible for each other's experience, and we can find real agreement and alignment by sharing this information. No matter how skilled or aware people are, they can't stop themselves from sense making, and inevitably interpersonal mush creeps into the relationship. Cleaning out the mush is crucial for the maintenance of a collaborative relationship, and that requires a periodic concerted effort such as an organizational learning conversation.

Organizational Learning Gets Us There

An organizational learning conversation is a process of talking and listening to each other until interpersonal clarity is achieved (Bushe, 2001a). I wrote my first paper on organizational learning as a doctoral student in 1979. It wasn't very grounded, and I spent many years looking for instances of learning that were truly organizational, where what was learned didn't reside only in some individuals but rather was encoded into the organization itself (Duncan and Weiss, 1979). This led me to think about what an organization is. Is an organization its buildings and machinery? Few would say so. Is it its strategy and goals? Strategies and goals come and go, and organizations persist. Is an organization its people? That's a popular cliché but hardly true—people come and go, and the organization remains the same. I've come to conclude that an organization is its patterns of organizing (Hedberg, 1981; Herbst, 1962), the patterns of interaction at work that take place day in and day out. These patterns are maintained by the conversations that take place (and don't take place) and the meanings people construct out of their interactions. If a team or organization really learns and changes, the change is manifested in those patterns of interaction; otherwise after an organizational change process that did not change the patterns of interaction, people will say that "nothing changed."

What's learning? Learning is the acquisition and use of new knowledge that comes from an inquiry of some sort. New knowledge that comes without inquiry is revelation, not learning. Learning requires use of the knowledge acquired for its effects to be sustained, perhaps even to be able to say that learning has taken place (Kolb, 1984). Learning should be evident in the changes we and others experience from its use.

Combining these definitions of learning and organization, I propose that organizational learning occurs when two or more people inquire in a way that results in new knowledge and alters their patterns of organizing. What I call an organizational learning conversation does that. In it, people (usually two but sometimes more) take turns describing their experience (observations, thoughts, feelings, and wants) and listening to the other's, usually about some pattern of organizing that is unsatisfactory to one or both. They use the conversation to obtain deeper insight into their own experience, a grounded sense of the other's experience, and figure out how they are each creating their own unsatisfactory experience. By doing so, they clear out the interpersonal mush and replace it with interpersonal clarity; very often this in itself leads to a positive change in the relationship and the resolution of whatever problem motivated the conversation in the first place.

Exhibit 8.1 presents an example of a learning conversation on a team living in the kind of interpersonal clarity that sustains a culture of collaboration. As I play back this interaction in the left-hand column, I take note in the right-hand column the organizational learning skills the participants are using to achieve interpersonal clarity.

EXHIBIT 8.1. A LEARNING CONVERSATION.

It has been four months since the president, Pierre, declared his and the board's intent to change the sole emphasis the organization has had for the past ten years on product A and introduce a new product, B. As he sits in a meeting of his executive committee, Pierre is worried that Stan, the vice president of the unit responsible for manufacturing product A, is resisting this change. He was very unhappy with Stan's performance at yesterday's board meeting, where he seemed confused and not in line with the new strategy, and concerned by the negative reactions some board members expressed once Stan had left the room. He values Stan, who has been an outstanding performer for many years, but realizes that he really doesn't know what Stan thinks about the change in strategy. As the discussion turns to the new strategy, the president takes the lead in being transparent about his own experience and seeking clarity about Stan's.

Notice that Pierre does not lead with judgments he has made about Stan's performance or his own sense making. Instead, he describes his observations, feelings, and wants and puts his sense making (doubts about Stan's support for product B) into a context that leaves him open to hearing something different—he is describing his experience in a way that invites the other person to describe his as well.

Pierre: Stan, I was somewhat puzzled after the board meeting yesterday, and so I would like to clarify where each of us stands on the product B strategy. I raise this now because it affects all of us, and we all need to be clear about what each of us thinks about this. So let me begin. I was concerned by your apparent confusion at the meeting, since I thought we had discussed the new product strategy thoroughly and were all in complete agreement. It raises in my mind some doubts as to whether you really support the product B strategy, and

EXHIBIT 8.1. A LEARNING CONVERSATION, Cont'd.

frankly, I'm starting to be concerned that you might resist it because you're afraid it will take resources away from product A. I want you to be upfront about where you stand on this, and I want us to find a way for you to feel fully behind both product A and product B.

Notice that Stan does not respond to or try to change Pierre's experience before he fully understands it. This seems to be crucial to successful learning conversations—one person tries to fully explore and understand the other's experience before responding to it in any way. Doing this requires a fairly high degree of self-differentiation—not taking responsibility for Pierre's experience and getting bent out of shape if Pierre is not having the experience Stan would prefer.

By first exploring Pierre's experience, Stan uncovers more information (about conversations with Stan's subordinates) that might not have come up if all they talked about was the board meeting, and this not only helps him understand Pierre's sense making but also turns out later to be crucial information for the whole group. Notice also that by trying to understand Pierre's experience, issues that are ultimately more important surface, and this would not have happened if this had been framed as a problem to be solved—how to get Stan to do better at board meetings.

(Stan, who is visibly disturbed by Pierre's remarks, does not respond to Pierre's statements but asks questions to get more clarity about Pierre's perceptions before reacting to what he is hearing.)

Stan: Could you tell me what, exactly, I did that caused you concern at the meeting?

Pierre: When you were fielding questions, you made a number statements that are contrary to the strategy the board has endorsed. For example, when Brian asked about the marketing strategy, you talked about building on the brand recognition of product A when we had already decided that it's better to keep the two products distinct in our clients' eyes.

Stan: Any other things?

Pierre: Well, yes. Your response to Marilyn about product launch and what you said to Hersch about expected cost of capital were not what we had agreed to.

Stan: Just so I'm clear, Pierre, can you tell me what you think I said and what we've agreed to?

(Pierre described what he heard Stan say at the meeting and what he thinks was wrong with what Stan said.)

Stan: OK, I think I see what you're unhappy about, but before I react to what you've said, Pierre, I want to check if there are any other reasons why you think I might not be fully behind the change.

Pierre: Well, I guess I was also taken aback a week or so ago in a conversation I had with Barbara

EXHIBIT 8.1. A LEARNING CONVERSATION, Cont'd.

(one of Stan's direct reports), who seemed to have some pretty confused fears about what effects this change might have on your department. Then I noticed a similar set of thoughts coming from Kevin, another of your managers. It got me wondering just how much of that is coming from you.

Stan: Were they talking about having to shift people to the new business unit? (Pierre nods.) Yeah, I know what you're talking about. Anything else causing you to wonder where I'm at?

Pierre: No, that's about it.

Stan begins by describing his here-and-now experience—thoughts, feelings, and wants—so that whatever sense making others are doing about this interaction will be more accurate. Then he responds to what Pierre has just said and describes his thoughts and feelings.

Stan: OK, well, let me start by saying that I'm somewhat surprised by all this. I had no idea that things went sideways at the board meeting, so I guess I'm glad you're telling me about it, and I do want you to know that I'm fully behind product B. Let me deal with the meeting issues first. With Hersch, I think I must have just not gotten my thoughts out clearly because I agree with what you are saying about our financing and how much debt we're willing to take on. But I have to tell you that I am confused about our marketing strategy and launch plans because I thought we had decided to build on the brand recognition and tie in with product A.

Here we see one big reason why it so useful for individuals to have learning conversations with their teams present. Many people prefer to have such conversations in private, if at all. But real collaboration and organizational learning require a willingness to have these kinds of conversations out in the open where the variety of experiences

Pierre: No, no—that was decided at least a month ago.

Robert: I have to tell you. Pierre, I'm with Stan on that one—I thought the opposite as well.

Susan: I didn't know a decision had been made.

Pierre: I don't understand this. We talked about this issue for weeks, and then at the last meeting of the board's Strategy Committee, a decision was made to keep the two products separate and distinct in our sales campaign.

EXHIBIT 8.1. A LEARNING CONVERSATION, Cont'd.

can be surfaced and integrated. It just takes a higher degree of self-differentiation for Stan to be able to remain calm and listen when such a potentially embarrassing interaction begins.

Robert: Well, I remember the discussions, but I thought we were all leaning toward product tie-in. I don't remember hearing that the Strat Committee had made a decision.

Errol: I knew about it from the meeting you had with the marketing group, Pierre, but I don't know if it ever came up here.

Pierre: Oh, hell, I thought I had announced that at our last meeting.

(Pierre tells the group about the decision made by the board's Strategy Committee and provides the committee's rationale. A discussion ensues, and it becomes clear that this is the first time the group has heard about and discussed this decision.)

Having gotten interpersonal clarity about the experience Stan and Pierre had about the product B strategy, they can now explore the real issues underlying those experiences. Here we see a leader, Pierre, willing to hear and explore experiences that are different from his own and in that process creating a space where real collaboration can flourish.

Imagine what might have happened if they did not have this conversation? Pierre would have developed doubts about Stan's commitment and would probably have continued to gather ever more data to support his fears. He would have thought the team was on board with the marketing strategy, not realizing it hadn't even been

Stan: To finish off with the issues you were bringing up, Pierre, it's true that people in my unit are afraid that they are going to lose resources to product B. I don't think it's going to be nearly as drastic as some fear, but obviously, some resources are going to be redirected, and we haven't yet decided what this is going to be. Frankly, I think the sooner we decide that the better because the uncertainty is fueling a lot of speculation and there's not a lot I can tell folks to calm them down. But you need to understand that as far as I'm concerned, bringing on product B is absolutely essential to the future health of our company and I am 100 percent behind it.

Pierre: I'm glad to hear that, Stan. But why are your people not on the bus too?

Stan: Oh, I don't think anyone questions the wisdom of moving into the product B space, Pierre. It's just that no one's sure what the ramifications for product A will be, and that is stirring up a lot of rumors and unfounded

EXHIBIT 8.1. A LEARNING CONVERSATION, Cont'd.

discussed. And perhaps most important, the group would not have developed a common understanding of the unwarranted fears and rumors swirling through the organization and been able to take action to ameliorate the situation. It is through their willingness to be clear about their experience with one another that they can truly support the success of the process (introduction of new product B) they are jointly engaged in, which is what collaboration is all about.

gossip. Last week someone asked me if we were closing down the product A unit!

Pierre: That's ridiculous! Product A is the core of this company. Isn't that obvious?

Stan: I think it is to us, but apparently there is some confusion in the ranks.

Errol: I have to agree with Stan, Pierre. A couple of days ago, I overheard a conversation in the cafeteria where some people were guessing how the product A unit was going to be reorganized.

Stan: I think the buzz coming from below is causing some of the concerns you are hearing from my managers, Pierre.

Pierre: Are any of the rest of you picking this up?

(The group launches into a discussion about the effects of implementing the new strategy on the organization's culture, with its ten-year history solely focused on product A. Some of this is news to Pierre, and together the group develops a picture of a pattern of misperceptions and misguided fears that are surfacing in the organization. Everyone affirms that product A is still the backbone of the company and that a new emphasis on product B should not have to mean a decrease in support for product A.)

Pierre: We'd better do something to clear up the confusion we've created. I think Collette's team on resourcing product B is just about finished. I'll ask her to speed up, and we can use her report to make some clear announcements throughout the company that will end the uncertainties about who is going to be working where. Susan, can you get the communications people geared up for this? I want to make it a priority. We don't need a lot of unfounded fears and rumors undermining our efforts to get product B to market quickly and effectively.

EXHIBIT 8.1. A LEARNING CONVERSATION, Cont'd.

The learning conversation comes to a close with Stan and Pierre describing what they have learned in creating this experience for themselves and agreeing on a plan for future interactions.

Pierre: I'm sure glad we had this conversation, though I'm a little sorry that it started from my misgivings about you, Stan. I see that I have some responsibility for what happened at the board meeting yesterday, so it looks like I owe you an apology.

Stan: Thanks, Pierre, but I have to take some responsibility for not having checked my facts before the presentation. I wonder if we can huddle before board meetings in the future, just to make sure I have my ducks in line.

Pierre: That sounds like a fine idea.

Having learning conversations that turn interpersonal mush into clarity requires some skills in addition to the capacity for self-differentiation. In general, these are awareness of one's experience, an ability to describe it to others in ways that avoid defensiveness and reactivity, an ability to inquire into other people's experience that helps them understand their own experience and makes them willing to tell their truth, and an ability to maintain an appreciative mind-set, to look for the positive intent behind what might appear to be negative actions (Bushe, 2001a).

Interpersonal Clarity in Organizations Depends on Certain Cultural Assumptions

There are a number of assumptions that support the creation and maintenance of a collaborative culture based on interpersonal clarity. I identify thirteen of them here (see Exhibit 8.2). My experience is that if people do not hold and act on these assumptions, real collaboration is hard to sustain.

To begin with is the assumption that each of us creates our own experience (assumption 1). Even when we witness the same event, are part of the same interaction, it is useful to assume that we may be having very different thoughts. feelings, observations and wants and not assume that others see it the same way we do (assumption 2).

EXHIBIT 8.2. THIRTEEN ESSENTIAL ASSUMPTIONS FOR A COLLABORATIVE CULTURE.

1. We each create our own experience.

2. In every interaction, every participant is having a different experience.

3. Everyone has a right to his or her own experience.

4. Each person's experience has equal status, although when it comes to objective issues, some may be more valid than others.

5. If I don't explicitly state what my experience is, others will make something up and treat that as if it's the truth.

6. It's generally useful to describe my experience to others with whom I want to collaborate and ask them to describe theirs.

7. Although it takes effort, it's good to be aware of my own in-the-moment experience.

8. Though I am compelled to make up stories about the experiences of significant others, I must maintain awareness of the difference between what I really know and what I'm making up.

9. By listening to others relate their experience without my trying to change or fix it, I can obtain more accurate information.

10. I need to work on being sufficiently separate from yet connected to the people I want to collaborate with.

11. To create clarity, I have to tell others my wants without expecting that those wants will be satisfied.

12. I am creating the impact other people have on me.

13. When I'm having unsatisfactory interactions with someone I want to collaborate with, we need to have an organizational learning conversation.

Collaboration is based on the assumption and behaviors of interdependence, a relationship where people are assumed to have equal rights (assumption 3). Such a relationship can't be sustained if some people's experience is given more status or validity than others or where people try to change each other's experiences, no matter how noble their intentions. I might go as far as to argue that sustainable collaboration requires that we fully respect other people's experiences and let them have their own experience, no matter how painful they might appear. That is different, however, from the extreme postmodern position that everyone's experience is equally valid. When it comes to objective issues—things that can be assessed independently of anyone's perceptions—some observations and thoughts may be more valid than others (assumption 4).

When people lack information about the experience of others, they are compelled to make up stories to fill in the gaps. Interactions are based on stories people have made up about each other, which they accept as "truth" (assumption 5). Over time, these stories tend to become more negative than reality and diminish the ability to collaborate successfully. Interpersonal mush is the normal, taken-for-granted environment in which work relationships (perhaps all relationships) exist unless people actively work at developing interpersonal clarity—a state in which each person knows what his or her own experience is, what the other's experience is, and the difference between them. Treating all experience as legitimate and not trying to change others' experiences when they are being described supports people's willingness to be clear with each other.

If I don't say what my experience is others will make it up and treat it as if it is the truth (assumption 5). Therefore, I need to be willing to describe my experience to others, which can feel risky at times, but that is when it is usually most important (assumption 6). To be able to do that, I have to be aware of what my experience is, and for most of us, that takes effort (assumption 7). We can probably never be fully aware of the totality of our experience, even after years of psychotherapy or meditation, and learning conversations are an important contributor to self-awareness.

Though we are compelled to make up stories about the experience of significant others, we can know and maintain awareness of the difference between what we really know and what we are making up (assumption 8). That is essential if we are going to be able to understand other people's actual experiences and to learn from our collective experience. By listening to others relate their experience, without trying to change or fix it, we can obtain more accurate information (assumption 9).

One of the things that makes it so difficult to create interpersonal clarity is the tendency to manage relationships by either becoming so closely connected that I take responsibility for your experience (or make you responsible for mine) or being so far apart that I don't even think of considering your experience. Interdependence and collaboration need people to value and practice self-differentiation (assumption 10).

One place where this shows up a lot is in managing expression of wants. People can be hesitant to ask others what they want if they think they will then be held responsible for fulfilling them (or fear that others will hold them responsible). So instead of getting a clear idea of what others want, people make it up, and the interpersonal mush deepens. That is different from a negotiation or contract kind of conversation, which also needs to take place in a collaborative relationship where you are getting a clear picture of what wants will be satisfied. The most important wants to be clear about are in-the-moment wants such as what I want from this interaction, what I want you to know about me, and the impact I want to be having on you (assumption 11).

Finally, sustained collaboration requires that we learn from our collective experience and that we occasionally take time to inquire into and learn about our patterns of interaction, both productive and unproductive, and work toward changing the patterns that are dissatisfying or in some way threaten our collaboration. Sense-making processes being what they are, whenever there is a problem in a work relationship, it is often too clear to each person how the other's behavior is the problem. If only the other person would change, everything would be fine! Such conversations need to be guided by the assumption that since I create my own experience, I am creating the impact you have on me (assumption 12). In any two-person relationship, each person is 50 percent responsible for what is going on. Therefore, the final and perhaps most important assumption for sustained collaborative relationships is that when we are having an unsatisfactory interaction with a person we want to collaborate with, a learning conversation is required (assumption 13).

Conclusion

The approach described in this chapter, which I have used with great success for more than a decade in a variety of organizations, works because most of the time it is interpersonal mush that is causing a hoped-for collaborative relationship to fall apart. Clear out the mush—create interpersonal clarity—and the problem often goes away.

References

Argyris, C., and Schön, D. A. *Theory in Practice: Increasing Professional Effectiveness.* San Francisco: Jossey-Bass, 1974.

Argyris, C., and Schön, D. A. *Organizational Learning II: Theory, Method, and Practice.* Boston: Addison-Wesley, 1996.

Barrett, L. F., and Salovey, P. (eds.). *The Wisdom in Feeling: Psychological Processes in Emotional Intelligence.* New York: Guilford Press, 2002.

Bowen, M. *Family Therapy in Clinical Practice.* Northvale, N.J.: Aronson, 1978.

Bushe, G. R. *Clear Leadership: How Outstanding Leaders Make Themselves Understood, Cut Through the Mush, and Help Everyone Get Real at Work.* Palo Alto, Calif.: Davies-Black, 2001a.

Bushe, G. R. "Self-Differentiation: The Missing Ingredient in Leadership." *Organization Development Practitioner,* 2001b, *33*(2), 41–47.

Bushe, G. R. "The Inner Core of Leadership." *Leader to Leader,* Summer 2002, pp. 37–41.

Duncan, R. B., and Weiss, A. "Organizational Learning: Implications for Organizational Design." In B. M. Staw (ed.), *Research in Organizational Behavior.* Greenwich, Conn.: JAI Press, 1979.

Fisher, R., Ury, W., and Patton, B. *Getting to Yes.* New York: Penguin, 1991.

Hedberg, B. "How Organizations Learn and Unlearn." In P. C. Nystrom and W. H. Starbuck (eds.), *Handbook of Organizational Design.* London: Oxford University Press, 1981.

Heller, F., Pusic, E., Strauss, G., and Wilpert, B. *Organizational Participation: Myth and Reality.* London: Oxford University Press, 1998.

Herbst, P. G. *Autonomous Group Functioning: An Exploration in Behavior Theory and Measurement.* London: Tavistock, 1962.

Kolb, D. A. *Experiential Learning.* Upper Saddle River, N.J.: Prentice Hall, 1984.

Rosenberg, M. *We Can Work It Out: Resolving Conflicts Peacefully and Powerfully.* Encinitas, Calif.: PuddleDancer Press, 2004.

Schein, E. H. *Organizational Culture and Leadership.* (2nd ed.) San Francisco: Jossey-Bass, 1992.

Schutz, W. C. *The Human Element: Productivity, Self-Esteem, and the Bottom Line.* San Francisco: Jossey-Bass, 1994.

Senge, P. *The Fifth Discipline: The Art and Practice of the Learning Organization.* New York: Currency/Doubleday, 1990.

Short, R. *A Special Kind of Leadership: The Key to Learning Organization.* Seattle, Wash.: Learning in Action Technologies, 1991.

Short, R. *Learning in Relationship: Foundation for Personal and Professional Success.* Seattle, Wash.: Learning in Action Technologies, 1998.

Torbert, W. R. *Learning from Experience: Toward Consciousness.* New York: Columbia University Press, 1973.

Torbert, W. R. "Interpersonal Competence." In A. W. Chickering and Associates, *The Modern American College: Responding to the New Realities of Diverse Students and a Changing Society.* San Francisco: Jossey-Bass, 1981.

Weick, K. *Sense Making in Organizations.* Thousand Oaks, Calif.: Sage, 1995.

Weiss, J., and Hughes, J. "Want Collaboration?" *Harvard Business Review,* March 2005, pp. 93–102.

Carol Sherriff is a founding director of Wilson Sherriff, facilitation consultants, a certified professional facilitator, and a certified trainer of neurolinguistic programming (NLP). She specializes in work with public sector and charitable bodies, focusing on creativity, change, and metaphor exploration and adapting NLP approaches widely used in areas such as sports and business coaching, sales, and marketing for facilitated events. With a background as chief executive officer of two national charities in the United Kingdom, she holds a master of business administration degree, is an associate lecturer with the Open University, and chairs the board of Welwyn Hatfield NHS Trust, a local health provider.

Simon Wilson is a founding director of Wilson Sherriff, facilitation consultants, a certified professional facilitator, and a certified trainer of neurolinguistic programming. He specializes in work with public sector bodies, focused on multiagency work and decision making in complex areas of policy. He uses metaphor exploration as a key component of this work. With a background as a consultant and adviser to the government of the United Kingdom and European bodies, he holds a master of business administration degree and chairs the board of trustees of Homeless Link, a national charity in the United Kingdom.

CHAPTER NINE

METAPHORS AT WORK

Building Multiagency Collaboration Through a Five-Stage Process

Carol Sherriff, Simon Wilson

Looking round the room just before the multiagency workshop began, you could see, hear, and feel the differences between the organizations seeking to work together. On the left, the head teachers from the local schools, smartly dressed, slightly aloof, and clearly demonstrating that their time was precious. On the right, the chief executive officers from youth organizations, casually dressed, lounging in their seats, chatting, and laughing. In between were senior officials from child care and social care organizations, a mix of formal and informal in dress, manner, and approach to the meeting. They were all there because of government priorities: local agencies were failing the neediest children because their services were not coordinated, they didn't keep each other informed, and they tended to be inward- rather than client-focused. Those present recognized the problem but found it difficult to reconcile the broader picture with the targets and objectives against which they were individually judged.

So how do you, as a facilitator, help organizations with such clear differences in culture, priorities, and ways of doing things work together to carry out a shared plan of action that is dynamic, empowering, and lasting? In our experience, one of the most effective ways is to develop and use the metaphors that different organizations have about each other, about working together and what they want to achieve.

Metaphors and Stories

Metaphors and stories are a powerful tool to help organizations harness individuals' underlying assumptions to guide collective action (Boyce, 1996; Denning, 2000; Morgan, 1997; Snowden, 2001). In particular, Gareth Morgan's work on the categories of organizational metaphors and the advantages and limitations of each type is extremely helpful for facilitators working in an organizational context. However, working with metaphors and stories to support collaboration between organizations is a relatively new field, and there are few published sources that directly support the work of facilitators seeking to assist in multiagency collaboration.

Parallel to this focus on organizational metaphors, interest in working with personal metaphors in therapeutic and personal development settings has been increasing (Gordon, 1978; Kopp, 1971). Coaches and therapists use neurolinguistic programming (NLP) (Bandler and Grinder, 1979, 1982) to develop a multisensory depth to working with personal metaphors that help support radical and lasting change for individuals. Developed out of this work in NLP and the use of therapeutic metaphors has been an approach to working with "clean language" (Lawley and Tompkins, 2000) to make sure that as far as possible, the coach or therapist is not "contaminating" the metaphor by imposing a personal version of it on the individual and the group.

One area of overlap between the organizational and individual fields is the use of "archetypal" figures in metaphor and a recognition that some roles in stories and metaphors seem to be universal in their application (Jung, [1936] 1990; Snowden, 2001). Carl Jung gave us the idea of the "collective unconscious" consisting of "contents and modes of behavior that are more or less the same everywhere and in all individuals." He wrote that the content of the collective unconscious includes archetypes that are "universal images" expressed in lore, myth, and fairytales. Carol Pearson's *Awakening the Heroes Within* (1991) is a helpful distillation of the Jungian archetypes set in an overall frame of the "hero's journey." The archetypes—innocent, orphan, warrior, caregiver, lover, seeker, creator, destroyer, magician, jester, ruler, sage—and the story of the hero's journey are claimed to provide a widely shared basis for communication among people from different backgrounds, organizations, and cultures.

We have combined these theoretical insights with our own experience of facilitating collaboration between organizations and groups using metaphor to develop a five-stage process for facilitators that creates multisensory depth, uses clean language, and promotes the development of archetypes within the metaphor. We have developed and tested this approach with various organizations and agencies in the United Kingdom for a number of years. In the following sections, we describe the benefits to organizations and facilitators of working explicitly with metaphors in a collaborative context, we examine three working assumptions to support facilitators in working with metaphors, and we outline the five key steps for collecting and using metaphors to assist the development of collaborative relationships.

Our final section warns facilitators that metaphors can be beneficial and positive and they can also be self-limiting and unhelpful. It advises facilitators how they can avoid pitfalls and create positive outcomes for their clients.

The Benefits of Working with Metaphors

How do metaphors support collaboration between organizations? The place to start is with a clear understanding of what a metaphor is and what it can do. Here are a few definitions we have found useful.

- Generally, a metaphor is defined as a manner of speaking in which one thing is expressed in terms of another in a way that casts new light on the character of what is being described (Kopp, 1971).
- All humans define reality in terms of metaphors and then proceed to act on the basis of those metaphors. We draw inferences, set goals, make commitments, and execute plans on the basis of how we structure our experience, consciously and unconsciously, by means of metaphor (Lakoff and Johnson, 1999).
- All organization and management are based on implicit images or metaphors that lead us to see, understand, and manage organizations in distinctive yet partial ways (Morgan, 1997).

In short, metaphors are a fundamental part of human and organizational life. They are shorthand or a code for how we think about our past, present, and future. We act as if they are true. By surfacing and exploring metaphors, we can shed new light on, discuss, and express feelings about a situation that is difficult to address directly. Because we act as if metaphors are true, they help guide action planning and the development of relationships.

Collaborative work between different organizations often seems problematic because each organization has its own culture and ways of doing things, opinions on what common goals should be, and how those goals should be achieved. In addition, there are differences within organizations as well as between them. These differences—both the internal and external ones—can be difficult to surface and deal with, but if they are not addressed, they can prevent a productive relationship from developing. Metaphors can reveal assumptions that directly guide action but are not recognized by the organizations. They can help organizations talk about their perceptions of each other in a way that is not regarded as rude or confrontational. Indeed, the facilitator can make such a discussion enjoyable and inspiring. Metaphors also have the power to motivate and galvanize organizations into action: for example, creating a rich sensory image of a flotilla of boats sailing toward the port of good services is more motivating than a step-by-step paper-and-pencil action plan.

Working with metaphor gives facilitators and organizations the opportunity to address some fundamental issues involving collaborative working. For example, in our work with a group of organizations, one participant described his company's situation as "waiting for the cavalry to arrive." The metaphor and its implications helped the organizations explore why the relationship seemed to be stagnating and talk about issues that were bubbling under the surface but difficult to speak openly about. Working together, they came to realize that one organization was acting as if it had circled its wagons against possible attack. The "cavalry" organizations explained how they would be tired, hungry, and very dusty by the time they arrived and probably in no fit state for an effective rescue. They worked together to create a more positive metaphor of joint collaboration.

Working Assumptions for Using Metaphors in a Collaborative Context

We have identified three assumptions and principles for working with metaphors in a collaborative context:

- Every organization already has its own set of metaphors, which may fall into one or more recognized categories. Existing organizational metaphors both help and hinder the organization.
- The role of the facilitator is to develop a rich metaphorical landscape, discovering or creating metaphors and bringing them to life in support of a shared goal.
- The facilitator's job is to ensure that a metaphor remains the property of the group, rather than imposing his or her own interpretation on the group.

Types of Organizational Metaphors

All theories about the way organizations work are themselves metaphors. Morgan (1996) identified eight types of organizational metaphors:

Machine	Political system or journey
Organism	Psychic prison
Brain	Flux and transformation
Culture	Instruments of domination

For each of these categories of metaphors, Morgan identified strengths and weakness. Recall our image of a fleet of boats sailing toward a common goal. This is an *organization as machine* metaphor—in our experience, the dominant type of organizational metaphor. It has considerable strengths. It is easy to build depth into this metaphor by identifying different kinds of boats—we have worked with flotillas that have included windsurfers and luxury liners—and it provides plenty of scope for different human roles on board, such as pilot, navigator, windsurfer, and social director. The limitations are common to most machine metaphors: attention is directed toward structure and hard systems rather than people and softer cultural issues; it's difficult to adapt the boat to changing circumstances without the notion of starting to refurbish, rebuild, or begin again; the metaphor is usually hierarchical; and the organizations have clear physical boundaries between them.

Other metaphor types that arise when organizations are seeking to work together are *organizations as organisms*—sometimes as a brain or nerve center, frequently as a garden or a tree. As described by Morgan (1997), the power of the garden metaphor is its focus on human endeavor and the continual interplay of humans and environment, taking information in, processing it, and feeding it back out. Metaphors that express the organization as an organism are dynamic: the organization has the power to learn and develop and support developments in its environment. The limitations of this type of metaphor can be a concentration on the environment without recognizing that the organism can affect its environment, and although a garden is more changeable than a machine, it still conveys the notion of fixed boundaries around individual organizations.

The *political system or journey metaphor* describes organizations as political systems—sometimes equated to the local political scene or ancient Greece or Rome or as a journey involving different groups and destinations. The strength of this metaphor in collaboration between organizations is its acknowledgment that all organizational functioning has a political dimension: goals are negotiated between individuals and teams and different interests, and conflict and power are features of all organizational life both inside and outside the organization. This type of metaphor is less bounded as a system and can be more adaptable. The weakness is that people's perception of politics can be negative and confrontational; negotiation, conflict, and compromise can be interpreted as manipulation and maneuvering.

At the early stages of organizations working together, it is useful to discover the dominant organizational metaphor for each member of the collaborating group. Organizations that have a similar group metaphor can find it easier to work together at the beginning of a process. However, as time goes on, they are likely to mutually reinforce the limitations of that metaphor and take it into the joint venture. If organizations' metaphors are very different, they may struggle to gain common understanding at the beginning of the process, as they are talking different organizational languages. However, this usually means that the group as a whole can develop more options about the nature of joint working: will it be like a machine, an organism, a political system, and so on?

Organizational metaphors provide a way for organizations to discuss their perceptions of each other in a nonthreatening way. For example, the windsurfer organization was seen as swift, zippy, and very economical but inclined to sail under the bows of the larger ships, either forcing them to change course rapidly or risking being mowed down. Facilitators can use their questioning and assumption-revealing skills to encourage the organizations to reflect on the implications of their different ways of experiencing the world.

When developing a new metaphor for the collaboration itself, it can be useful to the facilitator to use Morgan's types of metaphor and their strengths and weaknesses as a checklist for identifying key issues that need to be addressed. One of the strengths of working with metaphors is that these reflections can easily be shared and developed by the group. For example, ask, What would happen if all the organizations collaborating joined together as a flotilla of boats? What would happen if organizations were all part of the same garden or all embarking on a common journey? The power of this type of exploration and reflection is one of the reasons we argue strongly that the metaphors must be the choice of the group not the facilitator. If you reflect on the groups' metaphors, you will encourage deep insight and commitment; if you reflect your own metaphors, you risk creating confusion, passive resistance, and even conflict.

Creating a Rich Metaphorical Landscape

The richer the metaphor, the more power it has to involve and motivate individuals and organizations. However, there is a challenge for facilitators. The vaguer the metaphor, the easier it is for everyone to agree on it, as everyone will make a separate interpretation, and differences will not be immediately apparent. The more detailed the metaphor, the more the group has to discuss and agree on its characteristics. This is a judgment facilitators have to make. There are times when vagueness suits the purpose. If a metaphor is left vague and unexplored at the end of a meeting, often groups will come back having changed the metaphor by the next meeting. This can persuade groups of the power of metaphor to guide action. However, in general, the richer the metaphor the more power it has.

Three approaches help create richness in a metaphor:

1. *Encourage the group to accept the metaphor and forget for the time being the issue to which the metaphor relates.* When exploring a metaphor, it is valuable for the group to focus on the metaphor rather than the issue it represents. The more the group can bring the metaphor to life and tell its story, the better the result

when it is reconnected to the originating issue. For example, we were working with two groups who were joining together. One participant said that she felt like "a mouse at the feet of an elephant." This produced some discussion and questioning within the two groups, but there was no real shift in their perspective. The metaphor had not come alive. To encourage a shift, the facilitator suggested acting out the metaphor. The group played out a scenario in which representatives from each group, mouse and elephant, were being interviewed on a hard-hitting public affairs program. Three participants stepped into these roles. The interviewer asked the "elephant" and "mouse" about their experiences and goals and challenged them about what they each had to offer the collaboration. During the interview, the "elephant" revealed her fears about the tiny mice running around her feet—she did not know what they were doing, so she tended to trumpet defensively rather than speak to them. Acting out brought shifts in perception among participants and audience alike and created new insight into each perspective and understanding of the issue. The "mouse" group recognized that it might be seen as a threat—nimble, quick, and almost invisible—and both groups agreed that they needed to communicate more and to take responsibility for their actions rather than seeing themselves as victims.

2. *Make it multisensory.* To develop the richness of a metaphor, we use an approach taken from neurolinguistic programming, which states that humans use three main sensory systems to process and make internal representations of information—visual, auditory, and kinesthetic—and that their language demonstrates which system they are using at any given time (O'Connor and Seymour, 1995). This approach implies that for the metaphor to meet everyone's preference, the facilitator needs to make sure it has visual, auditory, and kinesthetic characteristics and needs to use visual, auditory, and kinesthetic language to question and probe the metaphor:

"What does it look like?"

"What are the sounds? What are people saying?"

"What are the feelings and emotions like?"

Even greater depth and richness can be achieved by exploring the characteristics of the main systems. For example, visual representations can be colored or black-and-white, moving or still; auditory representations can be loud or soft, high or low in pitch; kinesthetic representations can be heavy or light, intense or slight.

3. *Encourage the development of the metaphor as a story in which key archetypes play a role.* Most stories have a hero, but what type of hero is the archetype in this story? Innocent child or orphan? Warrior or caregiver? Destroyer or creator? Seeker of knowledge or lover? Ruler or magician? Sage or jester? Pearson (1991) set these archetypes within the framework of the hero's journey common to most stories. The hero prepares for the journey, faces a challenge, overcomes dark forces, and gains knowledge, returning from the journey changed. What types of story are the organizations running in their "collective unconscious"? In our experience, the different organizations and groups in a collaborative venture may well be running different storylines that need to be surfaced and explored before a common narrative can emerge.

Whose Metaphor Is It?

Facilitators need to make sure that metaphors are the property of the group and not driven by a dominant individual or organization or by their own representation of the metaphor. Techniques for making sure that a single organization or individual does not dominate a group are offered in most books about facilitation and are extremely useful in working with metaphor. In addition, special attention is needed to ensure that the facilitator's own representation of the metaphor does not contaminate the group metaphor. For example, returning to the metaphor of different organizations as a flotilla of boats, the facilitator will have his or her own representation of boats. Indeed, you may have one at this very moment. In seeking to deepen and expand the metaphor, you can actually alter it by the questions you use. "What kind of motors do the boats have?" assumes that they are motor-driven when the group may be thinking of sailboats. This type of questioning can disrupt the metaphor, limit its potential, and risk damaging the relationship between facilitator and group. In developing the richness of the metaphor, the facilitator's questions need to be as nonspecific as possible. We suggest that facilitators working with metaphors adopt the "clean language" approach developed by Lawley and Tompkins (2000). In essence, this means using the participants' own descriptions to find out more and using general rather than specific questions to keep assumptions out of the metaphor exploration—for example:

"And what kinds of boats are those boats?"

"And is there anything else about those boats?"

"And what happened just before?"

"And what happens next?"

The questions may seem awkward but are extremely powerful for keeping the metaphor the property of the group. *And* at the beginning of the question signals that the facilitator wants to build on the previous description, and the question is not likely to be taken as a challenge by participants who may be using their imagination in this way for the first time. The use of *those* also reinforces that the metaphor belongs to the group and not the facilitator.

Also, don't forget the power of nonverbal communication. Participants often gesture or draw their interpretation of the metaphor in the air. Gesturing in the same way or pointing to the air drawing and asking, "And what kind of . . . is that?" or even "And that?" will elicit additional multisensory details.

In summary, the key working assumptions underpinning facilitative practice with metaphors in interagency collaboration are to recognize what types of organizational metaphors the participants are using and whether they are from the same group of metaphors, to create sensorially rich metaphors, and to keep the facilitator's own perceptions out of the metaphor exploration. So how does the facilitator do that?

Metaphors at Work: A Five-Step Process

We have developed a five-step process for working with metaphors. It works with all metaphor exploration but is particularly useful when working on collaboration between groups and organizations. The process should be underpinned by the working assumptions described in the preceding section. Like most other processes facilitators use, it is not linear or strictly time-sequenced. It is in practice cyclical and iterative. The five steps are as follows:

1. Catch the group's metaphor.
2. Define the issue.
3. Gain permission.
4. Explore the metaphor.
5. Apply learnings from the metaphor to the issue under discussion.

1. Catch the Group's Metaphor

As noted earlier, the most useful metaphors are those that arise naturally and spontaneously. Scheduling a slot on an agenda for metaphor exploration and then asking the group to come up with metaphors is the least successful way of working with metaphors—probably because the group becomes self-conscious and tries too hard. We have therefore come up with a number of ways of encouraging groups to recognize their use of metaphors and, as facilitators, openly catching and logging them. We organize metaphor catching in a number of ways.

First, in preparing and planning for the event, explain to the organizers that you will be looking for how the groups use metaphors to describe themselves and their situation and that you will be interested in helping them use these metaphors to explore some of their issues. You may make metaphor exploration a specific agenda item. This should not be too early in the day, as you need to have caught some metaphors first. You may introduce some widely understood metaphors in your warm-up session. For example, we facilitated a joint working group on services that were described as a journey for the client group. We structured our opening session to use the metaphor of a journey and asked people to say how they had planned their journey to the venue. This approach introduces the participants to the idea that metaphors may be part of the later discussion.

Second, during the course of an event, metaphors will arise. We draw attention to these and log them, normally on a flipchart used solely for this purpose. You should explain that this record may provide the group with some material to work on later in the event. Invite group members to notice when someone has used a metaphor and alert you so that you can record it. Here are some examples of metaphors used early in an event and logged for possible exploration:

"In what direction is this ship sailing?"

"We can be like an army or like an orchestra."

"Our services are like a selection of pizza toppings."

"It's an entirely separate wing to the house."

This metaphor log has a number of purposes. It gets the whole group, including more skeptical members, used to the idea that we speak in metaphors and that they can be very powerful in communicating ideas and emotions between people. Often the metaphors that appear on the log will be picked up and used later on in the event. Sometimes it is a metaphor not on the log that transforms the group process; however, the log prepares the group to pursue a metaphor that opens up the discussion instantly. For example, we recently facilitated a discussion between senior managers in two British government departments. This was a polite event in which the managers wanted to find ways to collaborate better without necessarily giving too much ground to the other organization. Very early in the event, one manager described a particular policy as being "the Holy Grail for all of us." This naturally occurring metaphor transformed the meeting, serving as a challenge and a rallying point for discussion, and was returned to again and again by the participants.

Third, the facilitator may take the initiative. Sometimes metaphors do not arise readily. In this case, a prompt will elicit a metaphor in response:

"So what's it like doing your job?"
"It's like we're fighting fires all the time."

"What sort of a problem?"
"It's a great big mountain that blocks out the sun."

These metaphors should also be listed on the metaphor log.

Once the group is familiar with what a metaphor is and how frequently we use metaphors, you can use metaphors easily and effectively to explore issues and decide on appropriate courses of action.

2. Define the Issue

In talking to the client about the desired outcome of the event or project, you will make a judgment about the issues to deal with and which ones might benefit from exploration using metaphor. You will also notice when the client uses metaphor to tell you about the issues so that you become sensitized to the types of metaphors that may arise—or aware when very different metaphors arise.

We place "define the issue" after "catch the metaphor" in the process for two reasons. First, participants may use metaphors at the beginning of an event to signal what is important to them but too sensitive to say directly. So sometimes the early metaphors highlight an issue that needs dealing with at some point. Second, once a metaphor captures the imagination of the group and people wish to explore further, it is important briefly to define the issue to be explored. Whether a metaphor arises spontaneously and is pursued immediately or is logged and chosen later, you need to make a judgment about timing. Before the group goes "into Metaphorland," it should agree on a definition of the issue. Ideally, it should be written up and displayed. Paradoxically, it then needs to be put aside and the facilitator needs to encourage people to enter Metaphorland and disregard the issue. Our experience shows that the most powerful use of metaphor is to have an explicit purpose—hence the definition of the issue—and then let the mind focus on the metaphor rather than the purpose. This encourages much greater insight once the metaphor is reunited with its originating issue.

Sometimes the issue arises well after a metaphor has been logged. We were working with two organizations who had to collaborate on implementation of a major national policy goal in the British public service. During the first day of discussion, the metaphor of "marriage" was used on a number of occasions to describe the relationship. The relationship was described by the participants as being healthy and in good shape. During the second day, a major issue arose relating to a third agency not represented at the meeting. The marriage metaphor was revived with a different spin: the participants spoke of a "third person in the relationship." The metaphor enabled participants to identify the extent of the problem between the two agencies present and the third organization.

3. Gain Permission

Nowadays, most organizations use some creative, intuitive approaches to strategy planning and decision making. However, comfort levels with this approach vary among organizations and individuals. Where different organizations are working together, this must be actively managed.

In preparation for the event, you should ask the client about the use of intuitive techniques in general and metaphors in particular; finding out about different experiences of such techniques, particularly if any organization has had a negative experience; preparing people for the style of event by making it clear on the meeting notice or invitation. Think about how you yourself come across. We make it clear that we use creative techniques because they work, not just for the sake of using them.

Gaining permission also refers to work done by the facilitator early in the meeting to establish the mood of the event so that participants are prepared to cooperate with an approach that may be unfamiliar to them.

It is best to begin gently using metaphor, particularly if this is the first meeting in a series. It is helpful to use metaphor in your opening introduction: these sessions can be like a party when you have accepted the invitation but are not quite sure whether you are going to enjoy it or meet the right people. Encourage participants to use analogies and metaphors in introducing themselves. This is often fun, and it's more interesting than people saying who they are and what organization they belong to.

The metaphor log also signals that metaphors are not some weird and wonderful technique but something people use all the time without thinking. When logging metaphors, refer to the value of creativity and intuition as a complement to rational and analytical processes or the way the left and right sides of the brain work together—a metaphor in itself.

It can be worth having short exploration sessions before focusing on the main issues for discussion, inviting some people to "give it a go" without making a big deal of it. For example, this was how the elephant-and-mouse interview referred to earlier was framed. It is a way of demonstrating to the group how rich an exploration can be while enabling members who are willing to have a go as soon as possible.

4. Explore the Metaphor

Now the fun starts! Exploring metaphors is a creative process, and depending on the degree of permission you have, anything goes. The principal task during this stage is to enable the participants to keep their minds switched off the substantive issue under discussion, working with intuition rather than deliberate thought. This is best done by distracting the rational mind through tasks. For example, getting people to build a creative sculpture of their metaphor with materials they find, drawing pictures or storyboards, or setting up a current affairs debate are all highly effective because the mind is kept away from the originating issue. The task absorbs and produces a concrete result that can be adapted as the discussions progress.

We worked with a group of armed service organizations that needed to coordinate their actions. The group defined the problem—essentially, setting up communication systems that were horizontal and quick rather than vertical and slow and yet would be acceptable in hierarchical organizations. The participants decided that they would try a creative sculpture for a number of reasons, including that it was after lunch and this was an opportunity to go outside. They agreed that they would work in two groups and each go on a walk to find interesting objects and artifacts to build their sculpture with. The ground rules were not to talk directly about the issue and only about the artifacts, weather, scenery, and so on. They ultimately built a wonderful sculpture based around an umbrella with water channels made out of ribbons and branches to direct the flow of rain. This in itself was an act of collaboration between groups. Absorbed in building their structure, they realized that their channels were flowing sideways—water was no longer flowing between channels and did not reach the ground.

This led the group from metaphor creation to the exploration phase. The participants set about adapting their sculpture into a more free-flowing system. They later recognized that water doesn't flow uphill, so how could they get the channels to work upward as well as around and downward? At one stage, they inverted the umbrella—a powerful symbolic action in organizations accustomed to a top-down chain of communication and command.

Different exploration activities are appropriate to different contexts, but as with the example just given, the facilitator will be encouraging and steering the group to pay particular attention to such matters as changes in understanding of the metaphor, shifts in perspective, and evolution in time and space.

During this phase of the process, the group will begin to take the metaphor in the desired direction through discussion and questioning:

"Is the ship leaky or sound? Are we heading for the rocks? Are we passengers on a luxury liners or rowing like crazy to keep it going?"

"If we're an orchestra, who's the conductor?"

The facilitator can encourage active and creative ways of working—for instance, drawing pictures inspired by the metaphor: cartoon strips or idealized visions. Or the facilitator can encourage the group to act out or develop scenarios based on the metaphor.

During the exploration phase, the facilitator should attend to a number of things, many of which are common to all facilitated activity. The exploration of the metaphor needs to be a group task, so you may need to prompt a dominant member to listen to others or a shy member to get involved.

As the facilitator, through questioning and encouragement, you help deepen the metaphor and make sure that it is the group's interpretation and not the facilitator's. The use of clean language and sensorially rich questions is very important at this stage, as these techniques seek different goals.

Sensorially rich language is used to deepen the metaphor, engaging the creative part of the brain and perhaps linking to a collective unconscious and archetypes. Questions such as these can encourage rich representations:

"What does it look, sound, and feel like?"

"What will we hear, see, and feel when we have arrived there?"

"What is the color, tone of voice, texture?"

Clean questions complement this by minimizing the input of the facilitator and allowing the group members to develop the metaphor in their own way:

"And that's an elephant like what?"

"And what kind of marriage is that marriage?"

"And when you find the Holy Grail, what happens next?"

As noted earlier, the specific formulations of clean language may appear clumsy on the page but have been found effective in allowing groups to explore their own metaphors.

Another task for the facilitator is to prevent early closure. Some members of the group will want to keep referring to the issue under discussion. What seems to happen with metaphor exploration is that an initial number of insights arise from the metaphor. One or two of these may be profound, but most will be issues that the participants already knew but hadn't expressed before. As participants continue to engage actively in the task, setting aside analysis and logic, a second wave of insights evolves, often more profound, the result of one person's thinking being stimulated by the thoughts of another. It is therefore worth prompting participants to go that bit further in developing the metaphor. As a guide, at least fifteen minutes in Metaphorland is required.

5. Apply Learnings from the Metaphor to the Issue Under Discussion

There is a common cycle of energy in metaphor exploration—an initial burst of energy and activity, then a slowing of activity when the facilitator may need to prompt further exploration and activity, followed by another burst of energy and exploration. It is worth monitoring the energy of the group so that you end the metaphor exploration before that energy dissipates. This leaves participants still energized and ready for the next phase.

You then need to draw them out of the metaphor exploration and back to the issue. This can be done very simply:

> "So your issue was . . . ? What does this metaphor exploration tell us about it?"

The facilitator prompts reflection with clean language and does not steer the group. It is important to ensure that the group pulls out all of its learnings, rather than careering after the first and perhaps very obvious insights. In this context, the "Columbo question" is very useful. The disheveled detective would always ask one more question on his way out the door. Similarly, the facilitator will get a lot of value out of a simple "clean" question:

> "Is there anything else?"
>
> "And what else?"

This question may be repeated several times before moving the discussion on. Also, it is worth drawing out some of the learnings about the process itself. Collaboration is often a new experience; so for many people is metaphor exploration. So how was the process? What did it feel like to work together? What worked well and what didn't work so well?

The Challenges of Working with Metaphors

As Morgan's work on organizational metaphors (1997) made clear, metaphors are always limited in some degree. They work by highlighting the shared characteristics of an organization and, say, a machine. Therefore, facilitators need to be aware of these limitations and prompt the discussion to elicit the limitations of the particular metaphor used.

Some metaphors are in themselves more positive than others—we call these "firm friends." Travel or journey metaphors are of this type; they may correspond to archetypes in our unconscious mind and will usually open up areas for exploration. Some of the key questions posed by journey metaphors are the following:

Is it more important to reach the destination or to enjoy the journey?

What obstacles will you encounter on your way?

Are you all traveling by the same route or means of transport or by different ones?

What will you bring back from our journey?

On the other hand, sometimes phrases or words appear that are "false friends": for example, stock phrases that have lost their impact on our unconscious. One rather obscure but common example in our field of work is the word *silo*, which is used to refer to divisions or departments in the same organization that do not communicate with each other. We have tried in the past to open up this metaphor, which derives from a grain storage facility, with little success. In this case, we believe that most people have never seen a real silo but first came across the word in its figurative usage, so the basis of the metaphor, and hence its power, is lost.

Other "false friends" are common metaphors that when explored produce negative representations. "We get on like a house afire" is a curious figure of speech that is very difficult to explore positively. Military or warlike metaphors can also be very negative, although they may accurately reflect that organizations feel they are in a "war zone." In these cases, the facilitator's job may be to move on and help the group come up with a more empowering metaphor.

Finally, it is helpful for the facilitator to have his or her own positive metaphors of organizations working collaboratively. One we use is that you are hosting a party for a variety of talented and intelligent people, and your job is to make sure that the party comes together and everyone has a great time. Another uses a metaphorical basketball team, at a point in the game when all players get their hands on the ball and guide it collectively into the net. Of course, because these are metaphors, each has its limitations, but both have proved useful.

Conclusion

We hope that this chapter encourages facilitators to use the power of metaphor to help organizations work collaboratively together. We have sought to draw attention to the different types of organizational metaphors, how these and others can be enriched and explored, and the need to make sure that they are the property of the group rather than the facilitator. We have described in detail the process we use to work with metaphors and conclude with some of the challenges in working with metaphors and their inherent limitations. This is an evolving field, and as we continue to expand and refine our practice, we would be delighted to hear from other facilitators about their experiences in this area.

References

Bandler, R., and Grinder, J. *Frogs into Princes: Neuro Linguistic Programming.* Moab, Utah: Real People Press, 1979.

Bandler, R., and Grinder, J. *Reframing: Neuro-Linguistic Programming and the Transformation of Meaning.* Moab, Utah: Real People Press, 1982.

Boyce, M. E. "Organizational Story and Storytelling: A Critical Review." *Journal of Organizational Change Management,* 1996, *9*, 5–26.

Denning, S. *The Springboard: How Storytelling Ignites Action in Knowledge Era Organizations.* Oxford: Butterworth Heinemann, 2000.

Gordon, D. C. *Therapeutic Metaphors.* Capitola, Calif.: Meta, 1978.

Jung, C. J. *The Archetypes and the Collective Unconscious.* London: Routledge, 1990. (Originally published 1936.)

Kopp, S. B. *Guru: Metaphors from a Psychotherapist.* Palo Alto, Calif.: Science and Behavior Books, 1971.

Lakoff, G., and Johnson, M. *Philosophy in the Flesh: The Embodied Mind and Its Challenge to Western Thought.* New York: Basic Books, 1999.

Lawley, J., and Tompkins, P. *Metaphors in Mind: Transformation Through Symbolic Modelling.* London: Developing Company Press, 2000.

Morgan, G. *Images of Organization.* (2nd ed.) Thousand Oaks, Calif.: Sage, 1997.

O'Connor, J., and Seymour, J. *Introducing NLP: Psychological Skills for Understanding and Influencing People.* London: Thorsons, 1995.

Pearson, C. S. *Awakening the Heroes Within: Twelve Archetypes to Help Us Find Ourselves and Transform Our World.* San Francisco: HarperSanFrancisco, 1991.

Snowden, D. J. "Narrative Patterns: The Perils and Possibilities of Using Stories in Organizations." *Knowledge Management,* 2001, *4*(10).

Kim Sander Wright, B.S., M.A., is a researcher and facilitator whose interests focus on multicultural and multistakeholder processes, representational issues, and collaborative models for sustainable development. She is principal of Coracle Consulting and associate of Dovetail Consulting in Vancouver, British Columbia. She studied geology and natural environmental sciences at Sheffield University in the United Kingdom and biology at Simon Fraser University and conflict analysis and management at Royal Roads University in British Columbia. For nearly two decades, she has been involved as a participant or in the facilitation and coordination of a range of collaborative processes, from environmental and social change to interspiritual and political. She lives with her husband and her two children in Vancouver, British Columbia. Kim can be contacted via email at kim@coracleconsulting.ca.

CHAPTER TEN

UTILIZING UNCERTAINTY

Kim Sander Wright

A number of disciples went to the Buddha and said, "Sir, there are living here in Savatthi many wandering hermits and scholars who indulge in constant dispute, some saying that the world is infinite and eternal and others that it is finite and not eternal, some saying that the soul dies with the body and others that it lives on forever, and so forth. What, Sir, would you say concerning them?"

The Buddha answered, "Once upon a time there was a certain raja who called to his servant and said, 'Come, good fellow, go and gather together in one place all the men of Savatthi who were born blind, and show them an elephant.' 'Very good, sire,' replied the servant, and he did as he was told. He said to the blind men assembled there, 'Here is an elephant,' and to one man he presented the head of the elephant, to another its ears, to another a tusk, to another the trunk, the foot, back, tail, and tuft of the tail, saying to each one that that was the elephant.

"When the blind men had felt the elephant, the raja went to each of them and said to each, 'Well, blind man, have you seen the elephant? Tell me, what sort of thing is an elephant?'

"Thereupon the man who was presented with the head answered, 'Sire, an elephant is like a pot.' And the man who had examined the ear replied, 'An elephant is like a winnowing basket.' The man who had been presented with a tusk said it was a ploughshare. The one who knew only the trunk said it was a plough; others said the body was a grainery; the foot, a pillar; the back, a mortar; the tail, a pestle, the tuft of the tail, a brush.

"Then they began to quarrel, shouting, 'Yes it is!' 'No, it is not!' 'An elephant is not that!' 'Yes, it's like that!' and so on, till they came to blows over the matter."

"Brethren, the raja was delighted with the scene.

"Just so are these preachers and scholars holding various views blind and unseeing. In their ignorance, they are by nature quarrelsome, wrangling, and disputatious, each maintaining that reality is thus and thus."

Then the Exalted One rendered this meaning by uttering this verse of uplift: O how they cling and wrangle, some who claim: / For preacher and monk the honored name: / For, quarreling, each to his view they cling: / Such folk see only one side of a thing (Buddhist canon, Udana 68–69).

Conflict Within the Collaborative Process

The parable of the blind men and the elephant demonstrates a situation for which collaboration could be an appropriate process. Collaboration would require the men to work together to solve the problem at hand: What sort of thing is an elephant? "The objective of collaboration is to create a richer, more comprehensive appreciation of the problem among the stakeholders than any one of them could construct alone" (Gray, 1991, p. 5).

Collaboration is paradoxical, though, containing a great deal of conflict and often failing to live up to expectations. Groups come together because of shared purpose, and yet the differences between them in terms of "aims, cultures, structures, procedures, professional and sometimes natural languages, power and accountabilities" (Eden and Huxham, 2001, p. 374), as well as "culture and ideological differences" (Conca, 1995, p.454) make coordinated action difficult and can prevent collaborative processes from attaining shared goals.

A collaborative group, no matter how homogeneous it may initially appear to the participants, is a form of multicultural society (Rex, 1995). Whether the party's involvement is one of choice or necessary due to interdependence around an issue of shared impact, it is the diversity of individual viewpoints that leads to collaboration's paradoxical and unique social dynamics. Some form of conflict becomes inevitable. Diversity of perspective makes a collaborative process effective in finding unique solutions to complex problems and can prevent the participants from reaching their goals.

This paradox comes about because conflict has both constructive and destructive attributes. As conflict leads to the breakdown of social systems, it is also the harbinger of social change, with new systems replacing the old. It creates tensions and leads to dialogue. Conflict challenges individual viewpoints during attempts at resolution, breaking down existing belief systems and replacing them with new ones. It can also lead to the marginalization, oppression, or annihilation of parties. Given that conflict is a necessary aspect of collaboration, the question is not how to avoid conflict but how to manage or facilitate it to maximize its constructive and minimize its destructive aspects. In other words, how can the blind men convince one another that all of their respective viewpoints belong in the solution without the tail dominating the animal and the head becoming lost?

Certainty and State of Mind

The challenge for collaborative process facilitators is to analyze and understand the intergroup and interpersonal dynamics within each collaborative process on ongoing bases. They can then manage and facilitate the process to create a collaborative culture that embraces a diversity of viewpoints. If a process design for collaboration exists that has the ability to harness the creative capacity of conflict, it will be culturally appropriate, unique to the individuals and situations at hand, and reflective of the continually changing circumstances within the group. The framework presented in this chapter is designed to assist facilitators in this ongoing analysis by describing a continuum of states of mind with illustrative anchors that can be used relative to the degree of agreement within the group to design appropriate group process so that the creative capacity of conflict can be fully utilized.

State of Mind

How one is influenced by or influences conflict with others will be reflective of one's state of mind. For example, the Dalai Lama (2004) told a story about a man who was shot. He was in a battle where both enemy and friendly fire was occurring. The acquired injury was identical to one that would have occurred through enemy fire, but because it was friendly fire that inflicted his wound, the man emphatically insisted that he was OK. One could assume that the pain was far more bearable because he felt no animosity toward the soldier who shot him. Had he believed that the bullet came from enemy fire, would his affliction have been different? Similar to a battlefield, the collaborative process contains conflict that could be construed as constructive or destructive, depending on the state of mind of the participants who are caught in the crossfire. Whether the other parties are considered friends or foes will depend on whether they are perceived as contributing to the solution or to the problem. The state of mind would be cooperative on the one hand and competitive on the other.

Uncertainty and Certainty

Uncertainty and certainty are ways of measuring our attachment to a particular view on an issue and therefore our state of mind when in conflict with others about that issue. A person who is uncertain about something has an element of doubt as to whether his or her view is absolutely right. Certainty, by contrast, contains no doubt whatsoever. Uncertain and certain states of mind continually influence our perception of conflict during collaboration.

Uncertainty as to whether one's own viewpoint is absolutely right should lead collaborative process participants to regard the sharing of information with other participants as a potential solution. The uncertain ones would therefore see conflict during collaboration as friendly fire. The blind man who is uncertain as to whether his view is the only right one will question whether his experience is absolutely true of the elephant. He will be more likely to make friends with the other blind men in order to discover the whole truth about the elephant.

Certainty that one's own viewpoint is absolutely right should lead collaborative process participants to see information sharing as a battle, complete with the taking of sides and defensive or aggressive behavior toward other participants. The certain ones would therefore regard conflict during collaboration as enemy fire. The blind man who is certain that an elephant is exactly what he has experienced is less likely to legitimize anyone else's view, and his certainty will turn all the other blind men into foes.

Uncertainty Framework

As Norman Maier (1976, p. 241) pointed out, "Reaching consensus in a group is often confused with finding the right answer." Kenneth Thomas (1975) and Morton Deutsch (1973) both describe competitive and cooperative conflict-handling theories in which the outcome is dependent on the approach chosen by the parties. Those that use the competitive means tend to be adversarial and view conflict as a zero-sum (win-lose) game, whereas those that use cooperative means view conflict as a positive-sum (win-win) situation. Similarly, the uncertainty framework illustrated in Figure 10.1 shows a continuum that describes the manifestation of cooperative and competitive states of mind. The states of mind are framed as resulting from an individual's certainty or uncertainty about his or her viewpoint being absolutely right during collaboration.

During collaboration, an individual should ideally not reside in one spot on the continuum but move between the two extremes of absolute certainty and absolute uncertainty with a state of comparison somewhere toward the center during the course of the process. One continuously negotiates one's surroundings, questions, compares and draws on what one knows to be true to make assessments about one's own view, others' views, and where one fits into the process. By nature or nurture or both (a debate that cannot be entertained here), all individuals may hold an affinity for some spots on the continuum over others, but our experiences and our analyses of those experiences occur are broadened by using the entire continuum.

Collaborative processes are highly complex, and unlike the parts of an elephant, there can be strong value-based attachments to the views individuals hold. This attachment is an aspect of certainty and therefore a state of

FIGURE 10.1. UNCERTAINTY FRAMEWORK.

Cooperative (Constructive Conflict)	Comparison (Compromise)	Competitive (Destructive Conflict)
Uncertainty	Moderate Certainty	Certainty
	State of Mind	

mind that can lead to destructive conflict when in collaboration. As this chapter will demonstrate, when participants are unable to access the attributes of all parts of the continuum, the process can falter and lead to unsatisfactory results.

I shall outline the characteristics associated with the three points on the continuum illustrated in Figure 10.1. Once facilitators understand the characteristics of the continuum, they can better understand how the attributes of each position can be avoided or taken advantage of as necessary during various stages of the collaborative process.

Certainty

When one is certain that one's view is the right view, all other views are framed using absolute terms of right or wrong. All individuals are regarded as either friend or foe. This degree of certainty is used in the collaborative process when final decisions are made, rules are formed, and agreements are forged. Certainty is required when participants are asked to sign on the dotted line. It is assumed that such certainty is reached individually only if the group achieves the same collective certainty. This is most likely to occur near the end of the process rather than at the beginning.

Burton and Sandole's generic theory of human needs (1986) states that there are fundamental drives based on universal and genetic basic needs, such as the drive for identity, for development, for meaning, and for consistency in response, that need to be satisfied in order for social harmony to exist. Because these needs are deeply held and nonnegotiable, they can prevent the constructive resolution of conflicts when left unsatisfied. In human rights–based disputes, those involving strong moral judgments or the clash of value systems, one is more likely to find participants with certain states of mind and with entrenched positions. It is necessary for process conveners and facilitators to identify when human needs are not being met, as collaboration under such circumstances may not be suitable or possible.

As stated earlier, attachment to viewpoints with the certainty of being right will lead to destructive conflicts. Therefore, power and control techniques or legal intervention to ensure the removal of the perceived cause of conflict are processes that are most often employed to resolve such disputes. Collaboration may be possible via coalition formation between parties with this attachment to their view, as long as all see the issue in the same way. It will more difficult for them to collaborate with others who see the issues from different viewpoints.

Moderate Certainty

Somewhere between absolute certainty and absolute uncertainty lies a midpoint where one compares one's own views of the issues with those of others. By maintaining some degree of attachment to one's own views while also being interested in how they compare to the views of others, relative relationships between views are formed. A gray area of compromise is perceived between the black and white of opposing positions.

Ted Gurr's relative deprivation theory of conflict (1970) is closely associated with this state of mind, which views others from a midpoint between fiend and foe. According to Gurr, if I compare my own wealth with that of someone wealthier than I am, I may feel that my needs are not being met. There is not necessarily a well-defined source of conflict; one is in conflict when one perceives oneself as worse off relative to another party. It is the discrepancy between expectations ("I'm doing just as well as anyone else") and reality that causes the discontent. Often a reframing of the situation, which requires a move toward uncertainty, will lead to a solution. In our example, nothing in one's reality needs to change to restore the feeling of being well-off, only a comparison to individuals who have less rather than more money.

Conflicts from the state of mind that arises from the midpoint of comparison can be constructive or destructive, depending on how they are managed and how the issues are framed. If the parties try to make decisions while in a comparative state of mind, solutions will usually be based in compromise, with settlement on a small area of overlapping interest. If the parties are able to reframe the issues, movement toward the uncertain state of mind could result, which may allow for constructive conflict and more satisfactory outcomes for both parties. If individuals feel threatened, one-upmanship and competitive bargaining could occur as each party tries to gain the upper hand, moving participants toward the certain state of mind and destructive conflict. Compromise, although closer to the ideal objective of collaboration than the win-lose outcomes that result from a certain state of mind, still leaves the elephant somewhat deformed.

Uncertainty

At the other end of the scale from certainty in Figure 10.1 is a state of mind that is uncertain about whether one's own view is absolutely right. If they had been in an uncertain state of mind, the blind men would have realized that they each knew so little about the whole elephant that they should be filled with doubt about the reality of their own experience. Uncertainty allows for the creative process, the questions, and the openness to possibility that is characteristic of constructive conflict. In this uncertain state, there is an attempt to find a collective certainty through the sharing and organization of ideas.

Conflict experienced between uncertain individuals will be frustrating but, with enough time, constructive. Acknowledged will be the reality that no one has the right answer but collectively it might be found. It is the time-consuming nature of conflicts based in uncertainty, especially when the situation is urgent, that makes them uncomfortable.

Similar to other points on the continuum, uncertainty has negative attributes. Extreme uncertainty is too chaotic to be constructive, and continual uncertainty is often viewed as nihilistic. Although uncertainty provides opportunities for learning and the sharing of information, it can be limiting and frustrating for individuals in a collaborative process to stay uncertain all the time. If the ultimate goal behind collaboration is reaching a joint decision or coming to consensus, then certainty would need to be reached, collectively, eventually.

Diversity of Perspective

There are many models of personality type and analysis of worldviews, including Wilber's *Theory of Everything* (2000), Hofstede's *Culture's Consequences* (2001), and, Graves's *Levels of Human Existence* (2002), categorizing individuals and cultures according to their preferences and predispositions, but one factor will remain constant throughout and across cultures: every individual and group that comes into a collaborative process will be different. In addition, every individual could be positioned anywhere on the continuum of uncertainty. One person may feel certain that his or her position is absolutely right on some issues, may be full of comparison on others, and may be open to questioning on a third issue. Therefore, an individual's distinct view, attachment to that view as the only right view, and degree of engagement with individuals with other views should vary throughout the process, from time to time and issue to issue.

There will be times when each state of mind is a completely appropriate way of addressing an issue. For example, consistent with the need to be certain, each blind man would need to remember the distinctness of his own part of the animal in order for it to be accurately included in the final result. Certainty of right and wrong in such cases is understandable and necessary. Consistent with the need to assess things through relationship, each blind man would need to consider how his piece of the elephant compares to the others and the whole. Trunk feelers and tail feelers would need to compare notes to decide whether they had different parts of the animal or if they had simply experienced the same part differently. Consistent with the need to be uncertain, each blind man would need to consider the possibility that his experience is limited and that others may have perspectives that need to be sought out.

Many collaborative processes arise as a result of the uncertain nature of questions being addressed. Stakeholders are asked to contribute their experience and knowledge toward a collaborative process as a means of determining the bigger picture when decisions need to be made about issues of joint impact that hold elements of uncertainty.

Process conveners and facilitators need to ascertain, case by case, whether collaboration is an appropriate method for addressing the issue at hand. Through conflict assessment or stakeholder assessment, the assessor would identify the relevant stakeholders, map their interests, determine areas of agreement and disagreement, and explore the parties' willingness and ability to collaborate (Susskind and Thomas-Larmer, 1999). Once it has been established by all that collaboration is appropriate, a process will need to be designed that will enable the participants to use the whole continuum of uncertainty through to certainty, as necessary, so that ideas can be shared and agreement reached.

Changing States of Mind

William Isaacs (1999, p. 34) points out that "two habits . . . , losing respect for and so rejecting what is uncomfortable and unfamiliar, and becoming fixated on one's own certainties, pervade human consciousness."

Due to the number of parties involved, their various viewpoints and states of mind, and the number of issues that may be in question, a collaborative process could be described as a complex system (Kimball, Silber, and Weinstein,

2005). It is complex because of the diversity of elements that are present, and it is a system because of the interconnectedness or interdependence of each of the collaborating groups or individuals (Zimmerman, Lindberg, and Plsek, 1998).

According to complexity science, small changes can have a significant effect on complex systems as a result of this diversity and interconnectedness. The behavior of one individual can set off a chain reaction of events that will make or break the effectiveness of a collaborative process. Each individual continuously negotiates his or her own view in relation to the whole system as changes occur. Whether these changes serve to move individuals into new states of mind or fix them into a certain state of mind will depend on the dynamics of each situation.

Human behavior is assisted by feedback mechanisms that cause an individual to correct his or her behavior until whatever is necessary to attain a desired goal is attained. In positive feedback, the outcome reinforces one's behavior by reflecting expectations. In negative feedback, the outcome differs from what was expected, and so the behavior becomes modified to better attain the desired goal (Zimmerman, Lindberg, and Plsek, 1998).

Facilitators need to sense how to design the process to support or negate the different states of mind that are required during the different phases of collaboration. What type of feedback would reinforce or encourage uncertainty, comparison, or certainty? By using structure and competitive techniques, or through simple rules and the avoidance of overstructured processes (Kimball, Silber, and Weinstein, 2005), the desired degrees of certainty can be reinforced. According to Deutsch (2000), the process should actively reflect and support constructive conflict through cooperation between individuals. The process must not reward destructive conflict and competitive behavior.

Moving Toward Certainty

Zimmerman, Lindberg, and Plsek (1998) describe a self-fulfilling prophecy as a "vicious circle in a social system that takes place when an expectation . . . leads to actions culminating in results that serve to confirm the validity of the original expectation" (p. 270). This type of positive feedback can lead those who are competitive, with a certain state of mind, to dominate the collaborative process as they push their view and agenda forward as the one that is right. Their behavior, domination, is mirroring their certainty and need to be right. Because of the feedback and complexity of the system, the result of this behavior by some parties will become a movement toward the certain state of mind for all parties as they all start to compete for a piece of the pie. For those who win, attachment to certainty and the use of means and processes that demand certainty are reinforced. For those on the losing side, such a negative experience during collaboration, which is labeled as being socially progressive or inclusive, creates a breakdown or disengagement. When win-lose outcomes dominate a collaborative process, participants may feel worse off than if they had not participated at all (see Chapter Two of this book). Collaboration cannot be successful when it is avoided by those who are fearful of being taken advantage of and dominated by those who are making a pretense of it to attain the upper hand or push forward their agenda.

Highly structured processes are sometimes used when groups are in conflict. In such processes, participants are often expected to conform to the structure, avoiding conflict and attempting to reach resolution as soon as possible. Participants are often encouraged to set differences aside rather than expose each other to the discomforts of uncertainty that may arise from diversity of experience and perspective. Such service to structure can box participants in to their respective viewpoints. By contrast, in less structured, more emergent processes, time is spent up front exploring differences, and attempts to jump to conclusions or find answers are initially avoided.

The use of competitive techniques or high degrees of structure encourages certainty. The reinforcement of certainty, if it is to occur at all, should be controlled, consensually agreed to, and inclusive during collaboration. If achieved mindfully, collective certainty toward the end of the process will be beneficial to all participants. Formal signed agreements and contracts enforce the certainty of view that has been jointly attained.

Moving Toward Uncertainty

Fisher and Ury (1981; Fisher, Ury, and Paton, 1991) popularized the concept of separating the people from the problem in order to move individuals from focusing on their positions to focusing on their interests. As a result of focusing on interests, the individuals are moved from a competitive, position-based state of mind to a cooperative, interest-based one. Movement from position to interests is an example of a technique that helps people see the bigger picture into which they and their views fit. By reframing positions as interests, those who are locked in comparison can attain a higher degree of uncertainty, thereby opening them up to learning more about other points of view.

By avoiding the uncertainty inherent in collaboration, a false sense of certainty can arise. For this the false sense of certainty to be eliminated, the true uncertainty of the collaborative process needs to be more evident. According to Hofstede (2001), individuals who are attached to certainty may also be avoiding uncertainty. He claims that such avoidance is associated with laws, rules, regulations, controls, and less readily accepting change. Through the removal of heavy process structure and controlling or competitive processes, the reinforcement that comes from such structures is diminished. If simple rules and light structures keep participants away from the chaos and nihilism that comes from extreme and extended uncertainty, all will benefit from the creativity that emerges (Kimball, Silber, and Weinstein, 2005). With processes that encourage and enforce uncertainty, in which no individual is allowed to be absolutely right, individuals will need to let go of the certainty that their view is absolutely right in order to meet the collective process goals.

Using Uncertainty to Reach Agreement

Figure 10.2 shows the relationship between the degree of agreement within the group and the degree of individuals' certainty that their view is absolutely right. The certainty of the rightness of one's view and agreement within a collaborative process lead to constructive or destructive conflict, creative questions or solutions, or compromise.

During conflict within a collaborative process, the parties to the conflict are in the upper half of Figure 10.2. Whether they are certain that they are right and others are wrong or uncertain as to the rightness or wrongness of their viewpoint would determine whether they are likely to engage in constructive or destructive conflict with those with differing viewpoints. The horizontal movement from certainty to uncertainty will allow for sharing and creativity.

The right-hand side of Figure 10.2 shows the downward movement toward agreement through the constructive conflict of uncertain states of mind. Moving into uncertainty before moving to agreement is necessary in order for the solutions to benefit from the diversity within the collaborative process.

Any attempts at reaching agreement too soon (downward movement on the left-hand side of Figure 10.2) would result in destructive conflict that leads to win-lose rather than win-win outcomes.

FIGURE 10.2. DEGREE OF INDIVIDUAL CERTAINTY AND GROUP AGREEMENT.

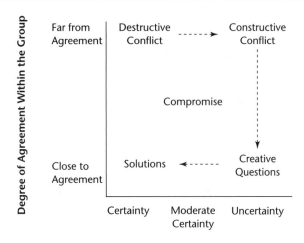

Degree of Individual Certainty (State of Mind)

Source: Adapted with permission from Stacey, 1996.

Downward movement from the center of Figure 10.2, when process participants are in a moderately certain and comparative state of mind, would lead to compromise.

The bottom half of Figure 10.2 shows the horizontal movement toward certainty from uncertainty that occurs near the end of the process when all are in agreement that the collective view that was created through the process is the one they want to sign off on.

For example, if the blind men were part of a facilitated collaborative process, the discussions might begin with all individuals feeling rather certain that their experience of the elephant is accurate (top left of Figure 10.2). Eventually, after initial discussions, they may all find themselves in a state of extreme uncertainty and even disbelief that they are all talking about the same animal (top right of the figure). After some constructive conflict and further information sharing, they may find themselves somewhere in the middle of Figure 10.2 as trunk feelers and tail feelers compare notes to see if their experience was the same or different. Through facilitated reframing, they decide to stay open to the possibility of both being right awhile longer. Each swing into uncertainty provides additional information to each blind man so that any swing back into certainty is accompanied by a change in view that incorporates some of the new information that was received, with agreement between the men coming ever closer. Toward the end of the process (bottom right of Figure 10.2), all would agree that certainty could be reached collectively through additional information sharing and possibly joint information searches. No blind man will leave the process with the same certainty that he entered with. The movement from uncertainty about what an elephant is toward collective certainty will follow, so that that the final picture is the amalgam that they created together.

Should a move toward certainty be attempted too soon through high degrees of structure such as the early drafting of formal agreements or though competitive behavior between participants, it is possible that any agreements reached will not accurately reflect the full diversity of the group. Such agreements could be short-lived or ineffective. Collaboration between interdependent parties is not always just about reaching a collective viewpoint. Collaboration can also be about building relationships between stakeholders and enabling them to learn from one another and learn together about the diversity of viewpoints they hold on a variety of issues. By broadening each participant's view of the issues at hand, trust can be created so that long-term relationships can be formed. The conflicts become resolved not though agreement or certainty but rather through relationship building and mutual understanding. As Roger Fisher (2000, p. 179) has noted, "Conflict resolution involves transforming the relationship and situation such that solutions developed by the parties are sustainable and self-correcting in the long run. Conflict and the relationships in which it is embedded must be transformed in an enduring fashion. . . . Conflict resolution thus does not imply assimilation or homogenization, although members of distinct identity groups may share a political or national identity as well; but it does imply a mosaic of integrated social groups, cooperating independently for mutual benefit."

Creating a Culture of Collaboration

According to William Isaacs (1999, p. 19), "Thinking together implies that you no longer take your own position as final. You relax your grip on certainty and listen to the possibilities that result from being in a relationship with others, possibilities that might not otherwise have occurred."

Small changes can have large effects. The context in which the collaborative process takes place or the climate in the room can have a dramatic impact on how the process unfolds. "Climate is a quality of the field as a whole. As such, it pervades all thought and action in the situation; it gives a 'flavor'— for example, of warmth, safety, fear, or distrust—to everything that happens" (Folger, Poole, and Stutman, 2001, p. 58). A climate of collaboration would be a climate in which the subtle balance between the uncertainty and the certainty in the room is palpable. Participants acknowledge the need for mindful movement between certainty and uncertainty, the need to stay uncertain until all information and views have been shared, and the awareness that attempts to reach agreement prematurely could lead to destructive conflicts. In such a climate, participants will find it easier to avoid certainty until all the diversity has been revealed.

Process facilitators have the ability to design collaborative processes that allow this collaborative climate to be created. The focus on asking questions rather than coming up with solutions—needs to be maintained until all participants in the process agree to move toward certainty and conclusion. (For an additional point of view, see Chapter Thirteen of this book.) Communication and understanding of diverse views through dialogue could be encouraged. Openness to receiving new information by way of joint information searches and educational workshops can be promoted. By encouraging the parties to come together repeatedly over time without needing to reach agreement on any specific facts or solutions until sufficient trust has been built to allow certainties to be loosened and joint problem solving to be managed in a collaborative manner.

Cooperation for mutual benefit over the long term is the most important aspect of collaboration. If collaborative process participants can learn from each other, their awareness of the relationship between their own view and the views of others will increase. They will see the issues in conflict differently, mindful of the limitations of their isolated views. "Creative engagement in deep and persistent identity-driven conflict begins when all sides can give voice to their essential concerns and can hear and recognize the essential concerns of the other side as well" (Rothman, 1997, p. 8). Exchanging ideas contributes to the expansion of views, individually and collectively leading to more sustainable outcomes. This is the collaborative process.

Bertrand Russell said, "About three-quarters of the evils from which the world is suffering spring from the fact that people feel certainty in matters as to which they ought to feel doubt" (1997, p. 348). Through exposure to different points of view in a climate that acknowledges and supports uncertainty, a collaborative culture can be created.

References

Burton, J., and Sandole, D. "Generic Theory: The Basis of Conflict Resolution." *Negotiation Journal*, 1986, *2*, 333–344.

Conca, K. "Greening the United Nations: Environmental Organizations and the UN System." *Third World Quarterly*, 1995, *16*, 441–457.

Dalai Lama, "Public Talk: Universal Responsibility" [http://events.onlinebroadcasting.com/dalailama/042004/index2.php?page=launch]. Apr. 24, 2004.

Deutsch, M. *The Resolution of Conflict: Constructive and Destructive Processes.* New Haven, Conn.: Yale University Press, 1973.

Deutsch, M. "Cooperation and Competition." In M. Deutsch and P. Coleman (eds.), *The Handbook of Conflict Resolution: Theory and Practice.* San Francisco: Jossey-Bass, 2000.

Eden, C., and Huxham, C. "The Negotiation of Purpose in Multiorganizational Collaborative Groups." *Journal of Management Studies*, 2001, *38*, 373–391.

Fisher, R. J. "Intergroup Conflict." In M. Deutsch and P. Coleman (eds.), *The Handbook of Conflict Resolution: Theory and Practice.* San Francisco: Jossey-Bass, 2000.

Fisher, R. J., and Ury, W. *Getting to Yes: Negotiating Agreement Without Giving In.* Boston: Houghton Mifflin, 1981.

Fisher, R. J., Ury, W. L., and Paton, B. *Getting to Yes: Negotiating Agreement Without Giving In.* (2nd ed.) Harmondsworth, England: Penguin Books, 1991.

Folger, J. P., Poole, M. S., and Stutman, R. K. *Working Through Conflict.* (4th ed.) New York: Longman, 2001.

Graves, C. W. *Levels of Human Existence.* Santa Barbara, Calif.: EXLET, 2002.

Gray, B. *Collaborating: Finding Common Ground for Multiparty Problems.* San Francisco: Jossey-Bass, 1991.

Gurr, T. R. *Why Men Rebel.* Princeton, N.J.: Princeton University Press, 1970.

Hofstede, G. *Culture's Consequences: Comparing Values, Behaviors, Institutions, and Organizations Across Nations.* Thousand Oaks, Calif.: Sage, 2001.

Isaacs, W. *Dialogue and the Art of Thinking Together.* New York: Currency/Doubleday, 1999.

Kimball, L., Silber, T., and Weinstein, N. "Dynamic Facilitation: Design Principles from the New Science of Complexity." In S. P. Schuman (ed.), *International Association of Facilitators Handbook of Group Facilitation.* San Francisco: Jossey-Bass, 2005.

Maier, N.R.F. "Assets and Liabilities in Group Problem Solving: The Need for an Integrative Function." *Psychological Review*, 1967, *74*, 239–249.

Rex, J. "Ethnic Identity and the Nation-State: The Political Sociology of Multicultural Societies." *Social Identities*, 1995, *1*, 21–34.

Rothman, J. *Resolving Identity-Based Conflict in Nations, Organizations, and Communities.* San Francisco: Jossey-Bass, 1997.

Russell, B. *Last Philosophical Testament, 1943–1968.* London: Routledge, 1997.

Stacey, R. D. *Strategic Management and Organizational Dynamics.* (4th ed.) London: Pearson, 1996.

Susskind, L., and Thomas-Larmer, J. "Conducting a Conflict Assessment." In L. Susskind, S. McKearnan, and J. Thomas-Larmer (eds.), *The Consensus-Building Handbook: A Comprehensive Guide to Reaching Agreement.* Thousand Oaks, Calif.: Sage, 1999.

Thomas, K. "Thomas-Kilmann Conflict Mode Instrument." In M. Dunnett (ed.), *The Handbook of Industrial and Organizational Psychology.* Chicago: Rand McNally, 1975.

Wilber, K. *A Theory of Everything.* Boston: Shambhala, 2000.

Zimmerman, B., Lindberg, C., and Plsek, P. *Edgeware: Insights from Complexity Science for Health Care Leaders.* Irving, Tex.: VHA, 1998.

Dale Hunter is a group facilitator and author in the field of facilitation. She is a founder and director of Zenergy Ltd., a New Zealand–based company providing facilitation, mediation, and coaching services. She is the principal coauthor of *The Art of Facilitation, The Zen of Groups, Co-operacy: A New Way of Being at Work,* and *The Essence of Facilitation* (also published under the title *Handling Groups in Action: The Use of Distinctions in Facilitation*). Hunter's doctoral thesis, titled "Facilitation of Sustainable Co-operative Processes in Organisations," includes a cooperative inquiry by facilitators and a survey of facilitators' values and ethics. Hunter has facilitated and trained group facilitators in Africa, Asia, Europe, and North America, as well as in New Zealand and Australia. She facilitated at the 2002 World Summit on Sustainable Development in Johannesburg, serves as vice-chair international on the board of directors of the International Association of Facilitators, and is a trustee of Heart Politics New Zealand.

CHAPTER ELEVEN

SUSTAINABLE COOPERATIVE PROCESSES IN ORGANIZATIONS

Dale Hunter

Groups and group processes are dynamic—they exist and change in both time and space. Through widening our awareness to include groups, organizations, societies, and the natural environment and through mentally encompassing time spans beyond the short term, collaborative endeavors become more than a fragmented series of disconnected acts. Our projects become more consciously part of the tapestry of unfolding human activity on the planet.

Such a holistic awareness gives access to rich sources of information that can assist us in becoming wiser and more effective facilitators, participants, and leaders. This awareness is embedded in the core values of the International Association of Facilitators (IAF) and its code of ethics (2004). The IAF core values are inclusiveness, global scope, participation, celebration, innovative form, and social responsibility. This chapter explores environmental sustainability (caring for our planetary home) as an essential prerequisite for social responsibility and ethical cooperative processes. In this context, sustainability does not mean longevity per se, without regard to other consequences.

The author thanks Catherine Lane West-Newman, Hamish Brown, Stephen Thorpe, and Zooey Neumann for their helpful questions and suggestions. Stephen Thorpe also provided valuable technical support.

Group Context

Groups are collections of individual people who exist in their own right as autonomous beings. They have a physical form, identities and personalities, families and friends, networks and circles of influence. They are connected with physical places (home or living space and places of work, recreation, and worship). As well as individuals in it, a group also has a "life," which exists through relationship and communication.

Groups are part of individual, organizational, and community life; a group comes together to achieve a particular purpose. Groups vary in size from two people to many and are located within a context—often an organizational fabric of some kind. They may have a particular meeting or workplace, a variety of meeting places, or in the case of virtual groups, many widely dispersed physical environments from which group members log into virtual group discussions. The group is a particular configuration in the dynamic web of relationships that constitute an organization, a community, and a society. The assumption underlying my discussion is that each individual and group is a connected and interacting part of the whole web of life, ultimately part of the ecology of our planet.

Although it is possible to work with a group without taking into account its wider context, if we do so, we miss the opportunity to be fully effective. It would be like gardening by attending only to the readily visible parts of the plants and ignoring the roots, soil, water, air flows, adjacent plants, and coexisting species. The garden environment (including all the plants) is an ecosystem, and the study of the relationships of organisms to their environment is known as ecology. The discipline that concerns itself with the relationships of human society and with the rest of the planetary ecology is known as social ecology (Hill, 1999, 2005).

Group facilitators make choices about the work we do, what clients we work with, and when, where, and how we work. These choices are based on our own personal (and professional) values, beliefs, relationships, commitments, and needs—our own context. Consider the diagram in Figure 11.1. Locate yourself at the center of the diagram. Choose an issue of interest to you personally. See how far you can go in noting your awareness of that issue from the perspective of each band. Note how your perspective alters as you extend yourself into the farther-out bands.

FIGURE 11.1 CONTEXT AWARENESS.

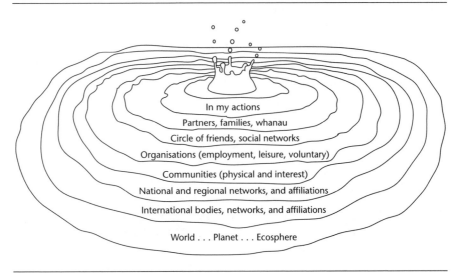

In my actions
Partners, families, whanau
Circle of friends, social networks
Organisations (employment, leisure, voluntary)
Communities (physical and interest)
National and regional networks, and affiliations
International bodies, networks, and affiliations

World . . . Planet . . . Ecosphere

Note: Whanau is Maori for extended family.
Source: Courtesy of Zenergy Ltd.

Now locate a group relevant to you toward the center of the diagram. Consider the group purpose and an issue it is facing. Envisage the context of the group. Note how your view of the group alters as you consider the group's place within the whole organization of which it is part, then the community, national and regional affiliations, and the world or ecosphere.

Now imagine an organization with a number of groups that are internal and also external to it, all interacting with and influencing one another and forming and reforming in dynamic interplay. Consider how an expanded awareness of these dynamics might influence your presence in and approach to relating to or working with these groups.

A Sustainable Context for Organizations

Facilitators usually work with groups that are part of larger organizations. Most organizations are experiencing growing pressure to become more socially and environmentally responsible. Organizational responses to these challenges have included the development and introduction of triple-bottom-line accounting systems where social and environmental effects are factored into profitability along with economic considerations (Elkington, 1998).

Contributing to new thinking for a sustainable society, Milbrath (1996) argues that top priority must be given to the good functioning of the whole ecosystem and second priority must be given to the good functioning of our society. Only when these two are viable is it permissible to seek quality of life in individualistic ways we may choose. He also argues that it is a mistake to give top priority to economic values, because this would lead to sacrificing vital life systems at a time when the increasing world population needs those life systems even more. The core values he affirms are love and compassion, justice, security, and self-realization. "A sustainable society extends love and compassion not only to those near and dear but to people in other lands, future generations, and other species. It recognises the intricate web of relationships that bind all living creatures into a common destiny. Life is not mainly conflict and competition between creatures; rather a sustainable society emphasizes partnership rather than domination; co-operation more than competition; love more than power" (Milbrath, 1996, p. 190).

This model, as shown in Figure 11.2, places life as a viable ecosystem at the center. The viability of the ecosystem underpins the core social values and is a necessary prerequisite to the good functioning of society. The outer rings further elaborate on the core values.

Futurists such as Barbara Marx Hubbard (1998), Hazel Henderson (1996), and Sohail Inayatullah (1999) are developing a context for conscious ethical evolution in which we can all play a part in a cocreative society. Hubbard believes that sustainable, life-affirming designs will emerge through the efforts of those who are part of the social potential movement. In the area of business, she describes the goal as conscious evolution and calls on businesses and entrepreneurs to apply their genius to the development of socially responsible businesses and investments. "The goal is a sustainable, regenerative economy that supports restoration of the environment, preservation of species, and the enhancement of human creativity and community, including expanded ownership, network marketing, community-based currencies, microcredit loans, and other such innovations" (Hubbard, 1998, p. 89).

Henderson (1996) stresses the need to redesign all our systems in a bottom-to-top design revolution. We should, she says, reshape our production, agricul-

FIGURE 11.2. A PROPOSED VALUE STRUCTURE FOR A SUSTAINABLE SOCIETY.

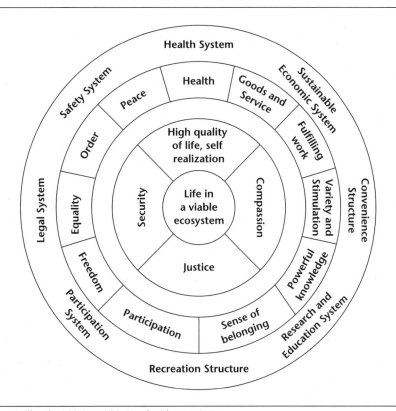

Source: Milbrath, 1996, p. 189. Used with permission.

ture, architecture, academic disciplines, governments, and companies to align them with nature's productive processes in a new search for suitable, humane, and ecologically sustainable societies. Henderson discusses the important role of reliable sustainability indicators to assist with this transition.

Jared Diamond explores such indicators in his book *Collapse: How Societies Choose to Fail or Survive* (2004). This in-depth analysis of a number of ancient and modern societies and why they failed identifies twelve significant environmental factors that need to be addressed. Diamond believes that present societies can survive if humans have the courage to practice long-term thinking and are willing to make bold, courageous, anticipatory decisions at a time when problems become perceptible but before they have reached crisis proportions. He also points out that another crucial choice is the courage to make painful decisions about values. He asks, "Which of the values that formerly served a society well can be continued to be maintained under new changed circumstances? Which of those treasured values must instead be jettisoned and replaced with different approaches?" (pp. 522–523).

Purpose, Values, and Ethics

The developing vision of a sustainable society can be taken as a context for facilitators and others working collaboratively.

Collaborative processes can be used in a wide variety of ways, for good or for ill. There is ample historical evidence that people can and do work cooperatively to wage war, pursue genocide, and destroy the environment. This raises important questions for facilitators and participants, such as what the purpose is for using a particular collaborative process and how the outcomes will be used. For example, if a group process would damage a person or the social fabric or diminish the ecological sustainability of an environment, it may be unethical to use it.

Individuals, whether group facilitators, leaders, or members, need to check the alignment of their personal values with the purposes of the groups and organizations with which they work (Birch, 1990). Without such alignment checking, congruence issues may remain unconscious, and anxiety and uneasiness may not be recognized as symptoms of deep disquiet. Purpose and values determine acceptable behavior, and this is what ethics is about—the alignment of purpose, values, and behavior. Because ethical use of processes involves making judgments about what and where one takes some action and when and how one does it, it can be regarded as limiting for some. Also, it can mean that one needs to become engaged in issues that are not clear-cut. Indeed, one recognizes many areas as gray.

People's understandings, definitions, values, and contexts differ, and so different choices will be made regarding the meaning of sustainability and social responsibility. But this does not mean that we should or can avoid action. Most activities involve ethical issues of some kind, whether we are conscious of them or not. We each need to become more conscious of such considerations and act on our developing understanding.

Group Development

As well as existing within in a context, group life and processes exist in time. They are dynamic and organic and subject to fluctuations and cycles, which can (like the seasons of weather and life cycles of plants and animals) be analyzed and mapped. Such process (or development) maps include the well-known forming, storming, norming, performing, and adjourning sequence of Bruce Tuckman (1965; Tuckman and Jensen, 1977) and Scott Peck's (1987) cyclical community-building model (pseudocommunity, conflict and chaos, emptiness, and authentic community).

Reflecting on the group development literature in an IAF journal, George Smith (2001) considers twenty-four group development models, categorizing them into three types and critiquing each model according to its usefulness. Finding that some of the models were more flexible, adaptable, and capable of dealing with a dynamic world than others, he favors those that emphasize that groups are open systems that are embedded in larger organizations and environments.

The FACTS Model

As part of my doctoral research, I undertook a cooperative inquiry with a group of facilitators on the topic of facilitating sustainable cooperative processes in organizations (Hunter, 2003). The model presented here developed as I reflected on the collective findings of that cooperative inquiry.

This model takes the form of a spiraling cycle and explains group development over time. It begins with the individual choice to be part of a cooperative process and with the commitment and willingness this entails to take on individual accountability. The alignment of group intention follows, and then the process of becoming congruent is expressed through clarifying purpose, values, and action. The conflict that arises as group members seek to become congruent with their intention is worked through with authentic and compassionate sharing toward life-enhancing and synergistic outcomes. The model seeks to honor individual autonomy and interpersonal cooperation and shows how facilitators and groups can check for alignment of purpose and values for individuals, the group, the organization, and the social and physical environment.

The FACTS model is illustrated in Figure 11.3 in the form of a repeating sequence of steps or spiral. A repeating spiral is an effective image for an organic evolving pattern, also described as "the basic universal tendency to attract, fuse, and liberate" (Ritter, 2001). Spirals are a natural organic form and have been used widely in art and literature as well as science. Relevant examples include Beck and Cowan's work in spiral dynamics (1995) and use of the spiral by Joseph Campbell (1988) and by Jean Houston (1993) to demonstrate mythic human processes.

FIGURE 11.3. FACTS MODEL FOR SUSTAINABLE COOPERATIVE PROCESSES.

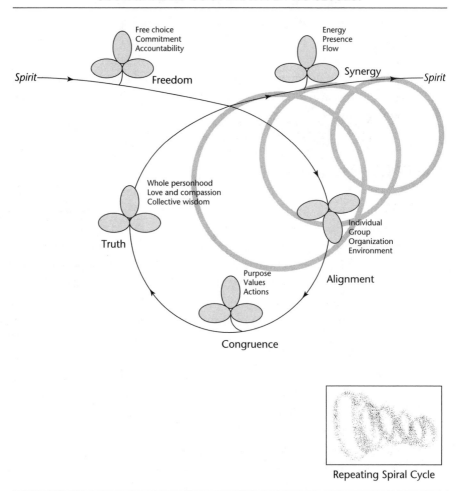

Repeating Spiral Cycle

The FACTS model summarizes five key factors that are crucial to addressing the sustainability of cooperative processes. I have defined these as *freedom, alignment, congruence, truth,* and *synergy,* forming the acronym FACTS. Each key factor glosses a set of related factors. The FACTS model offers a way to diagnose and guide the development of a group over time. As a diagnostic tool, it can be used to uncover what is missing or needs further development for a group to flourish. Let us take a closer look at each of the five key aspects.

Freedom

Ethical facilitation uses processes that enhance free and informed choice, commitment, and accountability (Hunter and Thorpe, 2005). People who take part in cooperative processes must do so freely, without coercion or fear of reprisal. Relevant information is needed for participants to make informed choices. Internal commitment to choice leads to responsibility and willingness to be accountable for one's actions.

Alignment

For the group process to be effective, all involved need to be aligned with the intention of the cooperative process and how it fits in the organizational or multiorganizational setting. Alignment involves the individual, group, and organization and the consistency of the intentions of each. In addition, alignment includes connectedness with the wider social, physical, and natural environment. Intentions may be expressed as shared vision, mission, and goals or a statement of intent. For sustainability to be achieved, the intention must extend to the health of the environment and the whole planet. The intention of the group becomes potent when it is expressed as a clear, concise written statement of purpose containing one main idea.

Congruence

For a group process to be effective, congruence is needed between the group's purpose, values, beliefs, assumptions, culture, and actions. These can be fully conscious, partly conscious, or even unconscious. Key group values may be expressed in ground rules, group agreements, charters, actions, codes of practice, and even images, such as logos. Actions include spoken and written words and individual and group behaviors.

Decreasing the distance between what we believe, what we say, and what we do is the domain of ethics and the "daily delicious fight to be congruent" (Maheshananda, 1999). This aspect of group life is likely to involve self-reflection, challenging of one another, and changes in behavior. Facilitators are useful in enabling people to receive feedback without defensiveness and make behavioral changes required for the group to be congruent with its purpose and values.

Truth

As used here, truth encompasses whole-person learning (Rogers, 1994), love and compassion, and collective wisdom. Personal development can provide access to embodied whole personhood through dissolving and reframing unhelpful conditioned, patterned behavior. Experiencing all aspects of ourselves, including a wide range of emotions, without fragmentation and dissociation, allows us to connect with love and compassion to self, other persons, groups, cultures, other species, and the whole cosmos or transplanetary field (Heron, 1999). Speaking individual truth and working through the conflicts that ensue takes the group to a deeper, more potent level, which in turn propels the group forward toward synergy.

Sensitively facilitated cooperative processes can enhance individual access to personal truth and enable the expression of collective wisdom in the group.

Synergy

When a group is aligned, congruent, and truthful, more energy will become available. Energy will be released and enhanced. Participants will become more present, attentive, and aware, and the group will experience a sense of "flowing with" (Csikszentmihalyi, 1990) as distinct from struggling and striving. Synergy is the experience of collective energy and of the sum being greater than the parts. This energy is available to an aligned, congruent, and truthful group.

The Flow of Spirit

Form follows spirit (Owen, 1994). "Spirit cannot be bought, ordered, directed. It responds positively to a very different treatment called *inspiration*" (p. 48). You may refer to spirit as God or higher purpose, depending on your belief system. Cooperative processes are the forms that follow the spirit of cooperative endeavor or "co-operacy" (Hunter, Bailey, and Taylor, 1997). Noticing spirit at work requires awareness. Following spirit requires intention and rigor.

Often spirit is most easily perceived through its shadow, which highlights unhelpful, conditioned behavior, distress from the past, and fear of the future. Encountering the individual, group, and collective shadow material is the work of everyone who seeks awareness and consciousness. The cooperative spirit moves through cooperative processes and is an expression of the desire to experience ways of being and doing that nourish the value of the individual and the collective wisdom of the group.

If freedom, alignment, congruence, and truth are present, synergy will become available, and spirit will continue to flow. The cycle of sustainability will continue and grow as a spiral. All the FACTS require ongoing attention and rigor. Embodied whole persons speaking their truth with love and compassion is the prerequisite for the achievement of sustainability. If we are going to generate a sustainable world, then, the fear and "pragmatism" in most organizations must be challenged.

Using the FACTS Model

The FACTS model was developed for facilitators to use while they are facilitating. Here are some reflections by facilitators using the model (Hunter, 2003).

Using the model in an organizational workshop to assist the forty participants understand their conflicted organizational context, Hamish Brown found that the model helped the participants identify their own areas of weakness. The aspects of the FACTS model identified as missing or weak in the organization were freedom and alignment. In relation to freedom, "people were not able to choose, given that they did not have the correct information about the management stance" regarding the issue in conflict. He also commented on finding the metamodel useful both as a sequential cycle and as a means of identifying how to maintain synergy once achieved.

Hazel Hodgkin noticed while facilitating a policy meeting for a political party that there was not full alignment with the purpose of the day. Two people expressed early on their unhappiness with the preagreed group purpose, and one of them became involved in a direct conflict with another participant later in the day. Hodgkin believed the two participants' lack of alignment influenced their ability to participate fully and cooperatively in the meeting discussions.

Hodgkin reflected that she could have worked more with alignment of the participants, particularly at the beginning of the day. She also believed that she might have usefully watched for opportunities to increase the level of honesty and emotions, where appropriate. However, she believed that there was sufficient freedom, alignment, and congruence for significant synergy to emerge at the end of the meeting. Reflecting on synergy, Hodgkin saw this as something for which she strived: "If it happens, it is almost always an indication of a successful facilitation. However, if it does not happen, it does not necessarily mean a lack of success. Lack of synergy may just mean that some other work was done by the group that still needs more processing before being fully worked through" (Hunter, 2003, p. 229).

Sarah McGhee facilitated a women's collective involved in health issues and noted that the key issues here were around alignment and congruence, particularly congruence between values and behaviors. McGhee's approach to moving the group forward included naming the incongruent behaviors and invoking the spirit of the organization. "I stood for being a collective of women with values (such as equity, empowerment, advocacy, love and safety) who were working on behalf of a multi-cultural community. I confronted them when I saw their behaviours didn't match what they were up to" (Hunter, 2003, p. 229). Because the group had developed sufficient trust prior to the confrontation and had faith in the facilitator, group members were able to move into speaking their own truth. "By the afternoon we had named the 'elephant' as issues around power, old systems that didn't work and history of personal attacks" (p. 229).

Reflecting on the model, McGhee supposed that there is a skill base involved in using it, in particular, when to intervene and on what basis. She wondered how one learned to listen for the key issues rather than little issues. She then went on to answer her own question by adding, "Once I tapped into the spirit of the organization as a community-based service, then I was able to see what really mattered and needed to be attended to. I have learnt this from being around Maori, Pacific Island, African and Maltese cultures. If the spirit is missing then there is always a potential danger of the facilitator becoming oppressive" (Hunter, 2003, p. 230).

Another facilitator, Catherine Lane West-Newman, in an academic setting, critiqued a daylong organizational retreat she had attended as a participant. She considered it an example of an event that was not able to achieve synergy and on reflection saw that none of the FACTS were well represented. Her vignette included the following reflections:

- *Freedom.* Most people did not want to be there. Commitment to achieve co-operative processes and collective outcomes were drastically lacking in some cases and lukewarm in others—at least partly because of a history of failed meetings of this kind.
- *Alignment.* No alignment existed before the meeting and none was achieved. The group decided to proceed directly to the task that the two [leaders] perceived had to be done. The facilitator was explicitly prevented from doing anything in the way of a warm-up or check-in because these are "touchy-feely" and not appropriate [for this profession]. Also, the past history of tears, tantrums, and terrorizing do not allow these people to want to expose themselves to each other.
- *Congruence.* Each individual at the meeting had their own purposes, values, and desires. In general each perceived that achieving their own goals and establishing themselves as the most important person there could only be done by thwarting everyone else, embarrassing and even humiliating them if necessary in the process. It might even be said that there was an active will present to prevent congruence. Tears, accusations, complaints, dragging up past histories all contributed to the atmosphere of isolated and frustrated human entities. People claimed what they wanted. One person walked out. As the loudest complainers got what they wanted others subsided into resentful silence. The facilitator's attempts to reframe problems and processes were simply firmly opposed and suppressed by those who had not wanted to have her there in the first place.
- *Truth* was the victim on the day. In fact some people's truths were spoken very loudly indeed but no collective or sustainable truth was allowed to emerge. Whole personhood, love and compassion, collective wisdom? Wash your mouth out.
- *Synergy.* Well, no. Energy, presence, flow? Inertia, absence, lumpy resentment and fear. A list of who would be doing what (more or less un-willingly) in the year to come. And dread that it will have to happen all over again next January. This is the very particular hell of non-co-operative processes in a large organization [Hunter, 2003, pp. 230–231].

This critique illustrates, perhaps even more graphically than the positive earlier critiques, the importance of attending to the FACTS for effective cooperative processes.

Time, Space, and Presence

Holding the awareness and appreciation of group context and group development (space and time) may seem at first to be a mental challenge. However, it is not necessary to reconcile these two dimensions but rather to hold the context open (like a wide cinema screen showing a broad landscape) and allow the group action to take place in that space (an intimate drama played out in an expansive vista). Then the expanded space may occur as a spacious, multidimensional, and dynamic interplay of color, change, and movement. A way to achieve this expansion is through accessing expanded consciousness or "presence."

This involves becoming present to oneself first and then consciously expanding one's senses and awareness outward in all directions to include all the group members, the room, and the locality (including any natural features such as trees and water) and also opening oneself to connect with the energies and spirit of the place. The connecting energy is that of compassion and love (through an appreciation of each of the individuals and the whole group as they are at that moment, keeping in mind the development phase of the group), engaging with participants and the group as a whole with a heartful yet nonattached energy. This helps the participants become less defensive, listen with more empathy, and connect with one another.

In Zenergy, we have developed a diploma of facilitation program. Toward the end of the program, participants take part in two four-day "master classes." These events were developed in response to requests by experienced facilitators who wanted to investigate the rich possibilities of facilitation and explore areas such as transformation, emergence, resonance, collective consciousness, presence, and expanded consciousness.

The process of grounding, expansion, and connection experienced in these master classes creates a fertile soil for individuals to experience themselves and one another in new and profound ways. I have led twenty-four such four-day events, and I sense that Peter Senge and his coauthors may be describing a similar process in their groundbreaking book *Presence* (2004, p. 12):

> We've come to believe that the core capacity needed for accessing the
> field of the future is presence. We first thought of presence as being fully
> conscious and aware to the present moment. Then we began to appreciate
> presence as deep listening, being open beyond one's preconceptions and

historical ways of making sense. . . .Ultimately, we came to see all these aspects of presence as leading to a state of "letting come," of consciously participating in a larger field for change.

In the end, we concluded that understanding presence and the possibilities of larger fields for change can come only from many perspectives from the emerging science of living systems, from the creative arts, from profound organizational change experiences—and from directly understanding the generative capacities of nature.

Conclusion

I have argued that through awareness of group context and group development, the facilitator and participants in groups and collaborative processes can access rich veins of generative possibility within which groups and organizations can interact and cocreate with increasing consciousness. This expanded consciousness is necessary for all who want to enable humanity, as well as organizations, to survive and flourish.

References

Beck, D. E., and Cowan, C. C. *Spiral Dynamics: Mastering Values, Leadership, and Change.* Malden, Mass.: Blackwell, 1995.

Birch, C. *A Purpose for Everything: Religion in a Postmodern Worldview.* Mystic, Conn.: Twenty-Third Publications, 1990.

Campbell, J., with Moyers, B. *The Power of Myth.* New York: Doubleday, 1988.

Csikszentmihalyi, M. *Flow: The Psychology of Optimal Experience.* New York: HarperCollins, 1990.

Diamond, J. *Collapse: How Societies Choose to Fail or Survive.* New York: Viking, 2004.

Elkington, J. *Cannibals with Forks: The Triple Bottom Line of 21st Century Business.* Stony Creek, Conn.: New Society, 1998.

Henderson, H. *Building a Win-Win World: Life Beyond Global Economic Warfare.* San Francisco: Berrett-Koehler, 1996.

Heron, J. *The Complete Facilitators Handbook.* London: Kogan Page, 1999.

Hill, S. B. "Social Ecology as Future Stories." *1999: A Social Ecology Journal,* 1999, *1,* 197–208.

Hill, S. B. "What Is Social Ecology?" [http://www.zulenet.com/see/chair.html]. Aug. 2005.

Houston, J. *Life Force: The Psycho-Historical Recovery of the Self.* Wheaton, Ill.: Theosophical, 1993.

Hubbard, B. M. *Conscious Evolution: Awakening the Power of Our Social Potential.* Novato, Calif.: New World Library, 1998.

Hunter, D. "Facilitation of Sustainable Co-operative Processes in Organisations." Doctoral thesis, School of Social Ecology and Life-Long Learning, University of Western Sydney [http://library.uws.edu.au/adt-NUWS/public/adt-NUWS20031107.153926/index.html]. 2003.

Hunter, D., Bailey, A., and Taylor, B. *Co-operacy: A New Way of Being at Work.* Auckland, New Zealand: Tandem, 1997.

Hunter, D., and Thorpe, S. "Facilitator Values and Ethics." In S. Schuman (ed.), *The IAF Handbook of Group Facilitation.* San Francisco: Jossey-Bass, 2005.

Inayatullah, S. *Situating Sarkar: Tantra, Macrohistory and Alternative Futures.* Maleny, Australia: Gurukul, 1999.

International Association of Facilitators. *IAF Code of Ethics* [http://www.iaf-world.org/i4a/pages/index.cfm?pageid=3346]. June 20, 2004.

Maheshananda, D. "A Personal Remembrance and Conversation with Paulo Freire, Educator of the Oppressed." *Global Times,* July-Aug. 1997. [http://proutworld.prout.org/features/freire.htm]. 1999.

Milbrath, L. W. "Envisioning a Sustainable Society." In R. A. Slaughter (ed.), *New Thinking for a New Millennium.* New York: Routledge, 1996.

Owen, H. *The Millennium Organization.* Potomac, Md.: Abbott, 1994.

Peck, M. S. *The Different Drum: Community Making in Peace.* New York: Simon & Schuster, 1987.

Ritter, P. "Diagrammatic Illustrations of the Philosophy of Relating." Paper presented at the University of Western Sydney Hawkesbury Winter School, Sydney, May 2001.

Rogers, C. *Freedom to Learn.* (3rd ed.) Upper Saddle River, N.J.: Prentice Hall, 1994.

Senge, P., Scharmer, C. O., Jaworski, J., and Flowers, B. S. *Presence: Human Purpose and the Field of the Future.* Cambridge, Mass.: Society for Organizational Learning, 2004.

Smith, G. "Group Development: A Review of the Literature and a Commentary on Future Research Directions." *Group Facilitation,* Spring 2001, pp. 14–45.

Tuckman, B. W. "Developmental Sequences in Small Groups." *Psychological Bulletin,* 1965, *63,* 384–399.

Tuckman, B. W., and Jensen, M. C. "Stages of Small Group Development Revisited." *Group and Organizational Studies,* 1977, *2,* 419–427.

Paul T. P. Wong earned his Ph.D. in psychology at the University of Toronto. He has held professorial positions at the University of Texas at Austin, York University, Trent University, the University of Toronto, and Trinity Western University. He is the founding president of the International Network on Personal Meaning (www.meaning.ca) and the International Society for Existential Psychology and Psychotherapy (www.existentialpsychology.org). With more than 150 published articles and book chapters, he has contributed to many areas of psychology and management. His volume *The Human Quest for Meaning* (Erlbaum, 1998), which he edited with Prem S. Fry, is considered a landmark publication in the scientific study of meaning. His most recent major publication is the *Handbook of Multicultural Perspectives on Stress and Coping* (Springer, 2006), edited with Lilian C. J. Wong. His meaning-centered approach has gained international recognition in the fields of psychology, counseling, and management.

CHAPTER TWELVE

IS YOUR ORGANIZATION AN OBSTACLE COURSE OR A RELAY TEAM?

A Meaning-Centered Approach to Creating a Collaborative Culture

Paul T. P. Wong

Have you ever tried to negotiate an obstacle course? The only thing you can expect is that there will always be something unexpected that throws you off track and thwarts you from reaching your goal. A course that would normally take no more than an hour to complete without the obstacles would now take a few days or even longer, depending on your ability to navigate the course.

Unfortunately, some organizations are just like that. You are so tired of dealing with the endless, unnecessary obstacles that you have little energy or time left to engage in productive work. In such an organization, there are many "pockets" of power, each headed by a little warlord who is more interested in grabbing power than in collaboration.

In contrast, some organizations are like a relay team, where everyone helps everybody else succeed. The mantra is "How can I be of help to you?" In the end, everyone succeeds as the team succeeds. Clearly, a relay-team organization is more efficient and productive than an obstacle-laden organization; the former has *added values,* whereas the latter has *added costs.* This difference is sufficient to make or break any company in today's highly competitive world.

What kind of culture fosters conflict-ridden organizations? What is the meaning-centered approach to cultural transformation? What role can group facilitators and managers play to transform a toxic self-destructive corporate culture into a healthy, collaborative one? This chapter attempts to answer these questions from the perspective of meaning and purpose.

The Most Valuable Resources

In a knowledge economy, human resources are the most important assets. A collaborative culture is essential for recruiting and retaining creative and talented knowledge workers. Since these individuals are most in demand, why should they stay in a company where they have to waste precious time and energy dealing with an unappreciative and bureaucratic management? In fact, why would any person stay in an organization where getting anything done is like running an obstacle course? Who would not want to be part of a company that functions like a relay team?

Given the importance of human resources, for any organization to stay competitive, it cannot function like an obstacle course. It is understandable that no leader would openly admit that his or her organization is like an obstacle course. This chapter will reveal the underlying mechanisms of such dysfunctional corporations, identify their inevitable waste of the most valuable resources, and show how these added costs can be transformed into added values.

The Added Values of a Collaborative Culture

Year after year, *Fortune*'s one hundred best companies to work for have demonstrated that these companies possess a positive, cooperative corporate culture that enhances job satisfaction and contributes to productivity. Such a rewarding, transformational culture does not occur by happenstance. It requires a lot of leadership skills to bring different individuals together and develop a cooperative, cohesive, high-performance team. It requires even greater dedication and competencies to create and maintain a positive, collaborative organizational culture.

Freiberg and Freiberg (1996) have revealed that their secret of success at Southwest Airlines is to create a culture where employees are treated as the company's number one asset. Their formula is quite simple: trust your people, treat them as people, celebrate the good, and make information easily available to everyone. In a positive, collaborative culture, people naturally work together and make the business a financial success.

As I have said elsewhere (Wong, 2002a, 2002b, 2004), culture matters. Organizations need a positive, collaborative culture in order to retain their best workers, motivate their workforce, and grow their companies. Similarly, Deal and Kennedy (2000) emphasize that to revitalize their companies in today's environment, business leaders need to pay greater attention to corporate culture because workers want to belong to purposeful, meaningful institutions. According to Schein (1990), "The unique and essential function of management is manipulation of culture" (p. 317). I would go even further and make the case that the essential function of management is to create a positive, healthy culture because there would be no added values for workers and customers without a collaborative culture.

This chapter first considers problems of the toxic cultures that reduce the workplace into an obstacle course. It then presents a larger picture of positive management, the meaning-centered approach to organizational life. Finally, it discusses what it takes to create and maintain a collaborative corporate culture.

Typology of Corporate Cultures

It is important to know how to differentiate between toxic and healthy corporate cultures because collaboration is possible only in healthy ones.

Toxic Corporate Cultures

There are five types of toxic corporate cultures (Wong and Gupta, 2004):

- Authoritarian-hierarchical
- Competing-conflictive
- Laissez-faire
- Dishonest-corrupt
- Rigid-traditional

These five types are not mutually exclusive. Several problems tend to occur in all toxic cultures.

Abuse of Power and Control. Abuse of power and control is most likely to occur in an authoritarian-hierarchical culture. Senior management's drive to perpetuate its grip on power becomes an all-consuming passion. In fact, every position holder tries to maximize his or her power and control. As a result, time and energy are wasted in power struggles and manipulations. Power plays become the predominant ethos of the workplace.

A rigid-traditional culture also encourages abuse of power and control in order to suppress change. Those who see themselves are guardians of corporate tradition will resort to any tactics to stop progressively minded innovators from having their way.

Abuse of power is evident in various manipulation tactics. The typical tools of manipulation are the following:

- Deception. This includes straight lies, half-truths, and intentional omissions of vital information.
- Denial. This takes the form of denial of any wrongdoing, reneging on earlier promises, or denying any involvement in anything that has gone wrong. As a result, no one ever owns up to any mistakes or apologizes for anything.
- Passing the buck. Closely related to denial is the practice of passing the buck and attributing blame to some third party.
- Paper pushing. The standard bureaucratic control is to make people fill out unnecessary forms and then send them to another department to fill out more forms.
- Obfuscation. This involves speaking from both sides of one's mouth, expressing vague support without commitment, and making convoluted and obscure statements to cover up a lack of knowledge or lack of courage to reveal the truth.
- Stonewalling. When all the foregoing tactics fail, you can always stonewall by refusing to answer e-mails, return phone calls, or meet with people. This delaying tactic is most effective in preventing others from accomplishing anything.
- Covering up. Often more serious abuse of power occurs because of attempts to cover up some less serious misdeeds and wrong decisions.
- Dirty tricks. Powermongers often resort to dirty tricks to discredit anyone who poses a threat to their authority; these may include innuendos, false reports, and trumped-up charges.

- Divide-and-conquer tactics. Authoritarian leaders favor this approach. When various vice presidents fight among themselves or when different divisions compete for advantages, the president gains power by acting as the arbitrator.

Lack of Responsibility and Accountability. The root problem of abuse of power almost always stems from a faulty governance structure. The enormous power of a president who also holds the position of chairman of the board tends to result in abuse of power. Similarly, abuse is also likely to occur when the president has a handpicked, insulated board. History has provided ample evidence that any authoritarian system of governance, without checks and balances and without an effective opposition, inevitably breeds abuse and corruption.

Occasionally, a leader with deep moral convictions and uncompromising integrity may be able to resist the corrupting influence of absolute power, but a more effective way to combat corruption and abuse is to restructure governance so that leaders are accountable to both their overseeing body and their subordinates. Transparency, accountablity, and democracy are needed to prevent the abuse of power.

The other extreme—a total lack of control—can also be harmful to an organization. Ironically, when a leader is incompetent, irresponsible, and disengaged, it creates a laissez-faire culture. Since there is no demand for productivity and no accountability, it is very tempting for workers to be slack and irresponsible. Furthermore, ambitious and unscrupulous individuals may take advantage of the leadership vacuum to promote their own agenda at the expense of group interests. As a result, the organization becomes fractured and demoralized.

Lack of Integrity and Respect for People. The absence of integrity and respect for people can occur in any organization, although it is more likely to happen in an authoritarian culture. When leaders or managers are self-absorbed and preoccupied with power plays, integrity becomes the first casualty.

In a dishonest and corrupt culture, where the mission statement is worth less than the paper it is printed on and core values are no more than window dressing, one can expect a lack of integrity in all sorts of transactions and decisions. It is difficult to restore a sense of trust and respect without a wholesale change of senior management.

Some organizations are burdened with a culture of competition and conflicts, with different factions constantly grappling for power and control. This often happens after a merger of two companies with different corporate cultures and agendas. In large multinational companies, vice presidents do not speak to each other as a result of the vicious and ruthless infighting. There is little room for integrity and respect in a competing-conflicting corporate culture.

Healthy Corporate Cultures

There are four healthy corporate cultures (Wong and Gupta, 2004), characterized as follows:

- Progressive-adaptive
- Purpose-driven
- Community-oriented
- People-centered

These four culture types contribute to intrinsically motivated high performance because they meet people's deepest needs for meaning, community, spirituality, and agency. The ideal company should possess the attributes of all four types of healthy corporate cultures.

Facilitators and managers need to learn how to understand toxic cultures in order to transform them into healthy ones. I have already identified some of the structural problems in governance and the functional problems in management typical of toxic cultures; however, the skills involved in a more thorough cultural diagnosis is beyond the scope of this chapter. The rest of the chapter will therefore focus on the positive psychology of management and the meaning-centered approach to cultural transformation.

Positive Psychology of Management

Effective cultural transformation may benefit from considering the larger picture of positive psychology (Crabtree 2004a, 2004b; Wong, 2002a; Wong and Gupta, 2004) and the best practices of positive management (for example, Collins and Porras, 1994; Blanchard, O'Connor, and Ballard, 1997; O'Brien,

1992; Weisbord, 2004; Wong, 2005). These recent developments can contribute a great deal to our understanding of "soft" skills such as community building, communication, and team building, which are necessary for facilitators in their endeavors to build a collaborative culture.

Every organization is a collection of individuals, with their unique combinations of personal needs and cultural backgrounds. Conflict is an inevitable aspect of organizational life. It requires a lot of leadership skills to bring different individuals together and turn them into a cohesive, productive, high-performance organization. The psychosocial dynamics involved are complex and intricate. An important part of the positive psychology of management is concerned with culture climate (CC) management. The psychosocial dimensions of corporate life are complex and dynamic. To unleash human potential, corporate leaders need to know how to manage the socioemotional economy of organizations (Coffman and Gonzalez-Molina, 2002; Frost, 2003; Maitlis and Ozcelik, 2004).

There is an increasing awareness of the need to move beyond self-interest and the profit motive. Drucker (1995) has identified the worship of a high profit margin as one of the deadly sins in management in a time of change. Canfield and Miller (1998) in *Heart at Work* also state that there needs to be more than just the bottom line to make a business successful. Drawing on general systems theory, Gassler (2004) identifies the importance of altruism and other motives that operate in nonprofit organizations. Wilms (1996) has found that in an age of downsizing, robotization, and globalization, both management and unions are more willing to listen to each other and cooperate in order to increase productivity.

The present knowledge economy also demands a collaborative culture. Myburgh (2003) has documented that successful knowledge management can only take place on a collaborative basis. Also, Capps (2002) has pointed out the trend of increasing dependence on virtual communications, such as Web conferencing and text messaging. In the virtual world of multinational corporations and outsourcing, we need to discover new ways of fostering a sense of community and collaboration. Advances in technology have created new opportunities for virtual facilitators to explore new ways of collaboration (Bradley and Beyerlein, 2005).

Not only can transformation to a collaborative culture reduce burnout (Frost, 2003) and workplace violence (Minor, 1995), but it can also increase morale and productivity. Transformation is necessary to turn a failing company into a profitable one and to make a good company great. Managers and facilitators need the competence to assess corporate culture and know how to transform it. To be successful, cultural transformation has to proceed from the top down and from the inside out. Superficial changes such as setting up more committees to solve problems and providing more opportunities for input provide only temporary solutions. Unless fundamental changes are made in the values and practices of the corporation, there will be no lasting improvement in morale and productivity.

The deep structure of organizational climate can be plotted along at least the following six scales (Wong, 2002a):

- Controlling—Empowering
- Oppressive—Supportive
- Secretive—Open
- Suspicious—Trusting
- Divisive—Unifying
- Political—Professional

Plotting a corporate culture along these dimensions provides a good indication of whether it is toxic or healthy. For example, an authoritarian culture will be oppressive and secretive. A competing-conflicting culture will be very divisive and political. A dishonest-corrupt culture will be highly secretive and suspicious. All healthy collaborative cultures, by contrast, will be rated toward the empowering, supportive, open, trusting, unifying, and professional ends of the scales. Facilitators can use these six dimensions to monitor progress in cultural transformation.

Facilitators can play a role in restoring positive feelings in the group process as well as in the day-to-day workings of an organization. Climate transformation can be achieved at the organizational level and at a departmental level. For example, it is possible to create a positive work climate in a particular department, even when the larger organizational culture remains toxic. Climate transformation will involve training in emotional intelligence, effective communications, effective coping, optimistic thinking, personal meaning, cultural sensitivity, and personal reflection.

Culture-Climate Competencies

Crabtree (2004a) points out that managers can learn from positive psychology's "discoveries involving innovation, employees' need for respect, and the search for meaning in the workplace." There is much we can learn from psychological research to make our practice of facilitation evidence-based. Lessons can be drawn from Weisbord's in-depth case studies of strategies that increase dignity, meaning, and community (2004). Leider (1997) has provided a practical guide on how to discover one's unique calling and a sense of purpose in achieving a full, productive working life.

More important, CC competencies demand a fundamental shift in managerial philosophy and critical self-reflection. After all, managers and facilitators need to become healthy, positive people before they can influence others in a positive way. Thus CC competencies call for not just acquisition of skills but also personal growth. Crabtree (2004b) stresses the importance of trusting employees and authentic leadership at work. Crabtree cites Bruce Avolio, director of the Gallup Leadership Institute, who defines authentic leadership as "transparent, positive, ethical, and aware, as well as other-oriented. [Avolio] and his colleagues have demonstrated that authentic leadership enhances psychological capital in the form of hope, efficiency, optimism, and resilience demonstrated by employees. That cluster of traits, in turn, predicts those employees' well-being and engagement." These themes will be emphasized throughout this chapter.

Lord, Klimoski, and Kanfer (2002) have documented new developments in the basic theory and research on how affect and emotions influence industrial-organizational psychology. An interview with Barbara Frederickson in the *Gallup Management Journal* (2003) focuses on the positive psychology of emotions. Current interest in emotional intelligence (EQ) is a good start, but competencies in CC management require a lot more than EQ.

The ethos of the market and the profit margin naturally dominate business corporations. Paradoxically, a more meaning-centered humanistic vision is needed to maintain a proper balance between hard-nosed aggressive competition and a respect for human dignity. We need to reclaim the ethos of community and humanity to counteract the profit-at-any-cost mentality. We need to care for the physical, emotional, and spiritual needs of employees. Ultimately, it is the human system that is responsible for the success or failure of any organization. Mean-spirited reengineering may yield short-term gains, but long-term success demands the creation of positive organizations (Positive Organizations, 2003).

Basic Tasks of Building a Collaborative Culture

Within the framework of CC competencies, here are some essential tasks in building and maintaining a collaborative culture. Each task entails a number of tools and skills that are important for group facilitators. For these tools to be effective, senior management has to be committed to becoming a collectivistic, participatory, and collaborative organization.

Community Building

Community building is a fundamental task in cultural transformation. It is essential for the creation of a culture of trust, openness, cooperation, and harmony. Human resource departments often organize "community" activities to foster a sense of community. However, these activities will do nothing to build a collaborative culture if the basic structure and practices of an organization are authoritarian and manipulative. Genuine community building has to begin with something deeper and more basic: treating each other with consideration and respect and regarding every individual as a fellow human being rather than an instrument. Group facilitators need to model these attitudes in all their interactions with people regardless of their status.

Dialogue is an important practice for community building. According to Pyser (2005, p. 209), "The hallmarks of dialogue are open communication and commitment to common purpose. In dialogue, well-trained facilitators interact with participants to create a safe place where everyone can trust and then think, talk, and gain insights and understanding to resolve challenges. Participants learn from one another in an environment where individuality, diversity, and creativity are not repressed. The dialogue process fosters deep listening and enables participants to connect, communicate, and bond."

Gadman (1997) emphasized the need to adopt new approaches to organizational culture. He advocated a "new logic, based on values of interrelatedness, and free access to information where ambiguity, confusion, and anxiety were primary initiators of new learning, awareness, and action" (p. 60). He also recommended dialogue as one of the new approaches to encourage exploring different perspectives and creating a powerful synergy.

Team Building

Team building is also essential for creating a collaborative culture because by definition, a team is a group of people working together toward a common goal. Teamwork becomes increasingly important in virtual organizations and project management. Many people recognize the importance of team building, but unfortunately, for a variety of reasons, teams do not always work (Robbins and Finley, 2000). The basic challenge is to maintain a proper balance between group needs and individual needs (Steelcase, 2006). Whenever a powerful individual imposes his or her own ambitions and needs on the group, it sucks the oxygen out of the team.

The biggest challenge for group facilitators is to recognize and appreciate individuals' needs for power, attention, recognition, and even affection and at the same time help people recognize that the most urgent task is achieving the group's common goal. Facilitators must use different strokes for different folks to keep them sufficiently satisfied to stay on task. This may involve trying to win over the trust and cooperation of individuals who have the greatest hunger for power and recognition.

Group facilitators also need to demonstrate the ability to remain focused and unfazed in the midst of conflicts and chaos. They are able to maintain their balance and cool even under provocation because they are able to distance themselves enough to stay objective and rational. At the same time, they need to possess sufficient wisdom and people skills to circumvent power struggles and turf wars to prevent the group process from being derailed.

However, even the best teams suffer setbacks because of misunderstandings, which are inevitable. Often the intentions we try to communicate are not interpreted in the same way by certain individuals. A word that seems perfectly innocent may be a hot button for someone from a different culture or with a different personal history. When conflict occurs, the group facilitator must make sure that the misunderstanding is clarified and corrected as soon as possible. It is important that facilitators model the courage and honesty needed to confess that they have misspoken or misunderstood something.

Like community building, team building cannot succeed without the support of senior administration. In other words, the policy and practices of the administration need to send a clear message that collaborative efforts and group-minded behaviors, rather than competitive one-upmanship behaviors, will be encouraged and rewarded.

However, there is a need to guard against the temptation to discourage honest dissent and creative conflict in the name of collaboration. Beware of the dangers of conformity and groupthink! Often teams fail to be productive and innovative because of a culture of fear—individuals are afraid to express their own ideas and instead toe the party line or wait to see which way the wind is blowing. Facilitators need to help create an atmosphere of trust and openness, which can survive vigorous debates and disagreements. In fact, creative conflict is necessary for the development of successful teams.

The Task of Communication

Facilitators live and die by communication. No other profession is more dependent on effective interpersonal and participatory communication (Chilberg, 2005). What makes communication such an essential task for professional facilitators? Kaner (2005) has recognized that different stakeholders have different interests and frames of references. This problem is compounded by the phenomenon that given the same set of facts, human beings construe reality differently on the basis of their own collections of assumptions, meanings, and perceptions. (For a related perspective, see Chapter Ten of this book.) These differences can create enormous obstacles to communication and therefore to reaching agreement. Not many managers or leaders are equipped with the necessary communication skills to bring different stakeholders to the point of seamless collaboration.

Baker and Fraser (2005) have identified the following communication competencies as important in creating a participatory environment:

- Applying a variety of participatory processes
- Demonstrating effective verbal communication skills
- Developing rapport with participants
- Practicing active listening
- Demonstrating the ability to observe and provide feedback to participants

Each of these skills actually represents a family of related skills. Some of these competencies require continuous education and practice. Take listening, for instance. Unnecessary conflicts often arise because someone fails to listen actively and accurately. Assumptions and biases often distort what one hears, leading the listener to impute wrong intentions to the speaker.

The Paradox of Communication. Harvey's article "The Abilene Paradox: The Management of Agreement" (1974) dramatically demonstrated the danger of pseudocivility and conformity. The article has become very influential in management circles because it encapsulates the paradox of communication: people can miscommunicate out of the good intention of being agreeable and collaborative. This further reinforces my earlier point that pseudocivility can be the kiss of death for community building. Group facilitators need to ensure that group members feel safe to express their ideas and feelings freely, honestly, and accurately.

The Need for Openness. Openness is the key to honest communication and effective collaboration. One thing that stifles the flow of communication is making a distinction between insiders and outsiders. Ideally, in a genuine community or team, every member is an equal collaborator and should be treated as such. Being open also requires the willingness to be vulnerable and to let go of control.

Without open communication, the "Abilene paradox" will be repeated over and over again, to the detriment of every group member. Group facilitators need to devise strategies and fine-tune their skills to make open communication an essential part of building a collaborative culture.

Building Trust

Now we come to the indispensable task of building trust, which is the bedrock for community building, team building, and effective communication. Weaver and Farrell (1997) use the acronym TARGET as a mnemonic for the characteristics of a collaborative culture: *truth, accountability, respect, growth, empowerment,* and *trust.* Strengthening any of these components would increase the effectiveness of collaborative relationships.

Stephen Covey (1990) compared trust to a bank account. It takes time to build up trust, but it can be spent quickly. The tragedy is that in human relationships, when trust is depleted, it may never be completely restored. The memory of betrayal often lingers for a long, long time. Trust is a very fragile thing; it needs to be carefully guarded. A single unintentional false statement or a minor misunderstanding, if not cleared up quickly, can permanently erode trust.

In the absence of trust, any working relationship becomes difficult. Even the simplest statement can be misinterpreted and the noblest intention maligned. Suspicion feeds suspicion. People begin to resort to manipulation, deception, and control to protect their self-interest. According to Rodas-Meeker and Meeker (2005, p. 89), "Absence of trust has an extremely negative impact on groups, and at a very high organizational cost. When trust is absent, negative emotions and actions, such as suspicion and blaming, can steal from an organization's productive energy and undermine the positive work that people should be attending to." In other words, lack of trust can result in added costs to the organization.

Ultimately, trust has to be based on such virtues as being truthful, responsible, dependable, faithful, loyal, and genuine. However, even the most trustworthy person with the most impeccable character can experience problems of trust for three reasons: (1) so many people have been so injured that they have difficulty trusting anyone; (2) we are living in a cheating culture (Callahan, 2004), in which our general experience is that most people tell lies (or white lies) as a matter of course; and (3) often in haste, things are not communicated clearly, resulting in misunderstanding and mistrust. That is why building trust can be difficult. Many people want to experience trust in order to place trust in others. Leaders need to possess both a character of integrity and the necessary skills to create an environment of trust.

Exhibit 12.1 identifies some practices that help build trust. Applied daily, they will not only strengthen one's character but also transform one's working relationships and the organizational culture.

However, even people who have applied all the practices identified in Exhibit 12.1 with wisdom and finesse will acknowledge that some of the skills do not always work. For example, when you validate and empower your employees, some may take advantage of your trust and feel that they are free to do as they wish, resulting in negligence of their responsibilities. That's why trust must go hand in hand with accountability. Failure to exercise proper supervision can result in harm to both employees and the public. Empowerment

EXHIBIT 12.1. PRACTICES THAT BUILD TRUST.

- Practice what you preach.
- Say what you mean and mean what you say.
- Make decisions based on core values and principles rather than expediency.
- Treat all people with courtesy, sincerity, and respect, regardless of their status.
- Care about people and their well-being.
- Do not use people as instruments or stepping-stones for self-advancement.
- Be prepared to be vulnerable, willing to admit your own limitations and mistakes.
- Be accountable, and assume responsibility for your decisions and actions.
- Confess and apologize for your mistakes.
- Have the courage to confront and take corrective actions when there is a problem.
- Don't promise anything you cannot deliver.
- Always follow through on your promises, no matter how insignificant.
- Always clarify and qualify your promises to make sure that you don't set up unrealistic or erroneous expectations.
- Take great care to maintain and nurture working relationships.
- Exercise self-control, and remember that an unkind word spoken in anger can cause irreparable damage to a relationship.
- Whenever a misunderstanding occurs, clear it up as soon as possible.
- Honesty is the best policy. Always tell the truth, even if it might get you into trouble.
- Give honest but constructive feedback.
- Trust people first until they prove themselves untrustworthy.
- Empower and validate others until they disqualify themselves by betraying your trust repeatedly.
- Practice forgiveness and grace when others let you down.
- Avoid favoritism. Be impartial in working with people regardless of how you feel about them personally.
- Follow procedures and due processes; cut corners only in clearly justifiable circumstances.
- Communicate openly and honestly, and explain your decisions.
- Earn people's trust by building a reputation for being competent and trustworthy.

does not exclude performance appraisal and the need for continued training. Rodas-Meeker and Meeker (2005) also warn that "leaders should not abdicate their responsibilities in the name of empowerment. Instead, they should commit to facilitate the development processes that will lead to greater levels of empowerment and trust" (p. 97).

Caproni (2001) points out that creating a high-trust organization requires more than interpersonal trust. There needs to be institutional mechanisms, such as norms, values, structures, and rituals, that sustain and promote trust. Such mechanisms will encourage the development of a collective identity and group goals through participation and sharing.

Stories telling about the organization's history and mission also help create a common culture and inspire a sense of shared vision. Stories work because they reach people at the emotional level and express their common hopes and fears. Stories give life to what people need and value. Thus building trust must proceed at both the interpersonal and organizational levels.

More than two decades ago, Ouchi (1981) made the same point in his Theory Z approach to management. The basic point of this approach is that the collective involvement of workers is the key to increased productivity. The first lesson of Theory Z is trust. What is the basis of this trust? It comes from two sources: first, it comes from the experience of complete openness and candor in working relationship, and second, it comes from the organizational culture, which is expressed through ceremonies, myths, symbols, and stories. Therefore, trust needs to be embedded organizationally through its values, norms, and structures. Interpersonal trust can only contribute to a collaborative culture; ultimately, there has to be formal organizational support of trust and collaboration. (Additional perspectives on trust can be found in Chapters Three and Four of this book.)

The Meaning-Centered Approach to Building a Culture of Collaboration

The meaning-centered approach has dual objectives: understanding what both the group and individuals mean and need and discovering the meaning and purpose of the group. This approach emphasizes our common humanity as the basis for empathy and mutual understanding. Kaner (2005) points out that "thinking within a framework of mutual understanding" means that we take time to understand "someone's perspective well enough to be able to think from that person's point of view, with or without affinity for that perspective" (p. 117).

Elsewhere (Wong, 2005), I have presented the humanistic-existential perspective of my meaning-centered approach to facilitation. The propositions of this approach can be summarized as follows:

- It emphasizes clear, honest, and open communication so that every group member and different stakeholders can all understand the meaning of what has been said and what is being proposed.
- It advocates the practice to hear deeply, think deeply, and see deeply so that every hidden agenda is exposed, nagging feelings are expressed, and a deeper mutual understanding can be achieved.
- It insists on confronting and accepting reality as the basis for problem solving and transformation.
- It encourages the development of shared mission, vision, and core values through a participatory process.
- It creates a safe and trusting environment for meaningful participation, collaborative problem solving, and creative solutions.
- It emphasizes the values of being courageous and authentic in making choices and assuming personal responsibility for decisions and outcomes. In other words, it discourages finger-pointing and blaming when the group experiences difficulty or when the outcome is negative.
- It seeks to balance group needs with individuals' needs. Ideally, the common goals are compatible with group members' personal needs and aspirations.
- Organizational goals take into account the higher purpose of making a contribution to society and humanity. Bringing in the larger picture and taking a broader perspective will enable group members to achieve a better understanding of specific minor issues.

We have already discussed various cultural climate competencies in building positive, collaborative cultures. The meaning-centered approach also identifies several corporate values as essential to the successful execution of these skills.

The Imperative of Meaning and Purpose

Albrecht (1994) states that "those who would aspire to leadership roles in this new environment must not underestimate the depth of this human need for meaning. It is a most fundamental human craving, an appetite that will not go away" (p. 22). Much has been written on how to create a work environment where meaning flourishes (Autrey, 1994; Epps, 2003; Handy, 1994; Pattakos, 2004; Terez, 2000; Wong, 2002a). When the larger issue of meaning and purpose is taken care of, there will be lasting improvement of morale and productivity (Terez, 2000).

Typically, the meaning and purpose of an organization are captured in its mission, vision, values, and strategic direction (Straus, 2005). Cynicism lives on in many organizations because there is a disconnect between mission statement and day-to-day practices (Terez, 2002). One of the challenges facing group facilitators is to make meaning and purpose the central focus in resolving problems and settling differences. Make mission the real boss. When every major decision is mission-centered and purpose-driven, there will be a lot more collaboration and unity in the organization. Furthermore, to stay focused on purpose is the best way to prevent falling into the traps of power and greed.

If we probe deeper, we will discover that meaning and purpose are rooted in values, virtues, and beliefs. Certain values such as fairness and integrity are the moral foundations for a culture of collaboration. Genuine core values always find a way to manifest themselves not only in policies but also in the day-to-day interactions.

From this broad perspective of a positive psychology of management and meaning-centeredness, we need to turn to the imperative of core values, which must be at the center of developing a collaborative culture. Skills and practices that do not reflect positive values will be perceived as manipulation tactics. A meaningful and purposeful workplace has to be based on positive core values, such as honesty and integrity. Collins and Porras (1994) have documented that companies that practice and stick to these positive values tend to outlast those who don't.

The Core Value of Integrity

One of the main themes of the meaning-centered approach is integrity. We come full circle to my earlier remark that corporate cultural transformation must be from the inside out. In other words, personal growth and character cultivation must be part of the professional development if we want to be effective in transforming corporate cultures. Integrity is one of the inner virtues that need to be cultivated because skills can take us only so far. Without integrity, we can achieve only limited success. I have characterized the challenge of living a life of integrity as follows: "Integrity does not offer an escape from the mundane, daily grinds of human existence; nor does it offer hope for prosperity and creature comforts. It only promises a long journey through the jungles and deserts, through the dark valleys and the precipitous mountain ranges. It is the daily discipline of doing the right things, undaunted by difficulties" (Wong, 2004).

Simply put, integrity means genuineness and authenticity—the touchstone of living a meaningful life. More specifically, integrity means that one's behavior not only remains consistent across situations but also truly reflects one's beliefs and values. Welch and Welch (2005) provide a vivid portrait of a leader of integrity. The presence of such a leader can have an enormous positive impact on the organization:

> Your people should always know where they stand in terms of their performance. They have to know how the business is doing. And sometimes the news is not good—such as imminent layoffs—and any normal person would rather avoid delivering it. But you have to fight the impulse to pad hard messages or you'll pay with your team's confidence and energy.
>
> Leaders also establish trust by giving credit where credit is due. They never score off their own people by stealing an idea and claiming it as their own. They don't kiss up and kick down because they are self-confident and mature enough to know that their team's success will get them recognition, and sooner rather than later. In bad times, leaders take responsibility for what's gone wrong. In good times, they generously pass around the praise [p. 71].

The meaning-centered approach demands that leaders and facilitators be persons of integrity because without integrity, they cannot inspire trust, no matter how articulate and skillful they are in self-presentation. Integrity cannot be faked; it can only be cultivated.

Organizational integrity represents an even greater challenge for facilitators. It means that at all levels of the company, the day-to-day culture needs to be congruent with its mission and vision. It means that all the corporation's policies, procedures, and practices are based on its professed mission and core values. This can happen only when the senior administration models the core values and establishes structures and mechanisms to reinforce these values.

Organizational Fairness and Justice

I have alluded to the importance of parallel processing in corporate culture—personal virtues need to be supported by organizational values. Thus fairness must be both personal and organizational in order to influence the corporate culture. When organizational structures and practices are at odds with personal morality, many individuals will eventually lose their sense of fairness and justice.

Perceived fair treatment is an essential component of meaningful life (Wong, 1998). When fairness and justice are lacking, in society or in the workplace, and when rewards are based on favoritism and cronyism rather than merit, people feel less satisfied with life. I have discussed various issues related to fairness and justice elsewhere (Wong, 2005). Here I want to emphasize that organizational justice—the perception of fairness of the organization for whom one works—is the key of employee motivation (Moorman, 2000). There can be no sense of unity when workers feel that they are being treated unfairly and unequally by their immediate supervisors (Pillai, Schriesheim, and Williams, 1999).

The Strategy of Cultural Transformation

Having laid the groundwork for a collaborative culture and identified its characteristics, we can now discuss the strategy of cultural transformation. The present meaning-centered approach borrows generally from the influential work of Straus (2002, 2005). The basic strategy is top-down and inside-out. It begins with the top administration and focuses on internalization of values essential for building a collaborative culture. Let's look at the general design:

- *Confronting the need for change.* The facilitator needs to work with the senior administration and expose these executives to the urgency and seriousness of the situation.
- *Commitment from the top.* The facilitator has to win the trust and earn the complete support of the senior administration and the board regarding the strategic interest to transform the organizational culture. The executives and

board must demonstrate this commitment by investing in the process and modeling new attitudes.

• *Mutual understanding.* The next step is to achieve a common understanding among all stakeholders regarding the purpose and plan of cultural transformation, which necessarily involves some organizational restructuring to support the change.

• *Shared acceptance.* This phase will involve debate, conflict, and disagreement until all parties can accept some form of revised mission, vision, and core values as the blueprint for reform. This agreement can come about only when all are convinced that these changes make good sense in that they not only ensure institutional survival and improve working conditions but also serve a higher purpose.

• *Sustained implementation.* Continued training is needed to educate people regarding the core values and positive practices that can transform the day-to-day culture. New policies, structures, and procedures are introduced and aligned with the collaborative culture. This phase is crucial in changing the organizational mind-set, internalizing the new corporate values and norms, and replacing the old manipulative practices with collaborative skills.

• *Continued monitoring.* The changes need to be monitored and measured at regular intervals to see what works and what does not. Concrete evidence of success will encourage reform. Setbacks can be corrected to ensure greater success.

In additional to these strategies for cultural transformation, I propose that we also need the courage to overcome the following challenges:

• *Confronting the bleak reality.* This is probably the most difficult step because the natural tendency of those in power is to deny that they have messed up the company. They want to maintain the status quo so that they do not lose their power and privileges. They may agree to some cosmetic changes to make people feel better without changing the corporate culture.

Some facilitators may not want to confront the reality because doing so is very unpleasant and risky—it may evoke resistance and even antagonism. However, realistic acceptance is more important than appreciative inquiry when the most urgent task is to diagnose the root problem and revive a sick organization. As Straus (2005) points out, unless senior management recognizes the strategic importance of cultural transformation, it will not be committed to this long and costly process.

- *Overcoming fear, mistrust, and cynicism.* This is another common challenge in cultural transformation. One way to overcome the burden from the past is to demonstrate a new openness, transparency, and accountability for the board and senior management. The flow of communication is no longer controlled by the president's office. The walls between different levels within the hierarchy become more permeable.

- *Implementation and accountability.* Old habits die hard. Those who have practiced manipulation and deception for many years may find it difficult to speak a different language and follow a new pattern of relating. Without accountability, they may continue to do things the old way and get away with it. Also, it is very difficult to replace the old mentality of "Don't rock the boat—just obey orders" to a new mind-set of caring for each other, assuming personal responsibility for the community, and making changes to improve the workplace. Therefore, the group facilitator can guide discussions on how to hold each other accountable in implementing the new values throughout the organization. For example, we can honor those who are voted by their peers as being most cooperative and helpful to others. We can also reward those who are very successful in eliminating added costs in their department.

One useful strategy is first to concentrate on the one or two departments that are the most eager to incorporate the new culture in their daily practices. Second, the facilitator can initiate discussions on how HR personnel can become champions for the employees. Ulrich (1997) has identified four distinct roles for HR professionals: strategic partner of the administration, administrative expert in personnel matters, change agent, and employee champion.

- *Monitoring progress.* Accountability requires monitoring and measurement. My six dimensions of organizational climate can be used to indicate whether a corporate culture is moving toward or away from greater collaboration. A reduction in stress leave and sick leave can also provide evidence of progress. More specifically, facilitators can introduce the following methods to monitor progress in eliminating added costs.

> *Operational analysis* can be used at the structural or operational level to measure how many steps to complete a routine task or provide a routine service.

> *Task analysis* involves asking,—does the organization have people with the necessary competence and skills to do the task at hand? Lack of competence in specific areas can also be monitored by taking note

of decisions and practices that deviate from acceptable professional standards.

In light of the fact that the biggest source of waste comes from inter-personal conflicts, *conflict analysis* can reveal the frequency and duration of interpersonal and interdepartmental conflicts and the frequency of uncooperative behaviors such as delaying tactics, paper-pushing, and buck-passing.

Conclusion

Facilitators can play a major role in cultural transformation because of their special skills and trainings in the following areas:

- The ability to maintain neutrality and objectivity even in a complex polit-ical situation, where every faction wants to gain some advantage.
- The ability to use descriptive, objective language to describe events that are emotionally charged and contentious, thus providing a model for stake-holders to communicate effectively.
- The ability to move the group process forward toward achieving consensus and solutions in spite of mistrust, resistance, and bad feelings.
- The ability to earn the trust of both management and the rank-and-file in order to bridge the gaps.
- The ability to create a safe and trusting environment for people to freely express their feelings and thoughts in an honest and respectful manner.
- The ability to identify obstacles to collaboration and transform obstacles into stepping-stones.

These skills are essential in cultural transformation. Engaging the services of competent facilitators maybe the most effective and economical way to transform a toxic organization into a collaborative workplace.

A decade ago, Drucker (1995) predicted that the greatest change in orga-nizations would be that management growth would be based not on *ownership* but on *partnership*, in the form of joint ventures, outsourcing, and semiformal alliances of all sorts. Furthermore, modern organizations depend on knowl-edge workers with narrow areas of expertise; a clear and common vision is needed to pull them together. Finally, organizations have replaced church and family as the major place for social integration. In view of these changes, a collaborative culture becomes increasingly important in the global marketplace.

If we really believe that people are our greatest resource, we need to make sure that we earn people's trust and inspire their passions. To unleash the full potential of people power, we need to create a collaborative culture and eliminate all the unnecessary hindrances, whether they come from traditionalism, hierarchical authoritarianism, or dysfunctional leadership. No organization can long survive if it refuses to dismantle its obstacle course and turn it into a relay track.

It takes dedicated visionary leaders to create collaborative corporate cultures. Group facilitators can play a major role in working alongside leaders and senior management to bring about cultural transformation. The meaning-centered approach provides a comprehensive conceptual framework and a flexible set of tools to facilitate this transformation.

References

Albrecht, K. *The Northbound Train: Finding the Purpose, Setting the Direction, Shaping the Destiny of Your Organization.* New York: AMACOM, 1994.

Autrey, J. *Life and Work: A Manager's Search for Meaning.* New York: Morrow, 1994.

Baker, L. L., and Fraser, C. "Facilitator Core Competencies as Defined by the International Association of Facilitators." In S. Schuman (ed.), *The IAF Handbook of Group Facilitation.* San Francisco: Jossey-Bass, 2005.

Blanchard, K., O'Connor, M., and Ballard, J. *Managing by Values.* San Francisco: Berrett-Koehler, 1997.

Bradley, L., and Beyerlein, M. "Facilitation of the Future: How Virtual Meetings Are Changing the Work of the Facilitator." In S. Schuman (ed.), *The IAF Handbook of Group Facilitation.* San Francisco: Jossey-Bass, 2005.

Callahan, D. *The Cheating Culture: Why More Americans Are Doing Wrong to Get Ahead.* Orlando, Fla.: Harcourt Brace, 2004.

Canfield, J., and Miller, J. *Heart at Work: Stories and Strategies for Building Self-Esteem and Reawakening the Soul at Work.* New York: McGraw-Hill, 1998.

Capps, L. T. "Toward Pervasive Computing: Toward Pervasive Virtual Collaboration." DM Review Online [http://www.dmreview.com/editorial/dmreview/print_action.cfm?articleId=5915]. Oct. 2002.

Caproni, P. M. *The Practical Coach: Management Skills for Everyday Life.* Upper Saddle River, N.J.: Prentice Hall, 2001.

Chilberg, J. "A Procedural Analysis of Group Facilitation: A Communication Perspective." In S. Schuman (ed.), *The IAF Handbook of Group Facilitation.* San Francisco: Jossey-Bass, 2005.

Coffman, C., and Gonzalez-Molina, G. *Follow This Path: How the World's Greatest Organizations Drive Growth by Unleashing Human Potential.* New York: Warner Books, 2002.

Collins, J. C., and Porras, J. I. *Built to Last: Successful Habits of Visionary Companies.* New York: HarperCollins, 1994.

Covey, S. R. *The 7 Habits of Highly Effective People: Powerful Lessons in Personal Change.* New York: Fireside Press, 1990.

Crabtree, S. "The Power of Positive Management (Part 1)." *Gallup Management Journal* [http://gmj.gallup.com/content/default.asp?ci=13894]. 2004a.

Crabtree, S. "The Power of Positive Management (Part 2)." *Gallup Management Journal* [http://gmj.gallup.com/content/default.asp?ci=14206]. 2004b.

Deal, T. E., and Kennedy, A. A. *The New Corporate Cultures: Revitalizing the Workplace After Downsizing, Mergers, and Reengineering.* Cambridge, Mass.: Perseus, 2000.

Drucker, P. F. *Managing in a Time of Great Change.* New York: Truman Talley Books/Dutton, 1995.

Epps, J. "The Journey of Meaning at Work." *Group Facilitation*, 2003, *5*, 17–25.

Freiberg, K., and Freiberg, J. *Nuts! Southwest Airlines' Crazy Recipe for Business and Personal Success.* New York: Bard, 1996.

Frost, P. J. *Toxic Emotions at Work: How Compassionate Managers Handle Pain and Conflict.* Boston: Harvard Business School Press, 2003.

Gadman, S. *Power Partnering: A Strategy for Business Excellence in the 21st Century.* Boston: Butterworth-Heinemann, 1997.

Gallup Management Journal. "The Power of Positive Psychology: What Managers Can Learn from the Science of Human Emotions" [http://gmj.gallup.com/content/default.asp?ci=1177]. Sept. 11, 2003.

Gassler, R. S. *Beyond Profit and Self-Interest: Economics with a Broader Scope.* Northampton, England: Elgar, 2004.

Handy, C. *The Empty Raincoat: Making Sense of the Future.* London: Hutchinson, 1994.

Harvey, J. B. "The Abilene Paradox: The Management of Agreement." *Organizational Dynamics*, 1974, *3*, 63–80.

Kaner, S. "Promoting Mutual Understanding for Effective Collaboration in Cross-Functional Groups with Multiple Stakeholders." In S. Schuman (ed.), *The IAF Handbook of Group Facilitation.* San Francisco: Jossey-Bass, 2005.

Leider, R. J. *The Power of Purpose: Creating Meaning in Your Life and Work.* San Francisco: Berrett-Koehler, 1997.

Lord, R. G., Klimoski, R. J., and Kanfer, R. *Emotions in the Workplace: Understanding the Structure and Role of Emotions in Organizational Behavior.* San Francisco: Jossey-Bass/Pfeiffer, 2002.

Maitlis, S., and Ozcelik, H. "Toxic Decision Processes: A Study of Emotion and Organizational Decision Management." *Organizational Science*, 2004, *15*, 375–393.

Minor, M. *Preventing Workplace Violence: Positive Management Strategies.* Menlo Park, Calif.: Crisp, 1995.

Moorman, R. H. "Relationship Between Organizational Justice and Organizational Citizenship Behaviors: Do Fairness Perceptions Influence Employee Citizenship?" *Journal of Applied Psychology*, 2000, *76*, 845–855.

Myburgh, S. "Culture, Collaboration, and Competition." Paper presented at the tenth Asia Pacific Special Health and Law Librarians Conference, Adelaide, Australia, Aug. 2003.

O'Brien, P. *Positive Management: Assertiveness for Managers.* London: Brealey, 1992.

Ouchi, W. G. *Theory Z: How American Business Can Meet the Japanese Challenge.* New York: Avon Books, 1981.

Pattakos, A. *Prisoners of Our Thoughts: Viktor Frankl's Principles at Work.* San Francisco: Berrett-Koehler, 2004.

Pillai, R., Schriesheim, C. A., and Williams, E. S. "Fairness Perceptions and Trust as Mediators for Transformational and Transactional Leadership: A Two-Sample Study." *Journal of Management,* 1999, *25,* 897–933.

Positive Organizations. "Organization and Management Consulting" [http://www.positiveorganizations.com]. 2003.

Pyser, S. N. "Effective Strategies for Designing and Facilitating Dialogue." In S. Schuman (ed.), *The IAF Handbook of Group Facilitation.* San Francisco: Jossey-Bass, 2005.

Robbins, H., and Finley, M. *The New Why Teams Don't Work: What Goes Wrong and How to Make It Right.* San Francisco: Berrett-Koehler, 2000.

Rodas-Meeker, M. B., and Meeker, L. "Building Trust: The Great Enabler." In S. Schuman (ed.), *The IAF Handbook of Group Facilitation.* San Francisco: Jossey-Bass, 2005.

Schein, E. H. *Organizational Culture and Leadership.* San Francisco: Jossey-Bass, 1990.

Steelcase. "Collaboration: The Culture of Teams" [http://www.steelcase.com]. 2006.

Straus, D. *How to Make Collaboration Work: Powerful Ways to Build Consensus, Solve Problems, and Make Decisions.* San Francisco: Berrett-Koehler, 2002.

Straus, D. "How to Build a Collaborative Environment." In S. Schuman (ed.), *The IAF Handbook of Group Facilitation.* San Francisco: Jossey-Bass, 2005.

Terez, T. *22 Keys to Creating a Meaningful Workplace.* Avon, Mass.: Adams Media, 2000.

Terez, T. "I'm Important, You're Important, We're All Important: 20 Down-to-Earth Ideas for Building Self-Worth in Your Workplace" [http://www.betterworkplacenow.com/important.html]. 2002.

Ulrich, D. *Human Resources Champion.* Boston: Harvard Business School Press, 1997.

Weaver, R. G., and Farrell, J. D. *Managers as Facilitators.* San Francisco: Berrett-Koehler, 1997.

Weisbord, M. R. *Productive Workplaces Revisited: Dignity, Meaning, and Community in the 21st Century.* (2nd ed.) San Francisco: Jossey-Bass/Pfeiffer, 2004.

Welch, J., and Welch, S. *Winning.* New York: HarperCollins, 2005.

Wilms, W. W. *Restoring Prosperity: How Workers and Managers Are Forging a New Culture of Cooperation.* New York: Crown Business, 1996.

Wong, P.T.P. "Implicit Theories of Meaningful Life and the Development of the Personal Meaning Profile." In P.T.P. Wong and P. S. Fry (eds.), *The Human Quest for Meaning.* Mahwah, N.J.: Erlbaum, 1998.

Wong, P.T.P. "Creating A Positive, Meaningful Work Climate: A New Challenge for Management and Leadership." In B. Pattanayak and V. Gupta (eds.), *Creating Performing Organizations: International Perspectives for Indian Management.* New Delhi, India: Sage, 2002a.

Wong, P.T.P. "Lessons from the Enron Debacle: Corporate Culture Matters!" International Network on Personal Meaning [http://www.meaning.ca/articles/lessons_from_enron.htm], Feb. 22, 2002b.

Wong, P.T.P. (2004). "Restoration of Integrity in the Cheating Culture." International Network on Personal Meaning [http://www.meaning.ca/articles04/president/integrity-sept04.htm]. Sept. 2004.

Wong, P.T.P. "Creating a Positive Participatory Climate: A Meaning-Centered Counseling Perspective." In S. Schuman (ed.), *The IAF Handbook of Group Facilitation*. San Francisco: Jossey-Bass, 2005.

Wong, P.T.P., and Gupta, V. "The Positive Psychology of Transformative Organizations: A Fresh Perspective and Evidence from the Anglo Context." In V. Gupta (ed.), *Transformative Organizations*. New Delhi, India: Sage, 2004.

Rosa Zubizarreta works as an organization development consultant, facilitating creative collaboration and greater effectiveness in business, government, nonprofit, and community settings. Her earlier professional background includes work in education, education reform, and social services, where she gained experience with transformative education, critical pedagogy, learning communities, and strengths-based approaches. In the area of collective intelligence and the evolution of democracy, she has collaborated with Tom Atlee on his book *The Tao of Democracy* (Imprint/BookSurge, 2002) and written on the social applications of dialogue for the Collective Wisdom Initiative (www.collectivewisdominitiative.org.). Zubizarreta holds a master of arts degree in psychology from the Organization Development program at Sonoma State University and in multicultural education from the University of San Francisco.

CHAPTER THIRTEEN

PRACTICAL DIALOGUE

Emergent Approaches for Effective Collaboration

Rosa Zubizarreta

The purpose of this chapter is to point to the emergence of a field of nondirective methods for facilitating practical creativity in working groups. In addition to delineating some of the common features of this field, which I am calling "practical dialogue," I will be highlighting some of the reasons why this set of practices is relevant for developing the kinds of collaboration that are badly needed at present—not just in organizational settings but also in our communities, our societies, and the wider world.

To illustrate practical dialogue, I will describe three dialogic methods designed for small group situations that require practical action and concrete results. Each of these methods—dynamic facilitation (Rough and Zubizarreta, 2003), dialogue mapping (Conklin, 2005), and transformative mediation (Bush and Folger, 2004)—has emerged independently. Consequently, each has its own distinctive features differs in significant ways from the others. At the same time, all three methods have certain basic elements and principles in common.

In addition to the people mentioned in this chapter, the author thanks Bruce Nayowith for his loving support, Gene Gendlin for his generous encouragement, and Saul Eisen for his inspiring example.

In addition to developing collaborative cultures, each of these methods helps us do all of the following:

- Work effectively with highly polarized situations and widely divergent perspectives
- Address complex issues with depth and creativity
- Welcome people as they are, without requiring any prior communication training
- Support the emergence of shared understanding, practical breakthroughs, and aligned action

Background Considerations

Instead of teaching *about* collaboration, one of the best ways to develop a collaborative culture is to provide people with an opportunity to *directly experience* its value. At the same time, we need to look more closely at the kinds of collaboration that we are seeking to develop. If we consider how cultures develop, we realize that no group experience is neutral. Instead, every group experience is already teaching us something about collaboration.

Developmental Levels of Collaboration

One of the first theorists to describe the difference between developmental levels of collaboration was Herb Shepard (1965). Shepard described "primary mentality" as the developmental stage in which we experience the collective and the individual as a zero-sum game. From this perspective, we experience an either-or choice. We can either subsume our individuality for the greater good of the collective (which can be seen as one form of collaboration), or we can to assert our independence at the expense of the common good.

In contrast to these two choices, Shepard described something that he called "secondary mentality." He described this developmental level as the embodied realization that the relationship between the group and the individual does not have to be a zero-sum game. Instead, the more a group welcomes the experience and divergent perspectives of each individual participant, the richer the collective experience becomes. In turn, the more we can share our unique gifts with others in a supportive group context, the more our own individuality is strengthened and nourished.

In Shepard's time, he believed that the most effective way of supporting group participants in developing secondary mentality was through sensitivity-training groups. This may or may not be true today. In any case, if we are looking at developing a collaborative culture, it is worthwhile to consider to what extent a particular facilitation method or group process supports primary mentality (collaboration as requiring some sacrifice of individuality) or instead helps participants develop secondary mentality (collaboration as both drawing from and strengthening individuality).

How Cultures Are Created

In his work on culture and leadership, Schein (1992) describes how culture is created as a by-product of the larger process of meeting practical challenges. When a group or an organization solves a meaningful problem, the assumptions embedded in that particular problem-solving approach begin to be adopted as part of the culture of that group or organization.

The more significant and meaningful the problem, the greater the learning. However, this learning process is not limited to any particular set of values. Instead, Schein's theory helps us understand how different cultures can evolve from different sets of experiences. For example, an organization that experiences successful collaboration as a result of having an authoritative leader with a clear-cut plan will tend to adopt the assumption that "to have effective collaboration, we need an authoritative leader with a clear-cut plan."

If instead an organization experiences successful collaboration through an approach that encourages individual initiative and welcomes divergence and complexity, these are the working assumptions that will be adopted by that organization: "to have effective collaboration, we need to welcome individual initiative, divergence, and complexity."

In either case, the group is learning something about collaboration. What the specific lessons are will depend on the assumptions embedded in the particular problem-solving approach.

Prevailing Approaches to Working with Small Groups

One way we might sort the various methods of working with groups that are prevalent today is according to their primary purpose. In one category, we might place methods that support interpersonal learning, the development of communication skills, and the growth of collaborative attitudes. This category would include sensitivity-training groups (Bradford, Gibb, and Benne, 1964), Ropes courses, and other forms of experiential learning.

In another category, we might include methods designed to help a group directly accomplish practical workplace tasks. This could include technical issues such as increasing production, redesigning work flow, or eliminating toxic hazards in the workplace, as well as "softer" goals such as developing a vision statement or elaborating a strategic plan. Facilitated problem-solving strategies traditionally used to help a group accomplish these kinds of tasks include methods like "situation-target-process" and force field analysis. The distinction between these two kinds of basic purposes and where various group processes might fit in to this scheme is shown in Figure 13.1.

Of course, reality is always more complex than any classification system we might devise. For instance, many experiential simulations ask the group to focus on a simulated practical problem in order to catalyze interpersonal learning. These methods might be more difficult to classify according to the scheme in Figure 13.1 because they help a group address a practical workplace task (albeit a simulated one) yet their primary focus is on the development of collaborative attitudes.

FIGURE 13.1. DISTINGUISHING SMALL GROUP PROCESSES BY PRIMARY PURPOSE.

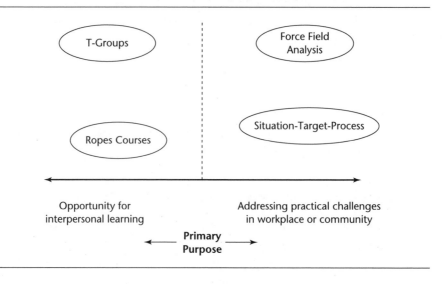

Where Does Practical Dialogue Fit In?

The three group processes that I am describing in this chapter as examples of practical dialogue are also difficult to categorize according to the scheme just presented, as they seem to contain elements of each category. On the one hand, they have been designed for addressing practical, on-the-ground situations. On the other hand, they feature a nonlinear orientation that has historically been associated with approaches designed to facilitate interpersonal and experiential learning.

As mentioned earlier, one of the distinctive features of practical dialogue is an open-ended approach to practical situations. Yet most facilitation methods that are open-ended and nondirective tend to have interpersonal learning as their primary aim and are generally thought to be inappropriate for supporting the accomplishment of practical workplace objectives. As a culture, we seem to take it for granted that to achieve practical ends or work-related tasks, we have no choice but to engage in linear, directive approaches. And indeed, most facilitation methods that are designed to help a group directly address practical workplace challenges tend to embody that step-by-step orientation.

Given these prevailing assumptions, introducing a nondirective approach for addressing practical tasks is no easy matter. It might help if we expand Figure 13.1 into a two-by-two matrix to depict the possibility of considering purpose and orientation independently of one another, and shown in Figure 13.2.

It's not too hard to imagine what might go into the bottom-left quadrant: people often use directive, step-by-step methods to support interpersonal learning. For example, we might easily imagine a design for communication training that introduces a series of skills in a linear fashion and includes directed practice for each one. Whether or not this is the best approach to take may depend on the situation. In any case, that question is beyond the scope of this chapter.

What I want to emphasize here is that there may be a cultural blind spot with regard to the upper-right quadrant. Until quite recently, it has been difficult for most of us to consider the possibility that there might be nonlinear, nondirective processes that effectively support a group in achieving practical ends.

There is, however, a historical precedent for open-ended exploration of practical realities, primarily within the *conscientização* process of Freirean dialogue—a form of dialogue that is seen as an intrinsic element of an ongoing cycle of reflection, action, reflection, and so forth. Unlike the more widely known tradition of Bohmian dialogue, Freirean dialogue has its roots in the

FIGURE 13.2. TYPICAL ORIENTATIONS OF SMALL GROUP PROCESSES AS CORRELATED WITH PURPOSE.

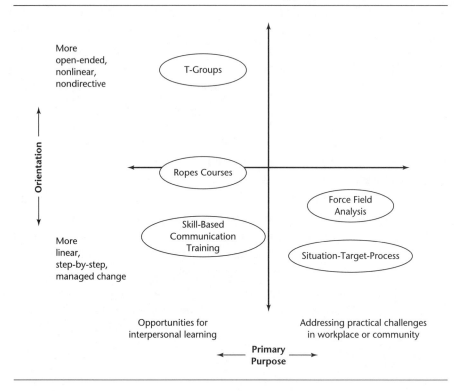

worlds of social change, community empowerment, and adult education (Freire, 1996).

There are also a number of large group methods that use nonlinear approaches to accomplish practical ends, such as Open Space Technology (Owen, 1992), Future Search (Weisbord, 1992), and World Café (Brown, 2005). However, when it comes to facilitating a task group that needs to address practical issues, there have been few models of effective nonlinear, nondirective practice.

Rationale for a New Approach

Even if we grant that it might be possible to achieve practical results in an open-ended manner, it may not be obvious why we should bother to do it that way. I'd like to look more closely at why a different approach to facilitating task-oriented groups may be helpful, especially in certain situations and contexts.

Drawbacks of "Managing Convergence"

As the use of both facilitation and mediation has grown, so has awareness and concern about their potential for abuse. The power that a facilitator or mediator wields over the process can be misused. This is especially true in task-oriented circumstances where there can be pressure to reach agreement. Directive processes are particularly vulnerable in this regard: divergent positions can be minimized in an effort to reach closure, or facilitators can discourage participants from bringing up concerns, framing them as distractions or hindrances to the process. When these kinds of things happen, participants understandably feel that they have been manipulated.

Of course, it is possible to use directive approaches with integrity. Still, especially in situations where trust has been damaged, it can be helpful to have effective, open-ended approaches where practical issues can be explored and convergences can emerge naturally, in a nondirective manner.

Drawbacks of Premature Problem Definition

Even when all participants feel that they have been treated fairly in a facilitated process, difficulties can arise when the effort to manage complexity leads to defining the problem or the situation too narrowly. This may allow us to feel that we have "kept the problem within bounds" and yield agreed solutions in the short run. However, it is also likely to create worse problems down the road, especially when dealing with complex issues.

It is often said that "identifying the real problem is 90 percent of the work of solving it." In cases where the way that a situation is being defined may itself be part of the problem, there is an immense value in using alternative approaches that do not require us to agree at the outset on a problem definition or a desired outcome. The possibility for achieving an entirely different level of understanding is enhanced when the method we are using does not require us to deem any perspectives as "irrelevant" to the practical issues under consideration.

Benefits of Inclusion: Welcoming Emotions

Especially when we are dealing with complex issues, it is likely that there are strong emotions attached to the various perspectives at hand. Many directive facilitation processes encourage people to "leave their emotions at the door" in order to be able to speak calmly and rationally. While this may make things more comfortable for some participants, there are a number of significant disadvantages to processes that frame strong emotions as impediments to the facilitation process.

Restraining strong emotions often ties up a great deal of participants' and facilitators' energies and attention. Norms regarding what is considered "polite discourse" can be used to privilege people from certain social groups and to stigmatize or silence others. They can also lead a facilitator or a group to marginalize the potentially valuable perspectives held by people who are strongly advocating for or against a certain position. As a result, the whole group loses potential sources of passion and commitment.

Processes that welcome emotions have the advantages of allowing people to "come as they are," without having to learn any special ways to communicate. They also place the responsibility on us as facilitators or mediators to listen deeply enough to recognize the gift in each person's contribution, regardless of how that gift might be wrapped.

Benefits of Creativity: Welcoming Nonlinear Thinking

If we are to adequately address complex issues, we need the full power of human creativity. And we know that creativity does not tend to proceed in a linear fashion. Step-by-step approaches may be more comfortable and familiar, but they do not tend to encourage the full flowering of a group creative process.

We have plenty of anecdotal evidence about the kinds of performance that are possible when a group is in a "flow state." We need greater familiarity with methods that can reliably create the conditions for the emergence and continuation of such states—not just during a brief brainstorming period but throughout the life cycle of a working group.

Benefits of Intrinsic Motivation: Supporting Shared Understanding and Energized Action

Agreements that have been brokered or negotiated often become agreements that everyone can "live with" but no one is particularly excited about. These tend to require significant expenditures of energy to ensure follow-through. In contrast, many of us have witnessed the power of group flow. We know from experience that group outcomes tend to be much more compelling when they have been arrived at freely, through a naturally unfolding creative process.

At the same time, regardless of how we manage to reach agreement, we know that external circumstances are continually changing. As a result, it is likely that our understandings and actions will need to be revised and reconsidered. The more enjoyable and rewarding our process, the more likely participants are to experience the ongoing conversation as an opportunity rather than a burden.

Building Capacity at All Levels

While we are helping people address practical issues, it is doubly helpful if we can simultaneously offer participants the opportunity to realize experientially the value of listening deeply to divergent perspectives and looking at whole systems. Beyond resolving the immediate situation, this builds participants' capacity for sustained collaboration.

When our approach allows us to work with people "as they are" instead of needing to learn to "communicate better" as a prerequisite for participation, we are able to engage with people across a wider spectrum. In turn, participants have the opportunity to learn interpersonal skills experientially by engaging in a supported process. These various points are summarized in Exhibit 13.1.

EXHIBIT 13.1. DISTINGUISHING FEATURES OF PRACTICAL DIALOGUE.

- Participants' differences are respected by a nondirective exploration of practical issues that continually welcomes divergence.

- Ability to handle complexity is greater, as no initial agreements are needed or sought with regard to problem definitions, desired outcomes, or selection criteria.

- Emotion and passion are welcome and are not regarded as an obstacle to the search for meaning.

- Practical creativity is accessed by making room for the nonlinear flow of conversation, as well as nonlinear thinking.

- Intrinsic motivation is tapped by allowing for the emergence of powerful natural convergences by refraining from "brokering" or "managing" agreement.

- Participants can "come as they are"; there is no need for preliminary training to participate in the process.

- Powerful interpersonal learning takes place experientially as a by-product of working on practical objectives in a creative manner.

It is also important to develop our own capacity as facilitators. Non-directive methods can be particularly helpful in this regard. As Peter Senge has said, "Good facilitators have actually internalized a belief based on experience, that whatever happens is supposed to have happened—even if it is very problematic and unfortunate. And because you have that belief, you don't waste your energy trying to fight what is going on. Instead, you try working with it" (Staples, 2000, p 10).

Whether or not we decide to specialize in nondirective methods, there are always some situations in which more linear or more directive methods are either not feasible or not appropriate. Becoming familiar with nondirective approaches can help us become more prepared for such an eventuality.

Overview of Practical Dialogue and Description of Specific Methods

Now I would like to describe three different methods that I see as examples that point to this emerging field of practical dialogue. Each of these methods has its own origins, history, and particular characteristics and arose independently of the other two.

Dynamic Facilitation: Co-sensing Emergent Wholeness

Jim Rough, the creator of this approach, began his explorations looking for a way to help task groups creatively address "impossible-to-solve" problems, challenges that a group might not even consider addressing due to their perceived intractability. At the time, Rough was an internal consultant at a lumber company in the Pacific Northwest, directing a project where shop floor workers were being invited to participate in quality circles for the first time in the mill's history.

Over time, Rough continued to develop his innovative approach to working with groups, which he has named *dynamic facilitation*. In this process, the facilitator's main task is "listening to understand" (Covey, 1989). In the process, the facilitator is drawing out all of the various problem definitions, ideas for solutions, concerns, and perspectives that are present in the room, in no particular order. Each contribution is recorded on one or more numbered lists as a way to begin mapping the shared field of meaning that is emerging.

Reducing Anxiety. Instead of using "ground rules," a strong sense of safety is created by the facilitator's listening work, which involves drawing out, reflecting, appreciating, and "protecting" the contributions of each participant. By "protecting," Rough means that whenever a conflict arises, the facilitator steps in, welcoming the divergent perspectives and inviting participants to address their comments to him or her as facilitator or "designated listener." This allows each person to be heard in full while giving others the opportunity to "overhear" each person's perspective in greater depth. (For another method of facilitating difficult conversations that also makes use third-party listening, see Pearce and Littlejohn, 1997.)

Initially, the dynamic facilitation process relies strongly on the listening work of the facilitator. However, in a fairly short period of time, participants begin to experience the value of hearing one another more fully than is usually the case in a fast-paced meeting. The growing excitement of the creative process leads them to show a genuine curiosity for divergent perspectives, and they begin to spontaneously draw one another out. This eventually allows the facilitator to fade into the background to a much greater degree, although he or she continues to listen and to record each individual contribution.

Maintaining Creative Tension. Throughout the process, the facilitator remains in a position of "radical inclusivity," welcoming each contribution and working hard to understand the meaning of each perspective in the participant's own terms. This inclusivity is made easier by the fact that the facilitator does not need to labor to keep the group "on task"; the only agenda is the one that emerges in from participants' concerns in the moment.

Equally important, the facilitator is refusing to "manage convergence" in any way, instead allowing an ongoing flow to emerge in which each naturally arising convergence opens into a new level of divergence.

As the group and the facilitator work together to map the territory of the present situation, including but not limited to the initial "impossible-to-solve" problem, the complex picture that begins to emerge can feel overwhelming to participants and create a momentary sense of crisis. Still, while creative tension is high, anxiety is reduced somewhat by the supportive listening work of the facilitator.

Creative Breakthroughs. Once each perspective has been received and appreciated and all the various "puzzle pieces" are on the table, a natural shift occurs as participants begin to realize the incomplete nature of all of their earlier perspectives. As each participant begins to consider all of the information that has surfaced, thinking rises to a new level.

Although the facilitator does not make any attempt to lead the group toward convergence at any point, he or she listens for any apparent convergences that emerge and verifies them with the group a short time after the fact. For example, a facilitator might say, "When John offered his solution to issue X, everyone nodded and people started talking about how to implement it. Is everyone really on board with this?"

If the convergence was only apparent, and one or more participants avail themselves of the opportunity to express something they had not revealed earlier, this is a good thing! The facilitator welcomes any divergent perspectives that surface, continuing to draw out participants and to engage in an open-ended process. Of course, participants will have ever more information to consider, and often a previously unvoiced perspective will shift the quality of the conversation in unexpected ways.

If the convergence was real, however, participants might pause for a moment in acknowledgment before resuming their conversation about different implementation strategies. However, what confirms the convergence is not the acknowledgment per se but rather the fact that each person's attention is now fully engaged with how to address the implementation questions that have arisen in response to the particular solution the group has converged on.

The process still has the same quality of open-ended exploration, and there is still a wide range of diverse perspectives on the table. Only now the process has jumped to another level, as participants are now engaged with the next set of challenges that have just emerged as an inseparable aspect of any authentic convergence.

Working with Time Frames and Acknowledging Accomplishments. At the end of the session, the facilitator helps participants summarize where they are at the end of the session and review what has been accomplished during its course. This is important at the beginning of the process, since the group may still be in the initial stages of mapping the shared field. However, it can be equally important if the group has already entered a highly creative flow state, since now the participants are likely to be working just as hard at the end of the meeting as they were at the beginning, only on an entirely different set of issues.

Bridging the Paradigm Gap. One of the most significant challenges when using dynamic facilitation is the absence of the familiar markers that most of us consider a necessary part of a decision-making process. I am not just referring to the absence of a formal voting procedure. Even most consensus methods generally include protracted negotiations as part of the process.

Instead, the emergence of shared understanding is more like a eureka experience ("Aha! I see it!"), where a perceptual shift occurs and a figure that has been hidden now becomes obvious to everyone in the group. The term *co-sensing* has evolved to distinguish what takes place in this process from most kinds of consensus.

Even when people are satisfied with the result, they can be uncomfortable with the experience of a new and unfamiliar process, and the absence of conventional markers can be disorienting. To reduce potential discomfort, it can be helpful to present dynamic facilitation as an avenue for creative exploration and a preparation for a later stage of conventional decision making, instead of as an alternative way to reach agreement. However, facilitators experienced with this method know that many of the "dilemmas" facing a group tend to simply dissolve as a result of the emergence of shared understanding.

In the past fifteen years, Rough has continued developing this process, which he describes as a synthesis of "head and heart creativity." He and his wife, Jean, regularly offer well-attended seminars on dynamic facilitation in their hometown of Port Townsend, Washington, as well as in other locations around the world.

Dialogue Mapping: High-Tech Help for "Wicked Problems"

Dialogue mapping is a software-assisted facilitation process. It was developed by Jeffrey Conklin as a way to help groups address difficult issues or "wicked problems" by creating a shared perceptual map that depicts the full complexity of the situation. (For more on "wicked problems," see Rittel and Webber, 1973.) In dialogue mapping, there is no need to reach premature agreement on any aspect of a problem, including divergent perspectives of the problem definition (Conklin, 2005).

Originally, Conklin created the software that supports his method as a tool for public utility companies to document complex decision-making processes involving vast amounts of information in a way that would withstand later public scrutiny. Over time, he realized that this software could be used for supporting real-time creative problem solving in a variety of contexts, including high-tech industries and multisectoral collaborations.

Using Software to Support a Nonlinear Process. The current version of the software used in dialogue mapping is an open-source shareware program called Compendium. It allows the facilitator to create a map that depicts all of the different problem definitions, potential solutions, pros and cons of each solution, assorted perspectives, and general data. Most significant from the point of view of this chapter, the design of the software allows the group to engage in a creative and nonlinear process while generating a highly ordered product.

Of course, dialogue mapping is only one way of using the Compendium software. Like any piece of software, Compendium can be used for a variety of applications (see Kirschner, Shum, and Carr, 2003). At one end of the spectrum, Compendium could be used to create an accurate record of a highly conventional meeting that followed Robert's Rules of Order. Yet Compendium also allows a group engaged in dialogue mapping to proceed in a creative, nonlinear manner while allowing the facilitator and group to generate a rigorously detailed map of the various considerations that are being explored.

To illustrate the concept of how a nonlinear process can lead to a highly organized result, consider the example of a large jigsaw puzzles with more than five hundred pieces. Which piece gets placed when does not usually follow a linear sequence: one might choose to work on a bit of sky here, a bit of border there. However, when all the pieces are put together, the final product is finely ordered, not at all chaotic. This analogy can help us understand how a nonlinear creative process can, in the end, result in something that is perfectly logical and rational. (For a more complex explanation of how nonlinear processes can lead to linear results, see De Bono, 1992.)

Unlike a jigsaw puzzle, however, the number of pieces of the puzzle are not fixed or even known in most problem-solving situations. While participants come into a meeting with different relevant experiences, information, and perspectives, they are also involved in an active process of sparking and inspiring one another, seeing new connections, and creating new possibilities. Any of these contributions can ultimately add to the emerging picture of the larger whole.

Welcoming "Initial Ideas for Solutions." Dialogue mapping and dynamic facilitation were developed independently. One is a high-tech, software-assisted facilitation method, while the other relies only on chart paper and markers. However, the two approaches have much in common, including the basic orientation of welcoming any contribution as a valuable piece of the emerging larger picture. One example is welcoming initial ideas for solutions as a key aspect of both methods.

Most problem-solving approaches ask participants to refrain from offering possible solutions until a much later stage in the game. In contrast, both dynamic facilitation and dialogue mapping welcome possible solutions at any point in time.

In his workshops, Jim Rough points out several advantages of welcoming initial ideas for solutions:

- It helps participants listen better to others by first helping each person feel fully heard.
- It supports creativity by welcoming and honoring all of the efforts participants have already made to come up with ways to address their current situation.
- It brings to light all the different assumptions that are held by participants, which are embedded in the various initial solutions or prototypes that people are bringing to the table.

When describing why dialogue mapping welcomes initial solutions, Conklin offers a further advantage drawn from cognitive research:

- It allows the group process to more closely resemble the natural creative design process.

Researchers in cognitive science were initially surprised to discover that the actual design process of moving from initial specifications to a final working product is *not* a linear progression toward a final goal. It is in fact a nonlinear process where early attempts at solutions help test the design requirements for the problem. This natural cognitive process, described in the literature as "opportunity-driven problem-solving," could also be characterized as "opportunity-driven creative design."

The natural process of opportunity-driven problem solving helps explain why traditional meetings can feel so stifling. Attempting to keep everyone focused on the same stage of a predetermined sequential process does not appear to fit the creative process of any individual in the group. Based on their previous experiences in groups, people tend to believe that it is impossible for individuals to be creative together as a group, that meetings are inherently tedious, or that creativity is incompatible with practical results. In reality, the constraint is not human nature but the structure of conventional meetings.

High Tech or High Touch? One of the major differences between dialogue mapping and dynamic facilitation is in how information is recorded. In dialogue mapping, Compendium software is used to generate a visual map in which graphics distinguish the various kinds of contributions (questions, ideas, pros and cons, general information) that are contained in each text box. In addition, the map uses arrows to show the connections among the different elements: which possible solutions address which problem statements, what concerns were raised with regard to each solution, and so on.

In contrast, dynamic facilitation uses chart paper and markers to create four numbered lists (problem statements, possible solutions, concerns, and general information) on which the facilitator records each person's contributions. There are no visible links between the various elements on the different lists; for example, which possible solutions correspond to which problem statements is not recorded explicitly on any of the lists, although the links remain surprisingly clear in the minds of the participants.

Of course, this leads to major differences with regard to the amount of information that can be processed with each method. In addition, software programs such as Compendium make it possible to store, retrieve, and reorganize data in a flash. At the same time, the dynamic facilitation method serves to illustrate that although the underlying principles and usefulness of practical dialogue can be enormously enhanced by advanced computer technology, it is by no means dependent on it.

Transformative Mediation: The Power of Principle-Based Practice

A third example of practical dialogue originated in the field of conflict resolution. Transformative mediation was developed by Bush and Folger (2004) as an alternative paradigm for working with conflict, and one of its distinguishing features is a principled refusal to "manage convergence" in the mediation process. Instead of placing any pressure on "achieving resolution," the emphasis is on supporting participants in the process of empowering themselves and in finding their own way to a greater sense of human connection with one another.

In contrast to other forms of mediation, the transformative mediator is seen as following instead of leading the process. He or she plays an active but nondirective role in which listening and reflection are key and the conversation is allowed to unfold in its own rhythms. In addition, a much wider range of expression and content is welcome than in conventional approaches.

In a relatively short period of time, transformative mediation has become a distinctive and established approach in the field of alternative dispute resolution. Practitioners of this approach are also exploring the applications of their model to work with larger groups, such as multiparty processes exploring controversial and highly charged public issues.

Working from Principles. One significant element of the success of transformative mediation in the mediation community has been the clear articulation of the principles on which it is based. Bush and Folger argue that if our primary goal in conflict is simply to have everyone obtain a satisfactory outcome, we end up missing opportunities to support human growth. In this "satisfaction model," we are seeing human beings as primarily focused on accomplishing their own ends.

In contrast, Bush and Folger describe a "relational model" in which people are seen as seeking both self-empowerment and respectful relationships with others. If the mediator focuses on listening respectfully to participants, supporting the processes of self-empowerment and recognition of others, the practical outcomes will tend to follow.

Research on the Strength of Emergent Agreements. In the alternative dispute resolution context, research has demonstrated the efficacy of transformative mediation. This nondirective approach not only results in stronger relational outcomes, as we might expect, but it also leads to long-term practical outcomes, often with regard to broader issues than the initial presenting problem (Bingham, 2003; Hallberlin, 2001; Antes, Folger, and Della Noce, 2001).

Although practitioners of transformative mediation have experienced success in the initial applications of their model to working with groups, I am not aware of any research yet along these lines. However, those of us who have been exploring nondirective approaches in the facilitation field know from experience that nondirective methods can be a viable and effective option with groups, not just with individuals in a mediated conflict. We have found that in return for allowing convergences to emerge in their own time, work teams tend to experience much greater alignment, commitment, and natural follow-through with regard to practical outcomes than is usually possible through managed processes. Of course, this is only experiential evidence; further research in this area is greatly needed.

Similarities, Differences, and Learning Opportunities. Many of the similarities between transformative mediation and the two methods described earlier should by now be apparent. Like dialogue mapping and dynamic facilitation, transformative mediation does not move forward in a linear fashion but instead tends to proceed in a more circuitous manner. The mediator's job can be seen as following closely rather than leading or managing. Welcoming, listening, and reflecting are key in all three methods.

One significant difference is that the transformative mediation model allows the parties in a dispute to direct their "heat" at one another instead of asking them to direct any charged comments to the facilitator or mediator, as is done in both dynamic facilitation and dialogue mapping. (Experience has shown, however, "third-party listening" may be useful in that context.)

Another difference is that transformative mediation has a very explicit and powerful philosophical foundation, which has not yet been developed in the same way for dynamic facilitation or dialogue mapping. Nevertheless, Bush and Folger's example has served as an inspiration for me in attempting the following initial description of the philosophical foundation of practical dialogue: *As human beings, each of us is continually attempting to make sense of our world, as best we can, on the basis of the information that is available to us. We do so for the purpose of responding creatively in a way that meets all of our needs, including our needs for autonomy and self-determination, our needs to understand and connect with others, and our needs to contribute—to ourselves, to others, and to the larger whole.* Each of the methods described in this chapter serves to create a container where we can, together, effectively draw on each individual's unique gifts and contributions in order to meet these very human needs.

Broader Perspectives on Developing a Collaborative Culture

This chapter has explored one particular aspect of developing a collaborative culture: supporting collaboration among members of task-oriented working groups. In an organizational context, this would include groups such as management teams, project teams, and functional teams; in a community context, it might include task forces, stakeholder councils, citizen deliberation councils, or coalitions.

I have attempted to show that the emerging approach of practical dialogue offers a powerful nondirective alternative for helping groups address practical issues, one that also fosters deep interpersonal learning of the sort that Shepard (1965) described in the shift from "primary" to "secondary" mentality. At the same time, I want to acknowledge that helping working groups become more collaborative is only one aspect of the larger work of developing a collaborative culture.

For example, if you are working with an organization, you may need to work with the leadership of the organization to examine and modify the current reward structure of the organization in order to remove systemic constraints to collaboration. Or you may want to involve the whole system of an organization or a community in a collaborative effort by organizing large-scale conversations of various kinds (see Weisbord, 1992; Owen, 1992; Brown, 2005). Other avenues for supporting collaboration may involve creating greater opportunities for informal communication through the design or redesign of architectural features.

Although the kind of collaboration that takes place in working groups is only one aspect of creating a collaborative culture, the implications of powerful group collaboration can reach beyond the particular tasks a group assumes. Highly functioning groups can offer an example to the larger organization or community of what is possible and can serve as effective catalysts for wider collaboration throughout the larger system. This is especially true when those groups reflect the diversity that is present in the larger social fabric, as is the case in stakeholder consensus councils or citizen deliberation councils (Atlee, 2003).

One way to help bridge differences in our society is through dialogue oriented toward promoting interpersonal understanding. At the same time, we also know that working together on common projects can also be a powerful way to help bridge differences. Stakeholder councils and citizen deliberation councils are examples of a growing trend in our society toward understanding democracy less as simply voting for those who will represent us and more as working together to forge creative and inclusive solutions to shared challenges (Barber, 1984). To do so, we need powerful tools that are suited to the task at hand: addressing practical issues in a way that fully honors the divergent perspectives among us.

Conclusion

I hope to have made a case for moving beyond conventional assumptions that regard dialogic approaches as not applicable to situations that require practical action and concrete results. The various methods described in this chapter point to a growing body of experience that serves to challenge limiting beliefs and expand our ideas about dialogue. I have illustrated where these methods fit into the larger spectrum of group processes in Figure 13.3.

The methods that I refer to as practical dialogue are among the most powerful ways that I have encountered to help working groups accomplish the following aims:

- To engage creatively with polarized situations and widely divergent perspectives
- To work effectively with complex issues
- To welcome people as they are, tapping into their natural gifts and desire to contribute
- To support shared understanding, practical breakthroughs, and aligned action
- To develop a culture of deep collaboration in which each individual's divergence is seen as a valuable contribution to the larger whole

Yet my intention has been not only to describe these particular methods but also to point beyond them, to the next generation of approaches that may better meet the needs of our times. To this end, I hope to have sparked some thoughts about how we might best create cultures of respectful and effective

FIGURE 13.3 PRACTICAL DIALOGUE: METHODS FOR BREAKTHROUGH RESULTS AND INTERPERSONAL LEARNING AS BY-PRODUCTS OF CREATIVE, OPEN-ENDED EXPLORATIONS.

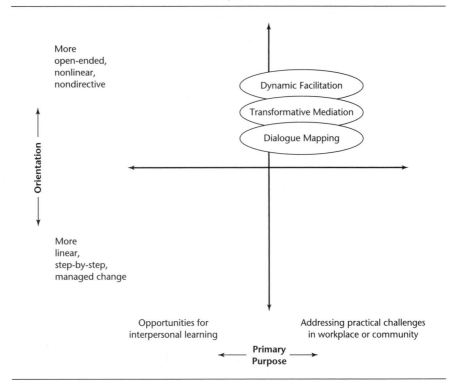

collaboration, not only in our organizations but also in our communities, our societies, and our shared world.

References

Antes, J., Folger, J. P., and Della Noce, D. "Transforming Conflict Interactions in the Workplace: Documented Effects of the USPS REDRESS Program." *Hofstra Labor and Employment Law Journal*, 2001, *18*, 429–467.

Atlee, T. *The Tao of Democracy: Using Cointelligence to Create a World That Works for All.* Cranston, R.I.: Writer's Collective, 2003.

Barber, B. R. *Strong Democracy: Participatory Politics for a New Age.* Berkeley: University of California Press, 1984.

Bingham, L. B. *Mediation at Work: Transforming Workplace Conflict at the United States Postal Service.* Washington, D.C.: IBM Center for the Business of Government, 2003.

Bradford, L., Gibb, J., and Benne, K. (eds.). *T-Group Theory and Laboratory Method: Innovation in Reeducation.* Hoboken, N.J.: Wiley, 1964.

Brown, J. *The World Café: Shaping Our Future Through Conversations That Matter.* San Francisco: Berrett-Koehler, 2005.

Bush, R.A.B., and Folger, J. P. *The Promise of Mediation: The Transformative Approach to Conflict.* (2nd ed.) San Francisco: Jossey-Bass, 2004.

Conklin, J. *Dialogue Mapping: Building Shared Understanding of Wicked Problems.* Hoboken, N.J.: Wiley, 2005.

Covey, S. *The 7 Habits of Highly Effective People.* New York: Simon & Schuster, 1989.

De Bono, E. *Serious Creativity: Using the Power of Lateral Thinking to Create New Ideas.* New York: HarperBusiness, 1992.

Freire, P. *Pedagogy of the Oppressed.* New York: Continuum, 1996. (Originally published 1976)

Hallberlin, C. J. "Transforming Workplace Culture Through Mediation: Lessons Learned from Swimming Upstream." *Hofstra Labor and Employment Law Journal*, 2001, *18*, 375–383.

Kirschner, P. A., Shum, S.J.B., and Carr, C. S. (eds.). *Visualizing Argumentation: Software Tools for Collaborative and Educational Sense-Making.* New York: Springer-Verlag, 2003.

Owen, H. *Open Space Technology.* Potomac, Md.: Abbott, 1992.

Pearce, W. B., and Littlejohn, S. W. *Moral Conflict: When Social Worlds Collide.* Thousand Oaks, Calif.: Sage, 1997.

Rittel, H.W.J., and Webber, M. M. "Some Dilemmas in a General Theory of Planning." *Policy Sciences*, 1973, *4*, 155–169.

Rough, J., and Zubizarreta, R. *A Dynamic Facilitation Manual and Reader.* Port Townsend, Wash.: Rough and Associates, 2003.

Schein, E. H. *Organizational Culture and Leadership.* (2nd ed.) San Francisco: Jossey-Bass, 1992.

Shepard, H. A. "Changing Interpersonal and Intergroup Relationships in Organizations." In J. G. March (ed.), *Handbook of Organizations.* Chicago: Rand McNally, 1965.

Staples, B. "Turning the Creative Tension On: Peter Senge Talks with *Edges'* Bill Staples." In *Edges*, 2000, *12*(1), 8–10.

Weisbord, M. *Discovering Common Ground.* San Francisco: Berrett-Koehler, 1992.

Roger Schwarz is an organizational psychologist and president of Roger Schwarz & Associates (www.schwarzassociates.com), a consulting firm that helps people get better business results and build stronger relationships, often in ways they didn't think possible. He teaches, consults, and writes about facilitation, leadership, managing change and conflict, and developing effective work groups. For more than twenty-five years, Schwarz has served as facilitator and consultant to Fortune 500 corporations; federal, state, and local government agencies; and nonprofit organizations. Distinguished consultants, executives, and academics have called his book *The Skilled Facilitator: A Comprehensive Resource for Consultants, Facilitators, Managers, Trainers and Coaches* (Jossey-Bass, 2002) a standard reference on facilitation. He is also lead author of *The Skilled Facilitator Fieldbook: Tips, Tools, and Tested Methods, for Consultants, Facilitators, Managers, Trainers and Coaches* (Jossey-Bass, 2005). Formerly an associate professor of public management at the University of North Carolina at Chapel Hill, Schwarz left his tenured position in 1996 to found Roger Schwarz & Associates. He earned his master of arts degree and doctorate in organizational psychology at the University of Michigan and his master of education degree at Harvard University.

CHAPTER FOURTEEN

USING THE FACILITATIVE LEADER APPROACH TO CREATE AN ORGANIZATIONAL CULTURE OF COLLABORATION

Roger Schwarz

Many leaders try to create a collaborative organizational culture, but they lead and design their organizations in a way that undermines the culture they seek to create. In this chapter, I describe how this occurs and describe the Facilitative Leader approach and how it can be used to create an organizational culture of collaboration. When leaders use this approach, they generate several outcomes: (1) increased quality of decisions or results, (2) increased commitment to implementing the results, (3) reduced time for effective implementation, (4) improved working relationships, (5) increased organizational learning, and (6) enhanced personal satisfaction. Several of these outcomes are particularly important to sustaining collaboration. From a task perspective, individuals consider collaboration more desirable to the extent that the results it produces are of higher quality than the parties could produce alone. From a process perspective, individuals find collaboration more desirable to the extent that it increases commitment to the outcomes

This chapter is adapted from "The Facilitative Leader" in *The Skilled Facilitator: A Comprehensive Resource for Consultants, Facilitators, Managers, Trainers, and Coaches, new and revised edition,* by Roger Schwarz (San Francisco: Jossey-Bass, 2002), and *The Skilled Facilitator Fieldbook: Tips, Tools, and Tested Methods for Consultants, Facilitators, Managers, Trainers, and Coaches,* by Roger Schwarz, Anne Davidson, Peg Carlson, and Sue McKinney (San Francisco: Jossey-Bass, 2005).

and increases the quality of their working relationships and their personal satisfaction.

Culture and Collaboration Defined

Organizational culture is the set of fundamental values and assumptions that members of an organization share and that guide their behavior (Schwarz, 2002). Although organizational culture is manifested in the artifacts it produces—including individual and group behaviors, organization activities, policies, processes, and structures—it stems from shared mental models. Consequently, to create and sustain a culture of collaboration, it is necessary for members to share a set of values and assumptions congruent with collaboration and to generate behaviors and structures that embody the values and assumptions. In this chapter, I will explore both behavioral and structural challenges to creating a collaborative culture, both of which arise from the mental models that individuals use to guide their behavior.

Chrislip and Larson (1994) define collaboration as "mutually beneficial relationships between two or more parties who work together toward common goals by sharing responsibility, authority, and accountability for achieving results" (p. 5). They distinguish it from communication, which is sharing knowledge and information, and from cooperation and coordination, a relationship that helps each party achieve its own goals. As they define it, "The purpose of collaboration is to create a shared vision and joint strategies to address concerns that go beyond the purview of any particular party" (p. 5).

For genuine collaboration to occur, parties must be able to learn from and with each other, especially in difficult situations, and must be able to jointly design the process by which they collaborate. Consequently, I define collaboration as a mutually beneficial relationship between two or more individuals, groups, or organizations who jointly design ways to work together to meet their related interests and who learn with and from each other, sharing, responsibility, authority, and accountability for achieving results.

Adapting the terminology of Argyris and Schön (1974), I distinguish between *espoused* and *genuine* collaboration. In an espoused collaboration, the parties declare their relationship to be a collaboration. In a genuine collaboration, the parties act in ways that are congruent with the definition of collaboration. Although sometimes espoused collaborations are genuine collaborations, often they are not.

What Makes Collaboration So Difficult?

Why is it so difficult to create and sustain genuine collaboration, even among people who ostensibly have similar goals? Creating a culture of collaboration requires changing two interactive factors: (1) the conversations by which people interact and (2) the structures that shape these interactions. Both of these factors are determined by individuals' mental models. We will examine each of these separately, beginning with how mental models determine process.

The research of Argyris and Schön (1974) and my more than twenty-five years working with leaders offer a basic explanation about why collaboration is so difficult: to effectively collaborate requires people to shift their mind-set (or mental models) from one of control to one of learning. But collaboration is often psychologically threatening because it requires us, among other things, to give up our preconceived ideas of what the solutions should be in order to find solutions that take full advantage of the collaboration itself. And under conditions of psychological threat, we cling to the very mind-set that makes effective collaboration less likely. In short, our thinking undermines the outcomes we say we want.

Consider the real-life example presented in Exhibit 14.1. Jonathan and Parker are investment partners and developers in a very large, complex real estate development that uses principles of traditional neighborhood development (TND), a high-density mixture of residential, commercial, office, and retail space in a tight pattern of pedestrian-oriented streets. The men's work relationship fits the definition of collaboration: they share a vision of investment through TND, each has knowledge and skills that the other lacks, and both are responsible and accountable to each other for maximizing their return on investment. In their conversation, about maximizing the return on investment, Jonathan wants porches on the houses and Parker wants brick houses without porches. Jonathan submitted this example at a workshop of mine as part of his effort to increase his effectiveness with his partner. The conversation between Jonathan and Parker appears in the right column; Jonathan's thoughts and feelings appear in the left column.

EXHIBIT 14.1. MAKING THE CASE FOR PORCHES.

Jonathan's Thoughts and Feelings	The Conversation
This argument was used by critics when TNDs first started, but no one except Parker has used it in the last four years.	*Parker:* Let me tell you, where I grew up we associate porches with poverty. Look at the poor parts of Washington. Very few of the houses built in the last 40 years have porches.
Where is the hard evidence when I need it?	*Jonathan:* Porches have made a huge comeback in recent years. Virtually every TND has porches and I understand porches are starting to bring a premium to builders.
Can't he find a way to use language to indicate that there is some middle ground? How can we reach a compromise when he needs to state his case in black and white.	*Parker:* Well, builders have told us that they will not build both brick and porches. It's too expensive to do both. It's either brick or porches and I want to have mostly brick.
The architect's plan is so logical. What is it he does not get about it?	*Jonathan:* Yes, I know the builders have told us that. The reason why the architect's plan works so well in my opinion is that they have taken that into consideration. They have come up with a plan that balances brick and porches, putting brick townhouses with no porches where they are most prominent and using siding on the houses whose facades are mostly covered up by a full porch.
He states everything as a "fact." He just does not give an inch.	*Parker:* Let me tell you, we are headed for disaster if we do not have more brick. I've been a builder in this region for more than 40 years. Residents expect brick. It gives them a sense of having a good solid house. If we don't have a preponderance of brick the builders will never be able to successfully sell these townhouses for the prices they need to get.

EXHIBIT 14.1. MAKING THE CASE FOR PORCHES, Cont'd.

Jonathan's Thoughts and Feelings	The Conversation
His apartment buildings that he built look like an engineer designed and built them. They have no re-deeming architectural quality, though they provide him with a healthy cash flow.	*Jonathan:* I really respect that you have been at this a lot longer than I have, but I have spent the last two years studying this new con-cept of TDN. It is very new and there is not a lot of hard evidence of its value. At the same time many of the developers and designers I have talked with say that there are all kinds of details that are critical to the success of a TND but we do not have absolute evidence of what is critical and what is not. From everything I have read, all new urbanists agree that porches are critical.

The Unilateral Control Model

What is going on in this example? It is a simple instance of collaboration be-tween two people in the same organization. By analyzing Jonathan's conversa-tion and his thoughts and feelings, it is possible to infer the mind-set Jonathan adopted to approach this high-stakes conversation with his partner and iden-tify the strategies and consequences that followed from this mind-set, which is a common one. In difficult situations—ones in which we feel some potential threat or embarrassment, including situations where our stake in the outcome is high—most of us operate from a set of values and assumptions that we are unaware that we're using but almost always lead to these consequences. This approach is called the *unilateral control model* (illustrated in Figure 14.1), which consists of three parts: *values and assumptions,* which together you use to gener-ate *strategies* or behaviors, which in turn lead to *consequences.*

Core Values. Beginning with values, you try to achieve your goal as you de-fined it before the conversation. You see the conversation as a contest in which you seek to win, not lose. Every comment that someone makes that is consis-tent with your goal is a small win; every comment that introduces information that may challenge your goal is a loss. You try to minimize the expression of

FIGURE 14.1. UNILATERAL CONTROL MODEL.

Core Values and Assumptions		Strategies	Consequences
• Achieve my goal through unilateral control • Win, don't lose • Minimize expressing negative feelings • Act rational	• I understand the situation; those who see it differently do not • I am right; those who disagree are wrong • I have pure motives; those who disagree have questionable motives • My feelings are justified	• Advocate my position • Keep my reasoning private • Don't ask others about their reasoning • Ease in • Save face	• Misunderstanding, unproductive conflict, defensiveness • Mistrust • Self-fulfilling, self-sealing processes • Limited learning • Reduced effectiveness • Reduced quality of work life

Source: Models derived from the work of Argyris and Schön (1974), who originally labeled them as Model I and Model II, and adaptations by Putnam, Smith, and MacArthur at Action Design (1997), who refer to them as the Unilateral Control and Mutual Learning models. Action design is an organization and management development firm that has built on the work of Argyris and Schön. Putnam and Smith are the coauthors with Argyris of *Action Science* (1985).

negative feelings, believing that if people start expressing negative feelings, it will only make things worse. Finally, you act rational. You think that the way you are approaching the issue is perfectly logical. And if it isn't completely logical, you should act as if it is. People use a mix of these core values, to different degrees.

In our example, Jonathan is seeking to achieve his goal of including porches. He frames the conversation as a contest in which he needs better evidence to win his case. His private question about what Parker doesn't "get" about the architect's logical plan illustrates the value acting rational. He has concerns about Parker's approach to design but withholds them. And he sees his reasoning for porches as flawless.

Core Assumptions. You operate from a matching set of assumptions. You assume that you understand the situation and anyone who disagrees doesn't. In this model, other people can't understand the situation and so see things differently. Consequently, you are right and others are wrong. You often question the motives of those with different views while believing that your motives are pure; you see yourself as a steward for the organization, while others are trying to advance their careers or otherwise meet their own needs. Finally, you assume that your feelings are justified. If you get angry, you have a right to be angry; others don't understand, are wrong, and have questionable motives. Remember that all this is at best at the edges of your awareness: you usually don't realize you are holding these values and assumptions in the moment.

Jonathan assumes that he is correct about the porches and doesn't entertain the notion that Parker's views may be valid. He attributes to Parker the sole motive of pursuing a healthy cash flow without attention to architectural quality.

Strategies. This combination of values and assumptions leads you to design strategies that seek to control the conversation and win. You don't fully explain your point of view because it might lead others to question and challenge it. You don't ask others to explain their points of view (except to shoot holes in them) because they may consider things that you hadn't, which would put your goals in jeopardy. To minimize people expressing negative emotions, you may ease in. Easing in is asking questions or making statements in a way that is designed to get the others to understand what you are privately thinking without your having to say it. It includes asking rhetorical questions starting "Don't you think that . . ." or asking leading questions so others will "see the light" and think that they have come up with the ideas that you want them to implement. If someone raises negative points, you may say they are irrelevant or unproductive or may suggest addressing them at a later time (privately thinking that the right time will be "never"). Because you assume that you understand the situation, you act as if your reasoning is foolproof without bothering to test whether your assumptions and data are accurate. Together, these strategies enable you to unilaterally control the situation and protect yourself and others. Through all of this, you keep your strategy for controlling the conversation private because divulging it would thwart the strategy or, even more likely, because you are not really aware of the strategy you are using.

Jonathan continues to advocate his point of view that porches are the solution. To his credit, he does not ease in. He does admit that there is not a lot of hard evidence to support his view, but he still continues to advocate it. He privately wonders what it is about the architect's logical plan that Parker doesn't get and does not ask Parker to explain his view. Because Jonathan has assumed that his view about Parker's favoring a healthy cash flow over redeeming architectural quality is valid, he does not ask Parker's view on the matter. Finally, Jonathan does not turn to a collaborative process to resolve their disagreement; instead, he tries to resolve it using a unilateral strategy.

Consequences. Ironically, by trying to control a situation, you contribute to creating the consequences you are trying to avoid. You create misunderstanding because you assume that the situation is as you see it, and you base your actions on untested assumptions about others. If you make negative assumptions about others' motives and do not test them, you build up your own mistrust of others and theirs of you. This leads them to be wary and cautious in their responses, which you perceive as defensive. In this way, you create a self-fulfilling process, generating the very consequences you set out to avoid. You also create a self-sealing process when you do not inquire into another person's defensive reaction because you believe it will only generate more defensiveness. Consequently, you seal off the opportunity for learning how your own behavior may be contributing to the collaboration's reduced effectiveness. All of this reduces the collaboration's ability to learn, its effectiveness, and quality of work life. It can be stressful when you cannot say what you are thinking without negative consequences. A great deal of mental energy gets tied up in trying to withhold what you are thinking or carefully craft what you are saying to dress up your intentions. The quality of decisions decreases, the amount of time needed to implement decisions increases, the commitment to those decisions decreases, and the quality of relationships suffers.

You can see the beginning of these consequences in Jonathan's case as he starts to make negative attributions about Parker's motives. By continuing to advocate his point of view and not be curious about Parker's views, Jonathan contributes to escalating the conflict, which he then uses as evidence to support his notion that Parker is not willing to compromise. They find themselves at an impasse, without a strategy for jointly learning which of their assumptions, if any, are valid. There is no commitment to a common course of action.

The Give-Up-Control Model: A Variation of Unilateral Control

When people recognize that they use the unilateral control model, they often want to change. Unfortunately, they often shift from one form of control to another—the give-up-control model, which I think of as a variant of the unilateral control model.

The core values of the give-up-control model are as follows: (1) everyone participates in defining the purpose, (2) everyone wins and no one loses, (3) you express your feelings, and (4) you suppress your intellectual reasoning (Argyris, 1979; Argyris, Putnam, and Smith, 1985). A key assumption is that for people to learn and be involved and committed, they must come to the right answer by themselves. Of course, the right answer is the one you have already decided on. When others don't see the answer that you prefer, a common strategy is to ease in or ask leading questions to help the people get the answer by themselves. The results of the give-up-control model are the same as those of the unilateral control model: increased misunderstanding, unproductive conflict and defensiveness, and reduced learning, effectiveness, and quality of work life.

People often move back and forth between the unilateral control model and its give-up-control variant. This commonly occurs when a manager seeks to empower his employees. After recognizing that he has been micromanaging and unilaterally controlling the group, the manager shifts to letting his group make decisions. He delegates an important decision to the group. However, in an effort not to influence his employees, he withholds relevant information he has, including criteria that the solution must meet. When the group proudly returns with a solution, the manager rejects it because it does not meet the criteria (which he did not communicate) or does not take into account the information he withheld. As a result, the group infers that the manager doesn't want to give up control and that he thinks the group is not ready to be empowered. The manager responds by shifting back to a unilaterally controlling approach. The give-up-control model is thus a variant form of unilateral control because it is imposed unilaterally.

Unilateral Control as Organizational Culture

When I describe these models to people involved in collaborative efforts, they often smile; they recognize themselves in the picture and the way their organization often operates. When I described it to one group of leaders, they told me that not only was unilateral control the model they often used but that their organization had been rewarding them for this behavior for years. They were trying to change but didn't have another approach to replace it with. Unfortunately, people are usually unaware that they are using the unilateral control model, although others can clearly see it. Fortunately, with practice, you can identify it for yourself and begin to learn a more effective approach.

The Facilitative Leader Approach: Creating Collaborative Outcomes by Changing Your Mind-Set

What would it look like if you approached challenging collaborative situations without using some form of the unilateral control model? In Jonathan's example, Jonathan might begin by saying, "Parker, let's discuss our views regarding the use of porches and brick. It looks like we disagree about whether porches will increase the value of the homes and, if they do, whether it is possible to have porches and brick together. Do you see our disagreement differently?" If Parker agrees that this is the disagreement, Jonathan can continue, "Rather than trying to convince each other, how about if together we figure out a way to find out whether porches will increase the value of the homes and, if they do, whether it is possible to have porches and bricks together? I'm open to the fact that I might be missing some key information. We would agree beforehand on what data we need to look at, what assumptions we want to make, and whom to talk with. What do you think? Do you have any concerns about doing it this way?"

The Mutual Learning Model

The example just given illustrates the Facilitative Leader approach. At the heart of this approach is the *mutual learning model* (see Figure 14.2), which can generate long-term positive results that the unilateral control model or give-up-control model cannot. You do not have to be in a formal leadership role to be a facilitative leader; team members and even individual contributors serve as facilitative leaders by virtue of using the core values and assumptions, principles, and techniques. In short, the Facilitative Leader approach enables you to lead collaboratively from any position. Although it can be easier to establish collaborative relationships when all the parties understand the Facilitative Leader approach, it is not necessary.

Like the unilateral control model, the mutual learning model has a set of values and assumptions, strategies, and consequences. As its name indicates, the model values learning and shared control rather than winning and unilateral control.

Core Values. The mutual learning model has four core values. First, you seek to collect and share valid information. Valid information includes all the rel-

FIGURE 14.2. MUTUAL LEARNING MODEL.

Core Values and Assumptions		Strategies	Consequences
• Valid information • Free and informed choice • Internal commitment • Compassion	• I have some information; others have other information • Each of us may see things the others do not • Differences are opportunities for learning • People are trying to act with integrity given their situations	• Test assumptions and inferences • Share all relevant information • Use specific examples and agree on important words • Explain reasoning and intent • Focus on interests, not positions • Combine advocacy and inquiry • Jointly design the approach • Discuss undiscussables • Use a decision-making rule that generates the commitment needed	• Increased understanding, reduced unproductive conflict, reduced defensiveness • Increased trust • Reduced self-fulfilling, self-sealing processes • Increased learning • Increased effectiveness • Increased quality of work life

Sources: Adapted from Argyris and Schön's Model II (1974) and Putnam, Smith, and MacArthur's Mutual Learning Model (1997).

evant information you have on the subject (whether it supports your position or not). Ideally, others can independently validate the information you share. Effective collaboration requires that you create a common pool of data and shared meaning. Second, you seek to encourage free and informed choice so that people agree to do things because they have the relevant information and because they believe the decision makes sense, not because they feel manipulated or coerced into it. You seek internal commitment to the decisions, which often flows from the first two values—with this level of motivation, people will do whatever is necessary to implement the decisions.

Finally, you value compassion, which means temporarily suspending judgment in order to appreciate others' perspectives. It means having empathy for others and for yourself in a way that still holds people accountable for their actions rather than unilaterally protecting others or yourself. When you act with compassion, you infuse the other core values with your intent to understand, empathize with, and help others. *Compassion* literally means "suffering with," although it is sometimes mistakenly thought of as having pity for others. The kind of compassion I have in mind enables you to have empathy for others and for yourself in a way that still holds you and others accountable for your actions. This kind of compassion does not involve unilateral protection and enhances the other core values, rather than diminishing them. Compassion comes from the heart. If you act out of compassion rather than out of fear and guilt, you are able to move beyond defensiveness and be open and vulnerable. This enables you to engage in conversations in which you can mutually learn with others how to increase your effectiveness.

Core Assumptions. As a facilitative leader, you assume that you have some information and that others have other information and therefore that other people may see things you have missed and vice versa. In other words, you know that you don't know all that you need to know. This includes recognizing that you may inadvertently be contributing to problems. This leads you to be curious and to ask about the ways in which others see you as contributing to the problems.

You assume that differences are opportunities for learning rather than conflicts to be avoided or contests in which you must show that you're right and others are wrong. And you assume that people are trying to act with integrity, given their situations. If people are acting in ways that do not make sense to you or that you think you understand but disapprove of, you do not conclude that they are acting that way out of some dubious motive. Instead, you begin from the assumption that people are striving to do the right thing; part of your task becomes understanding the reasons for their actions and then evaluating them accordingly.

You see these interactions as an intriguing puzzle—everyone has some pieces to offer, and the task is to complete the puzzle together. By exploring how people see things differently, you can help the group reach a common understanding that enables you all to move forward in a way that everyone can support. You are eager to explore differences because you see them as possible routes to greater understanding and solutions that integrate multiple perspectives. Compare these core values and assumptions with those of the unilateral control model.

Principles. Several key principles are associated with the mutual learning core values and assumptions.

Curiosity is a desire to learn more about something. It motivates you to find out what information others have that you might be missing and to explore how others came to a different conclusion rather than simply trying to persuade others that their conclusions are wrong.

Transparency is the quality of sharing all relevant information, including your strategies, in a way that is timely and valid. It includes divulging your strategy for discussion with the other participants so that together you can make free and informed choices about your collaboration. Transparency is difficult when you are acting unilaterally because revealing your strategy would render it ineffective. But being transparent when using a mutual learning approach actually increases the effectiveness of your strategy, which is now to learn together rather than to control the situation.

Joint accountability means that you share responsibility for the current situation, including the eventual consequences. Being accountable means that you are responsible for addressing your problems with others directly rather than avoiding them or asking others to do this for you. Instead of seeking to blame others, you recognize that because you are part of a system, your actions contribute to maintaining the system or changing it.

These three principles—curiosity, transparency, and joint accountability—are interwoven with the core values and assumptions of the mutual learning model. Together they are put into action in the strategies that follow.

Strategies. The strategies that facilitative leaders use to implement their core values and assumptions are also known as the *ground rules for effective groups* (for more information, see "Ground Rules for Effective Groups," by Roger Schwarz, published by Roger Schwarz & Associates, http://www.schwarzassociates.com). Many of these ground rules are designed to generate valid information. For example, you test whether the assumptions that you are making about others are valid before you act on them as if they are true. You share all the relevant information you have about an issue (whether or not it supports your position) by using specific examples, by explaining the reasoning that leads to your conclusions, and by stating the underlying needs, interests, or criteria that are important for you to meet. You create learning opportunities for yourself and others by asking others to identify things you may have overlooked after you have shared your thinking. To increase free and informed choice and internal commitment, you jointly design next steps with others. And you raise the undiscussable issues that have been keeping the team from increasing its effectiveness. Using these strategies does *not* mean that you have to make decisions by consensus. Although that is an option in the Facilitative Leader approach, it's not a requirement.

Consequences. Leaders who use this approach make several outcomes possible, including increased quality of decisions or results, increased commitment to implementing the results, reduced time for effective implementation, improved working relationships, increased organizational learning, and enhanced personal satisfaction. These outcomes are generated through the following consequences.

Increased Understanding, Reduced Unproductive Conflict, and Reduced Defensiveness. With the mutual learning approach, you increase understanding because you test assumptions and assemble valid information. You also assume that others have information you do not have and that they may see things you have overlooked. By assuming that people are striving to act with integrity, you reduce the negative attributions you make about others. You test attributions you do make with the people about whom you are making them. By doing so, you reduce the unproductive conflicts that arise from acting on untested, inaccurate assumptions and the defensive behaviors associated with them. Similarly, you increase trust. Using a mutual learning approach does not ensure that others will respond nondefensively; however, it does reduce the chance that you will provoke or contribute to others' defensive reactions.

Reduced Self-Fulfilling, Self-Sealing Processes. Acting on untested, inaccurate assumptions is the first step in self-fulfilling and self-sealing processes. By testing out your assumptions, you reduce the likelihood of such processes. Even if you do create a self-fulfilling process, your openness to learning how you created the problem will reduce the chance that it becomes self-sealing.

Increased Learning, Effectiveness, and Quality of Work Life. All of this information enables you and others to develop shared meaning that increases learning opportunities for yourself and the group. This includes learning how you and group members each contribute to the group's effectiveness and ineffectiveness. Together these results increase the group's effectiveness—its performance, its process, and the satisfaction of group members' personal needs. The mutual learning values and assumptions enable you to increase understanding and trust and reduce defensive behavior. This reduces feelings of anxiety, fear, and anger that create stress.

How You Think Is How You Lead

When I introduce the Facilitative Leader approach and the mutual learning model to people, it often seems like common sense to people, and sometimes they say, "I already do this." Not until they examine their own specific situations (often with help from others) do they begin to see the gap between how they think they lead and how they really lead.

The challenge in becoming a facilitative leader is not understanding the approach or even learning the strategies; it is learning to think differently. It means unlearning years of employing a unilateral control mind-set that you used skillfully and effortlessly. Here's why. If you only learn to apply the strategies of the mutual learning model, you will end up using them with a unilateral control model set of values and assumptions, which will generate the same negative consequences you've gotten in the past. That's because it's your core values and assumptions that drive your strategies and their eventual consequences.

How Unilateral Control Reduces Collaborative Structures and Outcomes

To develop a sustainable culture of collaboration, it is not enough to create conversations congruent with the mutual learning model.* Even when individuals have the ability to engage in mutual learning conversations, if group or organizational structures have unilateral control elements in them, they can have a powerfully negative effect on organizational members' ability to collaborate. (Borrowing from Allport, 1967, I define structure simply as a stable recurring process that results from individuals interacting with each other in certain ways. Using this definition, policies and procedures are forms of structure.)

*Portions of this discussion are adapted from Schwarz and Davidson (2005).

Unfortunately, the unilateral control model that leaders use and that generates dysfunctional conversations and relationships also leads them to design team and organizational structures that have unilateral core values and assumptions embedded in them. This is predictable. Leaders use their theory in use (or mental model) to design group and organizational structures. Given that many of these structures are designed to avoid some past or potential threat and that almost everyone uses a unilateral control approach under conditions of threat, you can expect to find unilateral elements embedded in many of these structures.

Examples of Unilateral Structures

Here are two examples of unilateral structures in client organizations and how they reduce genuine collaboration.

Managing Performance Problems in Teams. Many organizations tout the importance of their teams and at the same time set up structures that reduce teams' ability to tackle their own challenges. In many organizations, if a team member is not performing adequately and the supervisor is taking progressive disciplinary action to address the performance, the supervisor can't share with other team members that she has taken these actions or what they are. She can state only that she is "handling the issue." This is true even if the other team members initially raised the performance issue with the entire team and team leader present and if the team members continue to provide the member and leader with feedback about that team member's performance. This policy protects that employee's privacy and reduces the risk of liability associated with possible violations of privacy. It is also based on the unilateral value of minimizing the expression of negative feelings and the strategy of saving face. It potentially avoids difficult conversations that the manager might have to have with other employees who want to know what the manager is doing about the situation. Team members are left making inferences about whether and how the supervisor is addressing the team member who is having a problem. It makes undiscussable the poor performance that team members were likely to have not only seen but also brought to the attention of the leader. Essentially, it creates a situation in which team members can no longer work together to support the member having a problem. Removing this support increases the chance that the person will be moved or fired. The message implicit in this structure is that when situations get difficult, team collaboration and support are inappropriate. And the structure is the direct result of leaders' using a unilateral control model.

Establishing Organizational Budgets. Many CEOs exhort their executives to collaborate to enhance organizational performance and learning rather than simply focus on their own organizational areas. At the same time, the budgeting process is often designed so that executives each seek to win out over the others and hence share and withhold information strategically.

In one organization, department heads prepare their annual budget requests independently and then submit them to the finance director. Each advocates for as much as possible, knowing that there will be subsequent cuts. The finance director consolidates the requests and takes them to the COO, along with recommendations for cuts. The COO and finance director then go back to each department head individually to tell each one how much (and in some cases, where) to cut their budgets. Department heads never see one another's requests or detailed line-item breakdowns. Most feel that the process is unfair and assume that cuts are based in part on favoritism, so they try to outmaneuver one another by the way they present and justify their budgets. They sometimes make tenuous or questionable links to the COO's or finance director's favored initiatives. This process of competition, inflated requests, and hidden agendas is commonly referred to as "the budget game."

Not only does this kind of budget process encourage the withholding of information, but it also prevents department heads—key organizational leaders—from learning about critical organizational issues and opportunities. It reinforces the traditional "silo" mentality that often causes leaders to work at cross-purposes and limits their understanding of interdependence. They are subsequently blamed by those above and below them in the organization for not thinking systemically when in fact they lack important information that would lead them to see key interrelationships in different ways. The structure itself is designed to reduce collaboration. And the structure is typically established using the unilateral control model as a template.

Redesigning Structures for Collaboration

Unless you are working in a relatively new organization, yours probably has many structures (perhaps too many) for dealing with various issues. Consequently, the task in your organization is likely to be one of redesigning existing structures so they generate the outcomes of learning and collaboration without leading to unintended consequences. Ultimately, designing collaborative structures (like designing collaborative conversations) requires leaders who can operate from a mutual learning model or who are willing to work with someone who can help them rigorously reflect on their mental models. In either case, there are several steps you can take to redesign structures to make them collaborative.

Identify the Source

Find out whether the structure (policy, procedure) in question stems from a law, a generally accepted industry or professional practice, a formal or informal organizational policy, or a norm in the organization. A policy that originates in law is obviously more difficult to change than a policy developed independently by your organization or a policy that is a norm.

Identify Elements That Are Within Your Control

If a structure is actually a norm or a guideline that you have discretion to adapt, consider amending it so that it reduces unintended consequences. One client organization has adopted a collaborative budget process in which everyone involved sits down together at the same time each year and develops an organizational budget. Department heads frequently offer funding priority to other departments with more critical needs. All feel responsible for devising a fair and realistic budget that reflects organizational rather than departmental priorities. After several years of collaborative budgeting, these leaders say they no longer play the budget game, the budget-making process is faster overall, they engage in better long-range planning and capital budgeting, and the role of the finance and budget staff has moved from control of others to support and involvement in decision making. The department heads see themselves as partners rather than competitors.

Similarly, some clients have created teams in which the entire team addresses problems of team member performance that affect the team. To implement this fundamental change, team members reframed their idea of what it meant to be accountable to other team members. This included the assumption that if you have relevant information to share about someone on the team, withholding it or not sharing it in a straightforward manner prevents the team from identifying the issues and understanding how various members may have contributed to the problem. By reframing what it means to be accountable, team members were able to solve problems that had previously gone unsolved and increased the ability to work together as a team.

Understand Exactly What the Structure Says and Does Not Say

If it is a written structure such as a policy, examine it and learn firsthand what it says and does not say. If the structure is based on law, explore whether it is more restrictive than the law requires. If it seems more restrictive than your understanding of the law on which it is based, find out whether that is the intent. If it's not, you may have more freedom to redesign it. If the structure is unwritten, explore with the people responsible for it what it requires. Do not assume that a practice is a formal policy or law simply because someone tells you it is. Verify the information; ask the relevant people to document the details. In my experience, organizational members sometimes cite something as policy or law because they have been told it is policy or law, yet when asked to do so, no one is able to produce any evidence to that effect.

Explore the assumptions, values, and interests that the designers used to generate the structure. Share your assumptions, values, interests, and the unintended consequences you see of the current structure. Structures are solutions that leaders design to address perceived problems or opportunities. Interests are needs that the structure takes into account or criteria that the structure needs to meet. For example, a typical interest or criterion for any performance feedback system is that it be designed in a way that provides the recipients with accurate and usable information. Be curious about the interests that generated a particular structure. Identify interests that are not being met by the current structure, and ask for reactions from relevant parties.

Leaders also use their own values and assumptions to design structures—and this is how structures often become embedded with unilateral control elements. For example, using the unilateral control core value of minimizing expression of negative feelings, leaders usually structure performance feedback to be anonymous (unless it comes directly from the boss). Similarly, using the unilateral control assumption of "I'm right and anyone who disagrees is wrong," leaders design the structure so that when a manager gives a direct report feedback, the performance rating is already established and is rarely open to being changed. These core values and assumptions lead to the misunderstanding, defensiveness, and limited learning associated with the unilateral control outcomes. Helping leaders explore the unintended consequences of their core values and assumptions is a crucial step in redesign.

Explore Redesigns in Accordance with the Mutual Learning Model

Explore whether and how a structure or policy can be designed and implemented so that it reflects the values and assumptions of the mutual learning model and also addresses the interests you have identified. In one learning organization I know of, when policies come up for review (because they are not meeting organization needs or are perceived as being inconsistent with the values), the leadership team or a selected group of employees is given the task of reviewing the policy and identifying the interests that a new policy must satisfy. When a new policy is written, the interests that it is attempting to meet are stated in the first paragraph. Then the guidelines are given. There are usually several acceptable ways to meet the stated interests, and providing choices significantly increases commitment to following desired practices.

In the case of performance feedback, new solutions become possible with the shift from unilateral control to mutual learning values and assumptions. For example, if the person giving feedback does not assume that he or she is necessarily right, the feedback conversation becomes a setting in which both parties can be genuinely curious about how to work more effectively together, which includes the possibility of the manager's changing his or her behavior.

By rigorously examining organizational and team structures and redesigning them when appropriate, leaders create structures that foster genuine collaboration and learning.

Conclusion

Creating a culture of collaboration requires that all parties involved jointly design ways to work together to meet their related interests and learn with and from each other, sharing responsibility, authority, and accountability for achieving results. Sustaining a culture of collaboration involves facilitating collaboration conversation and supporting structures that make collaborative behavior possible. The Facilitative Leader approach, which has the mutual learning model at its core, is one successful approach to creating an organizational culture of collaboration.

References

Allport, F. H. "A Theory of Enestruence (Event Structure Theory): Report of Progress." *American Psychologist,* 1967, *22,* 1–24.

Argyris, C. "Reflecting on Laboratory Education from a Theory of Action Perspective." *Journal of Applied Behavioral Science,* 1979, *15,* 296–310.

Argyris, C., Putnam, R. W,, and Smith, D. M. *Action Science: Concepts, Methods, and Skills for Research and Intervention.* San Francisco: Jossey-Bass, 1985.

Argyris, C., and Schön, D. A. *Theory in Practice: Increasing Professional Effectiveness.* San Francisco: Jossey-Bass, 1974.

Chrislip, D. D., and Larson, C. E. *Collaborative Leadership: How Citizens and Civic Leaders Can Make a Difference.* San Francisco: Jossey-Bass, 1994.

Putnam, R. W., Smith, D. M., and MacArthur, P. Workshop Materials. Newton, Mass.: Action Design, 1997.

Schwarz, R. *The Skilled Facilitator: A Comprehensive Resource for Consultants, Facilitators, Managers, Trainers, and Coaches.* (rev. ed.) San Francisco: Jossey-Bass, 2002.

Schwarz, R., and Davidson, A. "Integrating the Skilled Facilitator Approach with Organizational Policies and Procedures." In R. Schwarz, A. Davidson, P. Carlson, and S. McKinney, *The Skilled Facilitator Fieldbook: Tips, Tools, and Tested Methods for Consultants, Facilitators, Managers, Trainers, and Coaches.* San Francisco: Jossey-Bass, 2005.

Ante Glavas is a doctoral student in organizational behavior at the Weatherhead School of Management at Case Western Reserve University and vice-dean of CBA, a business school in Croatia. His background is in systems thinking applied to personal development and business processes. Past experiences include developing Croatia's first private business school, which has professors such as Peter Senge and Margaret Wheatley; working as a regional manager in a major global company, Diageo; starting up his own company in organic food and deep ecology; and setting up a leadership school and a training institute. He has lived in five countries, having spent about half his life in the United States and half in Europe. He has published two articles and a book chapter all based on systemic leadership.

Claudy Jules is a doctoral candidate in organizational behavior at the Weatherhead School of Management at Case Western Reserve University. His research interests are in embedded intergroup dynamics, work team effectiveness, and the application of clinical inquiry in organizational research and consulting. He teaches courses in group dynamics, organizational behavior, and leading change. He has consulted on organization and change strategy issues for a broad range of industries.

He served as an adviser to the organization change consulting practice of CGI-AMS and has worked for the change management practice of KPMG Consulting and later as an organizational consultant and trainer for Georgetown University Hospital. Jules earned his master of science degree from the joint program in organization development at the American University and NTL Institute for Applied Behavioral Science. He also holds a master of science degree in management and a bachelor of arts degree in African American studies from the University of Maryland and has completed a one-year intensive postgraduate training program in organization and systems development at the Gestalt Institute of Cleveland. He is a member of the Academy of Management, the NTL Institute, and the OD Network.

Ellen Van Oosten is a doctoral student in organizational behavior at the Weatherhead School of Management at Case Western Reserve University. Her teaching and research focus is in the areas of leadership development, executive coaching, team coaching, and the link between individual development and organization development. Prior to beginning the Ph.D. program, Van Oosten worked for ten years in the Weatherhead School's Executive Education Department, most recently as assistant dean. In that role, she worked with top executives from Fortune 500 organizations to develop their leadership talent. She also holds a master of business administration degree from the Weatherhead School of Management and a bachelor of science degree in electrical engineering from the University of Dayton. She is a member of the Northeast Ohio Human Resources Planning Society.

CHAPTER FIFTEEN

USE OF SELF IN CREATING A CULTURE OF COLLABORATION

Ante Glavas, Claudy Jules, Ellen Van Oosten

You must be the change you wish to see in the world.

MAHATMA GANDHI

Change is an inescapable part of organizational life. For some people, it is the transition from individual team contributor in a silo structure to new department manager in a matrix structure. For others, it can be the merger of rival companies and the integration of these cultures. As a leader, manager, organizational member, or practitioner involved in facilitating and managing change across all levels in social systems, perhaps you have found yourself in such a situation at some point.

The essence of this chapter is the way in which practitioners use themselves—their own strengths—in service of the organizations they work with. Rather than focusing on skills and methods that the practitioner can use, we focus on who the practitioner is and how the practitioner applies himself or herself on the job. We focus primarily on awareness as the key component to the use of self. Awareness in this chapter is related to self-awareness and one's awareness of the organization as a whole, referred to as organizational awareness in a model described later. The intended audience is organizational lead-

The authors thank Charlie Seashore, Don McCormick, Meredith Myers, and Margaret Rudolf for their helpful comments on an earlier version of this chapter.

ers, managers, coaches, group facilitators, and consultants; we use the term *practitioner* to represent someone in any of those roles.

At the State of the World Forum, a peace conference for world leaders held in Belfast, Ireland, in 1999, Ben Zander, the famous lecturer and conductor of the Boston Philharmonic Orchestra, pointed out that anyone can learn to play an instrument or read music. However, true musicians will dig inside themselves, really get to know themselves, and then let go of their internal fears and ego in order to be able to give themselves completely to the music. It is this difference that separates great musicians from the rest.

We will not propose the instruments that practitioners can use, nor will we give advice on how to play those instruments. Rather, we will focus on what separates effective practitioners from the rest—which is their use of self in their work. Other chapters in this book, and other literature, describe what actions are necessary for the practitioner to undertake in order to create a culture of collaboration. Few models exist on who the practitioner has to *be*. It is perhaps ironic that practitioners overlook the part of the process on which they can have the greatest influence—themselves. Like Gandhi, we believe that change in any organization begins first with the practitioner.

We present a story of two important aspects of change: the use of self and how to work with others in building a culture of collaboration. The story is an example of an organization development (OD) consultant trying to build a collaborative culture, where his limited use of self hindered his effectiveness in helping the client organization meet its needs. Following the story, we present a model and some factors to consider in working with organizations to create a culture of collaboration.

A Consultant's Dilemma

Joe Dutton was an organization development consultant hired to provide consulting to a large financial services organization in the United States. The client organization was merging two business units into a single division and had hired a new managing director to oversee the division. Joe's assignment was a significant challenge: to integrate a historically command-and-control culture into one characterized by collaboration and employee participation. The target audience for his initial work was the managing director and his senior management team.

During Joe's entry stage, he relied on his consulting experience with senior teams in financial institutions. His first step was to conduct a series of interviews with key members of the senior management team and several employees from the two units being merged. After synthesizing the data from the interviews, Joe presented a plan to senior management for building a culture of collaboration.

The plan Joe constructed and followed relied heavily on standard, well-known team-building programs. He led a series of team-building workshops and exercises throughout the organization and invited a cross-functional representation of employees to each one. In the workshops, Joe served as a "trainer" and ran the courses in a very traditional manner in which he served as the subject matter expert. The workshops were well received initially. They enabled employees to know one another at a deeper level and provided the organization with a blueprint for how to increase productivity in teams—both important objectives.

Despite the significant amount of time and money invested to complete the workshops for the entire organization, results were hard to pinpoint. The senior management group grew uneasy and impatient as not much appeared to be changing in the organization. Many people both in the workshops and later offered suggestions to Joe for improving the workshops. One frequent recommendation was to draw on the participants' own expertise throughout the workshops. Another request was to customize the workshops to fit the specific context of the participants' business. Joe considered these ideas but opted to continue with his approach, reassuring his client that as time went on, change would happen. More time passed, but little changed in the company's culture. Joe's contract came to an end shortly thereafter and was not renewed.

Months later, Joe attended a philharmonic concert. It was at that event that he gained insight as to what he could have done differently. It was an experience he would remember for years thereafter. The orchestra put on a terrific performance. What intrigued him was that the philharmonic's conductor had arranged the orchestra so that the musicians sat among the audience while they were playing. After the performance, Joe approached the conductor and asked, "What inspired you to have the orchestra sit in the crowd?" The conductor replied, "The orchestra was not here to perform, nor was the orchestra here to play *for* the audience. The orchestra was here to play *with* the audience." It is only by sitting as a part of the audience that a collective experience could emerge.

Joe realized that there was a lesson to draw from this experience. The way he approached his consulting work with financial services companies was similar to the traditional way in which orchestras perform. He had played the role of the conductor or expert. He was up on a stage looking down at his audience. He knew exactly what notes to play. The trap he fell into was that he never stopped to sit side by side with his audience and integrate them into the performance. Joe later became a very successful consultant. He attributed his success to the lesson he learned at the philharmonic: that when creating collaboration, all members play a role.

Although this story has been oversimplified for the sake of example, we consider Joe's experience throughout this chapter as we offer ideas on how practitioners can use themselves in building a culture of collaboration.

Use of Self

What do we mean by "use of self"? Is it simply an empty OD catchphrase? One might suspect that OD practitioners and others affiliated with the applied behavioral sciences use the term to gain marquee appeal. However, the practice of use of self is neither new nor unexamined. A normative view held by many scholars and practitioners in the fields of human behavior and planned change is that the use of self as an instrument for change is the primary tool practitioners can use during their consultation. In recent years, a few authors have embarked on the journey to establish a common language and set of characteristics on use of self (Cheung-Judge, 2001; Curran, Seashore, and Welp, 1995; Hanson, 2000; Kashtan, 2005; McCormick and White, 2000; Seashore, Shawver, Thompson, and Mattare, 2004; Smith, 1990). A thread that weaves together these writers' different perspectives about use of self is that to understand how to use the self, practitioners must first understand themselves and demonstrate a practice of active commitment to examine, take in, and experience the world outside themselves. As one author notes, "It requires sitting on the boundary between being a part of the [system] and being apart from the [system]" (Smith, 1990, p. 277).

As a concept, use of self is inherently broad. We were unable to find a single commonly understood and accepted definition. In terms of a working definition, use of self can be described as the bridge connecting an individual's personal potential and the intended change the person seeks. It includes elements such as "what we do with our perceptions to make an impact in the world around us" and "intentional conscious actions taken with the hope of bringing about change" (Seashore, Shawver, Thompson, and Mattare, 2004, p. 44). Use of self includes our conscious and unconscious perceptions of who we are. Those thoughts are linked with our perception of what is required by the desired changes we seek in our life and the decisions we make regarding the role we wish to play in bringing about change.

Going a level deeper, social psychologist Roy Baumeister suggests that there are three patterns of experience people use to make sense of the basic meaning of "self": reflexive consciousness, interpersonal aspects of selfhood, and the executive function. *Reflexive consciousness* is "conscious attention turning back on its own source and gradually constructing a concept of oneself" (Baumeister, 1998, p. 680). Looking in the mirror, stepping on the scale, and reading your résumé are all examples of experiences that involve the reflexive consciousness.

The *interpersonal aspects* of selfhood are the inherent connections we, as individuals, have with others. Putting on your best suit to make a positive impression at an important job interview, keeping a promise to someone, and feeling warmth and happiness during a surprise reunion with a long-lost friend are all examples of experiences that reveal the interpersonal nature of self.

The *executive function* represents the command central, the director, and the air traffic controller. Stopping yourself from eating that third cookie, voting on election day, and pushing yourself to keep going in the face of exhaustion are experiences that involve the executive function. It is the part of us that gives us will or energy to take action.

Self as an Instrument for Building a Culture of Collaboration

To fully understand the dynamics of organizations as open social systems and the dimensions of using oneself, it's helpful to have a conceptual understanding of "self" as a system. Our starting point is that a practitioner must be able to take in input from his or her environment and focus that input to various change processes resulting in an output (for example, humans inhale oxygen, their bodies convert it, and they exhale carbon dioxide back into the environment).

A number of scholars and practitioners have attempted to develop theories and methods for using the self; our approach is based on a systems para-

FIGURE 15.1. MASTERING THE USE OF SELF AS AN INSTRUMENT FOR COLLABORATION (MUSIC).

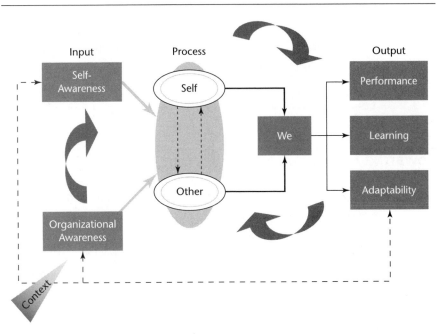

digm we call Mastering the Use of Self as an Instrument for Collaboration (MUSIC), illustrated in Figure 15.1.

MUSIC consists of three components: input, process, and output. They represent a conceptual division; in practice, they often occur simultaneously, with each part feeding back into the other parts. The input component consists of self-awareness and organizational awareness. In our model, the practitioner needs to be aware of himself or herself in terms of mental models, fears, ego, and anything else that can contribute or detract from quality of work and from the organization (performance expectations, organizational culture, decision-making structures, who is influential, and so on) before going to work. The process component consists of the self (the practitioner) and others (the group that the practitioner is directly working with in the organization). At the start of the work, usually the self and others are two separate entities. In our model, the effective practitioner is able to join those two entities into one entity, identified as "we" in the model. The output component consists of performance, learning, and adaptability. In our experience, these are the three outputs that an effective practitioner works toward. Output is critical because it gives direction to the process. If you don't know where you are going, you won't be able to get there.

The following sections of this chapter focus on the input, process, and output components in a change practitioner or group facilitator's use of self. These insights should be helpful not just for OD practitioners or group facilitators but for all who aspire to make a difference in the social systems around them.

Toward a Definition of a Culture of Collaboration

Our model integrates the self and the environment as well as the interplay between these two components. The purpose of this section is to introduce our MUSIC model first by defining what we mean by building a culture of collaboration and then by integrating content with process.

A culture of collaboration is a deeply shared belief system that places value on and fosters a practice of working collectively to boost organizational performance, learning, and adaptability. As Schein (1993) notes, culture is a learned product of a system's experience. As systems theory (Von Bertalanffy, 1950) informs us, a system is considered as a whole and as an aggregate of its parts. Thus a system is more than a collection of parts or the sum of its parts.

Input and Process

As stated earlier, effective use of self begins, logically enough, with oneself. The first component is made up of awareness of self and awareness of the organizational environment. The second component is self differentiating from other and the collective as a whole. The third component encompasses the converted outputs, including performance, learning, and adaptability.

Know Yourself

Use of self in building a culture of collaboration starts fundamentally with understanding oneself. From this point, it extends to a practitioner's awareness of the environment. The extent to which this awareness is accurate determines the extent to which the person will be effective in the role of change agent. Therefore, self-awareness is key.

Goleman defines self-awareness as "knowing what we are feeling in the moment, and using those preferences to guide our decision-making; having a realistic assessment of our own abilities and a well-grounded sense of self-confidence" (Goleman, 1998, p. 318). Goleman, Boyatzis, and McKee (2002) expand this idea of self-awareness as a competency to incorporate three specific behaviors: emotional self-awareness, accurate self-assessment, and self-confidence.

When practitioners tune in to their inner selves and notice their thoughts, feelings, moods, they are better able to manage their emotions appropriately. Thus practitioners are more likely to demonstrate empathy in dealing with others, which in turn positions them to better manage their relationships with others. This is a signature skill of emotionally intelligent leaders (Goleman, 1998). The impact of this is magnified in the context of creating a collaborative culture because demonstration of empathy increases when an organization exhibits self-awareness. As noted in *Primal Leadership* (Goleman, Boyatzis, and McKee, 2002), practitioners who demonstrate empathy help create a climate of positive norms in relationships. Empathy when practiced by members of an organization leads to organizational awareness and allows effective relationships to flourish.

In addition to Goleman's conceptualization of self-awareness, practitioners need to be aware of their thinking, mental models, and patterns of behavior. It is important to ask the team to work collaboratively to expose each member's mental models. If the mental models can be aligned, performance in the team will increase (Druskat and Pescosolido, 2002).

To strive for effective use of self means to strive for greater self-awareness and self-development. Effective self-applying practitioners must constantly engage in conscious and deliberate inquiry of their thoughts, feelings, and actions. More to the point, clarity of intentions is essential for effective practice.

In the story about Joe Dutton, Joe was not attuned to his inner mental model or aware that he was set in one. He thought that team building was the only possible model for creating a culture of collaboration. The more the employees disagreed with his model, the more he became upset and lacked empathy for the employees. He saw them as resistant rather than trying to understand the reasons for their behavior. By the end of the project, Joe had had several episodes when his emotions got the better of him, reflecting how disappointed he was in the employees.

Know Your Focus

Knowing oneself is only part of the process. You can know yourself and your own mental models and force them on the organization you are working with. Many practitioners can fall into the trap of getting more caught up in themselves than in the organization. For example, "by exposing aspects of ourselves, we can develop clarity of purpose in what we are trying to achieve. By not doing so, we run the risk of acting on our unconscious needs instead of exploring our conscious choices for what we to do" (Kashtan, 2005, p. 578). At the conscious level, practitioners may act as if they are truly there for the organization while at the subconscious level they may believe that they are the center of the organization.

For example, in Freudian terms, the practitioner may become caught up in his or her superego. The superego is a dominant force if the practitioner's main goal is to help the organization only so that the person can feel a sense of personal competence or excellence. In such a scenario, the practitioner's ultimate goal is not the benefit of the organization but rather his or her own personal benefit.

Alternatively, practitioners may fall victim to the Superman syndrome or Messiah complex. This is evident when practitioners pushes their own agenda and aren't really concerned with the needs of the organization. The reason they push their own agenda is that they feel they are experts who should be listened to. This results in one-way communication in which the practitioner talks down to the organization and discounts listening to other voices in the organization. The organization's collective potential is never tapped into. The focus rests exclusively on what the practitioner has to offer the organization rather than what the organization has to offer the practitioner.

We believe that an effective practitioner establishes a balance between his or her own needs and the needs of the organization. For example, Joe Dutton might have been more effective if he focused more on understanding his client. At the time, he seemed to be playing out the role of the superconsultant. His behavior reflected reliance on personal experience and approaches that had worked well for him in the past. Had he balanced that confidence with efforts to learn more about his client by asking questions, listening, and attempting to understand the existing culture himself, his plan might have produced greater results.

Know Your Surroundings

Once practitioners have established balance with the client to work collaboratively between taking in and being taken in by the client, the next step is to "know thy surroundings," or in other words, to become aware of the client. Here, use of self in building a culture of collaboration also incorporates organizational awareness or awareness of the context within which the practitioner operates. Organizational awareness is the ability of the practitioner to accurately understand the environment within which he or she is working. A practitioner demonstrating organizational awareness is politically astute, is attuned to important social networks, and can accurately interpret the distribution of power in an organization (Goleman, Boyatzis, and McKee, 2002).

To be aware of the organization, practitioners need to keep in mind that their perception of the organization is subjective. There are two explanations why perception can never be objective. One is biological and is described by Zull (2002) as a process whereby our brain receives visual and other sensory information objectively, which we then interpret subjectively. This is similar to the notion of mental models (Senge, 1990) or the way we make sense of the world. The other argument, derived from biophysics (von Foerster, 1973), argues, contrary to Zull, that our brain does not perceive the world objectively. The same objects are seen and sensed differently by each person.

Whether we take the stance presented by Zull or by von Foerster, the end result is the same. Perceptions and interpretations vary, are unique to each person, and are therefore subjective. The question then arises as to how practitioners can ever truly know their surroundings. We suggest that practitioners can take certain steps to assess the environment, such as asking for the perceptions of individual members of the organization, cross-checking these with their own perceptions, conveying what they perceive to the organization and obtaining feedback, and administering surveys or other tools for organizational assessment.

One of the traps that Joe Dutton fell into was imposing his own agenda. He did not even try to find out more about the division.

Know the Scope of Your Influence

Once you are aware of yourself and of the organization, the next step is to begin the process of building a culture of collaboration. In doing so, it is important to be aware of the scope of your influence. All that practitioners can do is influence and create the conditions for others to achieve their desired state.

If practitioners see that something they are doing is not influencing the organization toward desired outcomes, they should make a course correction, gather information, and try something new. In the case of Joe Dutton, he missed the opportunity to revise his approach when it became clear that things weren't going as planned.

Joe failed to realize that people do not respond in a simple causal manner like machines. With machines, one can push a button and expect a certain response. But with people, what one person does will not always influence others to act in the expected way. Joe should have allowed for the possibility that what he was doing might not work. He could have changed his plans after the first negative signs.

Know When to Change Your Behaviors

Seeing a culture of collaboration emerging is a major milestone. Realizing such a success, practitioners may feel they have taken the correct actions. Nevertheless, the actions needed in the future are not necessarily the same as those that were useful in the past. During each step of the process, different behaviors are needed. Each situation needs a specific type of leadership (Blake and others, 2000). Similarly, each component of our model requires a different form of acting by practitioners. They need to take another hard look at themselves once they get to know when to change behaviors and determine what actions are needed.

In Joe's case, although his work with the financial services firm failed, he learned from the experience. He succeeded in the end because he learned that the plan he had was wrong to start with and that in the future, he would need to listen more effectively to his clients to correct course and make appropriate changes.

Outputs

Our discussion of the output components of our model is our attempt not only to provide a descriptive perspective of what is considered a normative view on performance but also to describe how one's use of self can help an organization learn and adapt.

Organizational Performance

The performance of individuals in an organization is an important factor in the performance of the organization as a whole. Therefore, building a culture of collaboration is building collective ownership wherein the members of the organization are committed to the goals and outcomes achieved together. Although there are many perspectives on organizational performance (Burke and Litwin, 1992; Nadler and Tushman, 1977), the primary association here is with what members of an organization do each workday, which is generally thought of as operations, that inevitably contributes to the organization's performance (productivity, customer satisfaction, profits, and so forth).

Learning as an Ongoing Process

Learning can be characterized as having the dual nature of both a process and an outcome. Borrowing language from Karl Weick (1995), learning as an outcome can be described as knowing what works and to take what is learned to make the necessary adjustments in enabling an organization to change as a result of a learning process. Another perhaps more popular definition, "learning by doing" (Kolb, 1984), treats learning as a process whereby the members of an organization reflect on newly acquired knowledge and inevitably achieve some sort of transformation. Kolb conceived of learning as a four-stage cycle that can be best interpreted through one's learning style. Learning style shapes individuals not only in their own right, in the way they grasp and transform information, but also in how they might interact with groups (identifying opportunities, for example, or solving problems in an organizational context).

A learning point of view here is one that is characterized by the organization as a learning system where learning across differentiated units within the organization occurs as transactions between parts of the organization and different aspects of its environment.

Adaptability

Change happens in virtually all aspects of organizational life and affects organizations in often unanticipated ways. The challenge for an organization is to establish and maintain healthier ways of adapting to its environment. Here the practitioner should assist the organization in becoming more aware of its connectedness with all of its parts, both internal and external, as well as to the environment. Practitioners should understand the source and scope of an organization's ability to collaborate and achieve its desired outcomes. The component of our model for detecting errors and correcting course that extends beyond learning is called adaptability.

Adaptability doesn't just happen. It relies on the converted collective flow of organizational consciousness whereby the organization reaches a point of greater clarity about its purpose, routine business operations, human capital, and the web that weaves these various aspects together.

Conclusion

In the modern world, humans are constantly coming up with more and more knowledge about numerous fields, yet one field is often overlooked—ourselves. It seems that many people focus on elements external to themselves. For example, practitioners may focus what others are saying or doing, what their clients expect of them, which skills and methods to use in interacting with others, and so forth. But rarely in our experience do practitioners take a deep look inside to examine how they are influencing others. For example, how are their egos influencing others? How are their fears affecting people? How are their mental models influencing what happens in the group?

To overlook ourselves is to overlook our uniqueness. We as humans are not robots. Each of us is unique. As a result of our uniqueness, each of us brings something different to every interaction and thus to every job we do. If we are unique, then the methods and skills we use as practitioners will be used differently by each person. And what is more important, our uniqueness not only influences how the skills and methods are used but also affects the group and a deeper, often unrecognized level. Who we are and how we act can affect the group atmosphere and climate, how people respond and communicate, how and if people learn, and so forth.

But to dig deep inside, reflect, and to take a close, hard look at ourselves is a difficult and often painful task. To get in touch with our own fears, ego, and shadow, as Jung calls it, can be painful. Also, taking a look inside can open up a Pandora's box, which we might not have the time, energy, or knowledge to deal with. For example, a practitioner may uncover that he or she has serious challenges in dealing with power and authority. If that same practitioner ends up constantly working with middle management and challenging top management without actually collaborating, the results might not be as good. In our experience, such deep mental models are rarely evident. Effective practitioners will most likely know that they need to work with top management. But on a deeper, more subtle, unperceived level, these mental models might play out. As a result, practitioners who are not aware of their own mental models might wonder why they never have good relations with top management. This is just one example. There are infinite ways our mental models might play out. The challenge is to get to know them. One way for practitioners to recognize their mental models is to be aware of any patterns that keep repeating. A pattern is often a sign of an underlying mental model that is influencing others. Often we have seen people brush off their patterns as bad luck, wondering, "Why does this always happen to me?" Perhaps a deep look inside is warranted.

This chapter was intended to serve as a starting point for becoming self-aware so that practitioners can lead processes effectively. Using oneself in service of building a culture of collaboration is fundamentally an art, not a scientific process. To use oneself implies getting to know oneself. To borrow words attributed to Dag Hammarskjøld, the United Nations secretary general who received the Nobel Peace Prize in 1961, "The longest journey is the journey inward."

References

Baumeister, R. "The Self." In D. T. Gilbert, S. T. Fiske, and G. Lindzey (eds.), *The Handbook of Social Psychology.* New York: McGraw-Hill, 1998.

Blake, R., and others. "Contemporary Issues of Grid International: Sustaining and Extending the Core Values of O D." *Organization Development Journal,* 2000, *18*(2), 54–61.

Burke, W. W., and Litwin, G. H. "A Causal Model of Organizational Performance and Change." *Journal of Management,* 1992, *18*, 532–545.

Cheung-Judge, M. "The Self as an Instrument: A Cornerstone for the Future of OD." *OD Practitioner,* 2001, *33*(3), 11–16.

Curran, K. M., Seashore, C. N., and Welp, M. S. "Use of Self as an Instrument of Change." Paper presented at the annual meeting of the Organization Development Network, Seattle, Nov. 1995.

Druskat, V. U., and Pescosolido, A. T. "The Content of Effective Teamwork Mental Models in Self-Managing Teams: Ownership, Learning, and Heedful Interrelating." *Human Relations,* 2002, *55*, 283–314.

Goleman, D. *Working with Emotional Intelligence.* New York: Bantam Books, 1998.

Goleman, D., Boyatzis, R., and McKee, A. *Primal Leadership: Realizing the Power of Emotional Intelligence.* Boston: Harvard Business School Press, 2002.

Hanson, P. G. "The Self as an Instrument for Change." *Organization Development Journal,* 2000, *18,* 95–105.

Kashtan, M. "The Gift of Self: The Art of Transparent Facilitation." In S. Schuman (ed.), *The IAF Handbook of Group Facilitation.* San Francisco: Jossey-Bass, 2005.

Kolb, D. A. *Experiential Learning: Experience as the Source of Learning and Development.* Upper Saddle River, N.J.: Prentice Hall, 1984.

McCormick, D. W., and White, J. J. "Using One's Self as an Instrument for Organizational Diagnosis." *Organization Development Journal,* 2000, *18*(3), 49–61.

Nadler, D. A., and Tushman, M. L. "A Diagnostic Model for Organization Behavior." In J. Hackman, E. E. Lawler III, and L. Porter (eds.), *Perspectives on Behavior in Organizations.* New York: McGraw-Hill, 1977.

Schein, E. H. "How Can Organizations Learn Faster? The Challenge of Entering the Green Room." *Sloan Management Review,* 1993, *34*(2), 85–92.

Seashore, C. N., Shawver, M. N., Thompson, G., and Mattare, M. "Doing Good by Knowing Who You Are: The Instrumental Self as an Agent of Change." *OD Practitioner,* 2004, *36*(3), 42–46.

Senge, P. M. *The Fifth Discipline.* New York: Doubleday, 1990.

Smith, K. K. "On Using the Self as Instrument: Lessons form a Facilitator's Experience." In J. Gillette and M. McCollom (eds.), *Groups in Context: A New Perspective on Group Dynamics.* Lanham, Md.: University Press of America, 1990.

Von Bertalanffy, L. "An Outline of General Systems Theory." *British Journal of the Philosophy of Science,* 1950, *1,* 134–165.

von Foerster, H. "On Constructing a Reality." *Environmental Design Research,* 1973, *2,* 35–46.

Weick, K. *Sensemaking in Organizations.* Thousand Oaks, Calif.: Sage, 1995.

Zull, J. *The Art of Changing the Brain: Enriching the Practice of Teaching by Exploring the Biology of Learning.* Sterling, Va.: Stylus, 2002.

PART THREE

COLLABORATION IN ACTION

Cynthia Silva Parker is a senior associate at the Interaction Institute for Social Change, in Cambridge, Massachusetts, where for the past decade she has been training, consulting, and facilitating to foster collaborative processes and support collaborative learning in the nonprofit sector. Previously, she was a senior leader in nonprofit organizations including Boston Freedom Summer, the Ten Point Coalition's faith-based youth leadership, and the Algebra Project, a nonprofit education group with sites across the nation. As an associate for Technical Development Corporation, Parker provided organizational assessment, strategic planning, and program evaluation services to nonprofit organizations. She also served as an adjunct faculty member at the University of Massachusetts, Boston, where she taught strategic planning. Parker holds a bachelor of arts degree from Harvard-Radcliffe and a master's degree in public policy and city and regional planning from the John F. Kennedy School of Government at Harvard University.

Linda N. Guinee is a senior associate at the Interaction Institute for Social Change in Cambridge, Massachusetts, where she helps design, facilitate, and manage the content of collaborative change processes. For more than twenty years, Guinee worked with nonprofit organizations in the Boston area, including the AIDS Action Committee of Massachusetts, the NAMES Project, and the Long Term Research Institute,. She was ordained into the lay Buddhist order by Zen Master Thich Nhat Hanh. Guinee holds a bachelor of arts degree in humanism and cultural change from the University of Wisconsin–Green Bay and a master of arts degree in conflict resolution from Antioch University–McGregor.

J. Courtney Bourns is a senior associate at the Interaction Institute for Social Change in Cambridge, Massachusetts, where she delivers training, consulting, and facilitation that foster collaborative process and support cooperative learning in the nonprofit sector, including extensive work in Ireland. Bourns is a trained mediator with expertise in conflict resolution and training in alternatives to violence. Her upbringing as a Quaker instilled in her a fascination with nonviolence and a strong commitment and responsibility to contributing to social justice. Prior to joining IISC, Bourns worked as a facilitator, mediator, and mediation and conflict resolution trainer and consultant. She served as a codirector of the Youth Leadership Academy in Nonviolence at the Rhode Island Committee for Nonviolence Initiatives. Bourns holds a bachelor of arts degree from Brown University and a master of ethics from Union Theological Seminary.

Jennifer Fischer-Mueller is the deputy superintendent for teaching and learning in the Public Schools of Brookline, Massachusetts. She has served as assistant superintendent for curriculum and professional development in Amherst, New Hampshire; as dean of faculty at Souhegan High School in Amherst, New Hampshire; and as a science teacher at Souhegan High School, at Hollis/Brookline High School in Hollis, New Hampshire, and at Spaulding Junior High School in Rochester, New Hampshire. Fischer-Mueller holds a bachelor of science degree in biology and a master of arts degree in teaching from the University of New Hampshire and a doctorate of education from the University of Massachusetts–Lowell.

Marianne Hughes is the founding executive director of the Interaction Institute for Social Change in Cambridge, Massachusetts. She delivers training, consulting, coaching, and facilitation services that foster collaborative processes and support cooperative learning. Prior to leading IISC, Hughes was a senior associate at Regina Villa Associates, where she served as a public policy consultant and human service lobbyist. In this role, she designed public interest initiatives and legislative budget campaigns and also consulted on policy development. Hughes also served as one of the first VISTA volunteers in 1966. This experience was followed by years of antiwar, disarmament, and low-income grassroots organizing. Hughes combines her social policy expertise, organizing skills, commitment to social justice, deep faith in the human capacity for goodness and change, and extensive skills in leading collaborative process in serving clients and leading IISC to achieve its mission.

Andria Winther is managing director of the Interaction Institute for Social Change, where she delivers training, consulting, facilitation, and coaching services by modeling and transferring collaborative process skills that help schools and organizations address problems. She works with teachers, administrators, and students, using a whole-system, asset-based approach to create healthy learning environments that prepare young people for the future. Prior to joining IISC, Andria led City Year's Education Department through a paradigm shift from a traditional classroom model to a Freirean, participatory approach that fostered peer learning. Winther holds a bachelor of arts degree from Hartwick College and a master's in teaching English as a second language from the University of Massachusetts, Boston.

CHAPTER SIXTEEN

COLLABORATION FOR SOCIAL CHANGE

A Theory and a Case Study

Cynthia Silva Parker, Linda N. Guinee,
J. Courtney Bourns, Jennifer Fischer-Mueller,
Marianne Hughes, Andria Winther

Creating a culture of collaboration and recognizing that people must commit themselves fully and deeply to address complex issues and effect social change challenge the Western paradigm of addressing problems individually. Yet evidence of collaborative practices can be seen everywhere in the skillful involvement of people in a vast array of groups, ranging from indigenous communities to organizations focusing on deliberative democracy. Thus collaboration is not a new idea but rather a direction to which we return. We focus in particular on collaboration for social change. We use the term *collab-*

We would like to thank all of the participants in the collaborative process at the Public Schools of Brookline. This work was skillfully undertaken by the Core Team, Design Teams I and II, Action Teams, Fitness Task Force, Daryl Campbell (teacher-leader of Minority Student Achievement), and Dr. Jennifer Fischer-Mueller (deputy superintendent of teaching and learning) of the Equity Project, as well as Dr. Richard Silverman and Dr. William Lupini (the former and current superintendents) at the Public Schools of Brookline, and the Brookline Foundation, which provided financial support. We express deep gratitude to our colleagues at IISC: Paul Botticello, Pat Bruce-Lerrigo, Sekou Kaba, Robert King Kee, Andrea Nagel, Sara Oaklander, Meave O'Marah, Louise O'Meara, Toni Phillips, Robert Ryan, Christina Savage, Chris Toppin, and Bruce Truitt; to Thomas Rice and David Straus (board members and friends); to our colleagues at Interaction Associates; and to our families and friends.

oration not in the pejorative sense of colluding to oppress people or deny human rights but in the positive sense of working across differences to address and resolve systemic social problems.

We have successfully used collaborative processes to create social change in many arenas—in neighborhoods, organizations, and school systems; in community groups; and in coalitions working on issues ranging from neighborhood revitalization to peace and security. Here we present a case study in which a school system used a collaborative process to create a plan for eliminating gaps in student achievement based on race and achieving educational equity. It demonstrates how collaboration helps build the processes, relationships, skills, and culture necessary for ongoing transformation and social change.

We describe the conditions that support launching a collaborative process, the practitioners' contributions to creating collaborative culture, and how these conditions and practitioner contributions came into play in this case. We discuss key ingredients in designing successful processes that nurture collaborative culture and social change and discuss lessons learned from this experience.

Conditions That Support Launching a Collaborative Change Effort

We've found that specific conditions enhance the possibility of creating and sustaining collaborative change in many settings (see Exhibit 16.1). Although it is possible to move a collaborative effort forward without all of them, the more of these conditions that are present, the greater the chance for groups to succeed in mounting a collaborative response to the issues and opportunities they face.

Perhaps the single most important condition is an *imperative for change*—a compelling state that innovators want to move toward or an intolerable state about which people believe that something *must* be done (Mitchell, 1995; Moore, Longo, and Palmer, 1999; Straus, 2002). Participants need to understand the high cost of *not* doing anything and the potential rewards of spending time and energy to create change. People often reach this point after arriving at the "end of the road" trying to address a situation individually, realizing that the only way to effect the desired change is by working together (Chrislip, 2002). And of course, they must *believe the situation can change.*

EXHIBIT 16.1. CONDITIONS THAT SUPPORT LAUNCHING A COLLABORATIVE CHANGE EFFORT.

- Imperative for change
- Belief that the situation can change
- Willingness to trust the process
- Active learning and practicing specific collaborative skills
- Willingness to focus on the group's superordinate goals
- Facilitative conveners and leaders
- Commitment to meaningful stakeholder inclusion
- Orientation toward knowledge and information
- Skilled, collaborative project coordinator
- Outside process practitioner
- Time, financial, technical, and political resources

To work together, however, people must be *willing to trust the process*. They must have confidence—or faith—that the process will be fair and transparent and that both those affected and those with authority and resources will be fully involved. Participants must be willing to wait to discover what emerges, trusting that the group will produce something better than they could produce alone. This willingness must be practiced regularly, as there will be times during the process when individual participants may want to just "get on with it" and solve the problem their own way.

While there is often support for the *concept* of collaboration, true collaboration requires the hard work of *active learning and practicing specific collaborative skills* (Argyris, 1993; Brodsky, 1989). It also requires *willingness to focus on the group's superordinate goals* ahead of (or at least alongside) individual or institutional goals and needs (Deutsch, 1973).

Collaborative processes need conveners with passion, credibility, and access to people and resources (Carlson, 1999; Chrislip, 2002). They also require an initial set of community, organizational, or issue-specific leaders beyond the conveners who see the need for change. These committed *facilitative conveners and leaders* "engage relevant stakeholders in solving problems collaboratively and work to build a more collaborative culture" (Straus, 2002, p. 146).

The conveners and leaders must be willing to create disequilibrium and a sense of urgency around the issue (Heifetz, 1994) in order to generate broader interest in the effort. And they must model working and learning together.

Equally important, participants must demonstrate a *commitment to meaningful stakeholder inclusion*, beginning with a core planning group that includes those who will be affected by the decisions. They must do the ongoing and sometimes challenging work of moving beyond "usual suspects" to ensure that a wide range of people are involved, consulted, and informed throughout the process. This requires an ability to work across racial, class, cultural, and other divides and design processes that are welcoming and accessible to people from many backgrounds.

Collaborative work requires a countercultural *orientation toward knowledge and information*. In U.S. society, individuals and institutions tend to use information and control its dissemination as a form of power over others (Bachrach and Baratz, 1970). By contrast, collaborative processes use transparent, open access to information to create conditions for empowerment of all participants. Similarly, our society tends to acknowledge, reward, and defer to knowledge and expertise gained through formal education and positional leadership, as if the affected stakeholders had no relevant knowledge of the issues they face. At their best, collaborative processes acknowledge and legitimate formal and informal sources of wisdom and knowledge, lifting up the lived experiences of affected stakeholders alongside the research, degree-based, or positional credentials of other stakeholders.

A collaborative, *skilled project coordinator* is often essential to ensure that these commitments and beliefs are demonstrated in consistent action and follow-through. Project coordinators must model collaborative approaches in their relationships with conveners or leaders and all others involved. Project coordinators manage the process and related logistics, engage and motivate participants, manage intergroup politics, and attend to details while keeping the big picture in mind. More than anything, they act in service of the group. The project coordinator weaves participants together, looks for new relationships to develop and new stakeholders to involve, and constantly monitors how stakeholder groups are doing. In many practical ways, the project coordinator "holds the center" of the initiative.

Collaborative processes are significantly strengthened when skilled *outside process practitioners* (consultants or facilitators) codesign, facilitate, and manage the emerging content of the initiative. The efforts may also benefit from bringing in external content expertise, as needed. Many groups feel they should be able to do this work for themselves and must come to see that accepting "outside help" is not a reflection on their commitment or competence. The community must also provide or secure *time, financial, technical, and political resources.* These resources cover the costs of designing, facilitating, and staffing the effort; ensure participation; facilitate access to high-quality information; and build the capacity to ensure effective action.

How Does the Practitioner Contribute to Building Collaborative Culture?

While many essential ingredients are brought by the community, effective process practitioners demonstrate a few core competencies as they play critical roles in the effort. They combine skills and knowledge, clarity about their roles and about how power functions in the situation, and explicit collaborative values (McClelland, 1975). Skilled practitioners model confidence and experience blended with genuine curiosity, humility about their own limitations, and a desire to learn from others. They reflect on their practice and strive to close gaps between their values and actions, noticing, for instance, that they can be committed to social justice while struggling with their own biases (Applegate, 2005). At the same time, they model a belief that success is possible, even when the path forward seems unclear. By demonstrating confidence in the potential of collaboration, they can bring new and sustained energy and hope to the group.

The Practitioner as Process Guide

Many people have become familiar with the role of the practitioner as someone who serves the group without a stake in the group's decisions. Effective practitioners artfully apply the essential skills and knowledge of group dynamics and facilitation to help groups create shared meaning, engage in conflict constructively, and build solid agreements. They serve the group to get where *they* want to go, openly acknowledging that the process and goals are *the group's,* not the practitioner's. They demonstrate cultural competence in working across differences in race, class, and other dimensions of identity and are alert to ways their own identity could affect group dynamics. They apply these skills with intuition and artistry, studying people carefully; listening intently;

observing the text, subtext, and context of human interactions; and demonstrating the empathy and focus of one who combines a "tough mind and a tender heart" (King, 1981, p. 13).

As stewards of information, practitioners make sure that both the process steps and content information (especially ideas, issues, and agreements) are documented and shared appropriately, ensuring both the transparency and efficiency of the effort.

The Practitioner as Process Advocate and Codesigner

As process advocates and codesigners, practitioners *do* have a point of view and a stake in the process. They offer their expertise and advocate for the design of transparent, participatory, and effective processes. Far from being values-free or "neutral," principled practitioners model and defend explicit values as they design and facilitate collaborative processes. (For a discussion of neutrality in the conflict resolution field, see Laue and Cormick, 1978; Mayer, 2004; Rifkin, Millen, and Cobb, 1991; Wing, 2002; and Wing and Rifkin, 2001.) Chief among these are social justice, stakeholder inclusion, and balancing power.

In addition to advocating for these values, effective practitioners educate conveners, leaders, and participants about how thoughtful processes can address the group's needs, attend to group dynamics, ensure participation, and guide people toward meaningful agreements and effective action. They provide explicit training in skills that facilitate collaboration. They coach leaders and conveners to clarify their thinking, examine their behavior and its impact, learn new behaviors, and question assumptions.

Practitioners must leverage their own and others' skill, intuition, authority, and credibility to address power differentials and exercise "power with" others rather than "power over" others (Baker Miller, 1976; Coleman, 2000; Deutsch, 1973; Follett, 1973). They must also leverage participants' various sources of power for the benefit of the effort. In so doing, they avoid re-creating oppressive dynamics in their work. They surface assumptions and challenge unproductive thinking. They exhibit "multipartiality," applying appropriate efforts to ensure that everyone can participate fully (Rifkin, Millen, and Cobb, 1991); ensure that people on the margins of the issue are included in significant ways; advocate for clear, transparent decision-making processes as a way to balance power; and guide groups toward results that address root causes rather than "blaming the victim"—all the while creating holistic, systemic change.

They lend particularly valuable experience to the group in matters of stakeholder engagement. They guide groups toward identifying stakeholders and engaging them in culturally appropriate ways. They demonstrate respect for the dignity of each person and community with which they work, through individual interactions and by designing processes that assume that each person can contribute something of value. They help create spaces where people can see one another's humanity and demonstrate support, empathy, and care for one another while getting the work done.

Eliminating the Racial Achievement Gap in the Public Schools of Brookline, Massachusetts, 2003–2004

The Public Schools of Brookline (PSB) is a respected urban-suburban school system in the Boston area. It has a dedicated, skilled staff and a diverse student population. PSB is composed of eight elementary schools and one high school, each operating fairly autonomously. PSB is known for having high-achieving students.

In 2002, the superintendent in Brookline contacted the Interaction Institute for Social Change (IISC), wanting to create a more collaborative culture. They held initial conversations but had not identified a reason to collaborate at that time. That summer, PSB engaged IISC, in the person of Andria Winther, to facilitate a senior leadership retreat, helping build confidence in collaboration.

Discussions about the achievement gap were occurring across the system, and although the gap was consistently viewed as unacceptable, there was no agreement about how to close it as a system. A number of groups throughout the community and in each of the schools had worked separately on trying to address the racial achievement gap for a number of years, without much apparent impact.

The new deputy superintendent for teaching and learning, Jennifer Fischer-Mueller, took a fresh look at the PSB data on student achievement. Like most school systems in the United States, data from PSB showed a significant difference between the achievement of white and Asian students and that of black and Latino students. She came to the same conclusions as others: that this problem clearly needed attention.

With strong facilitative leaders committed to the issue, a commitment to equity in education, growing confidence in the help an outside facilitator could bring, and a belief that a systemwide, collaborative approach could create real change, the PSB leadership determined that it was time to try a collaborative approach. They knew that finding solutions would be a complicated and challenging process that would require examination of curriculum, teaching practices, administrative policies, and fundamental beliefs about education. They were also convinced that eliminating the racial achievement gap would improve achievement for all students.

Meanwhile, PSB had little experience with the mutual benefits of using a collaborative approach to solve problems and had rarely brought people in from the outside to help facilitate change. Both of these actions required a leap of faith.

In the summer of 2003, PSB was accepted into the Minority Student Achievement Network, a national organization working to address the racial achievement gap, thus catalyzing further action. Having earlier connected with Winther, PSB contacted IISC for support in designing the process, hired a two-person facilitator team from IISC, and launched a collaborative initiative to eliminate PSB's racial achievement gap.

As a precursor to designing the process, IISC trained future participants in Facilitative Leadership (Interaction Associates, 1997) in order to transfer and develop collaborative skills. Members of the community (administrators, teachers, parents, school committee members, funders, and other community members) spent time during the summer learning the skills of collaboration in order to work together effectively.

PSB brought leadership, resources, and commitment to the project, finding grant funding from the local community foundation and committing significant time and energy to the initiative. Fischer-Mueller describes some key PSB community characteristics that supported the initiative's success. Community members were "smart, motivated to learn, and willing to think hard and wrestle with complicated issues for which there's no easy answer."

Designing Processes That Nurture Collaborative Culture and Create Social Change

Process design is critical to successfully creating a collaborative culture and social change. At its core, a collaborative culture comes from the lived experience of people working well together. Although people work together in all kinds of situations, the possibility that a robust collaborative culture will emerge is maximized by consciously designing collaborative platforms that enable people to work effectively to bridge differences. In particular, the designer-practitioner should pay careful attention to three dimensions of success: results, process, and relationships (Straus, 2002), as shown in Figure 16.1.

Results That Matter

Collaborative approaches are especially necessary when addressing adaptive issues—complex issues that do not have straightforward technical solutions (Heifetz, 1994). The desired results need to match the depth and scale of the issues and must be expected to bear fruit slowly over time (Kubisch, 2004).

At the same time, the effective practitioner directs the group's attention toward articulating and seeking achievable, short-term milestones to gain and sustain trust, momentum, and commitment (Lewicki and Bunker, 1995). The practitioner facilitates building shared understanding of potentially successful strategies, drawn from the combined experience of affected stakeholders and other participants as well as research and promising practice.

Finally, practitioners must recognize that creating a collaborative culture—and the skills to support it—is itself an important result of the process of planning and working together, which contributes to achieving longer-term results. Evidence of this culture grows as the process unfolds. Decision making becomes

FIGURE 16.1. THE THREE DIMENSIONS OF SUCCESS.

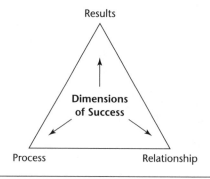

more transparent. Involvement of a wide diversity of perspectives and voices less frequently heard becomes a regular and expected occurrence. Collaborative and leadership skills are developed. Participants begin collaborating in other areas and addressing differences more skillfully. Previously excluded or fragmented stakeholder groups become coherent, organized constituencies and new centers of power (Reisman, Langley, Stachowiak, and Gienapp, 2004). Achieving these results requires careful attention to designing processes and nurturing relationships that support changes in values, behaviors, and attitudes.

Demystifying Process

Because people are trying to get important things done, effective collaborative processes must generate thoughtful *plans* that, once implemented, have the desired results. The best decisions are made when the group members making them are diverse and think and act independently (Carpenter, 1989; Surowiecki, 2004). When a group is reflective of the stakeholders affected by the issues and the decisions to be addressed, and when differences are actively surfaced and explored, groups come to decisions that can not only be implemented effectively but also create and sustain real change (Cornerstone Consulting Group, 2002).

In addition to generating plans, effective collaborative processes build formal and informal *networks* for ongoing creative thinking and joint action (Lederach, 2005). While increasingly sophisticated technology is being developed for linking people, information, and action (Cross and Parker, 2004; Krebs and Holley, 2006), the human side of networks—especially the involvement of "unusual suspects" in the thinking and planning—requires attention and skill.

For a collaborative process to have maximum impact and sustainability, the process must create *opportunities for participants to learn* practical skills and tools for working together—designing and facilitating meetings, taking proactive steps to include previously excluded people and groups, learning from actions taken, and keeping a group on track.

Furthermore, collaborative processes must acknowledge and address power differentials, both within the collaborative group and between the group and others in the wider context. Both real and imagined differences in power may be based in reputation; organizational role or status; degrees of formal education or technical expertise; racial, cultural and other dimensions of identity; or personal agency. Whatever the sources, the process must enable participants to share and use power responsibly and increase the ability of less powerful stakeholders to participate, develop voice, and effectively represent their interests (Folger, Poole, and Stutman, 2001; Laue and Cormick, 1978; Rouson, 2004).

Our experience suggests that good processes create a context for building relationships. Conversely, nothing harms relationships faster than bad process. People often experience process problems relationally, linking those interpretations with race, class, or other dimensions of identity. For instance, instead of noting that the decision-making process is unclear; people may think "They don't like my views" or "They don't want to hear from people like me." As we will see, healthy relationships are essential for nurturing and sustaining collaborative work.

The Importance of Relationships

Purposefully built relationships among individuals, groups, organizations, sectors, and communities are essential for developing both the bonding and bridging social capital and the vertical ties needed to make and sustain change (Briggs, 1997; Potapchuk, Crocker, and Schechter, 1997; Putnam, 1993, 2000). This insight arises from our own experience and from that of generations of community organizers and movement builders. People join an effort not simply because it is right, important, or likely to succeed but also because of the trusting relationships that draw them in and keep them engaged. When the work involves crossing significant boundaries (such as race, ethnicity, socioeconomic class, or even field of work), building relationships in a context where participants agree to work on a common problem as peers is essential in breaking down barriers, overcoming stereotypical thinking, and facilitating effective collaboration (Allport, 1954; Brewer, 1996; Brewer and Miller, 1984; Gaertner and Dovidio, 2005; Slavin and Cooper, 1999; Tajfel, 1969; Tajfel and Turner, 1986).

At their best, collaborative processes build relationships beyond those needed to sustain the effort at hand. They spawn formal or informal networks that share resources, learn together, plan future joint action, and provide moral support and sustenance for the long haul. These processes catalyze the creation of new kinds of broad-based social change movements that include those affected by decisions and issues as well as their allies.

The Equity Project: Building a Communitywide Commitment to Change

After initial conversations among PSB'ssuperintendent, deputy superintendent for teaching and learning, and IISC regarding the structure needed to move forward, PSB launched the initiative that came to be known as "Brookline's Educational Equity Project: Taking Action, Getting Results." The first step was convening a thirty-member Core Team in the summer of 2003. The Core Team's purpose was to gain a shared understanding of its members' beliefs about the relationship between race and achievement, study the racial achievement gap in Brookline, review research across the nation, and determine a plan of action for the ultimate elimination of the racial achievement gap in PSB. The Core Team was composed of a "diagonal slice" of the system, representing the different schools; administration, staff, faculty, parents, school committee members, and community members; the racial diversity of the system; and a wide variety of views about what was causing the gap. Most members volunteered through an open invitation to the community. To ensure representation of all stakeholder groups, some individuals were also recruited to the team.

Nine of the Core Team members formed the Design Team, which worked with the two-person IISC team (Winther and Guinee) to design and guide the process and to synthesize information from the larger group. They considered additional stakeholder input needed to devise a plan that would actually be implemented and developed an initial process map (Straus, 1999), which went to the Core Team as a proposal. The process map, shown in Figure 16.2, was a living document that changed throughout the planning process. This initial design process deepened the Design Team's understanding of collaboration.

With the support of IISC facilitators, the Core Team spent eight months reviewing student learning data, interviewing ninety-three additional stakeholders, learning what had and hadn't worked in Brookline, understanding the local wisdom and research from around the country, clarifying the current situation and the future desired state, and agreeing on beliefs that would guide the team's actions.

Agreeing on these beliefs was a complicated process through which Core Team members deepened their collaborative skills and willingness to have difficult conversations, allowing the group's wisdom to unfold. This four-month

FIGURE 16.2. PROCESS MAP FOR CLOSING THE ACHIEVEMENT GAP IN THE BROOKLINE PUBLIC SCHOOLS.

Phase

- Process Design and Big Picture
- Vision and Problem
- Solution and Planning for Implementation

Time Frame

- July to November 2003
- December 2003 to February 2004
- March to April 2004

Stakeholders & Activities

Timeline dates: 8/19, 9/17, 10/1, 10/8, 10/29, 11/10, 11/19/03, 12/5, 12/17, 1/8, 1/14, 1/26, 1/30 (Full Day), 2/4, 2/6, 2/24, 2/25, 2/26, 3/2, 3/4, 3/5, 3/8, 3/11, 3/17, 3/31, 4/14, 4/16, 4/28

Node labels:
- Core Team
- Design Team
- Synthesize Vision
- Learning and agree on Vision Draft
- Stakeholder Interviews: by 1/26
- FTF Themes
- Core Team: Themes & Gaps
- Design Team: Synthesize Themes & Gaps; Draft Gap Levels
- Core Team
- Core Team: Action Planning
- Design Team
- Core Team: Final Draft of Proposal for Action
- Design Team
- Design Team: Agreement on Proposal for Action

Learning & Communication

- Facilitative Leadership Training
- Relationship between Race & Achievement
- 12/10–12/12 Facilitative Leadership Training
- 12/16 Fitness Task Force Training

Products

- Brainstorm "Where We Are" and "Where We Want to Go" (Core Team)
- Synthesize and propose draft of "Where We Are" and "Where We Want to Go" (Design Team)
- Close on "Where We Are" and "Where We Want to Go" (Core Team)
- Design stakeholder input for Vision Phase
- Design team: list of members of Fitness Task Force
- List of stakeholders for Vision Phase
- Shared understanding of the relationship between race and achievement

- A shared vision
- Revisit "Where Do We Want to Go" based on the Vision
- Determine who to interview re: strengths and barriers
- Train the Fitness Task Force (FTF)
- Hold stakeholder interviews re: strengths and barriers (FTF)
- Synthesize themes regarding strengths and barriers (FTF)
- Review literature on why students aren't achieving (Core Team)
- Report themes re: strengths and barriers to Core Team (Design Team)
- Design and implement Gap Analysis
- Determine which components of the gap we'll solve for (Design Team)

- Draft Proposal for Action
- Gather input on proposal from stakeholders (Curriculum Coordinators, Principals, etc.)
- Agreement on Proposal for Action
- Determine how plan will be implemented in 2004–2005
- Agreement on Final "Where Are We Now? – Where Are We Going?"
- Agreement on Core Beliefs

Key of Symbols

- Design Team
- Core Team
- Fitness Task Force
- Other Stakeholders
- Skills Training
- Newsletter
- Proposal for Action Team
- Curriculum & Program Coordinators
- Principals
- Learning Events

process required repeatedly revisiting the emerging beliefs, often sending them to a subgroup that incorporated the Core Team's input and produced new drafts. Some participants experienced this process as frustratingly slow. Still, the Core Team maintained its commitment to agreeing on beliefs as a foundation for action. Team members passionately discussed issues related to individual potential, standards, and expectations. They struggled to talk directly about race and racism and to understand the relationship of race to achievement.

According to Fischer-Mueller and Winther, timing and trust proved critical to having these conversations. The Core Team had worked together and built trust for several months before conversations about the beliefs began. Fischer-Mueller also credits the facilitator's ability to read the group and know when to continue with the conversation, when to set it aside, and when to send the beliefs to a subgroup for further work.

Core Team members worked to balance the need for direct conversations about race with the need to keep the conversation open to others, regardless of how developed their thinking was about these issues. They increasingly questioned the system's curriculum, teaching practices, and administrative policies, in line with research demonstrating that teachers in the highest-achieving schools were those who were most reflective about and least satisfied with their practice (McLaughlin and Talbot, 2001). Through listening to one another, regular reflection, surfacing differences, and skillful facilitation, they mined the group's wisdom and agreed on the shared beliefs (shown in Exhibit 16.2) and assumptions (shown in Exhibit 16.3) that would guide their work.

The Core Team went through a similar process to develop an action plan. Based on significant input from Core Team members, a subcommittee developed and regularly brought new drafts of the plan to the Core Team and to other stakeholder groups, including parents, principals, coordinators, and teachers. The final plan (Public Schools of Brookline, 2005) was completed in May 2004. At the same time, the Design Team worked on creating a structure for implementation. Understanding the need for form to serve function, the Design Team created a structure that would support communication with all stakeholder groups and tap the expertise in the community. Action Teams were established for each area of the plan, with process and content leaders for each team serving on an overall Coordinating Team, as shown in Figure 16.3. Clear about the need for group process skills, the Design Team engaged IISC to ensure that the co leaders of the Action Teams had the meeting design, facilitation, and recording skills needed to support their work. Finally,

EXHIBIT 16.2. BROOKLINE PUBLIC SCHOOLS' EDUCATIONAL EQUALITY PROJECT: BELIEFS THAT GUIDE OUR WORK.

These beliefs were created by the Core Team of the public schools of Brookline, Massachusetts, in spring 2004 and are an adaptation of the beliefs originally created by the Minority Student Achievement Network.

1. Eliminating the racial achievement gap in our schools is the right thing to do.

2. Excellent schools are committed to the elimination of the racial achievement gap.

3. Students come to school with a variety of individual strengths and needs. Our responsibility is to recognize and build on their strengths while identifying and meeting those needs.

4. Students of all races can succeed in school.

5. Schools are most effective when they take responsibility for the ways in which their practices affect student achievement.

6. We need to focus primarily on what schools can do while establishing school, home, and community partnerships to ensure student achievement.

7. Excellent schools work to eliminate intentional and unintentional racism by constantly examining curriculum, teaching practices, and administrative policies.

EXHIBIT 16.3. ASSUMPTIONS GROUNDING THE WORK OF THE EDUCATIONAL EQUITY PROJECT.

These assumptions were adapted from the work of Beth Miller in *Critical Hours* (2003).

1. The achievement gap is a tremendously complex issue. It is a symptom of a larger issue of social, economic, and educational equity.

2. There are numerous actions and strategies that need to operate simultaneously and synergistically to close the gap; there is no single "silver bullet."

3. It is important to frame the problem. The achievement gap is an adaptive problem. Eliminating the racial achievement gap will require an investigation and inquiry into our beliefs, values, practices, and expectations.

FIGURE 16.3. TEAM STRUCTURE FOR IMPLEMENTATION OF THE EDUCATIONAL EQUITY PROJECT.

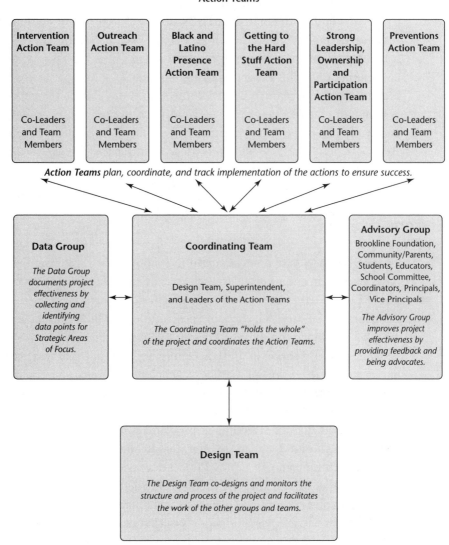

Action Teams

Intervention Action Team	Outreach Action Team	Black and Latino Presence Action Team	Getting to the Hard Stuff Action Team	Strong Leadership, Ownership and Participation Action Team	Preventions Action Team
Co-Leaders and Team Members	Co-Leaders and Team Members	Co-Leaders and Team Members	Co-Leaders and Team Members	Co-Leaders and Team Members	Co-Leaders and Team Members

Action Teams plan, coordinate, and track implementation of the actions to ensure success.

Data Group

The Data Group documents project effectiveness by collecting and identifying data points for Strategic Areas of Focus.

Coordinating Team

Design Team, Superintendent, and Leaders of the Action Teams

The Coordinating Team "holds the whole" of the project and coordinates the Action Teams.

Advisory Group

Brookline Foundation, Community/Parents, Students, Educators, School Committee, Coordinators, Principals, Vice Principals

The Advisory Group improves project effectiveness by providing feedback and being advocates.

Design Team

The Design Team co-designs and monitors the structure and process of the project and facilitates the work of the other groups and teams.

with the desire to ensure continued input from and accountability to a wider stakeholder group, the Coordinating Team created a broader advisory group. Each of these teams was carefully chartered with a clear understanding of its purpose, roles, and responsibilities.

By the end of the first year, PSB publicly declared that eliminating the racial achievement gap in the school system was a moral imperative and that it had a plan and a structure to create change. The school system asked the community to hold it accountable and launched the Action Teams to begin implementing the plan. When PSB introduced the plan to the entire school system (administration, faculty, and staff) and invited people to participate, eighty people (more than 10 percent of the faculty) volunteered to serve on Action Teams. The facilitators provided initial support to each of the Action Teams to ensure long-term sustainability.

Lessons Learned

This highly successful process taught us a number of important lessons that have broader implications. Carefully designed and facilitated processes coupled with opportunities to learn and practice collaborative skills can build a collaborative culture that transforms institutions. The collaborative culture and skill developed through the Educational Equity Project have resulted in a systemic transformation of PSB. Meetings are carefully planned, structured, and facilitated to ensure appropriate stakeholder involvement and clarity about who makes which decisions. Skilled facilitation is honored as an integral component of successful collaboration. People now talk openly about systems, practices, and curricula needing improvement and have built power among energetic, committed, skilled collaborators to address systemwide issues.

The PSB Educational Equity Project developed a comprehensive, collaborative approach to an adaptive problem (Public Schools of Brookline, 2005), one that involves continual learning, taking action, and getting results. Although the racial achievement gap has not yet been eliminated, the people in the system have come to understand the gap as a complex issue that is symptomatic of larger issues of social and educational equity. They share an understanding that many actions and strategies need to operate simultaneously and synergistically over time to close the gap. They also see the importance of framing the problem as an adaptive one that will require changes in beliefs, values, practices, and expectations (Heifetz, 1994), rather than a technical problem with one "right answer." With their growing culture of collaboration, they continue to pursue progress—together.

The Core Team struggled with when and how to communicate to the broader community. The team was committed to informing the community about its work but understood that communicating incomplete thinking could create problems. Team members also knew that they needed to spend the time building their own understanding of the issues and were balancing that with the need to keep others informed. By not always having confidence in their work and finding the right balance, they kept their work too close to themselves and chose not to engage the broader community, which at times resulted in missed opportunities.

We also found that as in many collaborative processes, the transition from planning to implementation necessarily begins with "planning for implementation." For those who were involved in the planning process, this was frustrating, as they were ready to start taking action. We must help groups build realistic expectations about the time needed to successfully launch implementation and the ongoing need to build collaborative skills and culture among new participants who may join. This challenge continues throughout implementation.

Maintaining passion, excitement, and commitment presents an ongoing challenge for collaborative processes, especially when they address adaptive problems for which the ultimate results may take years to realize. PSB has implemented several promising approaches. PSB frames the project as a long-term initiative rather than the "initiative of the day" and has made a long-term commitment of resources. The Educational Equity Project outlines not only long-term indicators of success but also shorter-term indicators of progress— and celebrates reaching them. The recruitment and inclusion of new members continue to generate new energy.

The time required of participants presented another significant challenge. Classroom teachers and administrators are already very busy, and collaborative processes take time. As the Brookline process unfolded, participants came to see this project as central to their work as educators rather than as an add-on. It started having direct benefits for other dimensions of their work, enabling them to see their participation as a worthwhile investment.

Documenting the work can create opportunities to model transparency and maintain momentum. Group memories of all meetings of the Equity

Project have been maintained and are available online for all participants, as well as executive summaries of all Action Team meetings, reflections on each team's work, and adjustments to the action plan and implementation structure.

Finally, PSB took up the challenge of allowing the plan and planning structure to constantly evolve rather than turning them into fixed entities. Reflecting the adaptive nature of the work, the PSB plan is a living, dynamic document. Communicating about this dynamic nature can be challenging and is well worth the effort.

Conclusion

IISC's work with PSB highlights the importance of nurturing collaborative culture as a vehicle for creating and sustaining social change. It is important to nurture collaborative culture and skills and to create relationships, contexts, and processes for continual innovation and creativity that adapt to the ongoing needs of the community (Lederach, 2005). "We live in a complex world," notes Margaret Wheatley (2002), ". . . and we won't be able to understand its complexity unless we spend more time in not knowing. . . . I believe we will succeed in changing this world only if we can think and work together in new ways" (pp. 34–35).

When imbued with social justice values, drawn from the power of innovative thinking and focused on systemic social problems, collaborative culture creates extraordinary potential for transformation of individuals and communities and represents a move toward true democracy.

The adaptive challenges facing communities around the world require collaborative thinking and action to create real, lasting social change. We've seen that bringing people together to address problems collaboratively produces significant intended and unintended outcomes. Participants in collaborative processes build an understanding of their shared vision of success. At their best, they uncover the nature and causes of problems and develop approaches that move beyond surface improvements to addressing root causes. Participants bring a shared commitment to implementation and leverage the power of their combined efforts, having far greater impact than any participant could have alone. Through participation in collaborative processes—especially when such processes involve deliberate skills transfer—we have seen participants deepen their skills and appreciation for the power of working together. We have seen participants begin to bring their collaborative relationships, skills, and culture into other arenas.

Groups are frequently driven by a sense of urgency to "do something," rushing through process design, stakeholder engagement, and project planning. As practitioners, we can guide the slower, more reliable work of designing inclusive planning processes, modeling and transferring collaborative skills, encouraging learning, and addressing issues of power that yields deeper levels of understanding and agreement. In the short term, this work fosters a culture of collaboration that produces shared visions, concrete plans of action, and many unanticipated benefits. In the longer term, it results in effective action and newly organized and networked constituencies for advancing the innovative and ongoing work of social change and transformation.

References

Allport, G. W. *The Nature of Prejudice.* Boston: Addison-Wesley, 1954.

Applegate, B. "Racial Equity as a Prism for Effective Consulting: A White Capacity Builder's Perspective" [http://www.allianceonline.org]. 2005.

Argyris, C. *Knowledge for Action.* San Francisco: Jossey-Bass, 1993.

Bachrach, P., and Baratz, M. S. *Power and Poverty: Theory and Practice.* New York: Oxford University Press, 1970.

Baker Miller, J. *Toward a New Psychology of Women.* Boston: Beacon Press, 1976.

Brewer, M. B. "When Contact Is Not Enough: Social Identity and Intergroup Cooperation." *International Journal of Intercultural Relations,* 1996, *20,* 291–303.

Brewer, M. B., and Miller, N. "Beyond the Contact Hypothesis: Theoretical Perspectives on Desegregation." In N. Miller and M. B. Brewer (eds.), *Groups in Contact: The Psychology of Desegregation.* San Diego, Calif.: Academic Press, 1984.

Briggs, X. S. "Social Capital and the Cities: Advice to Change Agents." *National Civic Review,* 1997, *86,* 111–117.

Brodsky, N. "Professional Excellence in Action: Process and Barriers." Unpublished doctoral dissertation, Department of Education, Harvard University, 1989.

Carlson, C. "Convening." In L. Susskind, S. McKearnan, and J. Thomas-Larmer (eds.), *The Consensus Building Handbook: A Comprehensive Guide to Reaching Agreement.* Thousand Oaks, Calif.: Sage, 1999.

Carpenter, S. *Community Problem Solving by Consensus.* Washington, D.C.: Program on Community Problem Solving, 1989.

Chrislip, D. *The Collaborative Leadership Fieldbook: A Guide for Citizens and Civic Leaders.* San Francisco: Jossey-Bass, 2002.

Coleman, P. T. "Power and Conflict." In M. Deutsch and P. T. Coleman (eds.), *The Handbook of Conflict Resolution: Theory and Practice.* San Francisco: Jossey-Bass, 2000.

Cornerstone Consulting Group. *Learning from the Journey: Reflections on the Rebuilding Communities Initiative.* Baltimore: Annie E. Casey Foundation, 2002.

Cross, R., and Parker, A. *The Hidden Power of Social Networks: Understanding How Work Really Gets Done in Organizations.* Boston: Harvard Business School Press, 2004.

Deutsch, M. *The Resolution of Conflict.* New Haven, Conn.: Yale University Press, 1973.

Folger, J. P., Poole, M. S., and Stutman, R. K. "Power: The Architecture of Conflict." In *Working Through Conflict: Strategies for Relationships, Groups, and Organizations.* (4th ed.) New York: Longman, 2001.

Follett, M. P. "Power." In E. M. Fox and L. Urwick (eds.), *Dynamic Administration: The Collected Papers of Mary Parker Follett.* London: Pitman, 1973.

Gaertner, S. L., and Dovidio, J. F. "Understanding and Addressing Contemporary Racism: From Aversive Racism to the Common Ingroup Identity Model." *Journal of Social Issues,* 2005, *61,* 615–639.

Heifetz, R. A. *Leadership Without Easy Answers.* Cambridge, Mass.: Belknap Press, 1994.

Interaction Associates. *Facilitative Leadership: Tapping the Power of Participation.* Boston: Interaction Associates, 1997.

King, M. L. *Strength to Love.* Minneapolis, Minn.: Augsburg Fortress, 1981.

Krebs, V., and Holley, J. "Building Smart Communities Through Network Weaving" [http://www.orgnet.com/BuildingNetworks.pdf]. 2006.

Kubisch, A. C. *Comprehensive Community-Building Initiatives Ten Years Later: What Have We Learned About the Principles Guiding the Work?* Baltimore: Annie E. Casey Foundation, 2004.

Laue, J., and Cormick, G. "The Ethics of Intervention in Community Disputes." In G. Bermany (ed.), *The Ethics of Social Intervention.* Hoboken, N.J.: Wiley, 1978.

Lederach, J. P. *The Moral Imagination: The Art and Soul of Building Peace.* New York: Oxford University Press, 2005.

Lewicki, R. J., and Bunker, B. B. "Trust in Relationships: A Model of Development and Decline." In B. B. Bunker and J. Z. Rubin (eds.), *Conflict, Cooperation, and Justice: Essays Inspired by the Work of Morton Deutsch.* San Francisco: Jossey-Bass, 1995.

Mayer, B. *Beyond Neutrality: Confronting the Crisis in Conflict Resolution.* San Francisco: Jossey-Bass, 2004.

McClelland, D. C. *Power: The Inner Experience.* New York: Irvington, 1975.

McLaughlin, M. W., and Talbot, J. E. *Professional Communities and the Work of High School Teaching.* Chicago: University of Chicago Press, 2001.

Miller, B. M. *Critical Hours.* Brookline, Mass.: Nellie Mae Educational Foundation, 2003.

Mitchell, C. R. *Cutting Losses: Reflections on Appropriate Timing.* Fairfax, Va.: George Mason University, Institute for Conflict Analysis and Resolution, 1995.

Moore, C. M., Longo, G., and Palmer, P. "Visioning." In L. Susskind, S. McKearnan, and J. Thomas-Larmer (eds.), *The Consensus Building Handbook: A Comprehensive Guide to Reaching Agreement.* Thousand Oaks, Calif.: Sage, 1999.

Potapchuk, W. R., Crocker, J. P., and Schechter, W. H. "Building Community with Social Capital: Chits and Chums or Chats with Change." *National Civic Review,* 1997, *86,* 129–139.

Public Schools of Brookline. "Brookline's Educational Equity Project: Taking Action, Getting Results" [http://teacherweb.com/MA/brookline/theequityproject/index.html]. May 2005.

Putnam, R. D. *Making Democracy Work: Civic Traditions in Modern Italy.* Princeton, N.J.: Princeton University Press, 1993.

Putnam, R. D. *Bowling Alone: The Collapse and Revival of American Community.* New York: Touchstone, 2000.

Reisman, J., Langley, K., Stachowiak, S., and Gienapp, A. *A Practical Guide to Documenting Influence and Leverage in Making Connections Communities.* Baltimore: Annie E. Casey Foundation, 2004.

Rifkin, J., Millen, J., and Cobb, S. "Toward a New Discourse for Mediation: A Critique of Neutrality." *Mediation Quarterly,* 1991, *9,* 151–164.

Rouson, B. "An Argument for the Need for Power Analysis in Capacity Building Social Change Work" [http://www.allianceonline.org]. Mar. 2004.

Slavin, R. E., and Cooper, R. "Improving Intergroup Relations: Lessons Learned from Cooperative Learning Programs." *Journal of Social Issues,* 1999, *55,* 647–663.

Straus, D. "Designing a Consensus Building Process Using a Graphic Road Map." In L. Susskind, S. McKearnan, and J. Thomas-Larmer (eds.), *The Consensus Building Handbook: A Comprehensive Guide to Reaching Agreement.* Thousand Oaks, Calif.: Sage, 1999.

Straus, D. *How to Make Collaboration Work: Powerful Ways to Build Consensus, Solve Problems, and Make Decisions.* San Francisco: Berrett-Koehler, 2002.

Surowiecki, J. *The Wisdom of Crowds: Why the Many Are Smarter Than the Few and How Collective Wisdom Shapes Business, Economies, Societies, and Nations.* New York: Doubleday, 2004.

Tajfel, H. "Cognitive Aspects of Prejudice." *Journal of Social Issues,* 1969, *25,* 79–97.

Tajfel, H., and Turner, J. C. "The Social Identity Theory of Intergroup Behavior." In S. Worchel and W. G. Austen (eds.), *Psychology of Intergroup Relations.* Chicago: Nelson Hall, 1986.

Wheatley, M. J. *Turning to One Another: Simple Conversations to Restore Hope to the Future.* San Francisco: Berrett-Koehler, 2002.

Wing, A. L. "Social Justice and Mediation." Unpublished doctoral dissertation, Department of Education, University of Massachusetts, 2002.

Wing, A. L., and Rifkin, J. "Racial Identity Development and the Mediation of Conflicts." In C. L. Wijeyesinghe and B. W. Jackson (eds.), *New Perspectives on Racial Identity Development.* New York: New York University Press, 2001.

Jamie O. Harris is a senior collaboration consultant for Interaction Associates and is the practice area leader for the company's collaborative change practice. Since joining Interaction Associates in January 1998, he has also served as the company's corporate counsel and a member of the board of directors. He was the engagement leader for the intervention described in this chapter. Harris graduated magna cum laude from Yale University with a bachelor of arts degree in political science and economics and earned his doctor of law degree at Yale Law School. He practiced business and real estate law in the San Francisco Bay Area for twenty-four years and before joining Interaction Associates was the managing partner of Evans, Latham, Harris, & Campisi, a firm he cofounded in 1985. He is the author of numerous articles published in various California and national legal periodicals. Harris has served as a "management mentor" for the Harvard Business School Publishing Company's *Manage Mentor* series on giving and receiving feedback (2003) and has recently published articles in *Executive Excellence* and the online magazine *HR.com.* Harris lives in Lafayette, California, with his wife of thirty-six years. They have three adult children. He enjoys sailing, fly fishing, and playing trombone in a jazz band.

David Straus founded Interaction Associates in 1969 and has over the years served in every major leadership position in the company, including president, CEO, and chairman of the board. Under his guidance, Interaction Associates has become a recognized leader in organizational development, group process facilitation, training, and consulting. Straus guided the development of Interaction Associates' consulting practice and training programs. He was also responsible for major change efforts in a variety of organizations, including the health care and service industries, and has worked with social action partnerships in Newark, New Jersey, and Palm Beach County, Florida. Straus earned a bachelor's degree from Harvard University and a master's degree in architecture from Harvard's Graduate School of Design. Under grants from the National Institute of Mental Health and the Carnegie Corporation, he conducted research in creativity and developed training programs in problem solving. Straus is the coauthor (with Michael Doyle) of the best-seller *How to Make Meetings Work* (Jove Books, 1976) and has written a new book, *How to Make Collaboration Work: Powerful Ways to Build Consensus, Solve Problems, and Make Decisions* (Berrett-Koehler, 2002). He lives in Cambridge, Massachusetts, with his wife Patricia. They have two daughters, Sara Farrer and Rebecca Straus.

CHAPTER SEVENTEEN

THEORY IN ACTION

Building Collaboration in a County Public Agency

Jamie O. Harris, David Straus

Moving an organizational culture from paternalistic hierarchy to collaboration is a daunting proposition. Yet as Straus (2002) and others have argued, both internal and external forces operating on today's organizations—worker demands for greater voice and access to information, increasing complexity, uncertainty, customer quality expectations, competition to reduce costs and time to market—are all pushing organizations to move to more collaborative forms and processes. Collaborative organizations tend to have the following characteristics:

- Alignment around shared purpose and meaning as expressed in vision, mission, core values, and strategic direction
- Organizational capability to transcend internal functional boundaries
- Widespread skill in facilitative leadership, teamwork, and collaborative problem solving

Jamie Harris acknowledges and thanks Donn Hatcher, formerly a senior consultant with Interaction Associates, for his energetic and valuable contributions to both the intervention and the writing of this case study. He was a true partner in the design and facilitation of the intervention and in thinking through the case study. He conducted the postintervention results assessment interviews and provided continuous encouragement and helpful critical analysis to help write the story.

- Commitment to lifelong learning and teamwork
- Social responsibility
- New technology that supports collaboration and involvement
- A social contract of rights and responsibilities between the organization and employees

Moving an organization toward collaboration requires a systemic effort addressing all aspects of the organization—values and culture, structure, work processes, reward systems, technology, leadership attitudes, and practices. Focus on one piece of the puzzle, such as teamwork training, will not result in lasting organizational change. Change must take place in multiple parts of the organization at the same time, and the change needs to be perceived as a strategic response, a do-or-die proposition.

Straus (2005) discussed five "prongs" required for a systemic effort to build a more collaborative organization:

1. Build leadership and ownership at all levels by linking the change to the mission and strategy of the organization and forming a cross-functional, multilevel team to guide and own the change effort.
2. Demonstrate the power of collaborative action throughout the organization by addressing and resolving issues collaboratively.
3. Increase the number of people at all levels who have internalized collaborative skills, and applied them to real issues.
4. Develop and deploy internal training, facilitation consulting, and coaching capability.
5. Measure and monitor the progress of the change effort.

The following example of building collaboration in a county public agency illustrates the application of this five-pronged approach to a particularly difficult culture and audience.

The Agency

The agency involved was the maintenance division of a county public works department. The division had about one hundred employees, most of whom were involved in manual outdoor labor such as street and highway repairs, vegetation removal, and flood control structure maintenance. Their jobs ranged from working with hand tools to the skilled operation of heavy equipment.

Initially, we were asked to facilitate an "all hands" off-site meeting. However, upon further discussion with the senior managers, it was agreed that we would perform an organizational assessment and diagnosis to gather data on long-standing issues and begin a process of employee involvement in defining and solving the problems. The assessment included numerous one-on-one interviews, two focus groups, and a written survey.

The Assessment

The interviews and focus groups revealed that the maintenance division was plagued with hostility, lack of trust, a vigorous rumor mill, racial tension, and an all-white "old boy" network. The management style was frequently described as militaristic and paternalistic. There was a consistent undertone of anger and pain, and complaints of unfairness, lack of respect for employees, punitive treatment, racism, favoritism, failure to deal with performance problems, fear of retribution, and mistrust of management were common. When we presented the assessment feedback and conclusions to the whole organization, agreement on the summary diagnosis we offered was widespread. Here is what we said:

> While many employees like their specific jobs, there are serious issues in the Maintenance Division that need to be addressed urgently by management and employees. Morale is low. Trust is lacking, especially trust in management. There is a widespread perception of favoritism in promotions and lack of accountability. Employees do not perceive that there is a common vision or set of goals for the future. Employees at all levels perceive that the superintendents and supervisors do not work will together to lead the Division effectively. There is fear of retaliation. Poor communication and mistrust lead to a destructive rumor mill. There is a lot of suspicion and skepticism about whether anything will change for the better.

The Intervention

Fortunately, the public works department senior leadership agreed with and wholeheartedly accepted our recommendation of a systemic intervention to try to change the organization and, using the word *teamwork* as shorthand, were very supportive of building a more collaborative organization. We shall describe the intervention using the "five prongs" we have described.

First Prong: Link the Change and the Mission and Strategy of the Organization and Form a Cross-Functional Multilevel Team to Own and Guide the Change Effort

Before we could address both parts of this prong, the first task was to try to build a top leadership team where none had existed before. Building a "team at the top" can often be challenging (Katzenbach and Smith, 1993). Although the director, deputy, and division chief frequently talked, it was always according to the strict hierarchical chain of command; they did not work together as a management team. We found that the top leaders had never really discussed, much less agreed on, core values, mission, or vision for the maintenance division. The public works department had a published vision and values statement, displayed on the walls in headquarters, but it was little known to employees in the maintenance yards. Nor had it been tailored to the maintenance division, which was significantly different in its work processes, general education levels, location, and culture from the engineering- and development-oriented functions of the rest of the public works department. The employees in the maintenance division had little idea of what the public works director thought about the future of the division.

Working with the director, we helped establish a "top team" of four individuals: the director, the deputy director in charge of maintenance, the division chief, and the newly hired director of maintenance operations (DMO).

Linking the Change and the Mission and Strategy of the Organization. We facilitated four half-day meetings during which these four hammered out basic agreements on how they would work together as a leadership team.

Decision making was a critical area for agreement. For example, what decisions would be made by team consensus, and what decisions would fall back to the director? Next, they reached consensus on a statement of core values that they, as leaders, aspired to have lived out in the maintenance division. This included brief descriptions of what the values would actually mean in action. They also agreed on their collective vision for the division's future and drafted a revised, maintenance-focused mission statement for the division.

Once these core tasks had been accomplished, we coached them next to step back and challenge their own thinking about change. What really was the business case for change? How would they justify, in a brief written case for change, the large expenditure of money, time, and pain that would be required to change the maintenance division culture? And specifically, toward what explicit changes did they want to lead the department?

The leadership team members felt that the goals they established for the change effort were challenging and simple yet comprehensive enough to address the issues documented in the assessment and diagnosis phase. They agreed that they would lead a change effort with the following objectives in mind:

- To align leadership behavior with the vision, mission, and core values of the division
- To open communication
- To improve morale and teamwork at all levels
- improve safety performance

In the alignment meetings, the four leaders developed a new openness and camaraderie. They frequently challenged each other's thinking but listened to one another respectfully. All of the key work products—values, vision and mission statements, case for change, and short list of key change goals—were subject to sometimes vigorous debate but ultimately were agreed to unanimously. For the first time, the senior leadership of the division was able to speak in one voice about where the division was headed and how the division was expected to work. Lastly, the leaders agreed on their own roles and responsibilities in leading the change effort. Though ultimate accountability to sponsor the effort remained with the public works director, much of the day-to-day change leadership would rest with the new DMO. The DMO turned out to be a very capable change champion possessing both personality and skills well attuned to creating a more open environment in the division. He was also a willing risk taker throughout the change process.

Creating an Empowered Transition Management Team. We proposed an all-hands meeting to establish a cross-functional, multilevel team to launch, guide, and own the change effort. In this large group meeting, the leadership team would present its collective decisions on values, vision, and direction; receive feedback; present the plan for change; and have the employees elect members of the transition management team (TMT).

The concept for the TMT was fairly typical for whole-system change efforts (for example, see Ault, Walton, and Childers, 1998) and is a critical part of the commitment-building and collaborative problem-solving elements of change. It is an organ for direct employee empowerment in the change process. We recommended, and leadership agreed to, a team of approximately a dozen members representing all levels of the organization from frontline labor to senior management. Importantly, we wanted to be sure that employees had a majority of the seats compared to management. The function of the TMT was to identify important problems in the division and take action to solve them. It was intended to be a true decision-making body with the power to choose for itself what problems to work on and what solutions to implement as long as its choices were aligned with the goals of the change effort. Obviously, there would be constraints (legal, budgetary, and so on), but the TMT would be empowered in its charter to act within those constraints, not just make recommendations. We expected that the TMT would be facilitated by the consultants for at least six months, during which time its members would build strong team bonds and learn important meeting and collaborative problem-solving skills. These skills would enable them to continue on their own, thus building organizational capability to solve problems.

As expected, the launch meeting was noisy. There were several not very respectful challenges to the leaders' presentations as well as to our facilitation. Cynicism, mistrust, and posturing were strongly in evidence. One important moment in the kick-off meeting occurred when a senior HR manager from "downtown" showed up at the meeting and spoke briefly in support of change in the division. For most employees in the division, this was the first time they had ever seen this person at the division yard. HR was often perceived as a distant powerful force used as an excuse by managers for keeping things as they were. The positive, supportive presence of a senior HR official in the kickoff meeting was a noticeable difference compared to past all-hands meetings.

The most significant moment in the meeting came when the crews were asked to enter into private meetings to select their respective representatives to the TMT. (The supervisors also adjourned to elect two of their number to the TMT.) Many of the employees appeared genuinely surprised that they could have a secret ballot process to elect people who would sit with management to engage in problem solving. This was not an experience they had had in the division before. We recognized that having the employees elect their own representatives rather than having management choose them was risky. What if we got a TMT consisting of all the hardest-headed, most resistant individuals who might act to frustrate what they thought was "just another management-sponsored initiative"? However, we felt that visibly transferring important responsibility for change to the employees from the very beginning was essential to begin to build trust and shared responsibility for change and to show an important initial shift in management's behavior. We were very explicit about the risks the employees were taking in choosing their representatives. We also explicitly stated that neither we nor management would "rescue" the TMT if it could not function. The message we tried to get across was that if the employees wanted things to change, they should choose people they thought would work in good faith because the TMT was empowered to actually make change happen if it could agree on what to do.

Response during and immediately after the launch meeting was mixed. Some employees and managers evinced enthusiasm, a spirit of "finally, it sounds like something might happen." Many others were openly derisive or hostile, including a few who dramatically walked out of the TMT election meetings or refused to vote. Overall, it was an intensely emotional experience, challenging the consultants to retain focus on the big picture and the long effort ahead rather than the drama of the moment.

By the end of the kickoff meeting, we knew who all the members of the TMT would be except for the seat reserved for HR. We still had not been able to secure agreement from downtown to provide a senior-level member who could act with authority. Ultimately, the unwillingness of HR to support the TMT process by providing a member to the team with decision-making authority severely limited its success because the TMT could not make decisions on a number of matters where HR policies or practices were involved. The public works director took on the task of advocating with HR for a meaningful presence on the TMT, but we did not want to delay while that discussion continued; we did not want to lose whatever momentum was established in the all-hands kickoff.

At the start, the TMT was a team in name only. We surmised that there would be a powerful lot of "storming" in getting it going, and we were not wrong about that. To accelerate team formation and functioning, we scheduled two full-day off-site work sessions to develop relationships and seek agreement on a comprehensive team charter.

Following the "Star Team" model (Interaction Associates, 1994), we consider a team charter at its most general level to be an essential set of agreements by the team on the following points:

- Shared, meaningful purpose
- Specific, challenging goals
- Roles and responsibilities
- Common and collaborative process
- Complementary skills

The charter also delineated boundary conditions and constraints. Some employee members bridled at the thought they would have boundaries, but with further discussion, the whole team was able to agree on the reasonableness of important boundaries such as working within legal constraints like the memorandum of agreement with the union, countywide employment policies applicable to all departments, and financial constraints such as the existing division budget and existing wages and benefits.

As might be expected, there was complaining about the time commitment of two full days and lots of pushback against having to take time to agree on a detailed charter. "Let's just cut the bull and get on with the work" was forcefully expressed. Our introduction of an activity to build a common vision for around purpose and goals was met with charges of "touchy-feely crap" by some. However, in debriefing this important piece of work, some startlingly creative and moving statements of individual team members' aspirations were made. One older gentleman, a slim and wizened thirty-year veteran laborer we'll call Herb, brought a hush to the room when he said, "I've worked here for most of my life. I won't be around here to see the outcome of all of this 'cause I'm gonna retire soon. But I just want to go out feeling like I've done something to make it a better place than I've had. I'll retire happy if I can do that."

We included in the chartering sessions some basic training on meeting and listening skills. Moving into the TMT work sessions, we frequently conducted just-in-time training modules on basic facilitation, agenda-planning skills, and collaborative problem solving (such as the need to agree on root causes of a problem before addressing solutions).

The work to develop an explicit and detailed charter paid off later by providing guidelines for what the TMT was supposed to be doing and what was "out of bounds." In one remarkable example, after several meetings in which one member repeatedly became stuck in advocacy that everything would be solved if they just all got a raise, the union shop steward, a longtime laborer respected by most employees, vigorously said, "Come on, cut that out; pay's not in our charter! Let's work on something we can solve!"

Second Prong: Demonstrating the Power of Collaborative Action Throughout the Organization by Addressing and Resolving Issues Collaboratively

Collaborative problem solving was a primary purpose of the TMT. From a very long list of possible issues generated in the early round of fact gathering from employees, the TMT narrowed its efforts to a few "hot button" concerns, such as when and how employees became eligible for higher pay for temporary service in a higher-class work position. "Higher pay for higher class," or HPHC, as it was called, was a long-standing issue that had generated deep feelings of unfairness. Filling vacancies was another key issue. As vacancies were left open for long periods of time, employees felt not only that their chances for advancement were reduced but that it indicated an intention of management to shrink the division and contract out more and more of the work, threatening basic job security.

In spite of some frustrations, the TMT agreed on some simple and direct changes to the HPHC process that were implemented in fairly short order. The group developed a new employee orientation program that was successfully implemented when the division hired eleven new laborers (much to everyone's relief) several months into the change effort. TMT members thoroughly analyzed a controversial "flex-staffing" program, gathered facts that rebutted a number of myths that had been floating around about it, and developed some appropriate changes in the program itself and in related training processes.

Having completed this first round of activities, and still under criticism from many employees that the team was not doing enough fast enough, the TMT decided to take on some larger issues. It chose to look at the safety program (safety training had lapsed, and an employee safety committee had fallen into virtual inactivity) and the extremely high level of disability absences (which put a lot of pressure on the employees who did show up to work). On each of these large issues, the TMT formed a working subgroup called a "problem advisory group," or PAG. Each PAG established its own short-term set of goals and a fact-finding plan.

The safety PAG succeeded in reinvigorating the employee safety committee, and safety training increased. Although the workers' compensation and disability group was not able to make any material changes (the system is controlled by various state law mandates and countywide policies beyond the control of the public works department), it did obtain a lot of detailed statistical information and educated all employees about the impact of time off on budgets, workload, and other employee concerns. We believe that the generally higher level of knowledge has increased employees' sense of responsibility regarding claims for benefits under the system.

Another illustration of the second prong was work with the supervisors to build their collaborative problem-solving capability. Employee perceptions of "backstabbing," lack of cooperation, and even basic lack of management competence in some cases were validated by the data and by the consultants' early interactions with the supervisors and superintendents. All were longtime division employees, having come up through the ranks, but there was great variation in skills, commitment, and methods of dealing with subordinates. Deep divisions persisted between the small group of supervisors, some racially based, some based on personal histories. A true "old boy" network did exist among some of the longtime managers, who had all attended the same high school. Some supervisors were loved by employees, and others were mistrusted. Supervisors rarely shared people or equipment from one crew to another. The two things they tended to agree on were that "senior management" was "screwed up" and that the employees weren't "held accountable." They did not seem to examine the role they played between these two groups or the impact they had on "screw-ups" or accountability. They seemed to feel completely disempowered to do anything but "hang on" and complain.

The challenge was clear. How could we, as outside consultants, help the supervisors look at themselves honestly, discuss their interpersonal issues openly, develop cohesion, address employee supervision problems, and become effective mid-level leaders of the organization? The challenge we saw was very consistent with the work of Barry Oshry (1996). He suggested that organizations in trouble very often need the most work in strengthening—empowering—the people in the middle so that they can speak truth to those above them and provide support to those below them. The "middles" are the fulcrum for change because they are in the only position in which to see and interact frequently with both "tops" and "bottoms." In their middle position, they are constantly pulled by all the stresses and strains of the system.

We facilitated several tough meetings with the supervisors, the purpose of which was to strengthen their ability to work as colleagues in management rather than continue to behave competitively. In the first session, we heard a steady chorus of challenges: "Why are we here? It's the senior managers' fault, not ours. Why are we being blamed? We can't do anything. We don't get any respect or support. What is the hidden agenda? Why don't they just tell us what to do? If we could just fire some of the bad apples, everything would be fine. That assessment was an exaggeration; it's really not that bad. I can't believe how much you guys are getting paid! What a waste of money." In the midst of such fulminations, they gradually began to talk about issues and problems they felt were getting in their way, although still asserting that the problems were always caused by others.

Finally, after almost two hours of this foment, one of the supervisors, an older man nearing retirement, said in a very soft voice, "You know, guys, I think we have to take some responsibility too. We have to look at ourselves." This didn't break the pattern instantly, as more of the finger-pointing talk continued, but a few minutes later, someone else picked up the message. "Wait. I think Jim was right. We need to look at ourselves some here too." From these small beginnings of awareness rather bravely spoken, the meeting moved into a realm of opportunity.

We had written all of the problems and issues that had been vented for two hours on flipchart sheets that adorned virtually the entire room. Now we helped the supervisors go back over them all and identify the key themes. They boiled it all down to nine or ten major problem areas. With rough agreement that they had at least named the problems of greatest concern (most of which, unsurprisingly, mirrored the data and themes from the assessment), we urged them to think about some goals for themselves as supervisors. We chose to focus on goals at this stage because we felt it was still too early to try to engage them directly in discussion of their own responsibility and dysfunction. We felt that they needed some agreement on direction first.

The rest of the meeting was energetic and positive as the supervisors proposed a list of possible goals, clarified and evaluated their ideas, and eventually settled on five goals to work toward: greater consistency in the way they managed staff, more teamwork among themselves, getting higher pay, and better communication upward and downward. Importantly, they also agreed that they wanted to meet as a group to present their goals to the public works director and the division chief, a significant first step in coming together as a management team.

To prepare for the supervisors' presentation of their goals, we coached the senior team thoroughly on basic listening skills, particularly paraphrasing and inquiry to check for understanding before challenging. "You don't listen to us" was the most frequent charge supervisors threw upward. We wanted to be sure not only that the senior team really listened but also that these managers had the skills to show the supervisors that they were hearing what was being said. We believe that one common cause of people's feeling that they are not being heard is simply that they do not get any evidence of being heard. Giving people evidence of being heard begins in the conversation itself.

The supervisors approached the meeting with the senior team with excitement and some apprehension. They were, we felt, quite surprised to find that the senior team, and especially the director of public works, not only listened carefully and heard what they said but actually expressed support for all five of the goals they had set, including trying to get more pay for them as the performance of the division improved.

The supervisors came to realize that they in fact had a great deal of power to influence the culture, performance, and day-to-day-experience of the division. We hadn't entirely eliminated skepticism and denial, but bringing the supervisors together had ignited a spark to open up to leadership and change.

A third demonstration of the power of collaboration to resolve issues was in dispute resolution. For example, we facilitated a dispute resolution session between one of the most "troublesome" (but also hardest-working) employees and the division manager and between the employees' union business agent and the public works director. Both of these efforts resulted in significant behavior change by the parties that was noticeable throughout the division.

Third Prong: Increasing the Number of People at All Levels of the Organization Who Have Mastered Collaborative Skills and Applied Them to Real Issues

To spread collaboration skills and opportunity and apply them to real problems, the TMT developed its own rules for rotation of membership. It successfully transitioned new members into service on the team as time passed. This served not only to refresh perspectives but also to increase the number of employees who gained leadership and problem-solving skills through the TMT experience. Many of these skills have been taken back to the division work crews, which have begun more successful meeting and planning processes. As planned, the consultants continued to work with the TMT for about six months. We agreed to extend for another two months.

Our intervention design sought to build collaborative team and leadership skills throughout the organization. Working at the senior team level built collaboration skills among the members of the top team. Empowering employees to solve real problems they cared about through the TMT and empowering supervisors to develop and advocate their own set of goals and needs helped build collaborative skills deeper into the organization.

To drive change deeper and make it last, however, employees throughout the division needed new skills and practices for working together differently. History and the assessment showed that there was a dearth of skills in teamwork, communication, collaborative problem solving, planning, feedback, and conflict resolution. Lacking these important capabilities for successfully working together, the organization tended to fall back on modes that created a culture of disrespect and dependency—waiting for orders, one-way (top-down) communication, a penchant for quick fixes, unresolved conflicts, finger-pointing, and political maneuvering. We saw a need to deliver fundamental teamwork, communication, and interpersonal skills to everyone to overcome these endemic problems.

Fortunately, the senior leaders supported these ideas wholeheartedly. They joined in the learning process themselves rather than operating on the assumption that skills training was only for employees farther down the hierarchy. The senior leaders' openness to skills training showed up not only in their willingness to pay for it but also early on when we spent several hours practicing basic listening skills with them before the meeting on goals with the supervisors. They very seriously engaged the practices, especially trying to balance inquiry and advocacy, and continued afterward to coach each other openly in practicing active listening and inquiry in our subsequent working sessions.

The "tops" and "middles"—senior team, superintendents, and supervisors—together attended a customized leadership workshop focused on collaborative leadership skills. This was a three-day session in which the participants learned elements of teamwork, balancing results, process and relationship, leading and planning meetings, coaching others, creating and communicating a vision, feedback skills (both giving and receiving), and the dynamics of the ladder of inference (Argyris, 1990, Senge and others, 1994). The workshop also acted as a forum for continued open dialogue between the middle managers and the senior team about what was going on, how they were or were not changing, and developing awareness of personal style differences. Even as supervisors remained critical of the senior team, and the director in particular, they were impressed with the openness and participation they saw from above. Sharing the workshop experience with the senior team helped somewhat to overcome the superintendents' perception that they were being blamed for the division's problems.

Spreading collaboration skills throughout the organization was continued through the biweekly work-planning meetings for all crews. Management of day-to-day work in the past had been up to each individual supervisor's style, but the predominant approach was a morning crew muster in which the supervisor told the crew what it would be doing that day. In addition, many of the supervisors also gave very explicit orders about who would do what and exactly how they would do it. The supervisors had lists of tasks to be done (generated by citizen requests, the engineering department plans, and management's long-term maintenance plans), but the employees rarely had any insight into the big picture.

The vision for a new management approach was that the crews and supervisors would plan two weeks of work at a time, together. Supervisors would lay out the work required over the two-week span and invite input from the employees not only on scheduling but also on staffing and execution of the work. Several of the supervisors were strongly opposed to such planning, saying that it was a waste of time or that they knew better than the employees how to do it. "After all, that's why we have supervisors!" Clearly, some of them feared a loss of authority and control if they invited employees into planning.

The senior leaders were adamant, however, that the more inclusive planning approach to managing the work be put into place. Some supervisors organized and led the biweekly planning meetings enthusiastically; others continued resisting the process, some barely complying, others not even holding the meetings. Although implementation was thus spotty at first, the change was very noticeable, and the process gradually took hold throughout most of the crews. Some of the supervisors began to talk about the good ideas they were getting from employees and how much the forward planning helped them avoid staffing problems when employees had a doctor's appointment, personal time off, or other anticipated work absences. When the employees got work assignments piecemeal on a daily basis, they had little reason to reveal anticipated absences, but when planning together with their crewmates over a two-week time span, they were much more willing to volunteer their own personal schedule conflicts so that absences could be planned around rather than come as a surprise.

The employees found that they had a voice in planning the work and a forum in which to offer their own experience and ideas about organizing what needed to be done. They saw the behavior of their immediate supervisors changing. It was actually possible to have meetings that resulted in discussion and action rather than just a one-way giving of orders!

The biggest training challenge was bringing team skills training to all of the crews. An important planning question was whether or not the supervisors should attend the workshops with their crews. There were pros and cons both ways. But before we had made a final recommendation, the supervisors, in a show of solidarity, told the director they would not attend the crews' workshops. They felt that the workshops would end up as a forum for them to be "bashed" by the employees, and they wanted no part of it. Happy that the supervisors had taken a stand (whether it was the right one or not) and reflecting on the obvious supposition that the crews would feel freer to speak their minds if their supervisors were not present, we proceeded to schedule the crews' workshops without the supervisors.

We delivered a two-day team skills workshop covering fundamental elements of teamwork such as the importance of shared purpose and goals, clear roles and responsibilities, and skills for interpersonal communication, feedback, conflict resolution, and problem solving. We anticipated that the parts of the workshop focused on team structure would be less important than the basic interpersonal skills of team members working together. We were right about that.

The standard agenda for the workshop was quickly abandoned, and each of the four two-day sessions took a path of its own. Most of the time was spent on communication and feedback skills and on teaching and practicing rudiments of conflict resolution. In several sessions, some crew members refused to come the first day, but their crewmates' positive comments about the experience convinced most of the holdouts to show up for the second day.

Consistently, the biggest issue that arose was the absence of the supervisors. "Why aren't they here getting the same stuff we're getting?" was asked over and over. Although the opportunity to discuss work matters without concern about reprisal from supervisors was appreciated, the crews were adamant that the supervisors should be taught the same things they were learning—a telling, if backhanded, appreciation for the learning taking place.

The team skills workshops served as a safe forum for crewmates to have some of the frankest and most honest conversations they had ever had with one another. We will never forget one feedback session in which two men told one of their crewmates, with elegantly specific fact-based feedback, how his uncleanliness, body odor, and sloppy personal habits affected them on the job. The next day, the individual showed up showered, shaved, and wearing clean clothes and shoes. His dramatic one-day makeover was openly celebrated by his coworkers.

We decided to act quickly on the demand that the supervisors should "get the same stuff." We designed a half-day review session for the supervisors to experience in summary fashion what had been covered in the crews' sessions. Moreover, we recommended, and with some difficulty got the supervisors to agree, to conduct facilitated crew and supervisor feedback meetings so that they could all practice what they had learned about feedback within the safety of a consultant-facilitated meeting. Some supervisors openly dreaded the prospect of receiving feedback from their crews; others said they would welcome learning what their crews thought about them.

To enable the crews and supervisors to have a productive conversation, we set a tightly structured agenda for the half-day sessions. Difficult conversations need to be strictly organized rather than "free-flowing" (Beer and Eisenstat, 2004).

After building quick agreement on ground rules, we facilitated "plus-delta" conversations on the "current state," that is, listing what's working when the crew and supervisor work together (the plus portion) followed by listing what changes should be made (the delta portion). We then facilitated a discussion to build agreement, as a team, on a vision of success for the team as a desired future state.

Despite a wide range of views on the current state, it was surprisingly easy for the crews and their supervisors to reach a broad consensus on a vision for the desirable future state. They did this by answering questions such as "What would it be like a year from now if you enjoyed working together?" The visions that the crews came up with were heartfelt, practical, and hopeful, focused on things like being able to trust one another, open communication, safety, opportunity for advancement, and having fun at work.

Each crew then brainstormed ideas for actions to move toward its future vision and reached agreement on three or four action items to pursue first. Some of these action items were more general ("Continue to give each other fact-based feedback"), and others were more specific ("Three of us will meet with the division chief in the next two weeks to talk about equipment maintenance problems we've had").

In debriefing the feedback sessions with the supervisors afterward, most expressed appreciation for having been able to receive feedback from their crews and felt that "it wasn't that bad after all."

Fourth Prong: Developing and Deploying Internal Training, Facilitation, Consulting, and Coaching Capabilities

Through the collaboration demonstration and training activities of the second and third prongs, a body of facilitation and coaching capability was installed in the system. The DMO in particular reconceptualized his role from being a manager of the supervisors to being their facilitator and coach. Several of the supervisors went through a similar recasting of their roles to become less a "crew boss" and more a coach and facilitator of crew planning and problem solving. The man who was leader of the TMT for its first year has become recognized in the division as a meeting leader and has taken on responsibility to plan agendas and facilitate some significant employee meetings even after leaving the TMT.

Given the size of the maintenance division (about one hundred people), it would not be realistic to retain a full-time internal trainer or consultant. However, the public works director has continued his commitment to leadership development and conflict resolution consulting for the public works department as a whole, and facilitative leadership has become the core leadership model for the whole department.

Fifth Prong: Measuring and Monitoring the Progress of the Change Effort

It would be wonderful if we had validated assessment tools with which to measure the collaborative characteristics of an organization before, during, and after an intervention. Developing the theoretical basis and statistical validation for such assessment instruments remains an important professional challenge for change-oriented facilitators and consultants.

Even without quantitative assessment tools, however, we feel that we were able to measure and document significant positive change through a series of postintervention interviews with the members of the senior management team, several supervisors, a sample of employees, and the employees' union business agent.

Our postintervention data gathering revealed a variety of perspectives, yet a coherent picture of positive change and significantly increased collaboration emerged. Major changes in work processes and some structural changes made during the course of the intervention and after were resulting in improved communication and more effective planning; for example:

- The former superintendent roles have been changed so that they provide direct support to the operations manager. He focuses on implementation and operational integrity of the new computer-based Maintenance Management System (MMS), quality of the division's work product, and planning for long-term resource and equipment supply.
- The superintendents no longer have direct-line supervision of the supervisors. The supervisors have been delegated more responsibility for problem solving and day-to-day management of the work in collaboration with their crews through the biweekly crew planning process.
- Through the leadership and team development training provided in the change initiative, both supervisors and crews have learned more effective problem-solving, communication, and feedback skills to plan and evaluate their work.
- Lines of communication are clearer, and the supervisors tend to work together more cohesively as a middle management team instead of playing one against the other.

In addition to important changes, increased interpersonal skills have opened communication, increased trust, and reduced conflict. In the postintervention interviews, people said things like this:

"The workers' trust in management has been reestablished."

"The atmosphere here is now much more open."

"We've learned how to solve problems by talking to each other."

"The power of the rumor mill has been reduced. Trust is starting to rear its head."

"The supervisors are communicating among themselves much more and sharing resources—people and equipment—in ways they never did before."

"Our senior leadership is more aware of how the employees view them and vice versa."

Although some employees are still viewed as "naysayers" or have a negative attitude, the influence of their negativity has been reduced. The regular process for obtaining employee feedback (using the "plus-delta" evaluation process) on a daily or weekly basis lets the steam out of employees whose former negativity frequently boiled over into confrontational behavior. We were informed that one of the employees who was previously considered a "worst case" "now comes up with wonderful ideas versus just objections. His focus now is to make things better, not just to get even."

Managers reported that less of their time has to be spent on resolving conflicts because employees are working out interpersonal conflicts among themselves through feedback and problem solving on the spot, and there is more trust and regular problem-solving communication between management and the union. Consequently, disciplinary actions and grievances have become less frequent, and the cost of conflict management has been reduced.

The biweekly crew planning sessions have become part of the standard operating procedure, resulting in more effective utilization of resources and greater satisfaction for employees who feel they have a voice in how the work gets done. One of the supervisors who was most resistant to involving his crew in decision making made a big turnaround and became very enthusiastic about his crew's frequent "plus-delta" reviews as a way to improve efficiency and quality and boost overall performance.

Successful use of the new computerized Maintenance Management System was viewed by management as essential to enable the division to compete for additional work outside of the county-owned facilities, thus protecting employee's jobs and holding out the promise of division growth. Many employees have gone from fear and opposition to the MMS to learning how to use it to increase division productivity. The links between productivity and job security are becoming clear to people.

Although the available record keeping systems are not able to produce hard data to confirm it, management and other employees believe that absenteeism for sick leave and injury claims has declined. The length and number of workers' compensation claims have declined as employees have gained a better understanding of the impact of workers' comp costs on the system;

they have also reduced the use of workers' comp absence as a form of protest against working conditions.

At the beginning of this chapter, we noted that moving an organization toward greater collaboration is a daunting proposition. The director of public works summarized the challenges and the possible rewards as follows:

> I was looking for a fundamental shift in thinking to get people to see that they are the problem and also that they are the solution to showing how good the division is, showing the quality and quantity of the work we can do. We're seeing that shift. . . . We are going to be able to teach our employees what quality means in our work. Now they are ready. We still have a lot of work to do. The managers are beginning to realize that for us to produce real quality, they have to let go some of their control, and the employees are beginning to realize that for the managers to let go of control, the employees have to step up to responsibility.

Building collaboration does require the fundamental shift the director was looking for. It is a shift in values, beliefs, skills, and behaviors, a shift in the very culture of an organization. Our experience with change in the maintenance division confirms that leadership, time, persistence, and a multipronged approach addressing the entire system are required to make it happen.

References

Argyris, C. *Overcoming Organizational Defenses: Facilitating Organizational Learning.* Upper Saddle River, N.J.: Prentice Hall, 1990.

Ault, R., Walton, R., and Childers, M. *What Works: A Decade of Change at Champion International.* San Francisco: Jossey-Bass, 1998.

Beer, M., and Eisenstat, R. A. "How to Have an Honest Conversation About Your Business Strategy." *Harvard Business Review,* Feb. 2004, pp. 82–89.

Interaction Associates. *Teams in Action Skills Workshop Manual.* Boston: Interaction Associates, 1994.

Katzenbach, J. R., and Smith, D. K. *The Wisdom of Teams: Creating the High-Performance Organization.* New York: HarperBusiness, 1993.

Oshry, B. *Seeing Systems.* San Francisco: Berrett-Koehler, 1996.

Senge, P. M., and others. *The Fifth Discipline Fieldbook: Strategies and Tools for Building a Learning Organization.* New York: Currency/Doubleday, 1994.

Straus, D. "How to Build a Collaborative Environment." In S. Schuman (ed.), *The IAF Handbook of Group Facilitation.* San Francisco: Jossey-Bass, 2005.

John M. Bryson is a professor of planning and public affairs and associate dean for research and centers in the Hubert H. Humphrey Institute of Public Affairs at the University of Minnesota. He is the author of *Strategic Planning for Public and Nonprofit Organizations* (3rd ed., Jossey-Bass, 2004), and the coauthor, with Barbara C. Crosby, of *Leadership for the Common Good: Tackling Public Problems in a Shared-Power World* (2nd ed., Jossey-Bass, 2005). The Public and Nonprofit Division of the Academy of Management awarded earlier editions of each book the title of Best Book for the year in which it was published. He has received numerous other awards for his work, including the General Electric Award for Outstanding Research in Strategic Planning from the Academy of Management. Bryson serves on the editorial boards of the *Journal of Public Administration Research and Theory, Public Management Review,* and the *Journal of Public Affairs Education,* among other journals. A fellow of the National Academy of Public Administration, he consults widely with nonprofit and governmental organizations in North America and Europe.

Barbara C. Crosby is associate professor at the Hubert H. Humphrey Institute of Public Affairs and a member of the institute's Public and Nonprofit Leadership Center at the University of Minnesota. During 2002–2003, she was a visiting fellow at the University of Strathclyde, Glasgow, Scotland. She has taught and written extensively about leadership and public policy, women in leadership, media and public policy, and strategic planning. She is the author of *Leadership for Global Citizenship* (Sage, 1999) and coauthor with John M. Bryson of *Leadership for the Common Good: Tackling Public Problems in a Shared-Power World* (2nd ed., Jossey-Bass, 2005). She is an associate editor of *Leadership Quarterly.* A frequent speaker at conferences and workshops, Crosby has conducted training for senior managers of nonprofit, business, and government organizations in the United States, the United Kingdom, Poland, and Ukraine. She is a former gubernatorial press secretary and speechwriter. She has also been a newspaper reporter and editor and has written several book chapters and articles for national journals. She holds a doctorate in leadership studies from the Union Institute.

CHAPTER EIGHTEEN

LEADERSHIP FOR THE COMMON GOOD

John M. Bryson, Barbara C. Crosby

Increasingly, scholars and practitioners alike are recognizing that tackling major social problems or challenges requires collaboration among all sectors (Goldsmith and Eggers, 2004; Crosby and Bryson, 2005). Yet such collaboration is often a difficult undertaking. As Chris Huxham (2003) notes, cross-sector collaborations typically experience tensions around purpose, trust, power, membership, and leadership.

The business, government, nonprofit, media, and community sectors operate according to different logics; they answer to different sets of stakeholders; they are prone to different kinds of successes and failure. Each sector, in effect, has a distinctive culture. The transaction costs of bringing together people from very different types of organizations can be high.

Development of a broad-based culture of collaboration is an important way of managing these tensions and transaction costs. Thus as leaders seek to

The authors gratefully acknowledge the assistance of Gary Cunningham in providing information about the African American Men Project for this article. This chapter draws substantially on "A Leadership Framework for Cross-Sector Collaboration," by Barbara C. Crosby and John M. Bryson, *Public Management Review*, 2005, 7, 177–201. That article is aimed specifically at elected officials and public managers.

build a cross-sector collaboration, they would be wise to nurture a collaborative culture not only within the collaboration but also in the broader community in which the collaboration takes place.

This chapter will examine a collaborative leadership initiative by elected officials, public administrators, and citizens in Hennepin County, Minnesota, the county that contains Minneapolis. Called the African American Men Project (AAMP), the initiative seeks to transform the life chances of African American men and to prompt cross-sector collaboration to support this transformation (http://www.aamp-mn.org). The case is a story of at least initial success, but success has required considerable struggle and has come on the heels of decades of policy failure. As Nancy Roberts (2000) has argued, policy change advocates often have to fail their way into collaboration.

First, we will say a bit more about culture and the cultural milieu in which this project began. We will then describe the project itself and present a framework for analyzing leadership in this case and other collaborative endeavors. Finally, we will offer lessons for leaders trying to build cultures of collaboration among diverse stakeholders. The lessons highlight the benefits of intensive stakeholder analysis and extensive stakeholder involvement; the importance of thoughtfully framing public problems; the difficulties of disrupting existing systems; the importance of seed money, champions, and sponsors; and the need to share leadership widely in order to build new, beneficial policy regimes.

Cultural Milieu

The culture of a group, organization, sector, or community refers to its habitual, or "right," way of doing things, its deepest assumptions about meaning, power, and legitimacy in social arrangements (Hall, 1981; Crosby and Bryson, 2005). Cultural analysts can find clues to these assumptions in behaviors, stories, artifacts, and spatial design (Schein, 2004). Leaders who recognize the need for cultural change cannot alter fundamental assumptions directly. Instead, they will need to tell new stories, engage in new behaviors, and create new artifacts and social designs—all of which evoke, while recasting, the cultural traditions of the group, organization, or society.

In the case of the African American Men Project, leaders needed to understand the culture of Hennepin County as a whole, other cultures within

Hennepin County, and especially the culture of Hennepin County government. Hennepin County is home to Minnesota's largest city, Minneapolis, and numerous suburbs. Both Minneapolis and many first-ring suburbs have high levels of ethnic diversity, yet often people of color are segregated in poor neighborhoods. The county has some traditions of cross-sector collaboration to deal with public issues and crises, but these traditions have eroded somewhat in the past couple of decades as many local corporations have become more nationally and internationally focused. Generally, the county has had a culture in which each sector did its own thing. Government provided public schools, social services, public safety, and facilities like roads and parks. Nonprofits (churches, foundations, and service, charitable, and advocacy organizations) provided specialized services and independent schools, organized or funded innovative projects, and catered to specific communities. The mass media covered African Americans' outstanding accomplishments but also highlighted crimes committed by African American men.

In poor neighborhoods, some residents were organizing self-help operations to rid their blocks of drug dealers and reach out to troubled young people, but many simply felt beleaguered and left out. A culture of frustration and hopelessness sometimes seemed in ascendance.

For their part, businesses provided jobs, products, and services and in some cases cooperated with government and nonprofit groups to provide training for workers with minimal or obsolete skills. Also, some business associations were active in promoting legislative agendas that affected county tax rates and programs.

Hennepin County government culture was manifested in siloed departments, many of which dealt separately with the same clients. Many staff were strongly rooted in a professional culture that has tremendous strengths (for example, concern for clients' well-being and adherence to standards of care or service) but also weaknesses (failure to treat clients holistically as multifaceted members of the community and attachment to the provider-client model that may obscure the potential for partnership between professionals and citizens in need of assistance).

Meanwhile, many African American men had become detached from the cultural traditions that had sustained black families in the face of hardship for many decades. An important factor in this detachment was the tendency of many public policies to ignore and even actively undermine the important role of men in family life.

The African American Men Project, 1999–2005

In 1999, Mark Stenglein, an elected Hennepin County commissioner, was driving through an impoverished neighborhood in his district and was surprised to see so many African American men standing around on street corners in the middle of the day. The state's economy was doing very well at the time, and Stenglein wondered why these men weren't working. Soon afterward, he ran into Gary Cunningham, head of the county's Office of Planning and Development, and asked if Cunningham could provide an explanation.

One might have predicted a confrontation between the two men—Stenglein, a conservative European American politician raising questions about the behavior of African American men, and Cunningham, a public servant who was himself African American and had a long history of working for the benefit of the black community. Cunningham, though, saw a chance for fact-finding and proposed a formal inquiry. He already knew that while many African American men in Hennepin County were doing very well in terms of employment, financial success, and leadership roles, substantial numbers were in trouble; for example:

- Each year, 44 percent of the county's African American men between the ages of eighteen and thirty were arrested, mainly for minor offenses.
- Only 28 percent of male African Americans in the Minneapolis public schools were graduating on time.
- The death rate among young African American men was twice that of their white counterparts.

Moreover, over the years, a host of goals, objectives, policies, and programs had been established for this population, yet improvements had been marginal. Schools had set graduation targets, public health agencies aimed programs at improving health care for African Americans, the court system had specific objectives for processing cases, and so on. Already an array of government and nonprofit organizations were involved, as well as some businesses participating in hiring and retention programs. Yet none had made a real dent in the group's high unemployment, low education levels, and poor health conditions. Moreover, given the conflict-ridden history of U.S. race relations, almost any proposed solution to problems affecting African American men was likely to invoke old and acrimonious debates over civil rights, the legacy of slavery, racism, affirmative action, welfare policy, and personal morality. Gary Cunningham well knew that any solutions to the problems affecting African American men would have to be multifaceted and would require contributions from a multitude of stakeholders, including African American men themselves, county commissioners and employees, businesspeople, black families, education officials and teachers, other government bodies, and journalists. To compile a preliminary report, he consulted his staff, black community leaders, other county commissioners, business leaders, and university faculty.

After Cunningham's office delivered its preliminary findings, Mark Stenglein and fellow commissioner Peter McLaughlin persuaded the Hennepin County board of commissioners to authorize a more in-depth study of the status of African American men in the county. Cunningham's office organized a steering committee of government representatives and community notables that would guide the study and prepare the final report. Herman Milligan Jr., a vice president at Wells Fargo Bank, agreed to chair the committee. Also on the committee were the current mayor of Minneapolis, Sharon Sayles Belton; three county commissioners; and longtime grassroots leaders like John Turnipseed, director of a fathering program for the nonprofit Urban Venture. Working teams—including committee members, community advisers, and academic researchers—were assembled to research different issues affecting African American men and to come up with recommendations. These teams collected information about the issues, engaged in a process to clarify the issues, and then moved on to specific goals. The teams and the steering committee were a seedbed for the cross-sector collaboration that would become a hallmark of the AAMP. (Author John Bryson worked with one of the teams.)

In early 2002, the committee published its final report, *Crossroads: Choosing a New Direction,* along with an extensive research compendium. The report recommended creation of an advisory board to coordinate an ongoing African American Men Project that would do the following:

- Emphasize the contributions of African American males
- Create partnerships and coordinating mechanisms to improve education, housing, and employment opportunities, as well as access to health information, for black men

- Promote public policy changes
- Coordinate efforts to reduce the disproportionate involvement of minorities in the criminal justice system
- Get young African American men involved in the community

The Hennepin County board approved the new advisory board, provided a $500,000 seed grant to help it get started, and directed the county administrator to implement all recommendations for which the county was responsible. The county commissioners expected about thirty people to apply to serve on the board, to be called the African American Men Commission, but 130 applied! Gary Cunningham urged the county board to capitalize on this community enthusiasm and encourage these prospective leaders by appointing them all. Thus in September 2002, all 130 were sworn in as members of the new African American Men Commission; James Cook, a longtime African American community leader and nonprofit director, and Herman Milligan Jr. were designated cochairs.

The commission established a schedule of quarterly meetings for the membership as a whole; in addition, members agreed to serve on three planning and project development committees. A small county staff, coordinated by Shane Price, who worked with the project from the outset, was assigned to assist the commission and help organize project initiatives. Also, the project received a substantial grant from the Minneapolis Foundation to assist with planning and evaluation.

Since January 2002, the African American Men Project has organized several community events to publicize the steering committee's report and involve citizens in the project's initiatives. The commission members and staff have recruited 120 Quality Partners, an array of business, nonprofit, media, and government organizations that are directly involved in AAMP initiatives, which include the following:

- Days of Restoration, in which a judge from the Hennepin County court reviewed hundreds of old traffic violation cases and offered individuals who had been ticketed a chance to clear their record by paying their fines or performing community service. The restoration process has saved hundreds of thousands of dollars in administrative costs and enabled many citizens to more easily apply for jobs and rent housing.

- Reinstatement of the right to vote for former offenders who committed low-level or nonviolent crimes.
- A cooperative employee recruitment program with the Metropolitan Transit Authority.
- The Right Turn Project, bringing together people in the faith community, the Minneapolis Police Department, social service organizations, and grass-roots groups to help young African American men who have committed "livability crimes" (such as disorderly conduct and low-level drug offenses). Each young man enrolled in the project works with a project team to devise and implement an individual development plan that includes goals like securing stable employment and housing, resolution of outstanding legal issues, and carrying out parental responsibilities. In its first year, 2004, the project served 425 men and has a long-term goal of assisting one thousand men annually.
- Black Men Reading, a weekly book club that brings older and younger African American men together.

The supporters of the African American Men Project have encountered various obstacles along the way. The economic recession that began in 2000 put pressure on county government revenues and thus forced supporters of the AAMP to work hard on maintaining needed funding levels. Also, some people in the Hennepin County government bureaucracy were hostile toward an initiative that pointed out the shortcomings of their approaches to working with young black residents. County administrator Sandra Vargas protected the project from this internal sniping. When the project began, its educational initiatives were bolstered by the strong support of an African American superintendent of schools in Minneapolis. When the superintendent resigned to take another job, her replacement was less interested in the project, and the proposed Brother Achievement program for the public schools was consigned to a back burner. Also, black community leaders were initially suspicious of the project, but Gary Cunningham obtained a commitment from them to at least remain neutral as the project got under way. Once the project began to demonstrate its effectiveness, more of these leaders became supporters.

The launch of the African American Men Project and the project's accomplishments despite numerous obstacles exemplify leadership for the common good. The next section will explain more fully what this type of leadership is all about and examine how it was practiced in this case.

The Leadership for the Common Good Framework

By launching the African American Men Project, the Hennepin County commissioners, Gary Cunningham, and their community partners were promoting "leadership for the common good," in which representatives of diverse stakeholders collaborate in defining public problems, finding promising solutions, and obtaining and sustaining the necessary policies, programs, rules, and norms that can establish a "regime of mutual gain" over the long haul (Crosby and Bryson, 2005). A regime of mutual gain is a policy regime that achieves widespread lasting benefits at reasonable cost and that taps and serves people's deepest interests in, and desires for, a better world for themselves and the people they care about. These regimes can be thought of as shared-power arrangements in which organizations from different sectors share information, coordinate activities, and collaborate on long-term projects.

As we studied and supported the work of leaders like the organizers of the African American Men Project, we have developed the Leadership for the Common Good Framework, which provides diagnostic tools and guidance for people seeking to foster widespread collaboration on tough public problems. The framework draws on the extensive and growing body of research about leadership theory and practice and draws together work on policy entrepreneurship, advocacy coalitions, and agenda setting (see Roberts and King, 1996; Sabatier and Jenkins-Smith, 1993; and Baumgartner and Jones, 1993). It considers multiple levels of action (personal, team, organizational, and societal), highlights the importance of context and of individual and collective efficacy, and provides a fuller understanding of how visionary, political, and ethical leaders operate and why visionary work in forums is so critical to the success of policy change efforts.

The Leadership for the Common Good Framework includes the following components (see Figure 18.1):

- Attention to the dynamics of a shared-power world
- The wise design and use of forums, arenas, and courts, the main settings in which leaders and constituents foster policy change in a shared-power world
- Effective navigation of the policy change cycle
- The exercise of leadership capabilities

FIGURE 18.1. THE LEADERSHIP
FOR THE COMMON GOOD FRAMEWORK.

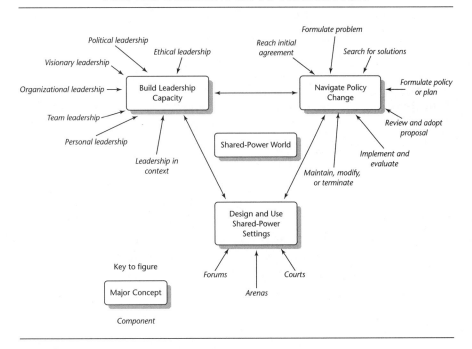

These elements do not provide a recipe for leadership success but rather what Chris Huxham and her colleagues call "handles for reflective practice" (Huxham and Beech, 2003; Huxham and Vangen, 2005). In the cases we have studied closely (Bryson and Crosby, 1992; Crosby and Bryson, 2005), leaders make headway in remedying public problems when they practice well the leadership capabilities highlighted in the framework, and they are unlikely to make progress when they do not. We have also found that these capabilities are not exercised by one or only a few individuals but rather by many people and even by groups and organizations over the long course of a policy change effort. Individual leaders are likely to be skilled in some capabilities and not others; indeed, an important metaskill for a leader seems to be knowing when he or she is best suited to provide a type of leadership and when to turn that work over to someone else.

Let's now examine how leaders in the case of the African American Men Project have enacted elements of the Leadership for the Common Good

Framework; that is, how they have been acting in accordance with the dynamics of a shared-power world; wisely designing and using forums, arenas, and courts; effectively navigating the policy change cycle; and exercising leadership capabilities.

Acting in Accordance with the Dynamics of a Shared-Power World

Many authors, including Harlan Cleveland (2002), Jean Lipman-Blumen (1996), and Charles Handy (1996), have noted the increasing interdependence of people and organizations throughout the world. To govern organizations and societies and to respond effectively to any major social need, leaders will have to operate in accordance with this increased interdependence. Whether they are working in the government, business, or nonprofit sector, they need to recognize that the power to meet social needs such as employment, housing, and education is widely shared within and across sectors. No single individual, group, or organization can make significant headway in fulfilling these needs without cooperating with other individuals, groups, or organizations that have a stake in producing better outcomes. Moreover, leadership will need to be dispersed across a variety of groups and organizations.

A central challenge for leaders is to bring diverse stakeholders together in power-sharing arrangements in which they can pool information, other resources, and activities around a common purpose. The focus should be on key stakeholders, the parties most affected by a social need or public problem or who have important resources for meeting the need or solving the problem. At the outset of the Hennepin County case, African American men and their families were obviously key stakeholders. Leaders of African American organizations, such as churches and parents groups, were very important. Other key African American stakeholders were business executives, public managers, educators, a foundation director, the local school superintendent, and the mayor of Minneapolis. Many of the key stakeholders were not African American—for example, the Hennepin County commissioners and many public managers, foundation directors, educators, and business executives who had considerable existing or potential ability to affect outcomes for African American men. (For more information on stakeholder analysis, see Chapter Twenty-One "Involving Multiple Stakeholders in Large-Scale Collaborative Projects.")

To make significant headway in achieving better outcomes for young African American men in Hennepin County, enough of these key stakeholders would be needed to join an advocacy coalition that could convince policymakers to adopt and fund new policies, programs, and rules. Building and sustaining successful advocacy coalitions requires wise design and use of forums, arenas, and courts over the course of a policy change cycle.

Wisely Designing and Using Forums, Arenas, and Courts

Forums, arenas, and courts are the shared-power settings in which human beings develop shared understandings of public issues, decide what to do about them, and manage conflict and adjudicate disputes over policy implementation. These settings are connected to what we see as the three main social practices that constitute power: the creation and communication of shared meaning; the making and implementation of executive, legislative, and administrative policy decisions; and the adjudication of disputes and sanctioning of conduct (Bryson and Crosby, 1992; Crosby and Bryson, 2005).

In *forums,* stakeholders consider differing interpretations, or framings, of public problems and evaluate potential solutions. These interpretations flow from the deep cultural bedrock containing assumptions about the meaning of life, community, and individual behavior. Examples of forums are conversations among neighbors and friends, task forces, discussion groups, brainstorming sessions, formal debates, public hearings, political rallies, conferences, newspaper columns, television and radio broadcasts, plays and other forms of dramatization, and popular and professional journals. The African American Men Project originated in an informal forum—the conversation between Gary Cunningham and Mark Stenglein in which the two men were probing the meaning of young men's seeming idleness. Later, meetings of the steering committee and associated work groups would be more formal forums for probing the causes of disproportionately poor outcomes for young African American men. These forums were a means of drawing on diverse perspectives about this undesirable situation and potential solutions. The operation of these forums—especially the use of stakeholder analysis techniques (described in Bryson, Cunningham, and Lokkesmoe, 2002)—resulted in a crucial framing shift that will be described further when we discuss visionary leadership. Forum participants identified key stakeholders—the important individuals, groups, and organizations that were affected by poor outcomes for African American men or that controlled key resources for improving those outcomes. They then analyzed the expectations, power, and interests of each in order to develop a common problem frame and vision that could appeal to as many of these stakeholders as possible. Many of the forums sponsored by the steering committee and its successor, the African American Men Commission, also have helped break down the isolation of young African American men from their community. In many of the gatherings, older men, often clergy, served as mentors to the young men; men wanting to turn their lives around connected with other men like themselves. AAMP conferences highlighted African cultural symbols.

Many of the forums gave access and visibility to young African American men as collaborators in improving conditions for themselves and their fellow citizens. For example, their voices ring out from the 2002 *Crossroads* report.

In *arenas,* executive, legislative, and administrative decision makers consider whether and how to adopt and implement proposed policy changes. Examples of arenas are boards of directors, city councils, cartels, markets, legislatures, cabinets, and faculty senates. In Hennepin County, Gary Cunningham used his authority as an administrative decision maker to do the initial study of the status of young African American men. The Hennepin County board approved funding for a full-fledged study to be directed by the steering committee and staffed by Cunningham's office. The board also unanimously approved the *Crossroads* report and provided funding for implementation. County administrator Sandra Vargas used her administrative authority to protect the project during implementation. Many of the implementation activities require supportive policy decisions from other arenas, such as foundation grantmaking bodies, the state legislature, and business boards of directors. Leaders in this case have built coalitions that have helped executive, legislative, and administrative decision makers recognize African American men as a constituency with clout.

Courts are the settings in which official and unofficial judges settle disputes about policy implementation and sanction conduct in accordance with laws, rules, and norms. Examples of courts are the "court of public opinion" (perhaps the most powerful), professional licensing bodies, municipal courts, the U.S. Supreme Court, military tribunals, and ecclesiastical courts. Because young African American men have disproportionately high rates of arrest and incarceration, they face barriers to employment and citizenship. The court system must be involved in efforts to divert these men from the criminal justice system and restore their rights once they have completed jail sentences.

Effectively Navigating the Policy Change Cycle

The cycle of policy change can be described as the interaction of seven phases (see Figure 18.2). Attention to the design and use of forums is especially important in the first three phases—Reach Initial Agreement; Formulate Problem, and Search for Solutions—which interact to create an issue. Attention to arenas is vital in the middle phases—Formulate Plan, Policy, or Proposal; Review and Adopt; and Implement and Evaluate. Also, courts are often crucial

FIGURE 18.2 THE POLICY CHANGE CYCLE.

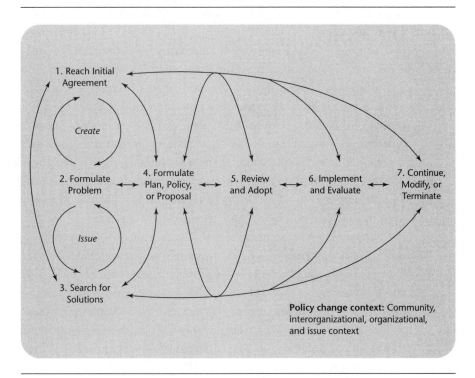

settings in the Implement and Evaluate phase. Forums are again important in the final phase—Continue, Modify, or Terminate—when change advocates must decide whether the original vision that prompted the change effort is being achieved or whether new understandings of the public problem and a new policy change effort will be needed. (The policy change cycle is explained more fully in Crosby and Bryson, 2005.)

Change advocates probably achieve the biggest payoffs from investment in the first three phases, which together result in issue creation—that is, public awareness of an important public need linked to one or more promising solutions that have pros and cons from the viewpoint of various stakeholders. The participants in the first stage of the African American Men Project (the stage culminating in the publication of the *Crossroads* report) worked long and carefully to describe the lives of young African American men and the barriers that were preventing them from achieving satisfying lives. Because of their considerable investment in stakeholder analysis and involvement of diverse stakeholders, they were able to move beyond old problem formulations and develop solutions that could be supported by policymakers across the political spectrum.

Although we have described the change cycle in terms of early, middle, and late phases, we are not arguing that policy change proceeds in an orderly, linear fashion. For example, change advocates may become involved at any point in the cycle. Also, expanded initial agreements may need to be forged well after the change groups have been working for a while on problem formulation as they seek to involve new stakeholders and expand the coalition for change. Moreover, change advocates may find themselves at an impasse, unable to move to the next phase, without cycling back through earlier phases and finding, for example, problem definitions and solutions that will bring more stakeholders on board and appeal to policymakers.

Such an impasse occurred early in the African American Men Project. Initially, participants framed the challenges affecting young African American men in terms that highlighted racism and social justice concerns. Their realization that this framing was unlikely to win adequate support from policymakers and the broader community prompted a period of near-despair among participants about whether change was really possible. Eventually, the group reframed these challenges (as described in the section on visionary leadership) in a way that enabled them to win broad support.

Exercising Leadership Capabilities

Leadership for the common good requires the exercise of eight main leadership capabilities. Clearly, no single person can be expected to exercise them all; many people will need to develop and exercise these capabilities in the course of building cross-sector collaborations to tackle public problems.

Leadership in Context

To respond effectively to social needs, leaders must understand the context in which the needs have developed and use that understanding to assess whether and how a change effort can get under way. Specifically, they should clarify how existing social, political, economic, and technological systems—the givens— have contributed to the needs and how trends or shifts in those systems are opening up new opportunities for leadership in the area of concern (Cleveland, 2002; Quinn 2000; Crosby, 1999). For example, the steering committee for the AAMP compiled and studied information about health, family structure, employment, housing, and criminal justice in relation to young black men.

Although the studies highlighted poor outcomes for many young African American men, they also revealed that many black men were doing very well. The *Crossroads* report noted, for example, that the percentage of African American men who were white-collar professionals working in the county's business sector significantly increased during the 1990s, from 33 to 39 percent. Another hopeful trend was the relatively recent advances made by African Americans in achieving elected and appointed public office. For example, at the project's inception, the mayor of Minneapolis and the Minneapolis school superintendent were African American.

Leaders need to understand how cultural assumptions and traditions contribute to the problem on which they are working and to the prospects for tackling the problem effectively. The shapers of the African American Men Project needed to recognize the multisector cultural forces noted earlier in this chapter. The *Crossroads* report highlighted what might be called a culture of social service fragmentation in Hennepin County. The report noted that most of the social service programs operated by government and nonprofit agencies served women and children rather than men and tended to operate independently. Further, the report found that the Minneapolis metropolitan area was one of the most racially segregated in the nation and that disparities (in areas such as education and employment) between white and black populations were high compared to similar regions. In the report, young African American men who aspired to better lives talked of feeling isolated from the larger community and from other men like themselves. The report summed up their feelings: "Sometimes you feel as if you're stuck in a no-man's land, accepted neither by the mainstream culture nor the people who feel they have no place in it" (Hennepin County, 2002, p. 35).

Leaders need to understand different cultural assumptions about leadership. Who are the formal and informal leaders in various communities? What leadership styles are valued? For example, supporters of the African American Men Project must cope with tensions between older and younger generations of leaders in the African American community. Gary Cunningham has emphasized that both groups need to be "at the table."

Leadership in context is about understanding when a situation is ripe for successful change—that is, when enough favorable conditions are in place that a trigger, even something as small as Mark Stenglein's query to Gary Cunningham, can be used to take advantage of those conditions. In this case, favorable aspects of the context included the growing visibility and clout of African American leaders in government, business, higher education, and nonprofit organizations; a strong network of African American grassroots organizations; a relatively healthy economy; and the obvious failure of many existing public policies and programs to significantly improve outcomes for young African American men. Gary Cunningham and other AAMP leaders were effective in promoting cross-sector collaboration because they had strong personal connections with people in the various sectors. Cunningham had worked for the University of Minnesota, nonprofit organizations, and the Minneapolis School Board, as well as the county government. He had chaired the Citizens League, a good-government group that involved citizen leaders from all sectors in working on public issues affecting the Twin Cities. These cross-sector connections helped make the context favorable for changing the status quo.

Personal Leadership

Attention to context is one starting place for leadership for the common good. The other is personal leadership—the work of understanding and deploying personal assets on behalf of beneficial change (for example, see Lipman-Blumen,

1996). Among the most important leadership assets is a sense of one's leadership "calling." The call to leadership stems from what an individual really cares about—in other words, what is important enough to invest one's time and energy in, to risk unpopularity and failure in service of a worthy goal (Quinn, 2000; Palmer, 2000; Bolman and Deal, 2001). Gary Cunningham, for example, finds his call to leadership in his personal mission: "To use whatever power, privilege, and skills I have to help people less fortunate than I am. I consider this the rent I pay" (Cunningham, 2003). An especially valuable personal asset for those seeking to build cultures of collaboration is talent and experience in working with diverse stakeholders—an asset evident among many members of the AAMP commission and staff.

Team Leadership

Leaders rely on productive work groups within and across organizations in order to achieve outcomes that could not be achieved by individuals working alone (see Wheelan, 1999). Important elements of team leadership are recruitment, communication, empowerment, and leadership development of team members.

Astute recruitment of team members is vital. For example, as Gary Cunningham put together his recommendations for members of the citizen group that would oversee the African American Men Project, he knew he needed African American people who had rich connections and credibility in their own ethnic community, businesspeople interested in a diverse workforce, representatives of various government agencies, executives of nonprofit organizations that worked with African American families, respected academics, and people with political clout. He obtained commitments from accomplished individuals in all these categories. The result was a steering committee, mainly African American, that had legitimacy and prestige in the eyes of many stakeholders and had access to important networks for implementing project recommendations. As he assembled teams to work on research reports, he sought out academic partners who had reputations for sound research and a commitment to achieving better outcomes for African American men. Members of these teams could be expected to produce research seen as legitimate by many stakeholders.

Team leaders should foster communication that aligns and coordinates members' actions, builds mutual understanding and trust, and fosters creative problem solving and commitment. Such communication requires an atmosphere of openness, information sharing, and respect (see Kouzes and Posner, 2002).

Team leaders also help each group member claim and develop his or her own power in service of the group's mission (Raelin, 2003). To do so, team members need a shared understanding of the team's mission, goals, decision-making procedures, rules, norms, work plan, and evaluation methods. They also need to know which roles and responsibilities they are expected to carry out. They need to see leaders and followers as mutually empowering. To maximize the contributions of team members, team leaders should seek to develop leadership capacity in everyone so that leadership tasks like recruiting new team members, modeling active listening, and reinforcing norms of openness and self-transcendence can be taken on by many if not all group members.

Organizational Leadership

Advocates of major policy change must ensure that effective and humane organizations are created, maintained, or restructured as needed (Bolman and Deal, 2003). Leaders of the African American Men Project so far have focused not so much on creating new organizations as on beginning new projects and programs within existing organizations and restructuring old ones. They are building interorganizational networks that can help organizations working with African American men coordinate their efforts. The commission has decided to incorporate AAMP as a nonprofit organization in order to make it more sustainable and independent from county government.

Whether leaders are launching new organizations or reshaping existing ones, they must perform three crucial overall leadership tasks: paying attention to organizational purpose and design, becoming adept in dealing with internal and external change, and building a sense of community inside and outside the organizations.

Visionary Leadership

Visionary leaders create and communicate meaning about historical events, current reality, group mission, and prospects for the future. They work with constituents in formal and informal forums to frame and reframe the problems or needs that concern them and develop a shared vision that can guide collective action in pursuit of the common good (Schön and Rein, 1994; Luke, 1998; Chaskin, Brown, Venkatesh, and Vidal, 2001; Chrislip and Larson, 1994).

The way a need is *framed*—how it is named, explained, and interpreted— has a tremendous impact on who will be concerned about it, what kinds of remedies will be considered, and the membership of a coalition that might be formed to advocate adoption of the remedies. Visionary leaders may evoke frames that are familiar to their constituents, make new linkages among frames, or invent new ones.

A variety of stakeholder analysis methods may be used to ascertain which problem frames are likely to attract the support of key stakeholders (see Bryson, Cunningham, and Lokkesmoe, 2002; Bryson, 2004; Bryson, Ackermann, Eden, and Finn, 2004). The African American Men Project steering committee developed stakeholder "maps" that showed the main goals or interests of each key stakeholder. It then produced a combined map that showed all of the key stakeholders and their interests. This map allowed the committee to identify clusters of interests that could be grouped together as "superinterests" that garnered support from many stakeholders. The "superinterest" map served as a guide for finding the common good and the structure of an argument that would tap into the interests of enough stakeholders to create a winning coalition. In other words, the committee was able to frame needed improvements in the lives of African American men in terms of the superinterests rather than in terms of less widely shared goals. The mapping exercise revealed that a "healthy community" or "shared fate" frame was much more likely to garner widespread stakeholder support than a frame like "social justice" that has a smaller, less powerful constituency.

This "shared fate" frame became a theme for the *compelling vision* presented in the committee's final report and in forums that have been held to publicize the report and to celebrate and stimulate follow-up action. The report frames the problem at hand as a complex one caused by a multitude of social and economic forces and requiring "an aligned and coordinated response—one involving multiple stakeholders and multiple strategies" (Hennepin County, 2002, p. 3). Emphasizing the "shared-fate" frame, the report argues that if conditions affecting African American men are not improved, the whole community will suffer, and if they are improved, the whole community will benefit.

Compelling visions weave together a hopeful understanding of a public problem and the most promising solutions. Visionary leaders work with others to create such visions—essentially *communal stories* that help diverse stakeholder groups develop a sense of what they have in common with each other and what they might do to tackle common problems and create a better future (Shamir and House, 1994; Stone, 2001; Kouzes and Posner, 2002). These stories are told from a "we" perspective to emphasize that the story isn't just about the values and needs of a single leader or small group but rather about everyone in the community. The executive summary of the *Crossroads* report opens with "We are at a crossroads," goes on to describe challenges confronting *all* the citizens of Hennepin County, and relates the circumstances of young African American men to these challenges (Hennepin County, 2002, p. 9). The report concludes with a strong vision of cross-sector collaboration and prophesies that by the end of the following year, every major stakeholder from all sectors would back a long-term plan for improving conditions for African American men and for the communities in which they live.

At the same time that visionary leaders emphasize the community as a whole, they *personalize* the story by giving illustrative examples from their own and others' lives. The *Crossroads* report presents survey results and direct quotations from interviews to reflect African American men to themselves and reveal their complexity and humanity to others.

In communicating a communal story, visionary leaders choose their *language* carefully (Shamir and House, 1994; Kouzes and Posner, 2002). They use metaphors that relate to and make sense of people's experience and impel people toward common ground (see Chapter Nine, "Metaphors at Work"). They use vivid, energetic, and optimistic language and an expressive style. For example, the *Crossroads* report presents statistical portraits of the county's young African American men under the title "How Are Our Neighbors Faring?" The report depicts these men as neighbors, family members, and workers (or potential workers).

Communal stories attend to *past, present, and future*. Fundamental *values and cultural tradition* are honored, and previous *mistakes and failings* are acknowledged. The stories evoke a *generative problem frame* (Schön and Rein, 1994), emphasize the disastrous (or at least harmful) *consequences of continuing on the current path*, and show how values can be realized in the future through specific behaviors; in other words, the stories help people develop a collective identity (Gardner, 1995) and grasp desirable and potentially *real futures* (Boal and Bryson, 1987; Van der Heijden and others, 2002).

The *Crossroads* report gives some attention to the past but focuses mainly on present conditions. It emphasizes that while most Hennepin County residents and many young African Americans are doing reasonably well, a large percentage of young African American men, especially those in poor neighborhoods, "are in trouble—with money, with employment, with their families, with their health, with their safety and/or with the criminal justice system" (Hennepin County, 2002, p. 19). The report evokes fundamental cultural values of community and mutual responsibility and presents specific recommendations for actions various stakeholders can take to improve conditions for young African American men.

In the stories they tell, visionary leaders describe a future that is full of immediacy and promise. The *Crossroads* report summons the image of all types of citizens stepping forward and working together to build a better community. The report concludes with a detailed scenario of "what might actually happen when new and seasoned leaders seize the day, and county government provides the right kind of support" (Hennepin County, 2002, p. 55).

The report signaled a significant reframing of the challenges facing African American men. The shift in focus away from black men as the problem to what they and the community can do to alleviate everyone's problems was extremely significant in that it converted what many in the greater community thought was the problem—the African American men themselves—into an asset, redefined the problem as everyone's problem, and helped show how everyone could contribute to better outcomes for everyone in the county. A large winning coalition organized around a shared purpose—creating better outcomes for African American men and everyone else—became possible. As John Kingdon (1995) notes, "Getting people to see new problems, or to see old problems in one way rather than another, is a major conceptual and political accomplishment" (p. 115).

Political Leadership

Leaders need visionary skills to develop shared understandings of public problems, build support for beneficial solutions, and develop commitment to collective action. They need political skills to turn the proposed solutions into specific policies, programs, and projects that are adopted and implemented by decision makers in executive, legislative, and administrative arenas. Crucial political leadership skills are mediating and shaping conflict within and among constituencies; building winning, sustainable coalitions; and overcoming bureaucratic resistance.

Mediating and Shaping Conflict Within and Between Constituencies. *Conflict* is necessary and must be used carefully in policymaking arenas if policymakers are to consider multiple options for satisfying diverse constituencies (Burns, 1978, 2003; Nutt, 2002; Bryant, 2003), and political leaders must possess transactional skills for dealing with individuals and groups with conflicting agendas. Political leaders must bargain and negotiate, trading the things of value that they control for others' support and developing advantageous positions. These leaders, notes James MacGregor Burns, "use conflict deliberately to protect decision-making options and power, and even more, . . . use conflict to structure the political environment so as to maximize 'constructive' dissonance, thus allowing for more informed decision making" (1978, p. 410). An effective advocacy coalition will have multiple channels of access that allow members' conflicts, tensions, and dilemmas to be aired and addressed on the way to full mobilization in support of policy decisions.

The trick is not to be immobilized by conflicting agendas and to maintain the integrity of the vision that is inspiring the proposed policy changes. Burns emphasizes that effective political leaders play a "marginal" role, avoiding complete assimilation by any one group in order to be able to deal with conflicts outside as well as inside their constituencies. "Their marginality supplies them with a double leverage, since in their status as leaders they are expected by their followers and other leaders to deviate, to innovate, and to mediate between the claims of their group and those of others" (1978, p. 39).

Thus a public official like Mark Stenglein or a public manager like Gary Cunningham needs to encourage different constituencies to supply him with their views of what's important, what their needs are, whom they can and cannot work with, and what they can contribute to change efforts. In working together to improve outcomes for young African American men, Stenglein and Cunningham can trade access to Hennepin County's policymaking process for resources (information, expertise, votes, connections to other groups, endorsements) that other individuals and groups control. Also, as a member of the county board, Stenglein has a vote on all matters before the board, and he can use his vote as leverage to obtain concessions or support from other board members. As the head of a county department, Cunningham can direct staff to organize meetings or studies that community groups request. County administrator Sandra Vargas has the power to ensure that internal resisters do not stymie the project.

Bargaining and negotiating have two main desirable outcomes: *compromise* and *copromotion.* In compromise, each participant gives up some of his or her desires in exchange for achieving the remainder; everyone, in a sense, loses something but also gains something. In copromotion, or what Leigh Thompson (2001) calls "integrative negotiation," the participants find ways to help each other achieve all or most of each other's aims, and possibly go beyond the parties' initial aims. Copromotion has obvious advantages, but compromise is usually needed too. In the *Crossroads* report, the AAMP steering committee emphasized copromotion as the way forward, rather than setting up win-lose struggles between ethnic groups. Some compromises have been made as project events and publications were put together, but the overarching approach has been copromotion.

Building Winning, Sustainable Coalitions. A starting place for putting together a winning coalition is analysis of the power and interest of key stakeholders. The power-versus-interest grid (see Bryson, Cunningham, and Lokkesmoe, 2002) is a tool that helped organizers of the African American Men Project identify stakeholders who shared an interest in good outcomes for young African American men, as well as stakeholders who had the power to affect policies affecting those outcomes. This analysis prompted the organizers to develop strategies for helping some powerful stakeholders see how their interests could be served by improving conditions for young African American men. The analysis also revealed how ostensibly less powerful stakeholders could increase their power to achieve better outcomes for themselves.

Political scientists emphasize the importance of creating a *minimum winning coalition*, the smallest coalition necessary to adopt proposed policy changes (Riker, 1962). Students of collaboration emphasize the importance of gaining agreement from all or most of the stakeholders involved or affected (Margerum, 2002). What seems to account for the difference between the advice of political scientists and that of collaboration scholars is that in collaborative, shared-power settings, implementers have more discretion about whether or not they wish to implement policy changes. Involving potential implementers early on in the design of the changes is often crucial to gaining their support when it is time to adopt and implement the changes (Huxham, 2003). Because Gary Cunningham knew that he would need to depend on many implementers over whom he and the county commissioners either had no direct control (those outside of county government) or else had perhaps tenuous control (those inside county government), he and Mark Stenglein sought *unanimous* county board adoption of the final project report. That way, the board would be making the strongest possible statement. The county board adopted the final report unanimously in January 2002 and directed the county administrator to implement all recommendations for which the county was responsible.

Advocacy coalitions may be formal networks (with official names and membership lists) or informal arrangements (Sabatier and Jenkins-Smith, 1993). In the case of the African American Men Project, a steering committee of community leaders along with Hennepin County commissioners and staff, academic researchers, and community organizations acted as an informal coalition that developed the recommendation for the ongoing African American Men Commission, consisting of "African American men and community, business, religious, academic, nonprofit, and government leaders." The commission was to "provide leadership and advice to policy makers, foundations, nonprofit, organizations, and the overall community on issues, programs, and policies that impact the lives of young African American men" (Hennepin County, 2002, p. 75). It could be expected to attract individuals, groups, and organizations that would support its initiatives.

One challenge for coalition leaders is keeping the coalition intact or growing once the initial burst of enthusiasm for a campaign or project wears off. The AAMP steering committee basically ensured continuation and expansion of the project coalition by successfully recommending to the Hennepin County board that a successor group, the African American Men Commission, be set up and that seed money be provided for the next phase of the project.

Overcoming Bureaucratic Resistance. Political leaders must continually find ways to enlist bureaucrats in their cause—for example, by appealing to a shared vision or goals (Behn, 1999). Institutional rules, procedures, and personnel may need to be changed or new parallel or auxiliary organizations created as part of the implementation process. When necessary, political leaders find ways to appeal over the bureaucrats' heads to the broader public or other powerful stakeholders who support the change.

Ethical Leadership

Once policymakers have enacted new policies, passed new laws and regulations, set up new programs and projects, or refused to do so, the policymakers' decisions are likely to be debated in formal and informal courts. In these courts, ethical leaders help constituents apply general rules to specific cases; resolve conflicts among competing ethical principles, laws, rules, and norms; and reward and punish the conduct of individuals and groups. Of course, there are ethical aspects of all types of leadership, but we define ethical leadership as adjudication and sanctioning of conduct in formal and informal courts because in this process, the fundamental concern is with what is ethical and legitimate.

A prime task of ethical leaders is educating others about ethics, laws, and norms that legitimize their policies, evoke broad support among stakeholders, and promote societal well-being (see Luke, 1998). In appealing to the court of public opinion in Hennepin County, leaders of the African American Men Project are emphasizing the norms of inclusion, personal responsibility and security, and equal treatment. By helping young African American men accept or renegotiate the sanctions applied by the courts, AAMP leaders are helping these men bolster their legitimacy and regain their rights as citizens, which will in turn give them greater access to key forums and arenas.

Policy Entrepreneurship

Policy entrepreneurs are able to take the long view and understand that complex policy change proceeds in cyclical fashion and is likely to extend over many years (Roberts and King, 1996). Different people may move into leadership roles in the course of the policy change cycle.

As noted earlier, in the first three phases of the cycle, visionary leaders help constituents design and use forums to gather information about a public problem, to foster a sense of urgency, to promote problem frames that can appeal to numerous stakeholders, to set directions, to create compelling visions of a better future, and to craft policy proposals that have good prospects for approval by policymakers in various arenas. Political leadership is most important in the middle phases, when policy proposals are being reviewed, voted on, implemented, and evaluated. Ethical leadership is also very important during implementation and evaluation; the need for visionary leadership may reemerge very strongly in the Continue, Modify, or Terminate phase. The personal leadership of champions and sponsors is vital throughout but is especially important in the early phases when the involvement of these people signals that a change effort may actually be sustained and successful. Policy change efforts are unlikely to get off the ground, much less succeed, without the endorsement of powerful sponsors, such as Mark Stenglein and Herman Milligan; nor are they likely to gather much steam without the ongoing hard work and determination of champions like Gary Cunningham. (For additional perspectives on champions and sponsors, see Chapters Seven, "Make-or-Break

Roles in Collaboration Leadership," and Twenty, "Avoiding Ghettos of Like-Minded People.")

Conclusion

Often public policymakers adopt policies, projects, or programs and then require stakeholders to collaborate in implementing them. In the case of the African American Men Project, public officials and managers took a collaborative approach at the outset of the policy change cycle. They involved diverse stakeholders in the work of exploring the causes of a complex public challenge, analyzing solutions, and crafting a proposal that would succeed in a legislative arena, the Hennepin County board of commissioners. The project is now in a lengthy implementation phase in which participants are building additional working partnerships, sponsoring a variety of forums, putting together proposals for several arenas, and working with formal and informal courts to accomplish the project's goals.

The African American Men Project offers several lessons for public officials and managers trying to foster collaboration to resolve complex public problems:

• The Leadership for the Common Good Framework can provide useful guidance for leaders seeking to meet complex social needs in an era of cutbacks in public social service budgets and of skepticism about government's problem-solving capacity. The African American Men Project illuminates how the framework can be used to analyze and improve efforts to involve diverse stakeholders in defining social needs and developing promising, cross-sector responses.

• Turning over much of the leadership work to nongovernmental stakeholders can create buy-in and release resources to supplement what government can provide (Chrislip and Larson, 1994; Luke, 1998). At the same time, public officials and managers are likely to face resistance in public agencies and other organizations to turning over more public problem solving to citizen groups (Osborne and Plastrik, 1997, 2000).

Furthermore, bringing together an array of citizens, service providers, advocates, and policymakers to define problems and craft solutions can allow public officials and managers to draw on expert and practical knowledge embedded in an array of organizations, grassroots groups, and professional communities (Scott, 1998; Forester, 1999). The various stakeholders can develop initiatives that help them coordinate their efforts rather than working at cross-purposes (Weisbord and Janoff, 1995; Holman and Devane, 1999). However, attempts to involve a representative group of stakeholders in a change effort also may bring out preexisting differences within and among various groups (Bryson, 2004). Thus leaders should be prepared to acknowledge and bridge differences where possible and sometimes be willing to proceed without the participation of every stakeholder.

Collaborative projects like the African American Men Project may not require big boosts in government spending, but they will need seed money and people like Mark Stenglein, Gary Cunningham, and Herman Milligan to act as powerful sponsors and champions (Roberts and King, 1996).

Stakeholder analysis methods can help policy change advocates frame public problems in ways that will attract the support of key stakeholders and foster development of a strong advocacy coalition (Bryson, Cunningham, and Lokkesmoe, 2002; Bryson, 2004).

Clearly, more research is needed on how best to pursue leadership in shared-power, cross-sector settings. Considerable practitioner experience is developing on how to produce good outcomes in collaborative settings, but research specifically on the leadership aspects of doing so is relatively sparse (Huxham and Vangen, 2000). We think that the Leadership for the Common Good Framework provides a useful place to start in researching what works best, under what circumstances, and why in collaborative settings. We hope to prompt other researchers to do additional rich, longitudinal qualitative and quantitative case studies to further test the framework's usefulness, applicability, and limitations.

References

Baumgartner, F. R., and Jones, B. D. *Agendas and Instability in American Politics.* Chicago: University of Chicago Press, 1993.

Behn, R. D. "The New Public-Management Paradigm and the Search for Democratic Accountability." *International Public Management Journal,* 1999, *1,* 131–165.

Boal, K. B., and Bryson, J. M. "Charismatic Leadership: A Phenomenological and Structural Approach." In J. G. Hunt, B. R. Balinga, H. P. Dachler, and C. A. Schriescheim (eds.), *Emerging Leadership Vistas.* New York: Pergamon Press, 1987.

Bolman, L. G., and Deal, T. E. *Leading with Soul: An Uncommon Journey of Spirit.* (rev. ed.) San Francisco: Jossey-Bass, 2001.

Bryant, J. *The Six Dilemmas of Collaboration: Inter-Organisational Relationships as Drama.* Chichester, England: Wiley, 2003.

Bryson, J. M. "What to Do When Stakeholders Matter: Stakeholder Identification and Analysis Techniques." *Public Management Review,* 2004, *6,* 21–53.

Bryson, J. M., Ackermann, F., Eden, C., and Finn, C. *Causal Mapping for Individuals and Groups: What to Do When Thinking Matters.* Chichester, England: John Wiley, 2004.

Bryson, J. M., and Crosby, B. C. *Leadership for the Common Good: Tackling Public Problems in a Shared-Power World.* San Francisco: Jossey-Bass, 1992.

Bryson, J. M., Cunningham, G. L., and Lokkesmoe, K. J. "What to Do When Stakeholders Matter: The Case of Problem Formulation for the African American Men Project of Hennepin County, Minnesota." *Public Administration Review,* 2002, *62,* 568–584.

Burns, J. M. *Leadership.* New York: HarperCollins, 1978.

Burns, J. M. *Transforming Leadership.* New York: Atlantic Monthly Press, 2003.

Chaskin, R. J., Brown, P., Venkatesh, S., and Vidal, A. *Building Community Capacity.* Hawthorne, N.Y.: Aldine de Gruyter, 2001.

Chrislip, D. D., and Larson, C. E. *Collaborative Leadership: How Citizens and Civic Leadership Can Make a Difference.* San Francisco: Jossey-Bass, 1994.

Cleveland, H. *Nobody in Charge: Essays on the Future of Leadership.* Hoboken, N.J.: Wiley, 2002.

Crosby, B. C. *Leadership for Global Citizenship: Building Transnational Community.* Thousand Oaks, Calif.: Sage, 1999.

Crosby, B. C., and Bryson, J. M. *Leadership for the Common Good.* (2nd ed.) San Francisco: Jossey-Bass, 2005.

Cunningham, G. Lecture delivered at the Humphrey Institute of Public Affairs, Minneapolis, Nov. 19, 2003.

Forester, J. *The Deliberative Practitioner.* Cambridge, Mass.: MIT Press, 1999.

Gardner, H. *Leading Minds.* New York: Basic Books, 1995.

Goldsmith, S., and Eggers W. D. *Governing by Network: The New Shape of the Public Sector.* Washington, D.C.: Brookings Institution, 2004.

Hall, E. *Beyond Culture.* New York: Doubleday, 1981.

Handy, C. *Age of Uncertainty: The Changing Worlds of Organizations.* Boston: Harvard Business School Press, 1996.

Hennepin County. *Crossroads: Choosing a New Direction.* Minneapolis, Minn.: Hennepin County Office of Planning and Development, 2002.

Holman, P., and Devane, T. (eds.). *The Change Handbook: Group Methods for Shaping the Future.* San Francisco: Berrett-Koehler, 1999.

Huxham, C. "Theorizing Collaboration Practice." *Public Management Review,* 2003, *5,* 401–423.

Huxham, C., and Beech, N. "Exploring the Power Infrastructure of Interorganizational Collaborations." Working paper, University of Strathclyde Graduate School of Business, Glasgow, Scotland, 2003.

Huxham, C., and Vangen, S. "Leadership in the Shaping and Implementation of Collaboration Agendas: How Things Happen in a (Not Quite) Joined-Up World." *Academy of Management Journal*, 2000, *43*, 1159–1175.

Huxham, C., and Vangen, S. *Doing Things Collaboratively.* London: Routledge, 2005.

Kingdon, J. W. *Agendas, Alternatives, and Public Policies.* (rev. ed.) New York: Little, Brown, 1995.

Kouzes, J. M., and Posner, B. Z. *The Leadership Challenge: How to Get Extraordinary Things Done in Organizations.* (3rd ed.) San Francisco: Jossey-Bass, 2002.

Lipman-Blumen, J. *Connective Leadership: Managing in a Changing World.* Oxford: Oxford University Press, 1996.

Luke, J. S. *Catalytic Leadership: Strategies for an Interconnected World.* San Francisco: Jossey-Bass, 1998.

Margerum, R. D. "Collaborative Planning: Building Consensus and Building a Distinct Model for Practice." *Journal of Planning Education and Research*, 2002, *21*, 237–253.

Nutt, P. C. *Why Decisions Fail: Avoiding the Blunders and Traps That Lead to Debacles.* San Francisco: Berrett-Koehler, 2002.

Osborne, D., and Plastrik, P. *Banishing Bureaucracy: The Five Strategies for Reinventing Government.* Boston: Addison-Wesley, 1997.

Osborne, D., and Plastrik, P. *The Reinventor's Fieldbook: Tools for Transforming Your Government.* San Francisco: Jossey-Bass, 2000.

Palmer, P. J. *Let Your Life Speak: Listening for the Voice of Vocation.* San Francisco: Jossey-Bass, 2000.

Quinn, R. E. *Change the World: How Ordinary People Can Accomplish Extraordinary Results.* San Francisco: Jossey-Bass, 2000.

Raelin, J. *Creating Leaderful Organizations: How to Bring Out the Leadership in Everyone.* San Francisco: Berrett-Koehler, 2003.

Riker, W. H. *The Theory of Political Coalitions.* New Haven, Conn.: Yale University Press, 1962.

Roberts, N. C. "Wicked Problems and Networking Approaches to Resolution." *International Public Management Review.* 2000, *1*, 1–19.

Roberts, N. C., and King, P. J. *Transforming Public Policy: Dynamics of Policy Entrepreneurship and Innovation.* San Francisco: Jossey-Bass, 1996.

Sabatier, P. A., and Jenkins-Smith, H. C. *Policy Change and Learning: An Advocacy Coalition Approach.* Boulder, Colo.: Westview Press, 1993.

Schein, E. H. *Organizational Culture and Leadership.* (3rd ed.). San Francisco: Jossey-Bass, 2004.

Schön, D. A., and Rein, M. *Frame Reflection: Toward the Resolution of Intractable Policy Controversies.* New York: Basic Books, 1994.

Scott, J. C. *Seeing like a State: How Certain Schemes to Improve the Human Condition Have Failed.* New Haven, Conn.: Yale University Press, 1998.

Shamir, B.A.M., and House R. "The Rhetoric of Charismatic Leadership: A Theoretical Extension, a Case Study, and Implications for Research." *Leadership Quarterly*, 1994, *5*, 25–42.

Stone, D. A. *Policy Paradox and Political Reason.* New York: Norton, 2001.

Thompson, L. *The Mind and Heart of the Negotiator.* (2nd ed.). Upper Saddle River, N.J.: Prentice-Hall, 2001.

Van der Heijden, K., and others. *The Sixth Sense: Accelerating Organizational Learning with Scenarios.* Chichester, England: Wiley, 2002.

Weisbord, M., and Janoff, S. *Future Search.* San Francisco: Berrett-Koehler, 1995.

Wheelan, S. A. *Creating Effective Teams: A Guide for Members and Leaders.* Thousand Oaks, Calif.: Sage, 1999.

William J. Ball, Ph.D., is chair of the Political Science Department at the College of New Jersey, where he also directs the Leadership in Public Affairs (LPA) program. LPA hosts two or three large community-based deliberative forums each year, involving citizens, leaders, and media outlets from the region in the policy formulation process. Ball's scholarly work focuses on the theory and practice of deliberative democracy, civic education, and teaching and learning methods in political science. He earned his doctorate in political science at the University of Missouri–Columbia.

CHAPTER NINETEEN

USING DELIBERATIVE DEMOCRACY TO FACILITATE A LOCAL CULTURE OF COLLABORATION

The Penn's Landing Project

William J. Ball

While it is important to examine the creation of culture of collaboration at the interpersonal and small group level, it is also essential to tackle the topic from the large-scale, political perspective. Here I examine the Penn's Landing project as a case study of creating a collaborative culture in an urban planning setting.

Collaboration among expert stakeholders has a long history in public planning. However, the ideal model of collaborative culture in planning has taken on a unique flavor more recently with the infusion of elements of the broader deliberative democracy movement in political theory and practice (Forrester, 1999). Deliberative democracy is an effort to involve citizens in public policy agenda setting and decision making through peer discussions in small group settings. Critical norms of deliberation include equality of participation and respect for expert, decision maker, and citizen alike; political tolerance; a sense of increased political efficacy by citizen participants; and the recognition of common grounds for action even in the face of continuing disagreement.

The author acknowledges the help of College of New Jersey students Joshua Sprague and Rachel VanHorn in collecting the presurvey and postsurvey data at the first forum and Meredith D'Agnolo in conducting the interviews.

Deliberative democracy has many advocates among political theorists (Gutmann and Thompson, 1996; Mansbridge, 1980) and public scholars and civic educations (Yankelovich, 1999; Matthews, 1998). Advocates of deliberative democracy have developed an increasingly creative array of proposals for its institutionalization into the national political system (Ackerman and Fishkin, 2002; Gastil, 2000).

Yet implementations of deliberation have had very limited and mixed results in demonstrating the creation of collaborative cultures in planning and policy development. On the one hand, the paucity of results is to due the relatively few systematic empirical studies of the practice, which in turn is due to the scattered and idiosyncratic application of deliberative practice (Barabas, 2004, and Gastil and Dillard, 1999, are two of the few empirical studies). On the other hand, the relative lack of success in demonstrating outcomes is due to the vastly complex nature of public policymaking and the tenuous connections between considered public input and policy outcomes, even when a collaborative environment exists. The difficulty in showing an impact of deliberative process on policy outcomes is an excellent case of the slim chances of success in, to use Wildavsky's infamous phrase, "speaking truth to power" (1979).

The present case illustrates the opportunities and challenges of infusing a culture of collaboration into public planning by means of deliberative democracy. In its design and especially in its outcomes, the Penn's Landing project is even more idiosyncratic than most implementations of deliberation. The case tells a fascinating story, one from which it would be easy to draw a very pessimistic conclusion. Yet the application of a variety of evaluative techniques has also generated strong evidence of success in creating elements of collaborative culture.

Penn's Landing and the Penn's Landing Project

Penn's Landing consists of thirteen acres on the Delaware River waterfront in the heart of central Philadelphia. The location commemorates the arrival of Pennsylvania colony founder William Penn. The waterfront region surrounding the site has a long history of shipbuilding and port-related industry. Penn's Landing itself was reconstructed on a foundation of fill in the 1970s to host a

large public space (dominated by the Great Plaza) for the national bicenten-
nial festivities of 1976. Although largely cut off from the rest of the city by
Interstate 95, which runs parallel to the river, Penn's Landing is a short walk
from most of the historic sites of center city Philadelphia, including Independence Hall. Figure 19.1 provides a simple map of the area.

Since the 1970s, the waterfront region of Philadelphia has experienced a
decline (although not a disappearance) of industry and a growth of residential and recreation-based commercial activity. In the past fifteen years, several
landmark attractions have been built just across the river from Penn's Landing in Camden, New Jersey, thanks to hundreds of millions of dollars of investments by the state of New Jersey. Penn's Landing itself has experienced
growth of major attractions around its periphery, but the core site remains essentially as it was in the 1970s.

FIGURE 19.1. PENN'S LANDING AND VICINITY.

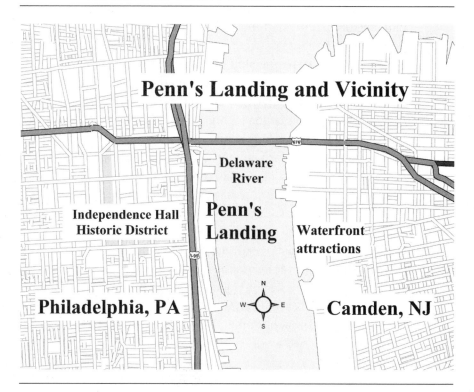

Despite the successful redevelopment of urban waterfronts around the country, a long series of initiatives by the city and developers over the decades have failed to produce any results at all at Penn's Landing, due to a combination of two primary factors: the perceived unprofitability of the site among developers as result of its isolation from the heart of the city and an unwillingness by the city to fund major components of the development costs (which would include massive infrastructure alterations to improve access to the site across I-95). Today, the Great Plaza of Penn's Landing hosts a diverse array of cultural festivals and artistic performances while the rest of the site provides a pedestrian thoroughfare to surrounding attractions and a place, as one citizen put it, "to just sit and look at Camden."

After yet another failed attempt to develop Penn's Landing, the office of Philadelphia mayor John Street announced in the fall of 2002 that it would take another tack. This led to a partnership with the city's leading newspaper, the *Philadelphia Inquirer,* and its most prestigious university, the University of Pennsylvania ("Penn" for short), to incorporate citizens into a deliberative planning process to chart the future of Penn's Landing (hereafter referred to as the Penn's Landing project).

The three-way partnership between the mayor, the *Inquirer,* and Penn augured well for success in establishing a culture of collaboration around planning for Penn's Landing. Knight-Ridder, the owner of the paper and financial sponsor of the Penn's Landing project, has a long history of leadership in public journalism, in which journalists collaborate with citizens to increase awareness of public issues (Sirianni and Friedland, 2001). Chris Satullo, the editor of the *Inquirer*'s editorial page and a key figure in the Penn's Landing project, has conducted hundreds of citizen deliberative forums over the years in the region. Penn likewise contributed impeccable expertise and experience to the leadership of the project. Harris Sokoloff of the university's Graduate School of Education has collaborated with Satullo in running deliberative forums and training workshops for forum moderators for many years and has also conducted forums on education policy around the state. Harris Steinberg, executive director of Penn Praxis, the clinical consulting arm of the School of Design at Penn, brought to the process architectural expertise as well as the participation of two world-renowned architects, Denise Scott Brown and Robert Venturi.

The team of Satullo, Steinberg, and Sokoloff developed and implemented an impressive array of integrated deliberative forums, media coverage, and design development and review in an attempt to generate a collaborative culture for determining the future of Penn's Landing. The primary effort began with a five-part background series in the *Inquirer*. This was incorporated into materials presented to citizens at the first event on January 29, 2003, held at Penn. A day of informational sessions was capped with an eveninglong deliberation designed to develop a citizen position on the key values, principles, and stakeholder perspectives that should be incorporated into future development plans. About 150 people participated in the deliberation in ten moderator-led groups, with each group producing a report.

The reports from the first citizen event were summarized in the form of seven principles intended to guide the remainder of the project. The team at Penn Praxis used these principles during an intense deliberative design session among architectural experts that produced three concept plans for developing the Penn's Landing site. The city also included the seven principles developed at the first citizen event in the initial materials it sent to potential private developers. Although the seven principles developed by participants in the first deliberative event included highly detailed recommendations, they were also presented in the following headline form, strongly revealing a citizen's point of view (Satullo, 2003):

1. Distinctively Philadelphia, with pride
2. It's the river, stupid
3. Get the connections right
4. Bolster destination Philadelphia
5. Make it affordable and sustainable
6. Keep it a public place
7. Use a public process

A second deliberative event was held on March 13, 2003, this time at the Independence Seaport Museum at Penn's Landing. It received extensive advance coverage in the *Inquirer* and was attended by about two hundred citizens, planners, city officials (several city council members and staff from the mayor's office), and potential developers. Again, citizens deliberated in small groups led by experienced moderators, this time focusing on the strengths and weakness of the three concept plans for the site developed by Penn Praxis. The evening culminated with votes on these visions of what Penn's Landing could be as well as short presentations from potential developers.

The request for proposals (RFP) issued by the city on April 23, 2003, highlighted the citizen recommendations from the first event but did not reference the outcome of the second public event. Nine potential developers had their qualifications approved, and four of them submitted proposals by September 2, 2003. The proposals reflected a vast range of expectations for spending on the site, with projects ranging from $250 million to $3 billion in total costs. By February 2004, the city had narrowed the selection to two developers.

The final form of public input to developing Penn's Landing was in the *Inquirer*'s online discussion forums and an online poll on the three concept plans developed by Penn Praxis (the developer proposals were not public at this point), which garnered more than five thousand votes. The paper would eventually publish a total forty-eight articles and editorial pieces on the process and outcomes, not counting online discussion forums.

After the completion of the *Inquirer*/Penn deliberative project of public input on developing Penn's Landing, events took an unexpected and decidedly uncollaborative turn. During early 2003, the city ran an entirely separate set of public forums, organized by Indira Scott, development manager of the Penn's Landing Corporation. These forums were integrated with the city's online publication of developer proposals and solicitation of feedback. However, the city-run forums were not coordinated with the Penn's Landing project developed and run by Satullo, Sokoloff, and Steinberg.

Then, during the successful fall 2003 reelection campaign of Mayor John Street, a series of bugging devices were discovered in his office. Eventually, these were traced to an FBI investigation of corruption. By March 2004, the local press started reporting that the developers who had been qualified for Penn's Landing proposals were being interviewed by the FBI. The FBI investigation of city hall quickly pushed the Penn's Landing project out of the public eye, especially since the Penn's Landing Corporation, the city's official agency responsible for choosing a plan, was an important element in the early phases of the investigation.

On October 14, 2004, Mayor Street announced that the city had rejected both of the final two developer-submitted proposals for Penn's Landing. Street cited finances as the reason, saying that up to $100 million in public investment "is too much, given our priorities" (Gelbart, 2004). By spring 2005, the FBI's prime target, Street fundraiser John White, had died of cancer, and a jury had convicted former Philadelphia treasurer Corey Kemp and four associates of corruption. The development of Penn's Landing ultimately did not figure prominently in the trial. Penn's Landing itself remained exactly as it was three years before (and as it had been for thirty years), a large public space with an active roster of community events, surrounded by tourist attractions and new businesses and homes.

Evaluating the Penn's Landing Project

Was this project successful in creating a culture of collaboration? On the face of it, the project would seem an utter failure. All of the effort put into involving the public had no apparent effect on the outcome. Even worse, the nobility of the idea of citizen participation in decision making was tarnished by the corruption investigation, and the resulting scandal pushed the deliberative project completely out of the public eye. Yet the story is not that simple.

While influencing policy outcomes is the most obvious goal in public deliberations, it is not the only one. In the present context of creating a *culture* of collaboration, it not necessarily the most important immediate goal. To get past the temptation to focus exclusively on policy outcomes, David Guston developed a framework for evaluating instances of policy analysis and applied it to a very similar form of deliberative democracy, that of the consensus conference. His framework serves well as a means of obtaining a larger picture of the effectiveness of the Penn's Landing project in having impacts in broader form. Guston's framework has four components (1999, p. 460):

1. *Actual impact on policy.* Has there been any change in relevant legislation, funding, regulations, or any other concrete consequence to any authoritative public decision?
2. *General thinking in the political system.* Has there been any change in relevant vocabularies, agendas, problem statements, or any other political aspect regarding the substance of the policy issue discussed or the deliberative process?
3. *Training of knowledgeable personnel.* Has there been learning by elite participants regarding the substance of the policy issue discussed, the deliberative process, or the participant's own role?
4. *Interaction with the public.* Has there been any learning by mass participants and nonparticipants regarding the substance of the policy issue discussed, the deliberative process, or the citizen's own role?

My student assistants and I collected data in four very different forms to apply Guston's framework to the Penn's Landing project. One major source of data was a collection of six interviews with elite participants in the project, conducted in the spring of 2004 (about a year after the project ended) in order to capture a long-term perspective on the impacts of the project. Satullo, Sokoloff, and Steinberg were interviewed as project organizers, as were three participating outsiders: Alan Greenberger, an architect and participant in the charette component of the project; Indira Scott, organizer of the city's forums and participant in the Penn's Landing project forums; and Steven McGovern, a Philadelphia-based expert on urban policy and development and an independent observer of the Penn's Landing project. Representatives of the mayor's office repeatedly turned down our requests to be interviewed—this period coincided with the height of press coverage of the FBI investigations. The interviews provided insight into all aspects of Guston's framework but most particularly on impacts on general thinking in the political system and the training of knowledgeable personnel.

A second major source of data was a pre- and postsurvey administered to participants at the first citizen forum. We were given access by the organizers to half of the randomly assigned discussion groups at the event, and sixty-two of the seventy-five participants in these groups completed both the pretest before the evening session and the posttest at the end of the session. The survey was primarily designed to assess the interaction with the public impact of the project on participants by measuring any short-term effects from participation. It also provided a gauge of how well the forum participants represented the population of Philadelphia.

These two major sources of data were supplemented with two others. The first was an informal content analysis of the ten group reports from the first citizen forum, the seventy-four feedback comments supplied by participants in response to an open-ended prompt at the second citizen's forum, and the coverage of the project in the *Inquirer*. The final source of data consisted of participant observations of the two citizen forums, where I acted as a small group moderator. The primarily goals of using the second set of sources was to broaden the scope of input, verify the impressions of the experts interviewed against public perceptions, and incorporate subjective but firsthand impressions of the forums. Following are the evaluation results, organized in Guston's framework.

1. Actual Impact on Policy

Given the nonresults of the latest round of efforts to develop Penn's Landing, it would be hard to make the case that the Penn's Landing project had an actual impact on policy in the sense of influencing outcomes. Although the most obvious question to ask, this is in many ways the least expected result of the process on the part of both organizers and participants. For example, participant comments at both forums expressed appreciation for inclusion in the process but skepticism that the result would change policy outcomes. None of the subjects interviewed in early 2004 expected there to be substantive policy outcomes that could be directly attributable to the project, nor did any of them claim that these outcomes had occurred. Unfortunately, the corruption investigation and cancellation of the development process negated the possibility that this case would be substantially informative on the issue of actual impact.

Yet even here there is more to the story. One of the more cynical but widely held perspectives on the willingness of the mayor's office to engage the public through the Penn's Landing project was that is was an attempt to quickly generate a new, publicly supported development project for the site in order to bolster the mayor's upcoming reelection bid (S. McGovern, interview, Mar. 23, 2004). However, deliberative processes by nature work slowly. The subjects interviewed universally observed that one outcome of the project was to slow the process of selecting a new development plan for the site. This delay in results coincided with the other events discussed previously that ultimately led to the cancellation of development altogether.

A careful examination of participant response indicates a strong desire not to commit too quickly to a single vision for the site. For example, at the second deliberative forum, when asked to choose among three distinctly different and competing visions for Penn's Landing, deliberators rated all three nearly the same. The online discussions and polling were somewhat more discriminating among the plans, but the key theme that emerged was the imperative of connecting the existing site to the rest of the city rather than major new development of the site itself (H. Steinberg, interview, Mar. 12, 2004). Anonymous feedback on the second forum, where the assigned task was to choose a concept plan, showed support and opposition to individual components of each plan. But significantly, 35 percent of the seventy-four comments rejected the idea of major changes to the site itself. As one participant put it,

"Absent a surprisingly persuasive development proposal, perhaps we should just let Penn's Landing be fallow for a while."

Although they were pushed from all sides to recommend major change for Penn's Landing, many of the participants at both forums were clearly resistant to that pressure, desiring that the site remain essentially as it was. The strong undercurrent of this resistance was evident in both of my group moderating experiences. A participant at the second forum wrote, "I am looking for the Great Plaza, only better. I think the planning of events at Penn's Landing is at least or more important than what is actually built there." It is ironic that no major change is exactly the de facto policy outcome that resulted from the deliberative process, even though it cannot be claimed that the Penn's Landing project produced the outcome.

2. General Thinking in the Political System

Impacts of the Penn's Landing project were directly evident in this area. In particular, the inclusion of the seven guiding principles developed in the first deliberative forum in the city's RFP had a clear impact on vocabularies used by developers to promote their plans. As Chris Satullo observed (interview, Mar. 10, 2004), the forums and their results where highly salient to potential developers as they looked to the forums for intelligence on what the city would value in proposals and what competing developers were thinking. The inclusion of the principles in the RFP put the burden on developers to reference the principles in their proposals (H. Steinberg, interview, Mar. 12, 2004; H. Sokoloff, interview, Mar. 14, 2004). As Alan Greenberger concluded (interview, Mar. 20, 2004), all of the developers were aware of not only the inclusion of the principles in the RFP but also the publication of the supporting group reports in the *Inquirer* and addressed them in some way: "Some did it better, but no one ignored it. More importantly, the public reception of schemes was totally colored by principles from these forums." It is worth noting that the project had a clear impact on the *vocabularies* employed in the political process, but this does not necessarily mean it substantially influenced the plans put forth. As Steven McGovern observed by way of illustration (interview, Mar. 23, 2004), developers responded to the demand for public space, but the actual size and accessibility of the public spaces proposed were far short of public expectations in three of the four proposals initially submitted.

An interesting political side effect of the public input project was the impetus it gave to neighborhood mobilization. The project and especially the massive coverage devoted to it by the *Inquirer* encouraged existing neighborhood-level citizen groups to increase their political activity, at least in the short term. This led to a coalition pressuring the city to develop a more comprehensive plan for the entire region around Penn's Landing. Although the city initially responded positively, delays in taking action resulted in the coalition's hiring a consulting firm to develop its own comprehensive plan (S. McGovern, interview, Mar. 23, 2004). The desire to take ownership of the political process determining the future of the site by neighborhood-level citizen organizations was evident in the deliberations of my group at the first forum and made very pointed in the following criticism of the process at the second forum: "The process initiated by University of Pennsylvania and the Philadelphia *Inquirer* has been imposed on the region and has not elicited actual community response through the political neighborhood groups, which exist locally. I can assure you that a more unified and organic vision would emerge if community groups had the opportunity to make their voices known in a democratic planning process," read one anonymous feedback comment.

3. Training of Knowledgeable Personnel

Where we had an opportunity to observe it, the deliberative process embodied by the Penn's Landing project had a substantial impact on the professionals involved. Given their unwillingness to be interviewed, little can be said about the impact on elected officials and their staff, except that they did participate fully in the deliberative process while still feeling the need to organize their own parallel process. Indira Scott, organizer of the Penn's Landing Corporation forums, simultaneously defended the value of a separate set of forums while acknowledging the value of the Penn's Landing project forums in clarifying the public response to various plans for the site (interview, Mar. 22, 2004).

The clearest impact of training on elites can be found in the architectural and planning community. As noted at the outset of this chapter, public planners are very comfortable with the idea of collaborative processes. However, for many people in this community, a fully deliberative process, with citizens as peers and citizen deliberations as the focal point, is unfamiliar but attractive territory. This was evident in the Penn's Landing project. While holding to his belief that the experts ultimately have superior judgment over design, architect Greenberger acknowledged how impressed he was with a deliberative public's ability to develop a coherent set of guiding principles (interview, Mar. 20, 2004). Urban politics expert McGovern was impressed with how well the deliberative process reflected normative expectations for citizen input: "A lot of people thought that was the way things ought to be. They thought this is the way it ought to work" (interview, Mar. 23, 2004). Architect Steinberg of Penn Praxis commented on his incorporation of deliberative elements into later work including projects on the nearby Ben Salem waterfront and high school design in Philadelphia (interview, Mar. 12, 2004). Harris and Sokoloff, old hands at leading deliberations, have continued with their deliberative work in the region after the Penn's Landing project. The three primary organizers of the project, Steinberg, Satullo, and Sokoloff, published their take on the lessons learned from the project as well as the value of public journalism in the political process in a handbook for planners and other organizers of deliberative processes (Sokoloff, Steinberg, and Pyser, 2005; Charles, Sokoloff, and Satullo, 2005).

4. Interaction with the Public

Public impact can be examined with regard to both the effect on forum participants and the effect on the general public through media coverage. The survey results from the first public forum provide insight into two issues concerning forum participants: the nature and representativeness of the participants at the forum and whether participation in the forums led participants to embrace the norms of deliberation embodied in the project.

Forum participation was solicited through announcements in the *Inquirer* and mailings to people who had previously expressed interest in participating in public events. (See Chapter Twenty, "Avoiding Ghettos of Like-Minded People: Random Selection and Organizational Collaboration," for an alternative view on the means for selecting participants.) Setting aside one or more evenings to attend forums represents a very high level of personal investment in the process on the part of participants. Thus it should be no surprise that when compared to 2003 census figures for the city, the people who attended the first citizen forum did not appear to be at all representative of the citizens of Philadelphia. The median age of participants at the event was fifty-three years, whereas it is forty-five for Philadelphians over the age of eighteen. Eighty-nine percent of forum participants identified their race as white, non-Hispanic, while the census rate for the city is 45 percent. All of the participants had at least a high school diploma, compared to 80 percent of Philadelphia residents over twenty-five. The median household income of forum participants was about $70,000, compared to $33,000 for Philadelphians. These differences were not due to an overrepresentation of suburban participants at the forum. In fact, 75 percent of them came from center-city Philadelphia, 20 percent from suburbs, and 5 percent from the New Jersey side of the river.

The group of citizens who attended the first forum also had a very active interest in community affairs in general and in Penn's Landing in particular. Sixty-one percent of them read the newspaper on a daily basis, over 70 percent reported that they watched or listened to political news daily, and more than 85 percent reported that they discussed politics with family, friends, and coworkers at least once a week. Just under half indicated that they had attended multiple meetings on issues facing their community or school in the past year, and just over 30 percent had attended deliberative forums sponsored by the *Inquirer* in the past. More directly bearing on the subject of the evening, 78 percent had visited Penn's Landing within the last few months, 47 percent had already read some of the background on the project in the *Inquirer*, and 71 percent had attended the information session given earlier the same day.

If the results from the survey taken at the first forum can be generalized to all of the public components of the Penn's Landing project, it would be fair to characterize participants as a socioeconomically and civically engaged elite and racially homogeneous segment of the population. As Indira Scott of the Penn's Landing Corporation concluded (interview, Mar. 22, 2004), this group does not resemble the profile of visitors to Penn's Landing, and its unrepresentative nature blunted the political force its recommendations would hold for the city.

In addition to characterizing the nature and representativeness of the participants at the forum, the survey investigated the degree to which short-term learning and attitudinal changes took place among participants over the course of the evening in terms of the substance of the issue, the process of deliberations, and their perceptions of their role in the political process. These results of the pretest and posttest survey questions are summarized in Table 19.1.

One goal of public forums, including deliberative events, is to provide participants with increased substantive knowledge of the issue at hand. Given that the *Inquirer* had already run a series of background articles on the subject and that almost three-quarters of the respondents had attended a previous information session, forum participants felt that they where highly informed on the

TABLE 19.1. SURVEY RESULTS FROM THE FIRST FORUM.

Concept and Variable	Means and Significance	
	Presurvey	Postsurvey
Issue Knowlege		
Familiarity with issue of Penn's Landing	4.03	4.35***
Importance of Deliberative Norms		
Encouragement to express unpopular views	4.15	4.40**
Understanding minority views	3.90	4.22*
Majority agreement	3.59	3.28**
Reaching consensus	2.46	2.12*
Agreeing to disagree	3.85	3.44***
Self-Interest		
People generally try to be helpful to others	3.07	3.57***
People have a responsibility to help others	4.32	4.35
Political Efficacy		
I feel comfortable presenting my ideas	4.03	4.32**
Citizens have considerable influence on politics	2.92	2.87
A few powerful people decide everything	2.47	2.23
Philadelphians are being listened to on Penn's Landing	2.83	2.97

Note: All items measured on a scale of 1 to 5, low to high; $N = 62$.
*$p < .05$, **$p < .01$, ***$p < .001$.

issue at the outset of the deliberative sessions, with the average self-placement on knowledge being a 4 on a scale of 1 (low) to 5 (high). Yet strongly significant further increases in self-perception of knowledge about the issue were evident by the end of the evening, as reflected in Table 19.1.

Advocates of deliberation advance two critical norms of behavior as goals for participants. The first is tolerance—the acceptance and even encouragement of the expression of viewpoints with which one disagrees. Participants at the first forum were asked to rate their agreement with a simple measurement of tolerance, the statement "[Individuals] should be encouraged to express their views publicly even when most people don't want to hear what they have to say." Again, the group assembled for the forum began the evening in a highly tolerant state but still showed significant increases in tolerance by the time the deliberations concluded.

The second critical norm of deliberative behavior is usually summarized as "finding common ground." "The core idea is simple: when citizens or their representatives disagree morally, they should continue to reason together to reach mutually acceptable decisions" (Gutmann and Thompson, 1996, p. 1). The essence of common ground is continued deliberations in the face of obvious differences without resorting to majority voting, exerting pressure to reach consensus, or terminating the deliberation by simply "agreeing to disagree." Willingness to find common ground is related to tolerance because in a well-functioning deliberation, participants should try to empathize with dissenting views in an effort to reach decisions that all can accept. The search for common ground is a rare and fragile state in political discussions, yet the deliberations at the first Penn's Landing forum show strong and consistent evidence of having achieved it. Table 19.1 reflects statistically significant changes in the expected direction on all four items included: increased importance was attached to understanding minority views, and less importance was attached to majority agreement, reaching consensus, and simply agreeing to disagree.

In addition to the critical norms of tolerance and common ground, advocates for deliberation argue that it improves participants' sense of political efficacy and moves people away from narrow conceptions of self-interest toward a more altruistic outlook (Mathews, 1999). These results were not strongly evident in the data collected at the first forum. Of the two questions concerning self-interest versus altruism, one showed a statistically significant increase in an altruistic perspective, but the second, similar question did not. Participants indicated a significant increase in comfort with presenting their ideas in a group discussion, but this did not translate into changes in their sense of efficacy in the political system in general or on the issue of Penn's Landing in particular, as shown in Table 19.1. It is likely that changes in self-interest and political efficacy are possible results only of long-term involvement with deliberative processes, and thus it is not particularly surprising that they were not evident at the end of a single event.

The remarkable role of the *Inquirer* in providing opportunities for mass learning warrants highlighting. Media coverage of deliberative events tends to be minimal (Guston, 1999) and even then often reported from a highly skeptical angle (Ball, 2004). For a major newspaper to devote so much effort to covering the issues, developing the deliberative process, and providing opportunities for public input is rare indeed. As noted previously, the *Inquirer* ran more than forty pieces on the project and related items on Penn's Landing, managed active online discussion forums, and offered an online poll on the three concept plans presented at the second forum, generating over five thousand votes. The project also received some limited attention in other local news outlets (C. Satullo, interview, Mar. 10, 2004).

We were not in a position to formally assess learning resulting from mass media. A review of the online discussion comments and public views cited in newspaper articles suggests a very different tone than what emerged at the project's public deliberations, one characterized by single-minded issue advocacy, personal attacks, and self-interest typical of traditional political debates. Comparing unstructured, essentially anonymous political discussion (such as occurs in open online forums), appropriately structured and moderated online deliberations (see, for example, Figallo, Miller, and Weiss, 2004), and face-to-face deliberation, appropriately moderated, would be an excellent direction for future research.

Conclusion

"I see such deliberative processes as precarious and vulnerable achievements created on existing political stages" (Forrester, 1999, p. 7). The Penn's Landing project should be taken as a cautionary tale for those who would try to engender a collaborative culture on the scale of public policymaking. It certainly embodies Forrester's words. Political powers and events beyond the control of the project organizers obliterated any measurable impact of the project on policy outcomes, despite the leadership of the top regional practitioners of deliberative technique and the backing of both the *Inquirer* and Penn. The project unfortunately represents another in a long history of failures of "speaking truth to power" in the history of public policy analysis.

Yet the deliberative project should also be remembered for its remarkable other impacts, as reflected in this chapter. It fully embodied the critical norms of deliberation noted at the top: equality of participation and respect for all parties involved, increased political tolerance and possibly political efficacy by citizen participants, and the recognition of common grounds for action even in the face of continuing disagreement. City leaders accepted the deliberative process sufficiently to include the resulting public principles in the city's official documents, which in turn had a substantial impact on the vocabularies used by the developer community. The project won new supporters among policy elites, especially in the architecture and planning community. Perhaps most important, it engaged a public highly mistrustful of politics. It briefly encouraged increased political mobilization at the neighborhood level. It provided an unprecedented stream of information on the issue for the mass public. Among its (admittedly unrepresentative) participants, it further increased their knowledge of the issue and produced startlingly strong short-term increases in their adoption of the two critical deliberative norms of tolerance and the search for common ground.

Even these accomplishments would be easy to dismiss if the Penn's Landing project had been a one-off event where the people of Philadelphia would be unlikely to have the opportunity to convene once again for public deliberations. But this is not the case. The team of Satullo and Sokoloff, now joined by Steinberg, and the institutions they represent, are in the business of building a collaborative culture of deliberation in Philadelphia for the long haul. With the Penn's Landing project, they achieved identifiable intermediate accomplishments toward the creation of a culture of collaboration among citizens and experts on public policy issues. Perhaps future opportunities will permit them to go the last mile in bringing local policymakers into this culture.

References

Ackerman, B., and Fishkin, J. S. "Deliberation Day." *Journal of Political Philosophy*, 2002, *10*, 129–152.

Ball, W. J. "Listening to the City and the Goals of Deliberative Democracy." *Group Facilitation*, 2004, *6*, 102–105.

Barabas, J. "How Deliberation Affects Policy Opinions." *American Political Science Review*, 2004, *98*, 687–701.

Charles, M., Sokoloff, H., and Satullo, C. "Electoral Deliberation and Public Journalism." In J. Gastil and P. Levine (eds.), *The Deliberative Democracy Handbook: Strategies for Effective Civic Engagement in the Twenty-First Century*. San Francisco: Jossey-Bass, 2005.

Figallo, C., Miller, J., and Weiss, M. N. "Listening to the City Online Dialogues: Overview and Observations." *Group Facilitation*, 2004, *6*, 25–31.

Forrester, J. F. *The Deliberative Practitioner: Encouraging Participatory Planning Processes*. Cambridge, Mass.: MIT Press, 1999.

Gastil, J. *By Popular Demand: Revitalizing Representative Democracy Through Deliberative Elections*. Berkeley: University of California Press, 2000.

Gastil, J., and Dillard, J. "Increasing Political Sophistication Through Public Deliberation." *Political Communication*, 1999, *16*, 3–23.

Gelbart, M. "Mayor Pulls Plan for Penn's Landing." *Philadelphia Inquirer*, Oct. 15, 2004.

Guston, D. H. "Evaluating the First U. S. Consensus Conference: The Impact of the Citizens' Panel on Telecommunications and the Future of Democracy." *Science, Technology and Human Values,* 1999, *24,* 451–482.

Gutmann, A., and Thompson, D. *Democracy and Disagreement.* Cambridge, Mass.: Belknap Press, 1996.

Mansbridge, J. J. *Beyond Adversary Democracy.* New York: Basic Books, 1980.

Mathews, D. *Politics for People: Finding a Responsible Public Voice.* (2nd ed.) Urbana: University of Illinois Press, 1999.

Satullo, C. "A Principled Strategy." *Philadelphia Inquirer,* Feb. 17, 2003, p. A23.

Sirianni, C., and Friedland, L. *Civic Innovation in America: Community Empowerment, Public Policy, and the Movement for Civic Renewal.* Berkeley: University of California Press, 2001.

Sokoloff, H., Steinberg, H. M., and Pyser, S. "Deliberative City Planning on the Philadelphia Waterfront." In J. Gastil and P. Levine (eds.), *The Deliberative Democracy Handbook: Strategies for Effective Civic Engagement in the Twenty-First Century.* San Francisco: Jossey-Bass, 2005.

Wildavsky, A. *Speaking Truth to Power: The Art and Craft of Policy Analysis.* New York: Little, Brown, 1979.

Yankelovich, D. *Transforming Conflict into Cooperation.* New York: Simon & Schuster, 1999.

Lyn Carson, Ph.D., is a senior lecturer in applied politics at the University of Sydney, Australia. She is the author, with Brian Martin, of *Random Selection in Politics* (Praeger, 1999). She has written widely on the subject of citizen participation, drawing on her earlier experience as an elected local government representative as well as her current research into deliberative, inclusive processes. She has participated in many examples of active democracy—for example, Australia's first consensus conference, Australia's first two deliberative polls, citizens' juries, and a combined citizen's panel and televote. She has also applied these methods in organizational settings. She maintains a Web site, www.activedemocracy.net.

CHAPTER TWENTY

AVOIDING GHETTOS OF LIKE-MINDED PEOPLE

Random Selection and Organizational Collaboration

Lyn Carson

Universities can be wonderful places to work: for academics there can be intellectual freedom among peers who can challenge and extend one's thinking, funding is usually available to extend one's research horizons, and there are bright students with whom one can engage in stimulating discussions. That is how I have experienced academic life as a political scientist in Australia's oldest university, the University of Sydney. However, like most universities, my own is not always a place for collaboration. Our offices are side by side on long corridors, and we rarely meet unless we have formal matters to attend to. We are an atomized group with a shared discipline-based identity but few opportunities for teamwork. Most of my colleagues like it that way. Like most universities, agonism—the presumptive application of adversarial, debatelike processes (Tannen, 1999)—is more prevalent than amicable approaches such as appreciative inquiry—the practice of asking positive questions to achieve positive potential (Cooperrider and Srivasta, 1987).

When it comes to selecting people for particular management or coordination roles, we pay lip service to democracy, and the selection process resembles "passing a parcel of dead fish," the parcel containing a smelly responsibility that few would seek—for example, to chair a committee or to represent the faculty on the academic board or to be part of an advisory group to meet with the dean. (It should be noted that in Australia, the term *faculty* refers to an orga-nizational unit, usually comprising schools, departments, or research centers. The terms *academics, staff members,* or *lecturers* would be used as the equivalent of the U.S. term *faculty.*) Management or coordination tasks are considered part of our administrative workload and not something greeted with much enthu-siasm. However, those who rise to the top through a merit-based promotions system reach higher levels of salary and are expected to assume greater levels of administrative or management responsibility. Deans and vice-chancellors are surrounded by senior staff and are inevitably too busy to spend much time in the company of those at less senior levels. I contend that their personal expe-rience of life in the university becomes more homogeneous because of the nar-rowing circle of colleagues. This lack of familiarity works to the detriment of everyone and is not, of course, exclusive to the university setting.

Random Selection

I have long been fascinated by the problems that arise when powerful elites self-select for office or are invited or nominated to do so. Subsequently, they can wield an inordinate degree of influence, whether this is in the political, corporate, organizational, or community sphere. The ancient Greeks provided an inspirational model for a more egalitarian alternative: routinely drawing citizens by lot to vote on important matters or even to serve as officeholders. Of course, if one was a foreigner, a slave, or a woman, one was not included in the ballot (Hansen, 1991). However, for its time in history, it was a pro-foundly fair method for inclusive representation in decision-making bodies. There have been few recent examples of governing by lot, the method being conspicuously avoided by the founders of all the Western republics, although medieval Italy (for example, city-states like Florence) offered at least one de-viation from the elitist norm (Knag, 1998).

Governance comes in many forms, and corporate governance has spawned the occasional surprising experiment with random selection. Shared Interest, a cooperative lending society with over eight thousand members in the United Kingdom, uses random selection to nominate five of its nine council members. It has been judged a success by its members because it has not compromised the council's scrutiny of the board and has led to broader representation (Shared Interest, 2005). The National Lotteries, also in the United Kingdom, rather appropriately uses selection by lot to select some of the members of its regional awards committees. It wanted to avoid the usual tap-on-the-shoulder process of selection and chose to headhunt for talent in the wider community (Hencke, 2002). In the Netherlands, university students wanting to complete a degree in medicine or veterinary science might find their names being drawn in a lottery because of the limited places available because of a belief that a weighted lottery system is the fairest method for selecting among eligible students. However, these real-life contemporary and historical examples are rare. More usually, random selection is confined to those who are wistfully speculating about a fairer world (Carson and Martin, 1999, Stutzer and Frey, 2004).

It seems somewhat counterintuitive to link randomness with collaboration. After all, usually we collaborate with people we know. This means that we move in narrow circles, gravitate to ghettos of like-minded people, and suspect that we will encounter higher levels of conflict or ignorance among strangers. This might not always be a useful attitude because it prevents collaborative possibilities. In practice, collaboration among strangers can be rewarding. Having experienced many instances of deliberative, inclusive processes (participatory methods such as deliberative polls, consensus conferences, and citizens' juries), it is evident that strangers, drawn together through random selection, are remarkably good at collaboration. These methods for public deliberation are not the subject of this chapter, but their efficacy, in terms of achieving successful collaborative environments, has been well documented (Atlee, 2003; Crosby, 2003; Gastil 2000; Gastil and Levine, 2005) and provides the backdrop for the organizational case studies that follow.

Organizational Experiments with Random Selection

I suggested two ideas involving random selection to colleagues at the University of Sydney because I wanted to counteract two problems that typically accompany hierarchical institutions: (1) an unequal opportunity for members to be involved in diverse organizational activities and (2) the narrow circle of participants in these activities because of a tendency to avoid unknown members or those at the base of the hierarchy. Both ideas to counteract these problems will be described in this chapter.

The university is a large institution with approximately twenty-five hundred full-time academics and nearly fifty thousand students. It is divided into colleges, faculties, schools, and disciplines, with decision making occurring at all four of those levels (as well as at the overarching university level). One of my proposals affected the faculty only; the other operated at the university level. One idea was embraced enthusiastically after its initial rejection; one foundered. I assumed the role of champion for the former and offered only a discussion paper (written with a colleague) for the latter. This role of process champion is crucial to the success of innovation and will be discussed later. A description of the two processes—Coffee with the Dean and Random Selection of Academic Board Members—follows, as does a discussion about the usefulness of Coffee with the Dean, the only process that actually reached trial.

Coffee with the Dean

The dean, Peter Wolnizer, and I arrived at the University of Sydney's Faculty of Economics and Business at about the same time, circa 1999. I brought with me a particular worldview about leadership, one that has been influenced by Fran Peavey's writing (especially *Heart Politics*, 1986) and her strategic questioning workshops, held in Australia most years between 1989 and 1999. From Peavey's perspective, leaders need support in order to lead well, and she maintains that criticizing them from afar is of little value. Leaders are often isolated and are rarely offered support or opportunities to reflect with another person on how they might lead better. Of course, this can place the collaborative, supportive person in a vulnerable position, close to a leader who might come under criticism by colleagues. However this supporting-leadership approach has the potential to hold a leader accountable in a positive way and, in my experience, is a far more constructive approach than any alternative. Asking a leader, "How can I support your leadership?" is a powerful question if the inquiry is genuine.

I cannot recall asking this specific question of the dean, but it was definitely the subtext of our exchanges over the years. When I first introduced myself, I struck up a conversation about the difficulties of his role, especially in relation to cross-discipline communication within the faculty. He clearly wanted to create good lines of communication across the disciplines, so I suggested that it would be a good idea to get to know staff (not just the senior academics and managers) from the outset and to avoid becoming isolated or being seen as distant or unapproachable. He asked how he could do that, and I suggested one idea for starters: Coffee with the Dean.

The faculty is large (approximately three hundred permanent staff and many casual teaching appointments), and regularly wandering the corridors of four different buildings and chatting with hundreds of staff members (academic and administrative) would not be feasible or even appropriate. The dean asked his senior people what they thought about my idea, and they advised against it, arguing that lines of management were in place. The dean rejected the idea, albeit reluctantly, but his enthusiasm for consultation with his senior colleagues overcame his belief in the proposal.

The Faculty of Economics and Business is made up of disciplines and centers situated in two schools: the School of Economics and Political Science and the School of Business. The two-school structure occurred during this dean's tenure when departments were abolished, to be replaced by disciplines (a situation that still irks some colleagues). Disciplines (the former departments) are small, close-knit units, and schools and the faculty are much less closely knit. The academics of the faculty or schools occasionally have morning teas or evening drinks among themselves, but apart from the executive staff, there was no equivalent "intimate" occasion with the dean that involved people from different disciplines and different staff levels. There was very little communication or collaboration across the two schools. In 2003, the dean decided that this situation needed attention, and Coffee with the Dean began in December of that year.

Coffee with the Dean was somewhat misnamed because it suggested that the dean was the focal point (the name was later changed to Coffee with the Dean and Colleagues). Most often the dean found himself in situations where he was being asked to talk, and no opportunities were created for other voices to be heard. I suggested to him that Coffee with the Dean was a chance to hear these voices and that for this reason, the occasions should be moderated and that he should remain quiet and simply listen. He agreed because he genuinely wanted to hear from his staff members about the work they were doing. The moderator (usually me, sometimes the director of teaching and learning, Mark Freeman) encouraged others to speak and drew in the dean at the end. The participants were told that this was an occasion to meet people with whom they might be unfamiliar and for the dean to have a chance to hear about what was happening in the faculty. (Exhibit 20.1 reproduces an e-mail sent to staff by the dean's administrative assistant, which preceded random selection of 2005 participants.)

People were randomly selected from the list of permanent staff members. This made it special: it had the flavor of a lottery win. Coffee with the Dean

EXHIBIT 20.1. INVITATION TO
COFFEE WITH THE DEAN AND COLLEAGUES.

Hello everybody!

The first of our 'Coffee with the Dean and Colleagues' meetings in 2005 will begin in February. In the next few days a number of staff members will be invited to join Faculty colleagues and the Dean for afternoon tea. Throughout 2005, other staff members will be randomly selected to participate in similar informal gatherings.

You may recall, the purpose of these gatherings is two-fold. Firstly, they will enable colleagues from both Schools, who rarely meet, to get to know a little about the work of others outside their own Discipline. Secondly, to decrease the remoteness that comes with his role as Dean, these gatherings will provide an opportunity for Peter to meet with and listen to a broad cross section of staff members—to catch up on the successes and challenges they face, and familiarise himself with the diversity of work that's occurring. The small group (six to eight people) will include academics and administrators from all levels. This is an opportunity for Faculty staff to talk together—and for the Dean to listen. The discussions will be facilitated by Mark Freeman and Lyn Carson.

The gatherings will be very informal and there is absolutely no obligation to attend. They'll be held in the Dean's Boardroom on a monthly basis, from 3.45–4.30 pm, and afternoon tea will be provided. For afternoon tea in 2005, names have already been drawn from a hat and invitations will soon follow. So stay tuned for yours!

Hoping to see you there!

Aleta

---

was, and continues to be, held in the boardroom. It is a bright, open space with a large table and comfy chairs, but it is a place that most participants had never seen, so this also made it special. The dean's administrative assistant arranged for coffee, tea, and delicious cakes. I welcomed people as they arrived. They had received and accepted an invitation from the dean. They knew who else would be there and what would be covered (an explanation of the latter, in the confirmation letter, was provided after an early participant said she would have liked some warning about what would be discussed).

The conversation was a guided "sharing of experience," with participants responding to a series of questions from the facilitator. Participants tended to speak in turn, although we encouraged cross-table responses. The flow of conversation varied from group to group; some were more stilted than others, but mostly they were relaxed and chatty occasions, and people seemed to enjoy the experience. No opinion or discussion was discouraged, though a prompt tended to take the discussion in a certain direction. For example, as facilitator, I might ask, "What are you excited about right now?" "What's giving you pleasure?" or "What are you feeling proud of?" We tried to model active listening and questioning, and other participants often followed this by commenting or asking questions as well. This was a qualitatively different type of group discussion than those usually experienced in university meetings; it was collaborative dialogue rather than adversarial debate. After the Coffee with the Dean session, the dean sent a thank-you note (another addition, following a suggestion from my fellow facilitator).

Randomly Selecting Members of Academic Board

Coffee with the Dean is a very different activity from the second one to be discussed, Random Selection of Academic Board Members.

The academic board maintains standards in teaching, scholarship, and research; safeguards academic freedom; and formulates and reviews academic policies, guidelines, and procedures. It reports to the university senate and provides academic advice to both the senate and the vice-chancellor. In 2002, when election of our faculty representatives for the academic board was imminent, the acting dean asked me and a colleague, Rodney Smith, to give some thought to how election methods might be modified. Until then, the procedure was that the faculty called for nominations, little interest was displayed, and the occasional willing (or badgered) academic put his or her name forward and was duly "elected" without opposition.

The rules and guidelines of the academic board (hereafter the board) have been determined by the university senate and include that each faculty be required to define for itself, from time to time, its election method within guidelines set by the board and approved by senate, and that must be submitted for approval by the board. Further, faculties must ensure that electoral processes encourage representative participation, with particular regard to issues relating to gender, discipline, and expertise, and also that at least one elected representative should be a professor. (Note that in Australia, the term *professor* denotes the highest academic position and is never used in the generic sense of an academic regardless of rank.)

Deans were encouraged to consult with their faculty in order to define its electoral methods, hence the acting dean's request to my colleague and me. There are more responsibilities than privileges associated with the role of board representative. It was my belief that the board role should be shared among colleagues; this explains my willingness to coauthor a discussion paper to begin a process that would involve colleagues in deciding how board representatives would be selected or elected.

The foregoing guidelines were descriptive rather than prescriptive, though recommending an electoral system that relied on nominations followed by preferential voting by postal ballot. Because it had always been far from a fiercely fought contest, my colleague and I puzzled over how we might achieve congruence between the process and the practice of board selection.

We decided that certain principles should be encouraged and suggested that the following should govern any decision about an election or selection method:

1. The election or selection method should deliver a broadly representative cross section of staff from our faculty.
2. Everyone should have an equal chance of being selected or elected.
3. Participation should be a responsibility shared over time.

We proposed two alternatives: by lot (Carson and Martin, 1999) and by a proportional representation ballot system (Reynolds and Reilly, 1997). In my opinion, the first option meets the three principles set out earlier, and the second option meets the first and third principles (since it would be difficult for any *electoral* system to meet such a principle). I will not cover here my colleague's option because random selection is the focus of this chapter. Here is how the "by lot" option would work.

All eligible academic staff members would be automatically nominated, that is, be available for selection. Anyone could ask to have one's nomination withdrawn by submitting a written request and justification to the faculty executive officer. Making the effort to provide adequate justification is important because availability for professional duties is a shared responsibility. In a process scrutinized by the registrar, individuals would be randomly drawn until five were selected that met the following requirements: no more than one from each academic level; no more than one from any discipline or center; no more than three from either school.

My belief was that this would result in a far more representative sample of the faculty's diverse voices than the narrow sample that resulted from elections (really, self-selection). Of course, this is the same problem that exists in the political realm, where citizens vote for preselected (usually self-selected) candidates.

To fully consider our guiding principles, our two options plus any other options, as well as the status quo, we suggested that a policy jury of twelve randomly selected staff members be convened (Crosby, 2003). This group would make recommendations that could be circulated to all staff for comment, culminating in final recommendations for our faculty's executive to consider. My colleague and I considered that our two suggested options plus the process for deciding on the best option provided a basis for deliberative, representative, efficient, inexpensive, robust decision making. The options and consultation process were considered at a faculty executive meeting. There was very little discussion and insufficient interest in pursuing these ideas, so the status quo has remained.

Discussion

Following is a discussion of both Coffee with the Dean and Random Selection of Academic Board Members.

Coffee with the Dean

In November 2004, I conducted an evaluation of Coffee with the Dean. This involved interviews with the dean, my fellow facilitator, the dean's administrative assistant who organized the sessions, and 20 percent of those who had participated in them (twelve participants who were randomly selected and interviewed briefly by telephone using very open-ended questions).

For the dean, Coffee with the Dean was a vehicle for communicating his values: respect, and tolerance through relationship building. In his opinion, Coffee with the Dean had enabled this to happen. It was important for him to model these values for his staff: to listen respectfully, to hear all views and accept any criticisms, in order to build relationships with people at all levels of the faculty.

The participants who were interviewed seemed relaxed and open with their responses. More than half of them had participated in sessions that I had not facilitated. I was surprised by respondents' consistent enthusiasm: "It's a really good initiative," "Keep doing it," "Definitely appreciated," "Nice to sit around a table," "Great participation," "Good to be with other people." I was also surprised by their occasional venom (from two of the twelve respondents): "No statement from the dean about vision or policy," "Does it make a difference, I wonder?" I began to note the importance of the Coffee with the Dean experience for administrators and junior academics and to detect deep-seated cynicism from senior academics who had been with the faculty for some time. I wondered if Coffee with the Dean should be kept exclusively for new staff members but realized that its strength was the way in which new staff were exposed to old and vice versa. Some commented that they had not met the dean before and this meant a lot to them; they were also thrilled to meet people with more experience and knowledge than themselves. Had we selected participants according to their duration with the faculty, academic level, discipline, or some other attribute, this would not have occurred.

The evaluation led to further realizations for the organizers, one related to clarity of purpose and the other to issues of trust. Participants had disparate personal goals in relation to Coffee with the Dean, possibly because there was residual confusion about the initiative's purpose. The intended purpose of Coffee with the Dean had been clearly spelled out in a circular to all staff, repeated in the individual invitations, and reiterated by the facilitator. Nevertheless, it seems that the statement was not enough; some staff members do not accept these words because they were busily looking for a hidden agenda. This raises the issue of trust. I would speculate that the search for a hidden agenda occurs when trust is lacking. Indeed, one respondent commented that there was "a very low level of trust" and that "the dean does not get to hear what's really going on." For those who had no reason *not* to trust, they read the words in the invitation, heard the facilitator's explanation, accepted them, and enjoyed the process.

Having completed the interviews, I wrote a draft report and gave it to my fellow facilitator as a basis for discussion. His questions pushed me to consider how we might use this experience to move the faculty further along a dialogic path, from pleasant conversation toward purposeful deliberation. Our ambitions had been small—to connect people who otherwise would not meet. It was a tentative step on the road to collaboration in a fairly noncollaborative environment, and we realized that much more was now possible.

Random Selection of Academic Board Members

Random Selection of Academic Board Members, an idea that was meant to exploit the efficacy of random selection, foundered so early in its life that any possible discussion is limited. However, its failure reinforces an important lesson. Senge, Scharmer, Jaworski, and Flowers (2004) have noted that organizations have a "mainstream culture" that can be "toxic to the innovators it spawns" and further that "when the organizational immune system kicks in, innovators often find themselves ignored, ostracized, or worse" (p. 35). In this case study, there was little malevolent behavior; rather, the reaction was indifference, although the organization's "immune system" seems to be have been activated.

The Australian Universities Quality Agency (AUQA) conducted an audit of the University of Sydney in 2004 and noted that there were vacancies on the academic board in positions that were meant to be occupied by students. AUQA made no mention of the selection or election processes used for academic representatives. Nevertheless, its suggestion, in relation to improving student representation, is equally relevant for academics: "that the University, in conjunction with its established student organisations, consider how it may improve its coordination of student representative arrangements. Such consideration ought to include processes for selection/election of students into University boards and committees at all levels, and induction and support for these students" (p. 14).

Conclusion

Some general conclusions can be drawn from these two case studies. They highlight particular aspects of organizational culture: the way in which random selection could widen organizational conversations, the usefulness of cynicism, and the entrenched nature of power. Also, the case studies demonstrate the catalytic effect of combining two roles, those of the process designer and the enabling leader.

Coffee with the Dean was not exactly a democratic breakout (Blaug, 1999); it was a friendly sharing of experiences among peers. However, as one participant noted, "Normally, faculty meetings are so top-down and being talked at, and this was not like that." Participants certainly perceived it to be a more egalitarian environment than they usually encountered and therefore a change to the mainstream culture.

Given my research and writing in the area of random selection, I was pleased to have confirmed again the efficacy of stratified random selection. Coffee with the Dean was demonstrably a fair process in terms of opportunities for selection because it consistently gathered together a very good cross section of the faculty and therefore widened the circle of participants in organizational activities. This was reflected in a recurring comment by respondents: "It was useful seeing and meeting people I don't bump into often because we have such a small circle of colleagues," "Great to say hello and see what others are doing," "Good to put faces to people I only knew as e-mail names." The circle of potential collaborators had widened.

When reflecting on the criticisms received from two participants, not so much about Coffee with the Dean but about management and the faculty in general, I realized how grateful I was for their cynicism. History has taught us that nationalism or patriotism is a hair's breadth away from fascism or totalitarianism; organizations possess similar vulnerability to groupthink and dysfunction, although the consequences are typically more benign (Lutz, 1986; Sims, 1992). Academics frequently describe the culture of their organization as one of "tension or conflict" and provide "vivid and graphic examples" to support their beliefs (Silver, 2003, p. 161). However, I am grateful to work among people who want to hold leaders accountable, who expect that appreciation should be earned and who find skepticism a healthy pursuit. I believe that this strengthens rather than diminishes the faculty.

I have argued elsewhere that institutional change will occur only with *process champions* (Carson, 2004); these case studies illustrate that the role of process champion is crucial. The proposal for Random Selection of Academic Board Members languished because it lacked a process champion; Coffee with the Dean flourished because it had several (including the dean and my fellow facilitator). It is perhaps more accurate to suggest that innovation requires a process champion *and* an enabling leader; only then will innovation be embraced. The acting dean had been preoccupied by more pressing matters during the window of opportunity that arose to alter the method of election for academic board, so no enabling leadership occurred. Once the opportunity passed, the discussion paper was shelved. (More on the role of process champions can be found in Chapter Eighteen, "Leadership for the Common Good.")

This is not a complete explanation of the differing reactions to these two ideas. Another possible contributing element could be that Coffee with the

Dean did not threaten to replace an existing institutional practice; it was an addition, although it altered the mainstream culture. It did not challenge existing power relationships because there was no decision making by its participants (Lukes, 1974). In contrast, the random selection of academic board members was a substitution for an existing mechanism and would have altered the mainstream culture as well as challenged existing power relationships.

It may be that it is not too late to revive interest in the Random Selection of Academic Board Members proposal, especially since Coffee with the Dean took four years from its suggestion stage to action. Ideas rarely ignite without fuel for the flames, and a champion is needed to fan the spark that the idea creates; often this requires considerable time and effort. A process champion needs the personal energy to convince others to sponsor or be involved in the collaborative innovation. Crucially, a process champion needs the support of an enabling leader with decision-making responsibility or a high degree of influence. Enabling leaders may be born but could also be made, and many strategies are available to stimulate good leadership. For example, strategic questioning is a most useful tool for energizing a nascent leader (Peavey, 2005). Certainly, more process champions and enabling leaders are needed for democratic innovations to take root in nondemocratic institutions.

Finally, these case studies contain seeds that could be planted in large hierarchical organizations other than universities. Coffee with the Organizational Leader could be used where communication channels are blocked or where ghettos of like-minded people have become the organizational norm. Random selection of representatives is a strategy that could lead to a more diverse decision-making body and might be a purposeful step in the creation of a collaborative organization. Embedding elements of both case studies could improve overall communication and decision-making processes, thus fostering a healthy culture of organizational collaboration.

References

Atlee, T. *The Tao of Democracy: Using Co-Intelligence to Create a World That Works for All.* Cranston, R.I.: Writers' Collective, 2003.

Australian Universities Quality Agency. *Report of an Audit of the University of Sydney.* Audit Report no. 28. Melbourne: Australian Universities Quality Agency, Dec. 2004.

Blaug, R. *Democracy, Real and Ideal: Discourse Ethics and Radical Politics.* Albany: State University of New York Press, 1999.

Carson, L. "Lotteries and Chit Chat: What Random Selection and Deliberation Can Do for Environmental Governance." Paper presented at the Ecopolitics XV International Conference, Macquarie University, Sydney, Nov. 2004.

Carson, L., and Martin, B. *Random Selection in Politics.* Westport, Conn.: Praeger, 1999.

Cooperrider, D. L., and Srivasta, S. "Appreciative Inquiry in Organizational Life." In R. W. Woodman and W. A. Pasmore (eds.), *Research in Organizational Change and Development,* Vol. 1. Greenwich, Conn.: JAI Press, 1987.

Crosby, N. *Healthy Democracy.* Edina, Minn.: Beaver's Pond Press, 2003.

Gastil, J. *By Popular Demand. Revitalizing Representative Democracy Through Deliberative Elections.* Berkeley: University of California Press, 2000.

Gastil, J., and Levine, P. (eds.). *The Handbook of Public Deliberation.* San Francisco: Jossey-Bass, 2005.

Hansen, M. H. *The Athenian Democracy in the Age of Demosthenes: Structure, Principles and Ideology.* Oxford: Blackwell, 1991.

Hencke, D. "Lucky Winners Given Chance to Hand Out Lottery Millions." *London Guardian,* Dec. 13, 2002 [http://society.guardian.co.uk/lottery/story/0,8150,859233,00.html].

Knag, S. "Let's Toss for It: A Surprising Curb on Political Greed." *Independent Review,* 1998, *3,* 199–209.

Lukes, S. *Power: A Radical View.* Old Tappan, N.J.: Macmillan, 1974.

Lutz, F. W. "Witches and Witchfinding in Educational Organizations." *Educational Administration Quarterly,* 1986, *22,* 49–67.

Peavey, F. *Heart Politics.* Philadelphia: New Society, 1986.

Peavey, F. "Strategic Questioning: An Experiment in Communication of the Second Kind." Crabgrass [http://www.crabgrass.org/site/strategic_1.html]. Feb. 2005.

Reynolds, A., and Reilly, B. *The International IDEA Handbook of Electoral System Design.* Stockholm: IDEA, 1997.

Senge, P., Scharmer, C. O., Jaworski, J., and Flowers, B. S. *Presence: Human Purpose and the Field of the Future.* Cambridge, Mass.: Society for Organizational Learning, 2004.

Shared Interest Society Ltd. "About Shared Interest" [www.sharedinterest.org.uk]. Feb. 2005.

Silver, H. "Does a University Have a Culture?" *Studies in Higher Education,* 2003, *28,* 157–169.

Sims, R. R. "Linking Groupthink to Unethical Behavior in Organizations." *Journal of Business Ethics,* 1992, *11,* 651–662.

Stutzer, A., and Frey, B. S. *Making International Organizations More Democratic.* Institute for Empirical Research in Economics Working Paper Series no. 217 [http://papers.ssrn.com/sol3/papers.cfm?abstract_id=639023]. Dec. 2004.

Tannen, D. *The Argument Culture: Stopping America's War of Words.* New York: Ballantine Books, 1999.

Tasos Sioukas is an educator, consultant, and the author of *The Solution Path* (Jossey-Bass, 2003). He has worked with hundreds of organizations, including Bank of America, Boeing, the City of Los Angeles, Hyatt Hotels, Northrop Grumman, and Sempra Energy. He is a professor of business administration at Los Angeles Valley College. He holds a doctorate from the University of Southern California and a master's degree from the University of California at Berkeley and has won multiple international awards for his work.

Marilyn Sweet is currently the dean of college advancement for the Los Angeles Community College District. She works with industry clusters, colleges, and the district to define needs and create collaborative programs. She then funds these strategic alliances by accessing funds, typically $1 to $3 million per project. Sweet holds a bachelor's degree from Ohio State University and a master's degree from the University of Southern California and has completed doctoral work in organization psychology.

CHAPTER TWENTY-ONE

INVOLVING MULTIPLE STAKEHOLDERS IN LARGE-SCALE COLLABORATIVE PROJECTS

Tasos Sioukas, Marilyn Sweet

Involving multiple stakeholders, people with a stake in a given project, is absolutely essential for creating solution ideas, making effective decisions, and generating commitment for implementation. It is required in all organizations no matter their scope or purpose. Therefore, it should not be surprising that most organizations bring multiple stakeholders together in teams for implementing project work. As reported in the *Journal of Management,* over 80 percent of companies with more than one hundred employees and more than 90 percent of Fortune 1000 organizations have institutionalized the use of teams for project work (Cohen and Bailey, 1997).

Working together in teams gives all participating stakeholders the chance to contribute and collectively shape and implement solutions that represent much more than the sum of their individual ideas. This is one way in which innovations happen, when team members can capitalize and expand on the diversity of their ideas and take collective action (Sioukas, 2003).

Large-scale collaborative projects, however, require more than working effectively with stakeholders on a project team. They require collaboration within and across multiple groups and individuals. Collaboration, the process of working together in a group, organization, or a community, is a delicate process that requires systematic effort and skill.

The more complex and sizable the project, the more effort and dedication we need to identify and involve stakeholders and to foster collaboration at almost every level of the organization.

Overhauling the Information Systems of a Four-College District

The following hypothetical case illustrates the complexity of involving various stakeholders in a large and complex project of an educational institution.* Early success was replaced by serious challenges that needed to be systematically addressed for the project to be completed effectively.

John and Ellen were the director and associate director of information technology of a college district, a public educational institution consisting of four colleges overseen by an elected board of trustees. Their project was to implement a series of districtwide information systems. These systems would modernize the institution's accounting, purchasing, and payroll practices and systems through a complete overhaul.

It was two years ago that a new district chancellor brought John on board with the mandate to head and develop a new department to upgrade the institution's "old and cumbersome" processes and systems. John had successfully directed the design and implementation of similar systems in both private and public organizations, including universities and colleges. Soon after the chancellor appointed him director of information technology, John realized the complexity of the situation and the great amount of districtwide participation and collaboration it would require. This is why he hired Ellen as his associate director. Ellen is an excellent group process expert with a proven track record of "making change stick" through collaborative action.

Together John and Ellen built a solid information technology department at the district office, the three original employees augmented by four new hires. John and Ellen worked diligently to meet individuals with key expertise at each of the district's four campuses and to inventory existing district information technology resources such as procedures, practices, and software.

---

*This case is entirely hypothetical. Any similarity to real organizations, circumstances, and names is purely coincidental.

John and Ellen partnered with the chancellor, their sponsor, the college presidents, and the district's three unions (administrative, faculty, and staff) to identify key stakeholders and build a districtwide project team. This team was to be the main vehicle by which the new systems would be designed and approved. Ellen invested endless hours meeting and recruiting stakeholder representatives from the staff union—members of departments such as accounting, purchasing, and payroll—as well as faculty and administrators. John and Ellen worked with the chancellor and the presidents to appoint a key representative from each campus and the district office to the project team. Moreover, the chancellor extended an open invitation for participation, and Ellen invited everyone she had met who had expressed an interest in participating. The efforts paid off. By the third meeting, John and Ellen had assembled their team of eighteen individuals: eleven members of the staff union, three faculty members, and four administrators.

The team went to work immediately, and three months after its formation, the team members had developed a conceptual solution and an initial budget. They also selected a vendor for the project. John and Ellen celebrated their first success as they secured overall approval from the chancellor, the college presidents, and the board of trustees.

During the year that followed, John and Ellen worked hard with the project team and separate task forces on accounting, purchasing, and payroll. This massive effort involved over fifty individuals from the district and several representatives of the vendor organization. They were able to detail each of the three information systems, the budget, and the implementation plan. They were proud to secure consensus by all the members of the project team and the three task forces.

Yet their efforts hit a roadblock. The district board of trustees did not approve their timeline for implementing the information systems. Instead, the board suggested that they needed to spend more time refining their design and more specifically to reconsider the lines of authority and responsibility implied by each system. Moreover, they were told that while the staff and administrative unions backed the project, the faculty union was opposed to it.

John and Ellen were disappointed and puzzled. Their team-based solution, which they developed through a highly participative process of idea generation, synthesis, and consensus decision making with over fifty individuals, proved inadequate. Clearly, they had a lot of work ahead of them before they could return to the board of trustees for approval.

A Systematic Approach for Collaboration

Diligent collaboration agents such as group facilitators, organizational development consultants, public participation specialists, collaborative leaders, and mediators spend time partnering with their project sponsor to identify key stakeholders, talk to them, and form a core project team. This is almost axiomatic for effective facilitation. Yet as the case of John and Ellen clearly demonstrates, large-scale projects require a much more systematic approach for collaboration to occur effectively. The aim of the discussion that follows is thus to help you take the steps necessary to launch and sustain a systematic approach of inclusion across the organization. This will include reviewing the role of process facilitators; understanding the various categories of stakeholders and designing a stakeholder table of the organization; creating a plan of collaborative action that feeds information to all stakeholder groups with the purpose of testing, refining, and communicating the solution; and additional key practices for fostering collaboration throughout the project.

The Role of Process Facilitators

Using group facilitation is an *absolute requirement* to work with stakeholders and various groups most effectively. Facilitation, a set of tools for structuring and conducting meetings, allows group members to share their views, brainstorm and prioritize ideas, synthesize solutions, make consensus decisions, and generate commitment for action. Facilitators are process experts who provide the tools that enable team members to make this possible (Kaner and others, 1996; Bens, 2000; Sioukas, 2003).

A key ingredient of the facilitators' role is their neutrality on *what* is being discussed and their focus on *how* each item is discussed. This frees leaders to do what they do best: participate, influence, and guide decision making. (For additional viewpoints on facilitator neutrality, see Hunter and Thorpe, 2005.)

Although facilitation is a broad field with an extensive literature, we think that four basic facilitator functions are especially pertinent:

1. Asking questions to stimulate participation
2. Listening actively to what is being discussed
3. Making the meeting visible by recording what is discussed; and,
4. Providing a safe haven for meeting participants

The fourth function is perhaps the most important. Facilitators strive to provide a safe and open environment for participation and interaction by regulating the order and manner whereby participants interact, resolving conflicts as they arise, and remaining neutral.

Depending on the size of your collaborative project, you may want to use multiple facilitators. If you cannot afford to hire external facilitators, the training of internal facilitators becomes essential. In selecting people for these positions, keep in mind that individuals whose daily duties are not affected by the outcome of the project are better suited because it is easier for them to remain neutral. (For additional views of facilitation, see Chapter Seven, "Make-or-Break Roles in Collaboration Leadership," and Chapter Sixteen, "Collaboration for Social Change.")

Categories of Stakeholders

When starting a large-scale collaborative project, your first step is to identify your initiative's major stakeholder groups. A stakeholder group, as opposed to an individual stakeholder, is a group of people (organized or not) who have similar concerns regarding a situation. You should include all relevant groups, including potential supporters as well as those who may block or delay project implementation. Although it is a natural human tendency to avoid potential threats to your project, do not avoid these detractors. Avoiding the involvement of detractors may allow the initial phases of the project to go more smoothly, but failing to involve them may in the long run severely delay your project or end it outright.

There is a rich cache of literature on stakeholder analysis and involvement (see Mitroff, 1998; Straus, 2002; Sioukas, 2003; Bryson, 2004; Carlson, 2005). Think carefully about whom to involve from each of the following four types of stakeholders: people affected by the project, decision makers and influencers, decision blockers, and people with relevant information or expertise. Let's take a closer look at each.

People Affected by the Project. In any project, it is usually apparent who will be directly affected by the solution or end result. For example, in John and Ellen's college district project, the people affected were primarily the staff and administrators who worked with these systems on an everyday basis, as well as faculty who served as project directors. Including all parties who will be affected is an effective tactic when implementing a large-scale project. Those closest to a problem are the most likely to generate and implement efficient, cost-effective solutions.

The need to involve everyone who will be affected may seem obvious, but it is frequently overlooked. When groups are excluded and then get wind of a project that affects them, their first reaction is often resentment or anger, and their resistance builds. If they are rebuffed as obstructionists or troublemakers or simply told "not to worry," they may turn their energies toward blocking the project.

Exclusion of those affected usually stems from a misplaced belief that they lack the requisite expertise to analyze and implement a solution or that including them will unduly increase the length of the project. As you work to satisfy the interests of all stakeholder groups, the largest and potentially most useful stakeholder group is the people affected by the project.

Decision Makers and Influencers. All individuals and groups with the formal power to make a decision about your project should be involved, such as administrators and managers who make final decisions based on the authority of their positions. In the college district project, these included the chancellor, presidents, and board members.

An early step in any project is to determine who will be making the final decision and whether any other person or body will have to approve that decision. It is also important to determine the level of their involvement and what resources they are willing to commit. Furthermore, are they committed to collaboration or merely giving it lip service? If you involve decision makers throughout the problem-solving process and the final consensus-building process, the outcomes of the project are likely to be formally supported. Involving formal decision makers saves everyone's time and energy. If these decision makers are excluded, the project may ultimately be dismissed or ignored, regardless of how well planned and executed it is.

Sometimes it is easier to access decision influencers—individuals who have credibility and influence within the formal power structure. Influencers are usually employees who report directly to the decision makers. For example, in the college district project, influencers included administrators, staff directors, and faculty members with direct access to college presidents, the chancellor, and the board.

Decision Blockers. Decision blockers are people who can delay or stop the implementation of your project. A blocker can literally be anyone who feels that the project, no matter how laudable, will have a negative impact on his or her work life. It may be as simple as resistance to learning a new skill or as complex as a loss of power. Involving the groups who may block a decision may well be your most difficult task. While it is relatively easy to involve formal decision makers, and perhaps to tend to rely on them too heavily to carry a project, involving those who may potentially block your project requires working against human nature. Ordinarily, when people suspect that a person or group will delay or stop a project, the tendency is to avoid the blockers and hope for the best.

Extra effort may be needed to include blockers throughout your project. Even if you fear overt challenges, it is preferable that your blockers oppose the project openly. Dealing with clear-cut opposition is preferable to being subjected to covert actions, such as individuals dragging their feet or simply going through the motions with no real intent to implement changes. Overt blocking in open meetings, no matter how difficult, can usually be resolved productively by using effective process facilitation. A skilled facilitator allows for the emergence and discussion of alternative views and guides stakeholders to synthesize a more inclusive and enlarged solution. Conflict is treated as an avenue to creative solutions, not something to be avoided. If overt blocking is not handled skillfully, the resistance will move underground, where it cannot be confronted.

Answering two key questions can reveal potential blockers: Who can sabotage, delay, or stop the project? And from which groups is support for the project needed? John and Ellen, for example, belatedly realized they had blockers in the form of the faculty union. The feedback they received from the board of trustees alerted them to the need to work harder to bring faculty concerns to the table and redesign their solution.

The power of the collaborative process is such that potential detractors can quickly become your most ardent supporters once their views have been expressed and taken seriously. If you are new to collaboration and group facilitation, you will have to take it on faith that detractors have valid viewpoints and for the most part need help to participate productively in a group process. Once that is achieved, they frequently become active contributors.

People with Information or Expertise. People inside or outside the organization who have specialized knowledge that directly relates to the project can be important allies. Your first step would be to evaluate whether you have the needed information or expertise to deal with the problem at hand. In evaluating resources, look first to the existing stakeholder groups. If outside expertise is needed to solve a problem, you can contract with content experts to participate in the project. Content experts are individuals with technical expertise in a particular field, such as accounting, software development, or business strategy. John and Ellen's project involved both internal experts in the information technology department and external experts in the form of software vendors.

After considering the four stakeholder categories and identifying the stakeholders of your project, it is useful to summarize them in a table that can guide you as you move on to designing a process for involving the stakeholders throughout the project. Table 21.1 depicts the stakeholder table for the college district project.

A Plan of Collaborative Action

How can we involve all stakeholders in a large-scale collaborative problem-solving process? The number of potential individuals to involve may seem daunting. Indeed, how is it possible to move an entire organization with hundreds of members through a complex problem-solving sequence that stretches out over an extended period of time?

In designing a process of collaborative action, it is useful to consider a project involvement map like the one shown in Figure 21.1. Each circle represents a different level of involvement. The innermost circle, the project team, has the smallest number of individuals. Moving out to the larger circles, task forces, feedback meetings, and communication and outreach meetings involve successively larger numbers of people but with less intensity of involvement. The number of circles may vary with the complexity of the project.

TABLE 21.1. STAKEHOLDER TABLE FOR THE COLLEGE DISTRICT PROJECT.

Category	Stakeholders
People affected	Staff, faculty, administrative unions
Decision makers	Presidents, chancellor, board members
Decision influencers	Vice presidents, deans, faculty members, staff directors
Decision blockers	Union leaders, prominent union members
People with information or expertise	Information technology staff, software vendors

FIGURE 21.1. PROJECT INVOLVEMENT MAP.

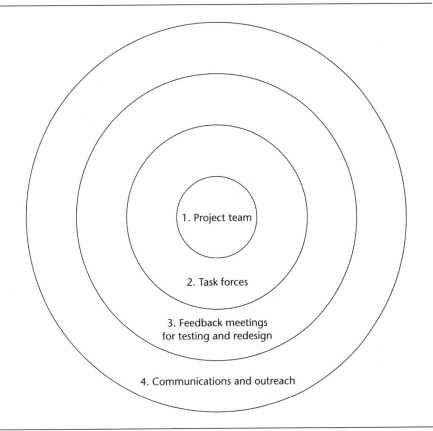

Source: Adapted from Straus, 2002.

In large-scale collaborative projects, the innermost circle, the core project team, serves as the steering or executive committee. This group includes appointees and representatives from all stakeholder groups and is ultimately responsible for the overall project and coordinating the work of the task forces. Task forces are responsible for smaller portions of the overall project. John and Ellen, for example, broke their information technology project into three task forces: accounting, purchasing, and payroll. The members of the task forces are those with the most knowledge about the subject at hand. The chairs of the task forces often also serve as members of the project team.

Even a core team with broad-based representation may find itself isolated. This can happen when team members do not communicate project results with their respective stakeholder groups on an ongoing basis. Such isolation may negatively affect your project when resources and commitment are needed from the rest of the organization. You can avoid this sort of isolation through the use of an "open-door policy" and an explicit plan for communicating project results to all stakeholder groups and obtaining feedback from the rest of the organization. The third and forth levels of involvement are designed to support you in these efforts, as well as increase participation and recruit new team members from all stakeholder groups. The third level of involvement, feedback meetings, tests and redesigns the solution with the participation of all stakeholder groups. In this way, all necessary groups have a chance to provide input to the final design. Thus you can avoid delays and surprises such as those John and Ellen faced in the college district project. The fourth circle, for communication and outreach meetings, needs to be in place as the solution begins to form. In addition, you can use the fourth level of involvement, like the third, for recruiting new team members from all stakeholder groups. Our experience shows that more stakeholders will want to join and enrich the resources of the team as the solution starts to take shape, leading to greater collaboration and commitment to the project (Sioukas, 2003).

Once you have developed your stakeholder table and your project involvement map, the next step is to develop a plan of collaborative action. This plan serves as a process road map, laying out who needs to be involved at each phase of the project and providing time estimates for the completion of each phase. You can create this plan with your project group in a facilitative way by asking questions such as these:

What phases need to take place to complete the project?

Who is responsible for each phase?

Which stakeholder group needs to be involved at each phase?

How long do we need for each phase?

This is exactly how John and Ellen proceeded to complete their project. They sat together with their team and developed a plan of involvement. They had already done a great job at initial concept development and approval, as well as detailing a solution that had achieved consensus with their team and task forces. Table 21.2 shows all the phases of their project, including the implementation phase. Before finalizing the solution, they built in multiple op-

TABLE 21.2. PLAN OF COLLABORATIVE ACTION FOR THE COLLEGE DISTRICT PROJECT.

Phase	Responsible Entity with Stakeholder Group	Time Needed
Concept development	Project team	3 months
Concept approval	Project team with decision makers (presidents, chancellor, board members)	
Solution design	Project team with task forces	10 months
Implementation plan design	Project team with task forces	2 months
Simple presentation design	Project team	1 month
Solution and implementation plan testing and refinement	Project team with all stakeholder groups (all unions), decision makers (presidents, chancellor, board members), decision influences (vice presidents, deans, faculty members, staff directors), and decision blockers (union leaders, prominent members of each union)	2 months
Solution and implementation plan redesign	Project team with task forces	3 months
Implementation plan approval	Project team with decision makers (presidents, chancellor, board members)	
Final approval	Project team with decision makers (board members)	1 month
Communication and outreach	Project team with all groups (all unions)	
Implementation	Project team	12 months (projected)

portunities for stakeholder groups to give input and feedback, hoping to clarify expectations and maximize understanding and support for the project. Their objectives were to surface objections and eliminate surprises. In one of the redesign meetings, they worked with faculty to surface their main concern, access to the system. Together they devised ways of building adequate access into the final solution. Thus they obtained approval for implementation. So be prepared to design, test, and redesign your solution until you reach final consensus (Sioukas, 2003).

Additional Key Practices

Achieving collaboration in large-scale projects is a complicated and challenging process with numerous best practices to consider. A few key practices will enhance your effectiveness.

Communicate to Build Trust and Common Goals.

Communicate to Build Trust and Common Goals. There are several times during a project when you need to communicate with various stakeholders. You can meet with them one on one. These meetings are very important, as they can be the means for obtaining support for your project. During these meetings, please keep in mind that effective communication is about listening. Instead of doing all the talking about your plans, ask questions to discover where each person is coming from, his or her interests and motivations, and how the person can be made part of the solution. While others are speaking, make them the priority in the conversation, and listen without interrupting. This communication process works wonders for generating *trust*, a crucial ingredient for obtaining their support (Sioukas, 2003).

By encouraging stakeholders to speak while you listen attentively, you can determine whether and how their goals are compatible with your project initiatives. You can adjust and frame your own goals in a way that is compatible with theirs. Most important, you will be able to develop *common goals* (Sioukas, 2003). These common goals will not only serve as a basis for working together but also help you throughout the duration of the project.

Believe in the Best of Others. The results you will experience by following this principle are extraordinary. When you believe that people are fully capable of performing at the highest level, they are bound to meet or even exceed your expectations. Sit with them, set goals, and support them with your enthusiasm and trust in their abilities. If they need help, such as coaching and training, be there to support them. Conversely, research shows that the opposite is also true. When you don't show your belief that individuals can and will perform effectively, they will most likely fail you and the project (Livingston, 1969).

Stay Flexible. Large-scale collaborative projects will quickly demonstrate the need to remain flexible. This is exactly what John and Ellen needed to do to turn their situation around. Change and the need for change are natural occurrences that continue to happen over time. Should you find that you get stuck, stay open to new ways of doing things. Flexibility and changes based on what your stakeholders and situations call for are keys to your project's success.

Think Positive. Hundreds of research articles in fields varying from management to medicine demonstrate the power of positive thinking in taking action and creating innovative results (Sutton, 2002). Yet when things get tough, people tend to hide behind their fears (Jeffers, 1987). When their fears do come true, managers and leaders learn the most and create their most significant breakthroughs (McCall, Lombardo, and Morrison, 1988).

Conclusion

Large-scale collaborative projects promise to stretch our skills as collaboration agents. Yet the benefits of organizational and personal learning and bottom-line performance are often tremendous. As you embark on your next large-scale undertaking, keep in mind tools such as the stakeholder table, the project involvement map, and the plan of collaborative action that you can develop with your project team. Finally, remember to think positive thoughts about your situation and believe in the best of the stakeholders you are involving. You may be amazed at the results.

References

Bens, I. *Facilitating with Ease!* San Francisco: Jossey-Bass, 2000.

Bryson, J. M. "Stakeholder Identification and Analysis." In J. M. Bryson, *Strategic Planning for Public and Nonprofit Organizations: A Guide to Strengthening and Sustaining Organizational Achievement.* (3rd ed.) San Francisco: Jossey-Bass, 2004.

Carlson, C. "Convening." In C. Carlson, *The Consensus Building Handbook.* Thousand Oaks, Calif.: Sage, 1999.

Cohen, S., and Bailey, D. "What Makes Teams Work: Group Effectiveness Research from the Shop Floor to the Executive Suite." *Journal of Management,* 1997, *23*, 239–290.

Hunter, D., and Thorpe, S. "Facilitator Values and Ethics." In S. Schuman (ed.), *The IAF Handbook of Group Facilitation.* San Francisco: Jossey-Bass, 2005.

Jeffers, S. *Feel the Fear and Do It Anyway.* New York: Fawcett, 1987.

Kaner, S., and others. *Facilitator's Guide to Participatory Decision-Making.* Philadelphia: New Society, 1996.

Livingston, J. "Pygmalion in Management." *Harvard Business Review,* 1969, *47*(4), 81–89.

McCall, M., Lombardo, M., and Morrison, A. *The Lessons of Experience.* New York: Free Press, 1988.

Mitroff, I. *Smart Thinking for Crazy Times.* San Francisco: Berrett-Koehler, 1998.

Sioukas, T. *The Solution Path.* San Francisco: Jossey-Bass, 2003.

Straus, D. *How to Make Collaboration Work.* San Francisco: Berrett-Koehler, 2002.

Sutton, R. *Weird Ideas That Work.* New York: Free Press, 2002.

APPENDIX

COLLABORATIVE VALUES, PRINCIPLES, AND BELIEFS

International Association of Facilitators: Statement of Values and Code of Ethics for Group Facilitators

Statement of Values

As group facilitators, we believe in the inherent value of the individual and the collective wisdom of the group. We strive to help the group make the best use of the contributions of each of its members. We set aside our personal opinions and support the group's right to make its own choices. We believe that collaborative and cooperative interaction builds consensus and produces meaningful outcomes. We value professional collaboration to improve our profession.

Code of Ethics

Note: For each statement, only the title and brief description are given here. Refer to the source publication for the complete description.

Client Service: We are in service to our clients, using our group facilitation competencies to add value to their work.

Conflict of Interest: We openly acknowledge any potential conflict of interest.

Group Autonomy: We respect the culture, rights, and autonomy of the group.

Processes, Methods, and Tools: We use processes, methods and tools responsibly.

Respect, Safety, Equity, and Trust: We strive to engender an environment of respect and safety where all participants trust that they can speak freely and where individual boundaries are honoured.

Stewardship of Process: We practice stewardship of process and impartiality toward content.

Confidentiality: We maintain confidentiality of information.

Professional Development: We are responsible for continuous improvement of our facilitation skills and knowledge.

International Association for Public Participation: Core Values for the Practice of Public Participation

- The public should have a say in decisions about actions that could affect their lives.
- Public participation includes the promise that the public's contribution will influence the decision.
- Public participation promotes sustainable decisions by recognizing and communicating the needs and interests of all participants, including decision makers.
- Public participation seeks out and facilitates the involvement of those potentially affected by or interested in a decision.
- Public participation seeks input from participants in designing how they participate.
- Public participation provides participants with the information they need to participate in a meaningful way.
- Public participation communicates to participants how their input affected the decision.

Public Conversations Project:
Our Observations and the Spirit Behind Our Practices

What We've Learned	*Spirit*	*What We Do*
People are more invested in a dialogue when they have been consulted in its design.	**Collaborative**	We respect participants' knowledge, including them in our planning and consulting them throughout the dialogue process.
	◆ ◆ ◆	
People are more likely to have a constructive conversation when they do not attack, are not defensive, and abstain from polarizing ways of speaking.	**Preventive**	We ask participants to agree in advance to set aside accusation and argument and avoid communication patterns that impeded previous conversations.
	◆ ◆ ◆	
Equal respect for everyone enhances trust and collaboration.	**Fair**	We use structure to provide equal airtime and agreements to promote respectful speaking.
	◆ ◆ ◆	
In an affirming, exploratory, future-oriented atmosphere, people are more open to new ways of communicating.	**Hopeful**	We elicit participants' visions and wishes for the future and highlight the appearance of promising, new interactions among them.
	◆ ◆ ◆	
When people share personal stories, their uniqueness and complexity emerge. Personal exchanges diminish stereotyping and promote caring.	**Rehumanizing**	We discourage depersonalized debate. We invite participants to share life experiences that they associate with their current views.

What We've Learned	*Spirit*	*What We Do*
When people are open with one another, they more easily develop relationships of trust, respect, collaboration, and mutual empowerment.	**Candid**	Participants are encouraged to speak openly about themselves. We explain why we do what we do, if asked. We express no opinion on the divisive issues at hand. We listen attentively.
	♦ ♦ ♦	
People learn more and relate better when they listen carefully and attentively to each other.	**Receptive**	We use structures and agreements that promote respectful listening.
	♦ ♦ ♦	
When people have an inquiring attitude about themselves and others, they interact more constructively than when they speak from certainty.	**Inquiring**	We encourage participants to ask instead of assuming or advocating. We invite participants to be open-minded toward themselves and others.
	♦ ♦ ♦	
When each person in a conversation considers varied perspectives, new ideas emerge and build on one another, dispelling simplistic polarizations.	**Expansive**	Our questions and tasks are designed to stimulate reflections and conversations that generate clarifying distinctions and fresh ideas.

Round Tables on the Environment and Economy in Canada: Building Consensus for a Sustainable Future: Guiding Principles

Consensus Processes

Consensus processes enjoy some inherent advantages over other decision-making processes in addressing the challenges of a sustainable future. Consensus processes are designed to:

- ensure that all significant interests are represented and respected
- enable participants to deal with each other directly
- give an effective voice to all participants
- allow the parties involved to design a process appropriate to their special circumstances and needs
- provide a forum that forges new partnerships and fosters cooperative problem solving in the search for innovative solutions that maximize all interests and promote sustainability

In terms of results, consensus processes can:

- improve the working relationships between all interests participating in the process
- help build respect for and a better understanding of different viewpoints among the participants
- lead to better informed, more creative, balanced and enduring decisions because of the shared commitment to and responsibility for the process, results, and implementation
- often be used to complement other decision-making processes

Even if all matters are not resolved through consensus, the process can crystallize the discussion, clarify the underlying issues, identify the options for dealing with outstanding disagreements, and build respect and understanding among the parties affected.

Excerpted with permission from *Building Consensus for a Sustainable Future: Guiding Principles. Round Tables on the Environment and Economy in Canada* [http://www.nrtee-trnee.ca/Publications/ html/Report_Consensus_Guiding-Principles_e.htm], 1993, pp. 7–17.

Guiding Principles of Consensus Processes

Consensus processes are participant determined and driven—that is their very essence. No single approach will work for each situation—because of the issues involved, the respective interests and the surrounding circumstances. Experience points to certain characteristics which are fundamental to consensus—these are referred to as the guiding principles. These principles are described in detail on the following pages.

Note: For each principle, only the title and brief description are given here. Refer to the source publication for the complete description of each principle.

Principle #1—Purpose Driven. People need a reason to participate in the process.

Principle #2—Inclusive, Not Exclusive. All parties with a significant interest in the issues should be involved in the consensus process.

Principle #3—Voluntary Participation. The parties who are affected or interested participate voluntarily.

Principle #4—Self-Design. The parties design the consensus process.

Principle #5—Flexibility. Flexibility should be designed into the process.

Principle #6—Equal Opportunity. All parties have equal access to relevant information and the opportunity to participate effectively throughout the process.

Principle #7—Respect for Diverse Interests. Acceptance of the diverse values, interests, and knowledge of the parties involved in the consensus process is essential.

Principle #8—Accountability. The participants are accountable both to their constituencies and to the process that they have agreed to establish.

Principle #9—Time Limits. Realistic deadlines are necessary throughout the process.

Principle #10—Implementation. Commitment to implementation and effective monitoring are essential parts of any agreement.

The Co-Intelligence Institute:
Principles to Nurture Wise Democratic Process
and Collective Intelligence in Public Participation

Wise democratic processes are those which utilize a community's or society's diversity to deepen shared understanding and produce outcomes of long-term benefit to the whole community or society. Not all public participation serves this purpose. Public participation can either enhance or degrade the collective intelligence and wisdom involved in democratic processes such as making collective decisions, solving social problems, and creating shared visions. The principles below offer some guidance for designing wise democratic processes.

1. Include All Relevant Perspectives

The diversity of perspectives engaged in a wise democratic process will approximate the diversity of the community of people affected by the outcome. In addition, community wisdom and buy-in come from the fair and creative inclusion of all relevant perspectives—all related viewpoints, cultures, information, experiences, needs, interests, values, contributions and dreams. Furthermore, those who are centrally involved, peripherally involved or not involved in a situation each have—by virtue of their unique perspectives—uniquely valuable contributions to make toward the wise resolution of that situation. Creative inclusion of perspectives generates more wisdom than mechanical inclusion of people.

2. Empower the People's Engagement

To the extent people feel involved in the creation or ratification of democratic decisions—either directly or by recognized representatives—they will support the implementation of those decisions. This is especially true to the extent they feel their agency and power in the process—i.e., that they clearly see the impact of their diverse contributions in the final outcome. Thus, it serves democracy and collective intelligence when expertise and leadership are on tap to—and not on top of—the decision-making processes of "We, the People" and anyone democratically mandated by the people to care for the common welfare.

3. Invoke Multiple Forms of Knowing

Community wisdom arises from the interplay of stories (with their full emotional content), facts, principles, reason, intuition and compassion. To the extent any one of these dominates or is missing, the outcome will be less wise.

4. Ensure High-Quality Dialogue

The supreme test of dialogue is its ability to use commonality and diversity (including conflict) creatively. There are three tests for the quality of dialogue towards desirable outcomes: Is it deepening understanding? Is it building relationships? Is it expanding possibilities? Most public forums need good facilitation to ensure high-quality dialogue. For approaches to dialogue, see "A Toolbox of Co-Intelligent Processes for Community Work," [http://www.co-intelligence.org/CIPol_ComunityProcesses.html].

5. Establish Ongoing Participatory Processes

Since intelligence is the capacity to learn, and learning is an ongoing process, collective intelligence can manifest most powerfully in democratic processes that are ongoing, iterative, and officially recognized by the whole community or society. One-time events (such as public hearings and conferences that are not part of a larger ongoing democratic process) are limited in their capacity to generate collective intelligence for a whole community or society. The institutionalization of official periodic citizen deliberations according to these principles maximizes collective intelligence. For examples, see "Citizen Deliberative Councils" [http://www.co-intelligence.org/P-CDCs.html].

6. Use Positions and Proposals as Grist

Early focus on positions and proposals can prevent the emergence of the best possible outcomes. In general, collective intelligence is supported by beginning with an exploratory approach which notes existing positions, proposals and solutions as grist for exploring the situations they were created to handle. Exploring the assumptions, interests, needs, values, visions, experiences, etc., that gave birth to these particular proposals tends to deepen understanding and relationship so that new and better solutions can emerge. See "Beyond Positions: A Politics of Civic Co-Creativity" [http://www.co-intelligence. org/CIPol_beyondpositions.html].

7. Help People Feel Fully Heard

To the extent people feel fully heard, they will be able to hear others and, ultimately, join in collaborative deliberation and co-creative problem-solving. Among the approaches to helping people feel fully heard are Active Listening [http://www.va.gov/adr/active.html], Nonviolent Communication [http://www.co-intelligence.org/P-nonviolentcomm.html], and Dynamic Facilitation [http://www.co-intelligence.org/P-dynamicfacilitation.html].

Organisation for Economic Co-Operation and Development: Ten Guiding Principles for Successful Information, Consultation and Active Participation in Policy-Making

1. Commitment

Leadership and strong commitment to information, consultation and active participation in policy-making is needed at all levels, from politicians, senior managers and public officials.

2. Rights

Citizens' rights to access information, provide feedback, be consulted and actively participate in policy-making must be firmly grounded in law or policy. Government obligations to respond to citizens when exercising their rights must also be clearly stated. Independent authorities for oversight, or their equivalent, are essential to enforcing these rights.

3. Clarity

Objectives for, and limits to, information, consultation and active participation during policy-making should be well defined from the outset. The respective roles and responsibilities of citizens (in providing input) and government (in making decisions for which they are accountable) must be clear to all.

4. Time

Public consultation and active participation should be undertaken as early in the policy process as possible. This allows a greater range of policy solutions to emerge. It also raises the chances of successful implementation. Adequate time must be available for consultation and participation to be effective. Information is needed at all stages of the policy cycle.

Excerpted from M. Gramberger, "Put Principles into Practice!" In *Citizens as Partners: OECD Handbook on Information, Consultation and Public Participation in Policy-Making.* Paris: Organisation for Economic Co-Operation and Development, © OECD 2001, pp. 83–88 [http://www1.oecd.org/scripts/publications/bookshop/redirect.asp?pub=422001141P1].

5. Objectivity

Information provided by government during policy-making should be objective, complete and accessible. All citizens should have equal treatment when exercising their rights of access to information and participation.

6. Resources

Adequate financial, human and technical resources are needed if public information, consultation and active participation in policy-making are to be effective. Government officials must have access to appropriate skills, guidance and training. An organisational culture that supports their efforts is highly important.

7. Co-Ordination

Initiatives to inform citizens, request feedback from and consult them should be coordinated across government. This enhances knowledge management, ensures policy coherence, and avoids duplication. It also reduces the risk of "consultation fatigue"—negative reactions because of too much overlapping or poorly done consultation—among citizens and civil society organisations. Co-ordination efforts should not reduce the capacity of government units to ensure innovation and flexibility.

8. Accountability

Governments have an obligation to account for the use they make of citizens' inputs received—be it through feedback, public consultation or active participation. To increase this accountability, governments need to ensure an open and transparent policy-making process amenable to external scrutiny and review.

9. Evaluation

Evaluation is essential in order to adapt to new requirements and changing conditions for policy-making. Governments need tools, information and capacity to evaluate their performance in strengthening their relations with citizens.

10. Active Citizenship

Governments benefit from active citizens and a dynamic civil society. They can take concrete actions to facilitate citizens' access to information and participation, raise awareness, and strengthen civic education and skills. They can support capacity building among civil society organisations.

Society for Organizational Learning: Guiding Principles and Ideals

Guiding Principles of SoL

Drive to Learn—All human beings are born with an innate, life-long desire and ability to learn, which should be enhanced by all organizations.

Learning Is Social—People learn best from and with one another, and participation in learning communities is vital to their effectiveness, well-being and happiness in any work setting.

Learning Communities—The capacities and accomplishments of organizations are inseparable from, and dependent on, the capacities of the learning communities which they foster.

Aligning with Nature—It is essential that organizations evolve to be in greater harmony with human nature and with the natural world.

Core Learning Capabilities—Organizations must develop individual and collective capabilities to understand complex, interdependent issues; engage in reflective, generative conversation; and nurture personal and shared aspirations.

Cross-Organizational Collaboration—Learning communities that connect multiple organizations can significantly enhance their capacity for profound individual and organizational change.

Ideals of the SoL Community—Our Commitments to Each Other

Subsidiarity—Make no decision and perform no function at a higher or more central level than can be accomplished at a more local level.

Inclusiveness—Conduct all deliberations and make all decisions by bodies and methods which reasonably represent all relevant and affected parties.

Shared Responsibility—Advance the Purpose in accordance with these Principles in ways which enhance the capacity of the community as a whole, as well as that of each member.

Openness—Transcend institutional and intellectual boundaries and roles that limit or diminish learning.

Adaptive Governance—Continually conceive, implement, and practice governance concepts and processes which encourage adaptability, diversity, flexibility, and innovation.

Intellectual Output—Use research generated by the community in ways that most benefit society.

Acknowledgment—Openly and fairly acknowledge intellectual contributions to Concepts, Theories, and Practices, both from within and from outside the community.

Participation & Quality—Contribute to and/or participate in research, capacity building, and practice, striving for the highest standards of quality.

New York State Forum on Conflict and Consensus Inc.: Bylaws Preamble

Facilitated consensus building techniques can be applied to a wide variety of public policy decisions such as: site specific problems, development of legislation and regulations, and restructuring of government services. A broad range of techniques can be used, such as policy dialogues, regulatory negotiation, mediation, citizen participation, risk communication, and analytical modeling. The common theme that ties these techniques together is collaboration—an emphasis on face-to-face dialogue facilitated in a way that invites interested parties and communities to participate, addresses the full range of issues and values, illuminates points of agreement and disagreement, develops a shared understanding of the problem, fosters joint problem solving and builds consensus.

More than just a collection of techniques, these methods reflect a set of values and assumptions:

- that all citizens—individuals, public interest groups, the business community, and other sectors of society—have the right to meaningful participation in decisions that affect them;

and that consensual, participatory decision making can

- result in higher levels of satisfaction among all participants including individuals and government officials;
- improve relationships among the various sectors of society;
- increase public confidence in government;
- lead to more innovative, stable, and in the long-run more cost-effective and timely solutions to complex public policy problems.

Excerpted from New York State Forum on Conflict and Consensus Inc., *Bylaws*, 1993.

Office of Management and Budget and Council on Environmental Quality: Memorandum on Environmental Conflict Resolution—Basic Principles for Agency Engagement in Environmental Conflict Resolution and Collaborative Problem Solving

Informed Commitment

Confirm willingness and availability of appropriate agency leadership and staff at all levels to commit to principles of engagement; ensure commitment to participate in good faith with open mindset to new perspectives

Balanced, Voluntary Representation

Ensure balanced, voluntary inclusion of affected/concerned interests; all parties should be willing and able to participate and select their own representatives

Group Autonomy

Engage with all participants in developing and governing process; including choice of consensus-based decision rules; seek assistance as needed from impartial facilitator/mediator selected by and accountable to all parties

Informed Process

Seek agreement on how to share, test and apply relevant information (scientific, cultural, technical, etc.) among participants; ensure relevant information is accessible and understandable by all participants

Accountability

Participate in process directly, fully, and in good faith; be accountable to the process, all participants and the public

Openness

Ensure all participants and public are fully informed in a timely manner of the purpose and objectives of process; communicate agency authorities, requirements and constraints; uphold confidentiality rules and agreements as required for particular proceedings

Timeliness

Ensure timely decisions and outcomes

Implementation

Ensure decisions are implementable; parties should commit to identify roles and responsibilities necessary to implement agreement; parties should agree in advance on the consequences of a party being unable to provide necessary resources or implement agreement; ensure parties will take steps to implement and obtain resources necessary to agreement

Voluntary Sector Initiative (Canada)
A Code of Good Practice on Policy Dialogue:
Principles Underpinning the Code

The Voluntary Sector's Value

A healthy and active voluntary sector plays an important role in helping the federal government identify issues and achieve its public policy objectives. By its very nature and particularly because of its connection to communities, the voluntary sector brings a special perspective and considerable value to its activities, including those it undertakes with the Government of Canada.

Mutual Respect

Both sectors will listen to and consider the views of all participants and respect their legitimacy and input.

Inclusiveness

Both sectors will involve the broadest possible range of groups or individuals who may be affected by a policy or who can make a meaningful contribution to the debate. Increasingly, policy development must take account of the specific needs, interests and experiences of the diversity of the voluntary sector including, for example, groups representing women, visible minorities, persons with disabilities, Aboriginal people, linguistic minorities, sexual orientation, remote, rural and northern communities and other hard-to-reach subsectors. Policies must also respect the *Canadian Charter of Rights and Freedoms*, the *Canadian Human Rights Act*, the *Employment Equity Act*, the *Official Languages Act*, the *Multiculturalism Act* and the United Nations *Universal Declaration of Human Rights*, as well as Canada's obligations as a signatory of relevant international treaties and conventions, for example, on the rights of children, women and indigenous peoples. Policies must also respect all amendments, extensions or replacements to these laws and policies.

Accessibility

Both sectors will take the appropriate measures to ensure that all those invited to participate in a dialogue have access to the process. This will take account of factors such as language, region, distance, ethno-culture, religion, socio-economic background, age, knowledge or capabilities.

Clarity

Recognizing that a clear mutual understanding of the objectives, purpose and process of participation and feedback is vital, both sectors will establish the terms of the policy dialogue in advance and communicate them to participants.

Transparency

To build trust, both sectors will establish open lines of communication, provide information readily and invest in working relationships. Participants must clearly understand the context within which each decision will be made, including the scope of and limitations on dialogue.

Responsibility

Both sectors will participate in good faith and recognize that adequate resources and time are required for an effective process.

Accountability

Both sectors will provide feedback to their respective constituencies on the full range of views expressed, and clearly communicate how this input has been considered in the public policy process.

KEY CONCEPTS

Aligned vision and values are shared or congruent belief systems or principles, including experiences of shared intent, passion, ideals, and motivations among the members. (Chapter 6)

Awareness is related to self-awareness and one's awareness of the organization as a whole; it is the key component to *use of self.* (Chapter 15)

Backstage activities are critical to the success of any collaborative effort. Official frontstage meetings are, in effect, the mechanisms by which informal backstage conversations, proposals, and resolutions are formally acknowledged, exchanged, and processed. As one person put it, "If you wait until the frontstage meetings, you've missed the most important places to affect what is going to end up happening." (Chapter 7)

Bench strength is a group's capacity to handle unanticipated, challenging dynamics; the group's resilience under pressure. (Chapter 1)

Benefit is a sense of well-being resulting from interactions, collaborations, projects, and membership. (Chapter 6)

Civil dialogue is cosmopolitan social trust building that engenders new shared values across the existing conflicting memberships. (Chapter 2)

Collaboration "The objective of collaboration is to create a richer, more comprehensive appreciation of the problem among the stakeholders than any one of them could construct alone" (Gray, 1991, p. 5). (Chapter 10)

Collaboration A mutually beneficial relationship between two or more individuals, groups or organizations, who jointly design ways to work together to meet their related interests and who learn with and from each other, sharing, responsibility, authority, and accountability for achieving results. (Chapter 14)

Collaboration is a relationship in which two or more people are committed to the success of whatever project or process they are jointly engaged in and use assumptions and behaviors consistent with interdependence while pursuing those outcomes. (Chapter 8)

Collaboration Chrislip and Larson (1994, p. 5) define collaboration as "mutually beneficial relationships between two or more parties who work together toward common goals by sharing responsibility, authority, and accountability for achieving results. . . . The purpose of collaboration is to create a shared vision and joint strategies to address concerns that go beyond the purview of any particular party." (Chapter 14)

In the *initial theory,* **collaboration** was modeled as the confluence of effective participation of all actors. Effective participation was defined as a combination of engagement and effort in the collaborative process. In the *revised theory,* collaboration was defined as the combination of the accumulation of the actors' ability to work with each other. Ability to work with each other accumulates over time as a function of effort, perceived risk, and interaction with other actors in the project. In the *final theory,* collaboration was redefined as the confluence of engagement of the parties involved; the higher the engagement, the higher the collaboration achieved. (Chapter 4)

Collaboration is a function of the recursive interaction of knowledge, engagement, results, perceptions of trust, and accumulation of activity over time. In this sense, the way to improve collaboration is to pay attention to how knowledge is managed in collaborative efforts, how results are produced and understood, and how communication can enable the creation of trust. (Chapter 4)

Collaborative tensility is the ability of collaborative partners to bend and remain flexible under pressure so that their work can maintain momentum despite challenges. (Chapter 6)

Confidence is a form of trust based on past experience within an organization. (Chapter 2)

Context awareness The group is a particular configuration in the dynamic web of relationships that constitute an organization, a community, and a society. To be fully effective in working with a group, it is necessary to take into account its wider context. (Chapter 11)

Co-sensing is the process of developing shared understanding in a group by exploring diverse perspectives in an open-ended way that encourages the emergence of insights or perceptual shifts. This is different from the kind of negotiated agreement or persuasion that is more typical of managed decision-making processes, including most forms of consensus. (Chapter 13)

Cosmopolitan social trust is trust between individuals based on negotiated understandings and not necessarily dependent on any particular similarities between them. (Chapter 2)

Culture is the habitual way of doing things in a given society or organization, reflecting deep assumptions about meanings, power, and legitimacy. (Chapter 18)

Culture is created as a by-product of the larger process of meeting practical challenges. When a group or an organization solves a meaningful problem, the assumptions embedded in that particular problem-solving approach begin to be adopted as part of the culture of that group or organization. (Chapter 13)

Culture-climate competencies are a collection of skills essential for managing the psychosocial aspects of organizational life, such as communication and building trust. (Chapter 12)

Decision blockers are people who can delay or stop the implementation of a project. (Chapter 21)

Decision influencers are individuals who have credibility and influence within the formal power structure. (Chapter 21)

Deliberative democracy is an effort to involve citizens in public policy agenda setting and decision making through peer discussions in small group settings. Critical norms of deliberation include equality of participation and respect for expert, decision maker, and citizen alike; political tolerance; a sense of increased political efficacy by citizen participants; and the recognition of common grounds for action even in the face of continuing disagreement. (Chapter 19)

Diversity can be seen in the ever-changing variety of community and individual experiences. Respect for diversity affirms the existence, recognition, understanding, and tolerance of difference, whether expressed through religious, ethnic, political, or gender background. Diversity is about being free to shape and articulate identities as well as acknowledging and valuing difference. (Chapter 5)

Equity is a commitment at all levels within society to ensuring equality of access to resources, structures, and decision-making processes and the adoption of actions to secure and maintain these objectives. Equity is about achieving equal opportunities and fairness in redressing inequalities. (Chapter 5)

Experience is the moment-to-moment stream of observations, thoughts, feelings, and wants flowing through a person. (Chapter 8)

Facilitation involves structuring and conducting meetings in a way that allows group members to share their views, brainstorm and prioritize ideas, synthesize solutions, make consensus decisions, and generate commitment for action. (Chapter 21)

The **FACTS model** summarizes the five factors that are crucial to addressing the sustainability of cooperative processes: freedom, alignment, congruence, truth, and synergy. As a diagnostic tool, it can be used to uncover what is missing or needing further development for a group to flourish. (Chapter 11)

The **five-prong approach** involves building a more collaborative organization address by (1) building leadership and ownership; (2) demonstrating the power of collaborative action; (3) internalizing collaborative skills; (4) providing training, facilitation consulting, and coaching; and (5) measuring and monitoring progress. (Chapter 17)

Forums, arenas, and courts are the shared-power settings in which human beings develop mutual understandings of public issues, decide what to do about them, and manage conflict and adjudicate disputes over policy implementation. (Chapter 18)

Generalized reciprocity is doing something for someone without expecting anything specific in return but in the confident expectation that reciprocation will occur sooner or later. (Chapter 2)

Group facilitation "Group facilitation is a process in which a person who is acceptable to all members of the group, substantively neutral, and has no decision-making authority intervenes to help a group improve the way it identifies and solves problems and makes decisions, in order to increase the group's effectiveness" (Schwarz, 1994, p. 4). (Chapter 2)

Group model building deals with the processes and techniques for handling problems that arise when involving a large number of people in the construction of a system dynamics model. (Chapter 4)

The **imperative for change** can be a compelling state that innovators want to move toward or an intolerable state about which people believe that something must be done. (Chapter 16)

Interdependence requires recognition by different interest or identity groups of their obligations and commitments to others and of the interconnectedness of individual and community experiences and ambitions leading to the development of a society that is at once cohesive and diverse. Interdependence is concerned with building better relationships and trust. (Chapter 5)

Interorganizational learning results from business leaders coming together to learn how to respond to challenges in their organizational environments. (Chapter 6)

Interpersonal clarity involves arriving at a state in which one knows one's own experience, the other person's experience, and the difference between them. (Chapter 8)

Interpersonal mush describes the interaction between two or more people based on stories they have made up about each other but have not checked out. (Chapter 8)

Key stakeholders are the individuals, groups, and organizations that are most affected by a social need or public problem or that have important resources for meeting the need. (Chapter 18)

Leadership for the common good is a process in which representatives of diverse stakeholders collaborate in defining public problems, finding promising solutions, and obtaining and sustaining the necessary policies, programs, rules, and norms that can establish a "regime of mutual gain." (Chapter 18)

Learning space is the environment of the collaborative space in addition to the experience of participating in a learning organization. (Chapter 6)

The **meaning-centered approach** is an approach to management and facilitation that is based on existential-humanistic psychology that emphasizes understanding the communications and needs of individuals and groups and meeting the basic needs for meaning and purpose for both workers and organizations. (Chapter 12)

Metaphors are shorthand or code for how we think about our past, present, and future. Because we act as if metaphors are true, they help guide action planning and the development of relationships. (Chapter 9)

Organizational culture is the set of fundamental values and assumptions that members of an organization share and that guide their behavior. (Chapter 14)

Organizational learning is an inquiry by two or more people into their patterns of organizing that leads to new knowledge and a change in those patterns. (Chapter 8)

Organizational learning conversation is a process for attaining interpersonal clarity and changing patterns of interaction. (Chapter 8)

A **plan of collaborative action** is a schedule of steps in the completion of a project and the time allotted to each that that serves as a road map for the team carrying out the project. It is created in a facilitative way by asking questions such as "What phases need to take place to complete the project?" "Who is responsible for each phase?" "Which stakeholder group needs to be involved at each phase?" and "How long do we need for each phase?" (Chapter 21)

Pluralistic social trust is trust between individuals based on something they have in common. (Chapter 2)

Practical dialogue is open-ended, nonlinear approaches designed for helping people arrive at effective solutions to task-oriented challenges. (Chapter 13)

A **private good** is any good that can be consumed by only one individual, usually its owner. (Chapter 2)

Process advocate Practitioners *do* have a point of view and stake in the process. They offer their expertise and advocate for the design of transparent, participatory, and effective processes. Far from being value-free or "neutral," principled practitioners model and defend explicit values as they design and facilitate collaborative processes. In the course of serving as a process guide, practitioners often take on the process advocate role. (Chapter 16)

A **process champion** needs the personal energy to convince others to sponsor or be involved in the collaborative innovation. Crucially, a process champion needs the support of an enabling leader with decision-making responsibility or a high degree of influence. (Chapter 20)

Process guide is a person who serves the group without a stake in the group's decisions and applies the essential skills and knowledge of group dynamics and facilitation to help groups create shared meaning, engage in conflict constructively, and build solid agreements. (Chapter 16)

A **public good** is any good that can be consumed by many individuals at the same time, at no additional cost and with no reduction in quality or quantity (Chapter 2).

Random selection It seems somewhat counterintuitive to link randomness with collaboration. After all, usually we collaborate with people we know. This means that we move in narrow circles, we gravitate to ghettos of like-minded people, and we suspect that we will encounter higher levels of conflict or ignorance among strangers. This might not always be a useful attitude because it prevents collaborative possibilities. In practice, collaboration among strangers can be rewarding. (Chapter 20)

Regime of mutual gain is a policy regime that achieves widespread lasting benefits at reasonable cost and that taps and serves people's deepest interests in and desires for a better world for themselves and those they care about. (Chapter 18)

Relational quality is the degree to which relationships either impede or facilitate collaboration and to which relationships among members affect the overall collaborative tensility of the organization, a sense of personal connectedness among participants and social interactions within and outside the formal meetings. (Chapter 6)

Relationships are intentionally established links between individuals, groups, organizations, sectors, and communities that are essential for developing the bonding and bridging social capital needed to make and sustain change. (Chapter 16)

Secondary mentality is the realization that the relationship between the group and the individual does not have to be a zero-sum game. Instead, the more a group welcomes the experience and divergent perspectives of each individual participant, the richer the collective experience becomes, and the more that individuals share their unique gifts with others in a supportive group context, the more their own individuality is strengthened and nourished. (Chapter 13)

Self-differentiation is the ability to be separate from and connected to other people simultaneously. (Chapter 8)

Sense making uses stories that people make up to fill in the gaps in their understanding of others. (Chapter 8)

Social capital is the stored value that individuals have accumulated in their networks. (Chapter 2)

Social ecology is the discipline that concerns itself with the relationships of human society and with everything else on the earth. (Chapter 11)

Social exclusion results from barriers to the rights of citizenship, to a basic standard of living, and to participation in the occupational and social opportunities of society. Although there is a strong relationship between social exclusion and poverty, isolation, prejudice, and discrimination, system failures also play an important part. (Chapter 5)

Social trust Trust in general depends on certain contexts and circumstances. Just as one finds variations in trusting behavior between individuals, it is possible to find variations in social trust between cultures. Citizens in some nations appear to be more open and trusting than in others. The attitude of "innocent until proven guilty" that operates in the United States works in reverse in societies with low levels of social trust where individuals treat each other as "guilty until proven innocent." (Chapter 3)

Specific reciprocity involves doing something for someone if the person does something for you. (Chapter 2)

Sponsors (sometimes known as conveners) are administrators, public officials, managers, and other community or organization leaders who arrange a collaborative process. They perform one or more of the following functions: authorize the collaborative effort, set up the basic "rules of play," invite the players, support the work of the group with resources, and connect the results to mainstream decision making and actions. (Chapter 7)

A **stakeholder table** is a table that summarizes the four categories of stakeholders in any project: people affected by the project, decision makers and influences, decision blockers, and people with information and expertise. (Chapter 21)

A **star team charter** is a list of agreements by the team on shared and meaningful purpose, specific and challenging goals, roles and responsibilities, common and collaborative process, and complementary skills. (Chapter 17)

Structure is a stable, recurring process that results from individuals interacting with one another in certain ways. (Chapter 14)

System dynamics modeling is used to study how the various components of a system interact and influence each other and how they define the behavior of a system over time. It provides a way to explore feedback-rich systems (where relationships among some of the elements are circular) and allows the investigation of the effect of changes in one variable on other variables over time. (Chapter 4)

A **transition management team** is a cross-functional, multilevel team assembled to launch, guide, and take responsibility for a collaborative change effort. Creating this team is a critical part of the commitment-building and collaborative problem-solving elements of change. (Chapter 17)

Uncertainty and certainty are ways of measuring one's attachment to one's views on an issue and therefore one's state of mind when in conflict with others about that issue. An individual who holds uncertainty about something has an element of doubt as to whether his or her view is exclusively *right*. Certainty, on the other hand, contains no doubt whatsoever. Uncertain and certain states of mind continually influence our perception of conflict during collaboration. (Chapter 10)

Use of self Rather than focusing on skills and methods that the practitioner can use, use of self puts the focus on who the practitioner is being and how the practitioner uses himself or herself while working. Awareness is the key component to use of self. (Chapter 15)

NAME INDEX

SUBJECT INDEX

A

"Abilene Paradox, The" (Harvey), 241

Absenteeism, 363–364

Academic collaboration, 18–19, 22–23, 419–431

Accessibility, 468

Accommodation, 133, 134

Accountability: in cultural transformation, 250–251; empowerment and, 242, 244; joint, 293; lack of, 233; of leaders, 21–22; of participants, 11, 21; in public policy-making, 460

Action Research, 104

Active citizenship, 461

Active learning, 324

Active listening, 458

Activedemocracy.net, 418

Adaptability, 315–316, 340–341

Advocates and advocacy: coalitions of, 390, 393; inquiry balanced with, 108, 113, 119, 122, 123; for policy change, 377; process, 327–328; styles of, 132–139

African American Men Commission, 372, 378

African American Men Project (AAMP), 368–393; background and development of, 370–373; cultural milieu for, 368–369, 381–382; initiatives of, 372–373; Leadership for the Common Good framework in, 375–393; stakeholders in, 376–378

Agency, 44

Agonism, 419

Agreements: barriers to, 159; shared acceptance and, 249; strength of, in nondirective approaches, 273–274; using uncertainty to reach, 204–206

Alignment: checking for, 216, 217; in collaborative tensility theory, 109, 111, 114–115, 118–125, 469; of mission, strategy, and culture change, 348–349; for sustainability, 216, 217, 219, 221–222, 223

Alternative dispute resolution, 273

Altruism, 235, 413

American Journal of Medical Quality, xxv

Anonymous feedback, 299

Anxiety reduction, 267

Applegate Partnership, 146

Appliance Design, xxiv

Appreciative stance: agonist stance *versus,* 419; confronting reality *versus,* 249; in interorganizational learning, 108–109, 122; in organizational learning, 167

Archetypes, 174–175, 181, 189–190

Architects, deliberative process training of, 409–410

Arenas, 378, 472

Argonne National Laboratory, 68

Art of Facilitation, The (Hunter), 210

Assertiveness, levels of, 132, 133, 135, 136, 137

Assessment: of change effort, 361–364; cultural, 313, 368–369; current and future state, 360; environmental, 313; self-, 313. *See also* Stakeholder analysis

Assumptions: cultural, 381–382; of mutual learning model, 292; in